Peasants and Globalization

In 2007, for the first time in human history, a majority of the world's population lived in cities. However, on a global scale, poverty overwhelmingly retains a rural face. This book assembles a group of internationally eminent scholars in the field of rural development and social change in order to explore historical and contemporary processes of agrarian transformation and its consequent impact on livelihoods, poverty and wellbeing. After examining the agrarian origins of capitalism in Europe, the impact of colonialism on rural change in colonized countries, and processes of agrarian transformation through the twentieth century until the present, this book offers a number of challenging perspectives on the extent to which contemporary international capitalism, neoliberal globalization, and transformations in the world food system have affected the capacity of developing and transition countries to facilitate sustainable rural development through egalitarian agrarian change and poverty eradication in the countryside. The book provides a critical analysis of the extent to which rural development trajectories have in the past promoted, and are now promoting, a reconfiguration of rural production processes, the accumulation of rural resources and shifts in rural politics – and of the implications of such trajectories for peasant livelihoods in an era of globalization.

Peasants and Globalization explores continuity and change in the debate on the 'agrarian question', from its early formulation in the late nineteenth century to the continuing relevance it has in our times. Collectively, the contributors argue that in deepening the market imperative governing contemporary agriculture, neoliberal social and economic policies not only have failed to tackle the underlying causes of rural poverty, but also have deepened the agrarian crisis currently confronting the livelihoods of peasant farmers and rural workers around the world. This crisis does not go unchallenged, as rural social movements have emerged, for the first time, on a transnational scale. Confronting development policies that are unable to reduce, let alone eliminate, rural poverty, transnational rural social movements are attempting to construct a more just future for the world's farmers and rural workers.

A. Haroon Akram-Lodhi is Professor of International Development Studies at Trent University, Peterborough, Canada.

Cristóbal Kay is Professor of Development Studies and Rural Development at the Institute of Social Studies, The Hague, the Netherlands.

Routledge ISS Studies in Rural Livelihoods

Routledge and the Institute of Social Studies (ISS) in The Hague, the Netherlands have come together to publish a series of books on key issues confronting contemporary rural livelihoods in developing and transition countries. The series will include volumes critically covering themes including rural poverty, agrarian transformation, land policies and land rights, food policy and politics, water issues, migration, rural social movements, and rural conflict and violence, amongst others. All books in the series offer rigorous, evidence-based, cross-national comparative and inter-regional analysis. The books are designed to be theoretically stimulating but also accessible to policy practitioners and civil society activists.

Peasants and Globalization

Political economy, rural transformation and the agrarian question

Edited by A. Haroon Akram-Lodhi and Cristóbal Kay

LONDON AND NEW YORK

Transferred to digital printing 2010
First published 2009
by Routledge
2 Park Square, Milton Park, Abingdon, Oxon OX14 4RN

Simultaneously published in the USA and Canada
by Routledge
270 Madison Avenue, New York, NY 10016

Routledge is an imprint of the Taylor & Francis Group, an informa business

© 2009 selection and editorial matter: A. Haroon Akram-Lodhi and
Cristóbal Kay; individual chapters, the contributors

Typeset in Times New Roman
by Taylor & Francis Books

British Library Cataloguing in Publication Data
A catalogue record for this book is available from the British Library

Library of Congress Cataloging in Publication Data
   Peasants and globalization : political economy, rural transformation and
the agrarian question / edited by A. Haroon Akram-Lodhi and Cristóbal
Kay.
      p. cm.
   Includes bibliographical references and index.
   1. Rural development–Case studies. 2. Peasants–Case studies. 3.
Globalization–Case studies. I. Akram-Lodhi, A. Haroon, 1958- II. Kay,
Cristóbal.
   HN49.C6P435 2008
   307.1'412–dc22
                              2008008935

ISBN 978-0-415-44629-7 (hbk)
ISBN 978-0-415-58875-1(pbk)
ISBN 978-0-203-89183-4 (ebk)

Contents

Contributors

A. Haroon Akram-Lodhi is Professor of International Development Studies at Trent University, Peterborough, Canada and has recently co-edited *Land, Poverty and Livelihoods: Perspectives from Developing and Transition Countries* and *Globalization, Neo-Conservative Policies and Democratic Alternatives: Essays in Honour of John Loxley*. His principal research interest is in the political economy of agrarian change, including its gender dimensions.

Farshad Araghi is Chair of the Department of Sociology and Director of the Graduate Program at Florida Atlantic University. He is a co-editor of the *International Journal of Sociology of Agriculture and Food*. His principal research interests are globalization, world-historical methodology and the political economy of agrarian change, and his work on global depeasantization relates peasant studies, food regime analysis, land reform and world-historical sociology. He is currently completing a book on peasants and the global enclosures of our times. His article 'Food regimes and the production of value: some methodological issues', published in the *Journal of Peasant Studies*, won the Eric Wolf Prize.

Amiya Kumar Bagchi is Director and Secretary of the Institute of Development Studies Kolkata, India and is perhaps best known for *The Political Economy of Underdevelopment, Capital and Labour Re-defined: India and the Third World* and *The Perilous Passage: Mankind and the Global Ascendancy of Capital*.

Henry Bernstein is Professor of Development Studies in the University of London at the School of Oriental and African Studies, UK. In addition to being former co-editor of the *Journal of Agrarian Change* and the *Journal of Peasant Studies*, he has co-authored *African Enclosures? The Social Dynamics of Wetlands in Drylands*, edited *The Agrarian Question in South Africa*, and co-edited *Rural Livelihoods: Crises and Responses*.

Saturnino M. Borras, Jr is Canada Research Chair in International Development Studies at Saint Mary's University, Halifax, Canada. His most recent books are *Pro-Poor Land Reform: A Critique* and *On Just Grounds: Struggling for Agrarian Justice and Citizenship Rights in the Rural Philippines*, co-edited with Jennifer Franco. His current research interests include transnational agrarian movements and redistributive reform in 'non-private lands'.

Terence J. Byres is Emeritus Professor of Political Economy in the University of London, and Emeritus Editor of the *Journal of Agrarian Change*. His earlier writing was on agrarian change in India. His last book, *Capitalism From Above and Capitalism From Below*, was a comparison of capitalist agrarian transition in Prussia and the USA. He is currently working on the relationships, in the eighteenth century, between the capitalist transformation of Scotland and the Scottish Enlightenment.

Cristóbal Kay is Professor of Development Studies and Rural Development at the Institute of Social Studies in The Hague, the Netherlands. He has co-edited *Disappearing Peasantries? Rural Labour in Africa, Asia and Latin America*, co-authored *Latin America Transformed: Globalization and Modernity*, and written *Latin American Theories of Development and Underdevelopment*.

Ray Kiely is Professor of International Politics in the University of London at Queen Mary College. His principal research interests are in international political economy, globalization, imperialism and social theory. Among his publications, his most recent books are *The New Political Economy of Development* and *Empire in the Age of Globalisation: US Hegemony and Neo-Liberal Disorder*.

Philip McMichael is Professor of Development Sociology at Cornell University. He has written *Development and Social Change: A Global Perspective*, which is in its fourth edition, has edited *Food and Agrarian Orders in the World-Economy* and *The Global Restructuring of Agro-Food Systems*, and has co-edited *New Directions in the Sociology of Global Development*. In addition, he has written *Settlers and the Agrarian Question: Foundations of Capitalism in Colonial Australia*. His current projects centre on the politics of globalization, including institutional changes in the global order and globalization counter-movements.

Bridget O'Laughlin is Associate Professor of Population and Development at the Institute of Social Studies in The Hague, the Netherlands, is a co-editor of *Development and Change*, and has published extensively in journals such as the *Journal of Southern African Studies*, *African Affairs* and the *Journal of Peasant Studies*. She is currently researching the gendered impact of the HIV/AIDS epidemic on rural livelihoods in Southern Africa.

Miguel Teubal is Professor of Economics at the University of Buenos Aires and researcher at the National Council for Scientific and Technological Research, known as CONICET. He has published widely on the political economy of food, agriculture and poverty in Latin America and Argentina. Some of his recent publications include 'Expansión del modelo sojero en la Argentina: de la producción de alimentos a los commodities' and 'Tierra y reforma agraria en América Latina', and he co-edited *Agro y Alimentos en la Globalización: Una Perspective Crítica*.

Michael J. Watts is Professor of Geography and Director of African Studies at the University of California at Berkeley. He is author of an extensive array of articles and chapters, and is currently working on two books, on the history of oil in the Niger Delta and the history of postwar US capitalism seen through the poultry sector. His concern with the agrarian question extends back over 30 years.

Ellen Meiksins Wood was for many years Professor of Political Science at York University, Toronto, Canada. Her books include *The Pristine Culture of Capitalism*, *Peasant-Citizen and Slave*, *Empire of Capital*, *The Origin of Capitalism: A Longer View*, and *The Retreat from Class*, which won the Deutscher Prize.

Preface

In 2007, for the first time in human history, a majority of the world's population lived in cities. However, on a global scale, poverty overwhelmingly retains a rural face. Nonetheless, when, in October of 2007, the World Bank *World Development Report 2008: Agriculture for Development* was released, it was the first such report in more than 20 years. Coming 18 months after the UN Food and Agriculture Organization convened the International Conference on Agrarian Reform and Rural Development in Porto Alegre, Brazil, the first such intervention within the UN system in 25 years, and during a period in which *The Economist* could declare on its cover 'The end of cheap food', as a consequence of rising demand for food in Asia and agrifuels in the USA, as well as climate-related cuts in food supplies, it is clear that, for the moment, the issue of rural development has reasserted itself onto the agendas of the international agencies concerned with the promotion of 'development'.

This reassertion is not just because global consumers face higher food prices and national politicians face the possibility of food riots. More importantly, global civil society has pressed the case for renewed attention to the importance of rural development as a precondition for the creation of a more just and egalitarian global order. Led by La Via Campesina, the international peasant movement that is the largest social movement in the world, the demand for food sovereignty and wide-ranging land and agrarian reform now echoes through the corridors of all the major actors involved in the global politics of development. This call has also reverberated into the intellectual community: while for many scholars, including the current Editors, land and agrarian reform has always been a pivotal social and political issue, there have nonetheless been a number of recent notable books published on the theme.

In January 2006, the Rural Development, Environment and Population Studies Group at the Institute of Social Studies in The Hague, the Netherlands brought these three groups together in an international conference on Land, Poverty, Social Justice and Development. The conference was in many ways a remarkable event, in that it was organized to ensure the voices of activists, policy-makers and scholars were all equally heard, so that a dialogue between these often conflicting expressions could, at the very least, be attempted.

One of the Parallel Workshops at this conference was entitled 'The peasantry and the development of capitalism in a comparative perspective', and this book is a direct outcome of that workshop. Three early drafts of chapters in this volume were presented at the workshop, after which the Editors commissioned the remainder of the contributions contained in this book. It is, in our view, a remarkable testament to the renewed importance of the issues raised in this book by the 'agrarian question' that this volume has been able to involve the current set of contributors, and we would like to acknowledge our thanks to them for their hard work – and their patience. Having said that, some who took part in the workshop but did not contribute to this book nonetheless played an important role in the early deliberations that resulted in this volume. In this light, the Editors would like to thank John Sender for acting as discussant at the workshop and Ken Post for chairing it. The Editors would also like to thank the Netherlands Inter-Church Co-operation Organization (ICCO), which provided principal funding for the conference and thus the workshop. We are also grateful to Terry McKinley who, while working for the United Nations Development Programme, commissioned some earlier research, from which emerged a set of ideas that have coalesced in this volume. Finally, at various stages in the preparation of this book, Harriet Friedmann and Prabhat Patnaik were interested and involved, although they were not, for reasons beyond their control, ultimately able to contribute to the volume.

This book is the second of a multi-volume series, Routledge ISS Studies in Rural Livelihoods. Each book in the series will focus on a key theme in rural livelihood studies, and will seek to explore that theme in a fresh yet critical manner, from a historical, comparative and policy perspective. The Editors would like to thank the other members of the Editorial Board of the series, Saturnino M. Borras, Jr and Max Spoor, for their ongoing contribution. At Routledge we wish to express our thanks to Terry Clague for steering the series as a whole, and Sarah Hastings for her work on this book.

Haroon Akram-Lodhi
Cristóbal Kay

List of abbreviations and acronyms

AQ1	the path-dependant agrarian question
AQ2	the global reserve army of labour agrarian question
AQ3	the class forces agrarian question
AQ4	the decoupled agrarian question of labour
AQ5	the gendered agrarian question
AQ6	the corporate food regime agrarian question
CE	Common era
CONAIE	*Confederación de Naciones Indígenas del Ecuador* (National Confederation of Indigenous Nations)
ENSO	El Niño Southern Oscillation
EU	European Union
EZLN	*Ejército Zapatista de la Liberación Nacional* (Zapatista Army of National Liberation)
FAO	Food and Agriculture Organization of the United Nations
GATT	General Agreement on Tariffs and Trade
GDP	gross domestic product
MLAR	market-led agrarian reform
MST	*O Movimento dos Trabalhadores Rurais Sem-Terra* (Landless Rural Workers' Movement)
NAFTA	North American Free Trade Area
NGO	Non-governmental organization
Q1	The agricultural production problematic
Q2	The politics problematic
Q3	The accumulation problematic
UN	United Nations
UNCTAD	United Nations Conference on Trade and Development
WTO	World Trade Organization

Part 1

Peasant Livelihoods and the Agrarian Question

1 The agrarian question

Peasants and rural change

A. Haroon Akram-Lodhi and Cristóbal Kay

The fate of the peasantry and the agrarian question

A peasant is an agricultural worker whose livelihood is based primarily on having access to land that is either owned or rented, and who uses principally their own labour and the labour of other family members to work that land. Peasants rely to a significant, if not exclusive, degree on cultivating arable land. They either prosper or go hungry according to whether the land, after meeting their production expenses, provides them with enough produce for the household to maintain an adequate standard of living and, if possible, some produce that can be stockpiled as a surplus to be sold or saved for future use. Peasants do not live an idyllic rural life; their lives are harsh, are too often short, and are deeply affected by forces outside their control. In trying to obtain land, they may have to deal with landlords; in trying to sell produce, they may have to deal with traders; in trying, when necessary, to work for others because they do not have a stockpile, they may have to accept what is offered. Peasants are thus rarely self-sufficient. Although peasants must be able to undertake a wide variety of tasks with a reasonable degree of competence, if they are going to be able to survive, they do not produce everything they need for their livelihood. As a consequence, peasants do not live in isolation from wider social and economic forces that are outside their control; rather, they are subordinated to those wider social and economic forces because of their need to obtain items they do not themselves produce. Finally, in obtaining items they do not produce, their identity affects the terms and conditions under which these items are obtained. Thus, the subordinate position of peasants affects the complex network of social relationships they enter into with others, the economic transactions they undertake with others, and the content of the culture within which they live day by day. This means that, in understanding the position of the peasantry, it is necessary to understand the relationships of peasants to their social superiors, to each other, in their families and in their communities on the basis of gender, age and kinship, to the state, and to the operation of the product and labour markets they may use. It is also necessary to understand how these relationships affect the conditions in which peasants may or may not produce the surplus that can allow them to prosper.[1]

More than a decade ago, Eric Hobsbawm (1994: 289), one of the most renowned historians of the peasantry, wrote that 'the most dramatic and far-reaching social change of the second half of this (last) century, and the one which cuts us off for ever from the world of the past, is the death of the peasantry'. Peasants existed before the dawn of the industrial world; their world adapted to the rise of capitalism, in Europe and around the world; and yet now, according to Hobsbawm, the world of the peasantry is dissolving before our very eyes. Indeed, in the words of Bernstein (2006: 454), 'nothing is gained, and much obscured, by characterizing contemporary small farmers as "peasants"'. The reason for this is the path capitalism has taken in the past two decades. As capitalism arose, peasants accommodated it, as their subordination to the wider social and economic forces transformed from that of a variety of pre-capitalist forms, including feudalism, to capitalism. However, over the course of more than two decades, capitalism has undergone inexorable change, and these changes have had profound implications for the global peasantry. The states and economies within which peasants are subordinated have become increasingly integrated into global circuits of production, trade and finance, a phenomenon universally known as 'globalization'.[2] As Ripple (2007) reminds us, food globalization is not new; it has been going on for 10 millennia, speeding up particularly in the late fifteenth century. Nonetheless, current forms of globalization demonstrate a historically significant strengthening of processes of concentration and centralization within capitalist enterprises operating internationally, a globalization of capital accumulation, and an apparently lesser role for the state. These developments have had extremely widespread effects in culture, society, politics and the economy. Granted, the immediate and long-term implications of these effects are not clear, and they are contested. Nonetheless, in this regard it is perhaps in seeking to understand the implications of globalization for the social and economic organization of rural and agricultural activity among peasants that the greatest degree of contestation is witnessed (Goodman and Watts 1997; Petras 1997; Borras 2004).

This is so, in large part, because of the emergence of a fundamental contradiction at the heart of the world food system: that in a world of unparalleled rural production and productivity, which has more than sufficient capacity to meet the food security needs of all, the numbers of those living in varying degrees of food insecurity and chronic hunger in the world's towns and countryside is historically unprecedented, even as the vast majority of the world's farmers, including the world's peasants, face a livelihood crisis (IFAD 2001; FAO 2005; IFPRI 2007; Patel 2007; Weis 2007). Indeed, the World Bank's flagship annual publication, *World Development Report 2008: Agriculture for Development*, has recently highlighted the fact that three-quarters of the world's poor live in the countryside, deriving their principal work activity from farming that does not foster a secure or sustainable livelihood (World Bank 2007).

This articulation of a global agrarian crisis with, in a sense, massive 'overproduction' in some parts of the global food system, has led some to argue that fundamental shifts are under way in the world food system, as capital in the form of agro-food transnational corporations, in conjunction with states operating through the World Trade Organization, seeks to reconfigure global agriculture. As a result, it can be expected that the position of the peasantry will be, at best, as little more than contracted petty commodity-producing pieceworkers subsumed within the buyer-driven commodity chains of corporate agro-food transnational corporations (McMichael 1994; Friedmann 2004; Bernstein 2006). In this way, the subordination of the peasantry to capital on a global scale continues, as it has in the past, but assumes a new character as, out of the disorder of the past three decades, a new global corporate agro-food regime consolidates (Friedmann 1993; Bonanno *et al.* 1994; Goodman and Watts 1997; Magdoff *et al.* 2000; Buckland 2004; Patel 2007; Weis 2007). Indeed, for some of these observers, including, apparently, Hobsbawm, the evolution of a seemingly globalized capitalism marks a decisive theoretical and practical break: old issues, such as the fate of the global peasantry, have disappeared into history, and new paradigms are required (Kearney 1996), because peasants are a 'historical anachronism, unable to survive the dynamics of the capitalist development of agriculture' (Veltmeyer 2006: 445).

This book is about the fate of the peasantry in a contemporary world subject to seemingly ceaseless agrarian change. Given the context of a global agrarian crisis, the book will examine whether, and if so, how, the location of food and agricultural production within contemporary capitalism has been reconfigured and is contributing to processes that will ultimately undermine the livelihoods of the global peasantry and bring about, in Hobsbawm's words, 'the death of the peasantry'.[3] To that end, this book will explore the processes underpinning the global agrarian crisis and the fate of the peasantry by examining the historical trajectories and contemporary relevance of critical issues surrounding the development of agriculture in emergent and mature capitalist societies, issues that were first identified more than 100 years ago and which are known collectively in the political economy literature as the 'agrarian question'.

In 1899 Karl Kautsky (1988) defined the agrarian question by asking 'is capital, and in what ways is capital, taking hold of agriculture, revolutionising it, smashing the old forms of production and of poverty and establishing the new forms which must succeed?' (Banaji 1980: 46).[4] Recently, Terence J. Byres (1996: 26) has elaborated this definition to mean 'the continued existence in the countryside, in a substantive sense, of obstacles to an unleashing of accumulation in both the countryside itself and more generally – in particular, the accumulation associated with capitalist industrialization'. Clearly, the agrarian question cannot be removed from the world-historical context within which it is situated, whether that be the period of imperialism or the period of globalization. These contexts witness a reconfiguring of the development of the forces and relations of production on a global scale, and these processes have profound implications for the prospects of capital accumulation among producers within the global rural economy and beyond. This book is itself both evidence of, and seeking to contribute to, the ongoing debate[5] within agrarian political economy as to whether, in the contemporary period, the agrarian question as it is conventionally defined continues to be of contemporary relevance for global capital; whether the meaning of the agrarian question in the contemporary period has fundamentally changed; or whether the agrarian question is now fundamentally a concept that can be relegated to the footnotes of history, as suggested by Hobsbawm.

The contemporary understanding of the agrarian question emerges from the insight that it is self-evident that mature capitalist economies are, in an economic sense, structurally different from developing capitalist economies. It is in seeking to understand the processes by which rural structures were transformed and capital accumulation unleashed that the agrarian question acquires its historical interest – in order for this transformation to occur, obstacles in the countryside to structural transformation, which are at the heart of development in its economic sense, had to be overcome. The key differences in the structures of mature capitalist and developing capitalist economies suggest that there must be changes: in the pattern of production, with a shift from an economy dominated by agriculture to an economy driven by higher-value industrial manufacturing; in produced inputs, with a shift towards capital-intensive production techniques and technologies in both the agricultural and non-agricultural sectors; in employment, with a shift from agricultural to non-agricultural occupations; and in demand, with the formation of a home market capable of sustaining accumulation. An understanding of these historical processes does have contemporary relevance: in a host of developing and transition economies, social and economic obstacles within agriculture continue to inhibit this structural transformation of the economy, potentially constraining rural accumulation. These potential limits to accumulation restrict the livelihood security of millions of people, in both countryside and town, and thus contribute to the global agrarian crisis.

However, this is not where the contemporary relevance of the agrarian question can be questioned. Rather, the heart of the current debate within political economy regarding the continued salience of the agrarian question is whether, in a real sense, agriculture 'matters' any more to processes of capital accumulation on a global scale. Indeed, 'does it even make sense to speak or write of "peasants" today?' (Veltmeyer 2006: 445). If capital and capital accumulation is increasingly internationalized, does agriculture continue to have a possible role in the emergence of capital within states, or is (in the current international economic conjuncture) agricultural transformation irrelevant to the emergence of capital within a state as the very circuits of capital have become globalized? This central issue is the overarching theme of this book.

The emergence of the agrarian question

The origin of a concern with agrarian issues within political economy can be traced back to the first volume of *Capital* (Marx 1976, orig. 1867), where, as

Bernstein (2006: 449) reminds us, the class basis of the emergence of capitalist farming within England was explored in detail through the concept of 'primitive accumulation'. However, it was in the 1890s that the agrarian question emerged as a clearly distinct field of enquiry within political economy, for it was in this decade that three foundational texts were written, establishing the terrain of its problematic. These were: *The Peasant Question in France and Germany*, written in 1894 by Friedrich Engels; Karl Kautsky's *The Agrarian Question*, published in 1899; and Vladimir Ilyich Lenin's *The Development of Capitalism in Russia*, also published, coincidentally, in 1899.[6]

In *The Peasant Question in France and Germany* Engels (1950: 381) argued that 'from Ireland to Sicily, from Andalusia to Russia, and Bulgaria, the peasant is a very essential factor of population, production and political power'. However, 'the development of the capitalist form of production has cut the life-strings of small production in agriculture; small production is irretrievably going to rack and ruin' (Engels 1950: 382). The reason was that European farm production in general, whether produced by large landowners or small peasants, was unable to compete with cheap grain produced outside Europe. This was leading to the slow dissolution of the peasantry as, unable to compete with imports, they were becoming dispossessed from the land. Only in England and in Prussia east of the Elbe was this not taking place, because these places witnessed 'big, landed estates and large-scale agriculture' (Engels 1950: 381) – in short, capitalism in agriculture had emerged. It was therefore necessary, according to Engels, that the European peasantry adopt a political response to this emergent agrarian crisis. However, 'the doomed peasant (was) in the hands of his false protectors' – large landowners that 'assume the role of champions of the interests of the small peasants' (Engels 1950: 382). The political party of the urban working class, which had a 'clear insight into the interconnections between economic causes and political effects', therefore had to become a 'power in the countryside' (Engels 1950: 382) by adopting a programme that reflected the political needs of the peasantry and, in so doing, forming an alliance with the peasantry. That was the road, argued Engels, to political power, in both town and country.

Engels' emphasis was clearly on the political implications of the agrarian question – that, in a sense, the emerging globalization of the food system as a result of imperialism was undermining peasant livelihoods in Europe, and that the agrarian question was an agrarian question for and about labour. His concern was not with the issue of the emergence of agrarian capital, rural capital accumulation, or capital more generally. These broader concerns were raised, though, by Kautsky and Lenin, because for both men the force behind the rural transformation identified by Engels, including political and social transformation, was the process facilitating the generalized emergence of capital, and hence the capital–labour relationship, in the form of capitalist industrialization. For example, Lenin (1964, orig. 1899) took it as a given that from the 1880s Russia had been undergoing capitalist industrialization, which had eroded the basis of the peasant economy, albeit incompletely and unevenly, and which would as a consequence revolutionize property relations, spurring the predominance of private property. Capitalist industrialization ended the interrelationship of rural agriculture and rural petty industry in the countryside. It had increasingly commodified agricultural production. It had broken down precapitalist labour regimes in town and country as the need for a waged labour force had emerged. Finally, capitalist industrialization had introduced new, productivity-enhancing techniques and technologies into agriculture and the rural economy.

While not the central focus of Kautsky's and Lenin's analysis, these processes occurred because industrial capital placed demands on agriculture for resources, and peasants, as we have seen, have the capacity to produce resources surplus to their needs, an agricultural surplus that cumulatively could provide the physical, financial and wage-good products necessary for capitalist industrialization and which, moreover, could grow as new agricultural techniques and technologies were introduced into the countryside. This necessitated a rural transformation of the precapitalist mode of production, a transformation that facilitated the emergence of a dynamic, surplus-generating class of producers within rural economy. Such a rural transformation was witnessed in the development of agrarian capital, and thus, according to Kautsky and Lenin, incipient capitalist industrialization propelled, as a necessary if not sufficient condition, the corresponding establishment of agrarian capital. It was the process by which agrarian capital was established that lay at the heart of the classically construed agrarian question.

The establishment of agrarian capital began, according to Kautsky and Lenin, with the deepening use of non-rurally produced simple manufactures in rural society. While rural areas had previously produced a range of their own manufactures, to meet the needs of the peasantry, it was nonetheless the case that the countryside had always relied on some small measure of urban manufactured commodities. What changed with the import of urban manufactures, produced under capitalist relations of production, was that these manufactures were cheaper than rural manufactures produced under precapitalist conditions, because rural manufactures were not subject to the constraint of coercive competition that was borne by capitalist manufactures. Then, as Kautsky noted, as the expanded insinuation of capitalist commodity manufactures into the rural economy proceeded, the need for money would be engendered and, as a consequence, the commoditization of agricultural production, often initially a staple food, would occur. As commodity production for agricultural markets expanded, however, the coercive disciplines of capitalist competition kicked in within rural society. In particular, as more was produced to be sold, the need to sell in order to survive deepened. The compulsion to sell facilitated increasing specialization in agricultural commodity production as a means of controlling costs, which further heightened dependence on the market, even as those producers who sought to sustain their market competitiveness found that markets could provide the basis of agrarian accumulation if the principles of capitalism were followed: expansion, innovation, and a lowering of unit costs through scale economies. This required investment, which in turn required that producers generate and retain a surplus. This in turn maintained growth in the surplus, which as a result became the basis of the capitalization of agriculture and agrarian accumulation.

Those peasants unable or unwilling to sustain their competitiveness found that attempts to use markets to increase consumption, while not being able to be competitive in product markets, generated deficits that were only reinforced by distress sales of output and the mobilization of debt. In order to meet the costs of market dependence, deficit households increasingly engaged in wage labour, which was performed both for the more dynamic surplus producers and for industrial capital. Thus, as agricultural commodity production expanded, peasants became subordinated to product and labour markets even as some producers, capable of sustaining agrarian accumulation, produced for the purpose of accumulation. The result was the gradual emergence of qualitatively distinct types of rural holdings, which differed in the purpose of their productive activity. One group produced for accumulation, while the other strove to maintain subsistence in increasingly difficult circumstances.

As differences emerged between peasants in the purpose of productive activity, changes in the pattern of capital and labour utilization also occurred among peasants. The result of these changes in the technical coefficients of production were, over time, a change in the structure of resource demand by producers of differing productive purpose and ultimately in the structure of resource distribution. Accumulating peasant households sought to expand their control over productive assets in order to give further impetus to accumulation. Deficit peasant households were unwillingly forced to liquidate their assets by selling them to more dynamic producers, in order to be able to cope. A change in the distribution of productive assets – both means of production and labour-power – thus took place. Deficit peasants became part of the labour force, and indeed of the market needed by those surplus-producing peasants boosting output and expanding holdings of the means of production. In turn, surplus-producing peasants had relatively higher incomes that, by contributing to the creation of a home market, spurred capital accumulation as a whole.

Lenin emphasized the interconnected and interdependent character of this rural transformation when he wrote that:

> the 'home market' grows as a result of the conversion into a commodity of the product of commercial, entrepreneur farming, on the one hand, and of the conversion into a commodity of the labour-power sold by the badly-off peasants, on the other.
>
> (Lenin 1964: 73)

Thus, in the genesis of agrarian capitalism, changes in social relations emerging out of a reconfiguration of access to, and control over, productive assets gave rise to changes in the structure of economic processes and rural transformation. Eventually, so the argument went, non-capitalist predatory property relations and labour processes are subordinated and integrated into capitalism (Brenner 1977).

However, both Kautsky and Lenin did not propose that rural transformation was subject to what today would be called 'path-dependence'; that is to say, self-reinforcing tendencies. Lenin and Kautsky wrote at a time of historically unprecedented globalization, of which they were aware, and which was not confined to industrial capitalism, but extended into agriculture. As Michael Watts (2002) has reminded us, the end of the nineteenth century witnessed intense international competition in an increasingly integrated world market in farm products, facilitated not only by the expansion of the global agricultural frontier, but also by marked improvements in long-distance shipping, by changing tastes arising from an ongoing gastronomic transition, and by supply-constrained national grain production being unable to match increases in national demand. Thus Lenin and Kautsky wrote during the heyday of what has been termed by Harriet Friedmann (1993) the first world food regime; the recognition of these processes by Kautsky in particular, and to a lesser extent Lenin in the 1890s, informed their theoretical perspective.

As a consequence, Kautsky in particular, but also Lenin, argued that the process of agrarian change could take multiple forms, rooted in the specificity of each case. Lenin, for example, wrote that 'a theoretical economic analysis can, in general, only deal with tendencies' and as such cannot uncover 'a law for all individual cases' (Lenin 1964: 111, 117). The manner in which what Watts (1998: 450) memorably terms 'recombinant' agrarian capital would develop was driven by agro-industrial capital, which might, in particular circumstances, prefer to sustain a non-capitalist rural economy because of the unique characteristics of agricultural production. These characteristics include seasonal and biological aspects, as well as the capacity of family-based agricultural production to, in effect, depress real wages by working longer and harder, and in so doing sustain an ability to compete with agrarian capital that was driven by the need to survive. In such circumstances, according to Kautsky (1988), agro-industrial capital would restrict itself to food processing, farm inputs and rural financial systems, using science, technology and money to subsume petty commodity production to the demands of agro-industrial capital.

The variant tendencies of recombinant agrarian capital meant that, for Kautsky, there were no inevitable 'laws' of agrarian development and change: capitalism does not impose path-dependence on agriculture. Thus there was no tendency for the size distribution of farms to change over time, as might be inferred if capitalist agriculture overwhelmed peasant farming. Farms did not have to be technically efficient in a capitalist sense in order to survive, but peasants had to be prepared to work more intensely, depressing the real return to peasant labour, in order to sustain competitiveness with capitalist producers. As a consequence, farms responded to the increased coerciveness of market relations in the late nineteenth century by altering their product mix, by incurring debt, and by out-migrating. Thus the agrarian crisis of the late nineteenth century, which was driven by a massive increase in the global supply of grain, and as a consequence witnessed falling grain prices, falling land rents and falling profits, was solved by the intensification of rural production, and by agro-industrial capital taking over some of the functions previously done within the farm sector, such as processing and agro-industry, in effect capitalizing a range of rural manufacturing processes.

Developing the ideas of Engels, Kautsky also identified a contradiction at the heart of an imperialist world food regime: that as rural economic activity in general, and agriculture in particular, started to assume a lesser role globally in the economy, the political importance of rural producers became all the more important. This was driven by both the slow extension of the democratic franchise, which gave political importance to the numerically important rural economy, and by the integration of an increasingly competitive global food market. This gave rise to a structure of state protection that, as a consequence, sustained a peasant subsector prepared to depress its own real earnings in order to survive against capitalist competition. For Kautsky, this did not have to be a transitional phase – it could be sustained over time. Thus Kautsky was able to link the character of the agrarian question to the character of the imperialist world market.

Clearly, Kautsky in particular, in considering the agrarian question, did not isolate the processes he was describing from the world market. Rather, he saw the processes being described as highly uneven and contingent, processes that had to be explored in all their complexity if the development of agrarian capital was to be understood. Interestingly, this is most clearly demonstrated by Lenin (1966), who, in his 'Preliminary draft theses on the agrarian question', written in 1920, posited the emergence of six rural classes from within a peasantry undergoing processes of fragmentation and change as agrarian capital developed in Europe.[7] At the apex of the rural class structure was:

> the big landowners, who, in capitalist countries – directly or through their tenant farmers – systematically exploit wage-labour and the neighbouring small (and, not infrequently, part of the middle) peasantry, do not themselves engage in manual labour, and are in the main descended from feudal lords ... or are rich financial magnates, or else a mixture of both.
>
> (Lenin 1966: 159)

Below the big landowners came a second stratum of exploiters:

> The big peasants (*Grossbauern*) are capitalist *entrepreneurs* in agriculture, who as a rule employ several hired labourers and are

connected with the 'peasantry' only in their low cultural level, habits
of life, and the manual labour they themselves perform on their
farms.

(Lenin 1966: 157, emphasis in original)

Lenin next introduced a stratum locked between the clear exploiters and the
clearly exploited, when he wrote that:

in an economic sense, one should understand by 'middle peasants'
those farmers who, 1) either as owners or tenants hold plots of land
that are also small but, under capitalism, are sufficient not only to
provide, as a general rule, a meagre subsistence for the family and the
bare minimum needed to maintain the farm, but also produce a certain surplus which may, in good years at least, be converted into
capital; 2) quite frequently ... resort to the employment of hired
labour.

(Lenin 1966: 156)

Among the clearly exploited, Lenin defined three strata. There were 'the
small peasantry, i.e. the small-scale tillers who, either as owners or as
tenants, hold small plots of land which enable them to satisfy the needs of
their families and their farms, and do not hire outside labour' (Lenin 1966:
154). There were also:

the semi-proletarians or peasants who till tiny plots of land, i.e. those
who obtain their livelihood partly as wage-labourers ... and partly by
working their own or rented plots of land, which provide their families
only with part of their means of subsistence.

(Lenin 1966: 153).

Finally, there were 'the agricultural proletariat, wage-labourers (by the year,
season or day), who obtain their livelihood by working for hire at capitalist
agricultural enterprises' (Lenin 1966: 153).

Analytically, then, Lenin's understanding of the processes of change
embedded within the agrarian question hinged critically on the emergence of
exploitation, defined in its strict Marxist sense. The commodification of
labour was, in these processes, the pivotal event, even if it was contingent,
because wage labour produced a surplus product that could be extracted
from the direct producer to the dominant class through the prevailing set
of relations of production, and which could thus serve as the basis of
rural accumulation. Under capitalist relations of production, this surplus
took the specific form of surplus value, which was the basis of capital
accumulation when it was extracted under relations of exploitation. In order
for surplus value to be appropriated from labour, it had to be free in the

classical 'dual sense': free to sell labour-power; and free from the means of production. Thus the emergence of agrarian capital and its corollary, agrarian labour, required a set of interlocking processes by which landed estates were transformed, at least to some degree, into capitalist farms, and the peasantry were also transformed, at least to some degree, into waged labour. It thus comes as little surprise that Lenin consistently argued that 'hired labour is the chief sign and indicator of capitalism in agriculture' (Lenin 1964: 101).

Lenin identified several mechanisms that might serve to facilitate the emergence of agrarian capital by enhancing either the relative or the absolute amount of surplus labour that was being extracted from the direct producer by the dominant class, and in turn promote accumulation. Three of these mechanisms can be mentioned, because of their continuing contemporary relevance: scale economies; changes in tenancy relations; and debt.

With regard to the first, Lenin and Kautsky both argued that the emergence of scale economies in agriculture enhanced relative surplus labour extraction.[8] Thus, Kautsky distinguished between a concentration in the scale of production permitted by an increase in the ownership of the total means of production and increases in the size of the physical units of production in order to capture the differences in farm asset ownership, cropping patterns, technology, production, sales, debt and migration, differences that would be witnessed in the development of agrarian capital. As Lenin wrote in this regard:

> if the land is not being improved, acreage gives *no idea at all* of the scale of agricultural operations; it gives *no correct* idea at all if besides this there are so many substantial differences between farms in the method of cultivation, the intensity of agriculture, the method of field cropping, quantities of fertilizers, the use of machinery, the character of livestock farming, etc.
>
> (Lenin 1964: 68, emphasis in original).

A similar understanding of the dynamics of agrarian change allowed Kautsky to identify that 'a small holding cultivated on an intensive basis can constitute a larger enterprise than a bigger farm that is exploited extensively' (Banaji 1980: 75).

These differences in peasant farms emerged as a result of the extent to which markets governed peasant behaviour. The compulsions of market dependence propelled both the generation of investment-facilitating surpluses and the establishment of a more effective, more capitalist division of labour if peasant farms sought to survive. This, in turn, permitted the reaping of scale economies at the level of the production process, the household and the farm, and engendered the emergence of dynamic and efficient units capable of accumulation. These differences could not be captured by examining the size of the unit of production, because this neglected the increased use of technology per unit of land and thus the technical coefficients of production.

For Kautsky and Lenin peasant farms used different technical coefficients of production when they differed in the purpose of production. Yet even uncovering the technical coefficients of production could be difficult, as 'in agriculture, because relationships are so much more complicated and intertwined, it is harder to determine the scale of operations, the value of the product and the extent to which hired labour is employed' (Lenin 1964: 65–66). It was apparent to both Lenin and Kautsky that the larger the size of farm, the more that had to be produced in order to cover costs and thus obtain a given level of income. This did not mean, however, that smaller-sized peasant farms were necessarily more profitable. Peasants on small-sized farms which were also small in scale would be pushed by subsistence to work harder in order to survive while remaining mired in poverty. As Kautsky memorably wrote, for small-scale, small-sized peasant farmers 'the profit did not mean his barns were full; it meant their stomachs were empty' (Banaji 1980: 70).

While the utilization of scale economies in agriculture required stricter conditions than in industry, Kautsky and Lenin argued that diminishing returns would, in practice, not apply because technological change and the extension of techniques meant that the productivity of both investment and of land would not decline. This was so not only for large-sized, large-scale holdings where the potential for technical change was great; Lenin also argued that the productivity gains typical of a healthy capitalist agriculture might lead to an absolute decrease in the size of the capitalist farms, as output growth could permit the leasing out of unneeded low-productivity land. This latter point meant that Lenin could argue that:

> capitalism grows not only by accelerating the development of large-acreage farms in extensive areas, but also by creating in the intensive areas enterprises on smaller tracts whose operations are on a much larger scale and are more capitalist ... As a result, the concentration of production in the large enterprises is actually much greater – and the displacement of small-scale production actually goes further and deeper – than is indicated by ordinary data.
>
> (Lenin 1964: 102)

Thus, in stark contrast to Engels, the argument that large-scale holdings did not necessarily require large amounts of land led both Kautsky and Lenin to suggest that the emergence of agrarian capital did not have to solely rely on out-and-out dispossession of peasants (Engels 1950).

Another mechanism of rural transformation could be changes in the forms of holding land. Lenin argued that agrarian peasant class differentiation might take the form of a decline in mortgage and a rise in tenancy. As Lenin wrote, 'the class interests of the landowners compel them to strive to allot land to the workers' (Lenin 1964: 137). This might be done by large-scale enterprises leasing out unneeded land in order to obviate labour shortages during peak periods. In addition, as differentiation led to a concentration in the ownership and control of means of production, small plots might fetch high prices and high rents for the landowners; but 'the higher price of small plots of land is not due to the superiority of small-scale farming, but to the particularly oppressed condition of the peasant' (Lenin 1964: 138).

Kautsky and Lenin also argued that another mechanism of rural transformation and the emergence of agrarian capital was debt. Lenin wrote that the types of debt incurred by the poorer and by the richer peasants was different. Small and semi-proletarian peasants became more dependent on the market over time to maintain subsistence. Although they consumed relatively less than richer peasants, poor peasants spent relatively more on basic consumption goods. If they lacked cash to meet needs, they went into debt. Given the tenuous economic position of small and semi-proletarian peasants, it was not surprising that Lenin argued that a larger proportion of small-scale farmers were indebted. Big peasants, on the other hand, were both less dependent on the market for basic consumption goods and more dependent on the market to supply production-oriented goods. The bulk of their cash expenditure went on the latter. Given a more secure financial position big peasants were more easily able to secure credit for large investments. As a result, while a lower proportion of large-scale farmers were indebted, those farms held a much larger mass of total debt. The emergence of agrarian capital thus gave rise to different types of debt; one was a sign of weakness while the other was a sign of strength.

Back to the future? Marx and the agrarian question

As this discussion of the arguments of Kautsky and Lenin makes clear, the agrarian question was recognized by both to be subtle and nuanced. Both offered an analysis capable of uncovering significant differences in processes of change in particular contexts, and thus substantive diversity among individual cases rooted in historically embedded routes of transformation. What is perhaps not adequately appreciated is the extent to which Kautsky and Lenin, in doing this, were, unbeknown to them, in fact following Marx, who 'himself returned repeatedly to the recombinant ways in which agrarian capitalisms developed (within the "swamp" of precapitalist labour relations)' (Watts 2002: 32). Thus, Marx wrote that a dominant form of surplus appropriation:

> does not prevent the same economic basis – the same in all its major conditions – from displaying endless variations and gradations in

appearance, as the result of innumerable different empirical circumstances, natural conditions, racial relations, historical influence acting
from outside, etc., and these can only be understood by analysing these
empirically given conditions.

(Marx 1981: 927–8, orig. 1894)

For a long time, political economy has been aware of the need to separate Marx's theoretical expositions from his empirical investigations. The
clearest evidence of this lies in the differences expressed in *The Eighteenth
Brumaire of Louis Bonaparte* (Marx 1967, orig. 1852) and *The Class
Struggles in France* (Marx 1973a, orig. 1850). Political economy has been
less explicit that these differences can also be witnessed in Marx's agrarian
writings.

Marx's consideration of the relationship between peasant agriculture and
the emergence of agrarian capital under 'empirically given conditions' was
evident as early as the *Grundrisse* (Marx 1973b, orig. 1939–41), in which is
noted a variety of ways in which transitions from precapitalism occur. In
these discursive notes, peasant agriculture appears in the guise sketched out
in many of Marx's writings over a 30-year period, including his famous
journalism on India, in which the peasantry is essentially conceived as being,
for lack of a better phrase, a precapitalist remnant that will be dragged into
modernity by the capitalist mode of production.

Marx's most fully developed analysis of the development of capitalism in
agriculture was worked out later in his life, and published in Volume 1 of
Capital as his account of the 'so-called primitive accumulation' in England.
There, Marx wrote that:

> in the history of primitive accumulation, all revolutions are epoch-
> making that act as levers for the capitalist class in course of formation;
> but this is true above all for those moments when great masses of men
> are suddenly and forcibly torn from their means of subsistence, and
> hurled onto the labour-market as free, unprotected and rightless prole-
> tarians. The expropriation of the agricultural producer, of the peasant,
> from the soil is the basis of the whole process. The history of this
> expropriation assumes different aspects in different countries, and runs
> through its various phases in different orders of succession, and at dif-
> ferent historical epochs. Only in England, which we therefore take as our
> example, has it the classic form.

(Marx 1976: 876)

In Marx's 'classic' example, which came, in many ways, to be seen as a *sui
generis*, English peasant farmers began to be dispossessed from the land as
the enclosure of the commons, which were an important part of the social
and material reproduction of the peasantry, deepened the crisis of the rural
economy and in so doing thus facilitated a process of socioeconomic

differentiation in the late fifteenth century (Tribe 1981). Within two centuries, a rural labouring class and a class of capitalist tenant-farmers faced each other beneath the dominant landlord class.[9]

In the journalism, in the *Grundrisse*, and in many interpretations of Volume 1 of *Capital*, the charge of path-dependence might be fair: it usually appears that, for Marx, the outcome of the introduction of capitalist relations of production into agriculture must inevitably be the emergence of agrarian capital and agrarian wage labour. However, note the last two sentences in the above quote: even in *Capital*, Marx clearly distinguished the possibility that there could be different ways in which a set of capitalist social relations would be established or consolidated.

In this light, a letter Marx composed in 1881 appears somewhat less remarkable than is sometimes claimed (Shanin 1983). Rather, the four drafts and final text of the letter to Vera Zasulich resemble *The Eighteenth Brumaire of Louis Bonaparte*; they do not disavow his overarching theoretical perspective on agrarian change, but rather demonstrate how Marx applied his analytical framework to the analysis of a messy and complex 'recombinant' set of 'empirically given conditions'. The result is a far from path-dependent, flexible and fluid analysis.

In the drafts and in the letter, Marx (1983, orig. 1925) discusses the possible fate of the Russian peasantry. The context is clear: a formally independent but internationally weak state, with a dominant peasant population, which was nonetheless rapidly industrializing under the auspices of an interventionist state, and with industry under the control of the state or non-Russians. It is, in many ways, a remarkably contemporary setting. In this setting Marx situates the fate of the Russian peasantry within the context of global economic processes: the Russian commune was 'linked to a world market in which capitalist production is predominant' (Marx 1983: 102). He stresses the specificity of the economic structure: a 'type of capitalism fostered by the state at the peasant's expense' (Marx 1983: 104). In so doing, Marx argues that, in this setting, the Russian commune is not threatened by the economic logic of the capital–labour relationship *per se*, but is rather threatened by oppression by the state and by 'capitalist intruders whom the state has made powerful at the peasant's expense' (Marx 1983: 105).

Marx thus identifies a set of 'powerful interests' seeking to subordinate the agrarian commune and the peasantry: 'overburdened by state exactions, fraudulently exploited by intruding capitalists, merchants, etc., and the landed "proprietors", it is also being undermined by village usurers' (Marx 1983: 114). In this messy setting, two different paths of transition were identified by Marx as being possible. The first would see the dominant class coalition – the 'new pillars of society' – largely eliminate the peasantry, converting them 'into wage-labourers' or, for a small number, into 'a rural middle class' (Marx 1983: 116), thus completing the agrarian transition in a classically capitalist sense. The second path was very different.

The second path of agrarian transition in the letter to Zasulich would see the agricultural commune gradually transform itself into 'an element of collective production on a national scale' (Marx 1983: 106). This could occur, according to Marx, because of the corporate specificities of the commune. These specificities included the fact that membership of the commune was not based on kinship; that all members of the commune received a private house and garden; and that the arable land itself had never been private property, but was allocated and reallocated to individuals who were allowed to appropriate the product of the land individually (Marx 1983: 108). This 'dualism' (Marx 1983: 104), according to Marx, gave the commune a set of social relations that articulated the positive and progressive features of capitalism with a set of features derived from an archaic but historically adaptable structure. This opened up the possibility that the commune could 'reap the fruits with which capitalist production has enriched humanity without passing through the capitalist regime' (Marx 1983: 112).

However, in order for the second path of transition to take place, the collective tendencies within the commune would have to gain a dominant logic over private interests, which in turn required a working class revolution that succeeded in creating a countervailing force to anti-commune stresses. Moreover, Marx hypothesized that following the revolution, new technologies could also be introduced to sustain the position of peasant agriculture. Finally, the deepening of democratic processes arising out of the revolution would be essential to the survival of the commune. Thus, Marx argues in the letter, 'to save the Russian commune there must be a Russian revolution (Marx 1983: 116).

It is far from obvious that one should prioritize the content of a short letter over a lifetime's intellectual work, and in this regard Shanin's assessment of the letter is too generous: that 'it was from Russia and the Russians that Marx learned about global "unevenness", about peasants, and about revolution' (Shanin 1983: 19) suggests far too much (Chattopadhyay 2006). Nonetheless, the letter is more than a historical footnote, for it suggests, at the very least, a clear acceptance on the part of Marx, like Kautsky and Lenin later, to envisage multiple paths of agrarian change in the empirical analysis of peasants located and operating within a dominant world economic system. Indeed, Marx writes repeatedly in the drafts of the letter that the analysis of *Capital* is 'expressly restricted to the countries of Western Europe' (Marx 1983: 117), and that it is wrong to place all agrarian transformations 'on the same plane' (Marx 1983: 107, fn c). Perhaps this intellectual flexibility, this willingness not to consign analysis to variants of path-dependence, this openness to confronting reality starkly, is the most important analytical legacy, which should be borne in mind when contemplating the contemporary salience of the agrarian question and possible paths of agrarian change. For, as Marx writes in the letter, the agrarian commune's 'innate dualism admits of an alternative: either its property element will gain the upper hand over its collective element; or else the reverse will take place.

Everything depends upon the historical context in which it is located' (Marx 1983: 120–121).

The agrarian question and agrarian transition

The logic of the classical exposition of the agrarian question grants a central place to rural transformations in peasant livelihoods as the labour process, production relations, surplus extraction and accumulation reconfigure and agrarian capital begins to be observed to emerge. The debate over the contemporary relevance of the classically construed agrarian question has its origin in an important recent deconstruction of various aspects of this classical exposition. This deconstruction breaks apart the way the agrarian question has been conceptually deployed since the 1890s into its 'component parts' (Byres 1996: 22), and then reformulates these meanings in an analytically inclusive and consistent manner in order to provide greater clarity. This has given fresh insights into the concerns of the classical exposition of the agrarian question and, as a result, questions regarding its continuing relevance have been raised.

The first tentative statement of the deconstruction of the agrarian question into its component parts was made by Byres (1986). However, it was Henry Bernstein's (1996/97; but cf. Bernstein 2006) review of Byres' *Capitalism From Above and Capitalism From Below* (1996) that offers both the most clear and the most critical elaboration of the three 'problematics' employed by Byres and which, together, comprise the contemporary understanding of terrain of the classical agrarian question.[10]

The first problematic Bernstein calls 'accumulation'. Derived from an understanding of agrarian change rooted in the work of the Soviet theoretician Yevgeni Preobrazhensky (1965, orig. 1926), which can be traced back to some of the considerations of Kautsky and Lenin discussed above, this problematic is based on a classical argument that has already been elaborated: that agriculture has the potential capacity to create productive resources surplus to its reproductive requirements, and that these surplus resources could be used to support the substantial resource costs of industrialization, structural transformation, accumulation and the emergence of capital. This problematic therefore seeks to understand the extent to which agriculture can supply a surplus and meet these resource costs, the ways in which such a surplus can be appropriated to fund industrialization and accumulation, and the ease with which such an appropriation may occur (Byres 1991a). The accumulation problematic has, under a variety of guises, underpinned a large and significant body of rural research for more than eight decades, around the world, using analytical approaches, methodologies and methods derived from Marxist and non-Marxist political economy.

The second problematic Bernstein calls 'production', and has its origins more centrally in the work of Kautsky and Lenin. This problematic explores 'the extent to which capitalism has developed in the countryside, the forms that it takes and the barriers which may impede it' (Byres 1991b: 10). A central moment in the development of rural capitalism is, as has been noted, the emergence of generalized rural wage labour and, as a corollary, the emergence of agrarian capital as a consequence of 'the dispossession of precapitalist predatory landed property and the peasantry' (Bernstein 2006: 451). Thus, this problematic explores the issues affecting the structural transformation of petty commodity-producing peasant labour into its commodified form, labour-power, through the restructuring of rural labour processes, shifts in the technical coefficients of production, and processes of peasant class differentiation, processes that were highlighted by Kautsky and Lenin in the classical exposition. This is reflected in the manner in which rural production is organized and the purpose that motivates producers. Like the accumulation problematic, the production problematic has also underpinned an extensive body of rural research over more than eight decades, a large proportion of which uses non-Marxist political economy.

The third problematic Bernstein calls 'politics', and is drawn directly from the theorization of Engels. In countries that have (or have had) large peasant populations, political formations and forces predicated on human emancipation have had to seek explicitly to create and sustain alliances with strata within the peasant population when such political formations and forces have been successful in facilitating social, political and economic change. Thus the politics problematic examines the impact of political forces and forms on the evolution of agrarian change and structural transformation. The politics problematic is significant because the factors conditioning or constraining the agrarian change explicit in both the accumulation and production problematics can shape, and be shaped by, rural struggle. As with the accumulation and production problematics, the politics problematic has underpinned an important body of rural research.

Thus, at their most fundamental, the problematics of the agrarian question explore the processes that contribute to or constrain the emergence of agrarian capital and rural capitalism. The key dynamic process in the emergence of agrarian capital and agrarian capitalism is the transformation – or non-transformation, or indeed even partial transformation – of petty commodity-producing peasants into wage labour, and hence labour-power. This process is central because, as has been noted, in order for peasants to be so transformed, they must be in some way divorced from the land on which they work, which in turn forces them fundamentally to reconfigure their livelihood strategy. No longer able to produce a part of their consumption needs, they must start to sell their labour and buy the food, clothing and shelter that they previously provided, at least in part, themselves. Wage labour is sold to emerging agrarian (proto-)capitalists who, constrained by the coercive discipline of the need to sell in the market in order to realize profit, must seek continually to enhance their efficiency and profitability. In other words, and as clearly understood in the classic foundational texts of agrarian political economy, the commodification of labour underpins deeper processes of wholesale commodification across the rural economy as a whole, and the concomitant transformation of the purpose of farm production, from production for use to production for exchange. The agrarian question is about the process by which this does or does not occur, and the implications of this process for accumulation and the social changes concomitant with the emergence of capital. It is, in this sense, and as has been articulated explicitly by Bernstein (2004, 2006), an agrarian question of capital, in that these changes are necessary, initially for the emergence of agrarian capital and later for the expanded reproduction of capital, which is, in turn, predicated on the appropriation, in a fully developed capitalist economy, of surplus value through relations of exploitation.

One final aspect of Bernstein's deconstruction is important to stress, and that is the way in which Byres, in particular, reconfigures the three problematics in order to produce an analytically inclusive account, because it is in this that current debates regarding the continued contemporary relevance of the agrarian question emerge. In Byres' formulation, in order for agriculture to no longer pose any obstacles to the capitalist transformation of an economy, the agrarian question must be 'resolved' through some form of successful 'agrarian transition'. Byres defines an agrarian transition as the occurrence of 'those changes in the countryside of a poor country necessary to the overall development of capitalism and its ultimate dominance in a particular national social formation' (Byres 1996: 27). Thus, in order to understand the pattern of capitalist development in a state, it is necessary to examine closely how accumulation, production and politics contribute to or constrain agrarian transition. Moreover, as Bernstein (1996/97: 24–25) stresses, the implication of the 'radical core of Byres' reformulation of the agrarian question as "agrarian transition" is the possibility of what Byres terms "historical puzzles"' (Byres 1996: 15): agrarian transitions that do not necessarily imply the full development of capitalist social relations of production in agriculture as part of the establishment of the dominance of capitalism within a particular social formation.

We have already seen how these 'historical puzzles' could be consistent with the analysis developed by Kautsky, Lenin and, indeed, Marx. Nonetheless, the concept of agrarian transition had to be introduced by Byres because of his 'growing unease about the constricted, and analytically impoverishing, way in which the agrarian question in contemporary poor countries is handled within the political economy tradition' (Byres 1996: 3). The first source of unease was that 'the full range of historical instances of successful transition is not referred to' (Byres 1996: 4) in the study of the agrarian question. The second was that the understanding of successful transitions 'is too stereotyped and too narrow' (Byres 1996: 4), often being predicated on a dogmatic insistence on historical inevitability and path-dependence that cannot be sustained. Byres therefore sought to undertake a 'broad comparative study' of 'the historical experience of capitalist agrarian transition' (Byres 1996: 3–4) in England, Prussia, the USA, France, Japan, South Korea and Taiwan, a preliminary sketch of which was published more than 15 years ago in the form of an important and influential essay (Byres 1991a).[11] To this work he has, more recently, added additional examples to his range of broad comparative experiences (Byres 2003). This had to be done because it was clear that many context-specific 'paths' of agrarian transition have been attempted (Byres 1991b; Bernstein 1994) within the context of both capitalist and post-capitalist modes of production.[12]

The meaning of the agrarian question: perspectives from this volume

Globalization is apparently transforming the development of the forces and relations of production on a global scale, which has implications for the agrarian question and agrarian transition (but cf. note 2). It is in seeking to understand this transformation that divergent understandings of the contemporary character of the agrarian question can be identified. In particular, it has been asked whether, in an era of globalization, agriculture continues to have, in contemporary developing and transition economies, the capacity to facilitate or constrain structural transformation and the emergence of capital. This can thus be reformulated: in the early part of the twenty-first century, under a regime of globalization, is agrarian transition possible or even relevant? Several positions in this debate can be identified in the historical and contemporary accounts offered in this book.

The first position, which can be labelled AQ1, we term the 'path-dependent agrarian question', and is critically assessed in the contribution of Ray Kiely to this volume. AQ1 argues that colonialism, by introducing capitalist relations of production, albeit unevenly and differentially across both time and space, throughout the developing world, unleashed an inexorable, if contingent, dynamic process of labour commodification that is ongoing everywhere across developing and transition economies. In this interpretation, the capitalist mode of production is deepening its ongoing diffusion into the rural sector of poor countries, transforming the agrarian production system by developing the forces of production, and in a relentless and inescapable yet contingent and differentiated process, establishing capitalist agriculture. In a very real sense, the emergence of rural capitalism is, as our term for this perspective makes clear, path-dependent and hence inevitable: the agrarian question is thus about the terms and conditions by which agrarian capital inexorably materializes. In his chapter, Kiely critically evaluates this argument, and argues, from the standpoint of industrial accumulation, that it is a poor description of the contemporary realities witnessed, and particularly the global distribution of value-added, which continues to demonstrate inequalizing unevenness on a world scale.

The second position, labelled AQ2, we term the 'global reserve army of labour agrarian question', represented in this volume by the contribution of

Farshad Araghi. AQ2 demonstrates some overlap with AQ1, but comes to a conclusion that is in many respects more consistent with the arguments of Kiely. Araghi argues that much of the debate on the agrarian question from the 1960s onwards has been implicitly predicated on a focus on the nation-state, which is unwarranted, as well as the teleological orientation of the original debate, which is then applied to an altogether different purpose – turning what was a political agrarian question into an economic one focused on development concerns. Araghi argues that the latter clearly misreads the original debate, while at the same time strongly suggesting that, from a world-historical standpoint, the former is highly misleading: current processes of globalization are, he argues, a direct continuation of the global imperialism witnessed during the colonial period when classical liberalism was ideologically dominant in the North. Thus the period between 1834 and 1870 and that from 1973 to the present have more in common than is usually assumed: economic liberalism, antiwelfarism, free market fetishism, and designs for constructing a truly global division of labour using a project seeking to create 'workshops of the world'. For Araghi it is the period between 1917 and 1973, when 'national developmentalist' approaches to the agrarian question were especially widespread, that was, in world-historical terms, exceptional. In seeing a continuity of processes over a long historical period, AQ2 has a temporal affinity with AQ1. However, Araghi does not see the creation of wage labour as the principal outcome of what he calls 'colonial–liberal globalism' or 'post-colonial neoliberal globalism', as might be argued in AQ1. Rather, he argues that modern forms of globalization, like those of the colonial period, are creating a massive reserve army of migratory labour through absolute processes of dispossession by displacement as a 'planet of slums' (Davis 2006) is fostered. For Araghi, the agrarian question is about the terms and conditions by which agrarian labour – and indeed labour more generally – reproduces, and in this there are clear echoes of Engels.

The third position, labelled AQ3, we term the 'class forces agrarian question'. AQ3 is represented in this volume, in often quite different ways, by the contributions of Ellen Meiskins Wood, Amiya Kumar Bagchi, Terence J. Byres, Michael J. Watts and ourselves, along with Saturnino M. Borras, Jr. This position holds that transformations in agrarian production systems and the forces of production are shaped by, and shape, relations between class forces. Thus Bagchi demonstrates that, reinforced by coercion, colonialism did, in some respects and instances, introduce capitalist relations of production and dynamic processes of labour commodification in the rural economies of the developing world, as suggested in AQ1. However, this introduction was by no means universal – if anything it was, as Bagchi demonstrates, quite limited. In other parts of the developing world, as part of a set of mechanisms to reinforce processes of capital accumulation, particularly in core metropolitan economies, colonialism reinforced pre-existing precapitalist class relations in an effort to sustain surplus appropriation among dominant class forces. Finally, in parts of the developing world, again as part of a set of mechanisms to reinforce accumulation in core metropolitan economies, colonialism partially transformed pre-existing relations of production, grafting, in conjuncturally specific ways, aspects of capitalist relations of production with aspects of precapitalist relations of production, again as part of an effort to sustain surplus appropriation. In some ways, Bagchi's analysis overlaps with that of AQ2; colonialism in many places increased systems of inequality and facilitated processes of export-led exploitation that, in the way they squeezed the capacity of labour to reproduce, in many ways resemble that which is witnessed today. In this interpretation, it was only rarely that an unambiguous process of labour commodification emerged. As a consequence, in AQ3 it is necessary to understand the diverse and uneven ways in which production and accumulation are, or are not, being transformed by capitalism, and the impact of such transformation on relations between and within class forces. Critical analytical variables in this understanding include the nature, extent and progress of the social differentiation found within the peasantry, the nature of the landlord class, and the role and character of the state, as stressed strongly by Byres in his contribution. Also important is the character of the market imperative and the way the market imperative shapes the actions of social classes and rural change, as argued by Wood, who stresses that only in England did changes in social property relations in the agrarian economy lead to the emergence of industrialization. The market imperative fosters processes of expanded commodification that have an impact on the agrarian structure, as argued by Akram-Lodhi, Kay and Borras in their contribution. As Watts argues, it is also important to recognize, and integrate into the analysis, the impact of: reconfigurations in the world food system and the emergence of 'new agricultures' and 'new peasants'; the changing spatial dynamics between town and country; the emergence of new forms of rural inequality as capital accumulation internationalizes and agriculture is drawn into global circuits of production, trade and finance, including in the post-socialist world; and the cumulative impact of these changes on relations between class forces and political movements, witnessed most notably in the emergence of questions surrounding the character of indigeneity. In the interpretation of AQ3, the emergence of rural capitalism, through some kind of 'agrarian transition', is quite contingent, being based on the balance of class forces.

The fourth position, AQ4, represented in this volume by the contribution of Henry Bernstein, we label the 'decoupled agrarian question of labour'. AQ4 doubts whether the agrarian question continues to be of relevance for capital. In AQ1 and AQ3, capital and labour are two relational elements in a single process, which is approached within the confines of the social formation, although it should be noted that Watts moves beyond the social formation. Thus within states the focus of analysis is how, from within precapitalist dominant and subordinate classes, a process of agrarian transition may or may not be unleashed that should, logically if not empirically, resolve the agrarian question on its conclusion by transforming predatory precapitalist landed property and the peasantry, having capital and labour eventually emerge to stand in contradiction with each other. However, Bernstein suggests that AQ1 and AQ3 fail to recognize the contemporary character of capitalism as a global world system, as does Araghi in AQ2. One impact of this has been to differentiate agriculture, which is organized through global commodity chains that integrate agrarian classes unevenly with capital at different stages of the chain, from farming itself.

Bernstein argues in this light that two key issues need to be confronted. The first is that the development of the forces of production on a global scale has, in the past 50 years, meant that agriculture globally has in effect become 'decoupled' from the process of capital accumulation. This proposition is supported by the extent to which agricultural production is located on the periphery of global capital accumulation, which is driven by manufacturing and services, particularly financial services, on a global scale. In this sense, the agrarian question of transnational capital has been resolved: transnational capital does not require access to surplus agricultural resources to facilitate accumulation, and there are also, at the same time, non-rural and non-national sources of capital that can be used to sustain national capital accumulation. It is therefore no longer necessary that capital reorganize agriculture. Agrarian transition is no longer a necessary precondition of the development of capitalism. Rather, transnational capital requires the technical capacity to allocate resources on a global scale ever more efficiently so as to enhance the surplus value generated within production, as well as the ability to develop and control markets to realize the surplus value created.

The second key issue is implicitly embedded within the first. The internationalization of capital has 'decoupled' transnational capital from national labour regimes, which are becoming ever more fragmented even as they become less capable of providing a livelihood. It is not only the case that agriculture does not really 'matter' for global capital accumulation; it is also the case that national labour regimes that do not enhance the value generated within production can also be by-passed by transnational capital, segmenting labour on a global scale, enlarging the global reserve army of labour and fostering a crisis of reproduction among fragmented classes of labour. It is important, in this regard, to differentiate AQ4 from AQ2: AQ4 sees this process as being specific to the current conjuncture; AQ2 suggests that this has been ongoing since the nineteenth century.

For AQ4, the agrarian question of capital has been resolved since the 1970s. In these circumstances, the agrarian question that remains is that of labour, which is struggling to construct a livelihood in the face of the development of the productive forces of capital. In this view, in a very real sense the globalization of capital has meant that the emergence of agrarian capital within a state is now irrelevant, except in how it shapes political struggles by subordinate classes over resources, production and accumulation. In this sense, in its focus on classes of labour and their reproduction crisis, AQ4 has clear affinities to the agrarian question of labour put forward by Engels.

Tangential to all four approaches, containing elements of more than one, is the contribution of Bridget O'Laughlin, which we term the 'gendered agrarian question' (AQ5). O'Laughlin argues that to answer the agrarian question, it is necessary to politically challenge neoliberal market fundamentalism, and that this can be done adequately only by addressing the gender dynamics of class, accumulation and politics. While she is quite sympathetic to AQ4 and the argument that labour is fragmenting, she stresses that gender is a relation of production that encompasses both cooperation and contradiction. Similarly, while at other times she can be amenable to AQ3, she takes the theorists of the agrarian question to task for failing adequately to include analytically the contribution of non-commodified labour to accumulation. Finally, in terms of the political dimensions of the agrarian question, which many contributors highlight, she notes the importance of gender relations in the operation of formal and informal political institutions. For O'Laughlin, an agrarian question that does not interrogate the character of gender relations and the ways in which they impinge on the resolution, or otherwise, of the agrarian question is analytically and politically lacking. The agrarian question must address contradictions of class and gender if it is to offer an analytically full account of social change in contemporary rural settings.

The final approach to the agrarian question in this book, AQ6, which we call the 'corporate food regime agrarian question', is provided by Philip McMichael. Like Araghi, McMichael questions the problematic of the agrarian question as it is formulated in AQ1, AQ3 and AQ4. However, he does so for reasons that differ from those offered in AQ2. McMichael argues that the agrarian question continues to be about capital and labour relations. However, he takes issue with that understanding posited in AQ1, AQ3 and AQ4, by arguing that the agrarian question cannot be reduced to a question formulated within the terms of capital theory itself. Posing the agrarian question in this misguided way results in two quite fundamental mistakes. The first mistake is a failure to adequately politicize the economic, narrowly focusing on the political consequences of proletarianization within terms of reference that are limited to the narrative of expanded reproduction, notably industrialization. McMichael strongly argues that such economic reductionism is consistent with an accumulation fetish.

The second mistake embedded within AQ1, AQ3 and AQ4 is a failure to recognize that the historical conditions governing the process of accumulation are not equivalent to the theoretical conditions of accumulation – a point similar to that made by Araghi in AQ2. AQ3, and by implication AQ1, is, according to McMichael, inadequate because it focuses on agrarian transitions in nation-states, and thus tends to discount the world-historical relations underpinning agrarian transition in the European capitalist state.

This precludes it, in turn, from connecting nationally based processes to the dynamics of struggle on a global scale. AQ4, in contrast, emphasizes the resolution of capital's agrarian question, but fails to identify the emergence of new contradictions between capital and labour on a global scale. Thus AQ1, AQ3 and AQ4 dehistoricize capitalism, according to McMichael. Ironically, this promotes, in the view of McMichael, a historicist understanding of capitalist transition.

To understand the contemporary agrarian question, McMichael argues, it is necessary to reframe its problematic in two ways. First, it is necessary to define it within and through the new world-historical conjuncture of financialization, neoliberalism, and the establishment of a global corporate food regime. Second, it is necessary to take capital as the point of analytical departure, but capital as a relation of production and of circulation, wherein the politicization of the economic can be witnessed. This leads McMichael to define the problematic not in terms of capital or labour, but rather as a contemporary agrarian question of food.

Situating the agrarian question as one of food squarely addresses the fetishization of agriculture, whether in terms of a commodity fetish or an accumulation fetish, politicizing a corporate food regime that subordinates public good for private profit through 'free' markets, which exclude agrarian populations that are increasingly dispossessed. At the same time, situating the agrarian question as one of food facilitates the subjects of accumulation imparting a specific historical sensibility that cannot be deduced from a categorical representation of the processes of accumulation. Thus global peasant resistance has developed a praxis premised on a critique of the conditions of the global movement of capital at this historical moment, focusing on the global politics of the corporate food regime in an effort to transform, as well as transcend, capital's relations of subjection and its developmentalist teleology.

McMichael argues that the contemporary global agrarian crisis requires reframing the agrarian question as one of food, which does not consign rural social relations to a narrative of industrial subordination and the elimination, or marginalization, of peasant farmers, but which rather embeds relations of production in relations of circulation. This opens up the possibility of rural transformation predicated on the social and ecological justice that is central to the food sovereignty movement and the consequent class struggles that shape the contemporary character of accumulation under a corporate food regime (McMichael 2006a, 2006b).

Like AQ6, Miguel Teubal also stresses the changing nature of world capitalism, in particular the way in which large transnational agro-industries dominate food technology, food processing and distribution within the corporate industrial agro-food system. Looking at McMichael's agrarian questions of food from a different perspective, Teubal notes how in some countries a new 'agriculture without farmers' is consolidating, shaped by the use of new technologies associated with the widespread production of transgenic crops and the massive expulsion of farmers and peasants from agriculture, an account that resonates with AQ2. This reconfigured agriculture is, according to Teubal, an essentially extractive system not very different from mining, as resources are taken from the soil. In this context, the struggle for land and agrarian reform is in fact a struggle against the industrial agro-food system being shaped by transnational corporations. It is a struggle for autonomy and in favour of communal values that are, in essence, contradictory to the main tenets of capitalism, a struggle that, as McMichael emphasizes, is wholly consistent with the demands of the food sovereignty movement.

To us, it seems that all contributors to this book use, as the critical analytical variable, the balance of forces, locally, nationally and internationally, between capital and labour, which are conjuncturally and contextually specific. Here is the heart of the debate about the contemporary relevance of the agrarian question: the contributors have manifestly differing assessments of the balance of forces in an age of globalization. AQ1 sees struggles over the terms and conditions of access to wage labour as both a central dynamic and a source of socioeconomic and spatial differentiation. AQ2 sees struggles between a globalizing capitalism and peasants dispossessed through displacement as part of the world-historical internationalization of the circuit of capital and hence value relations. AQ3 sees struggles between differentiating peasantries and the emergence of agrarian capitalism as highly contingent. AQ4 and AQ6 both see, from class-theoretic and world-historical perspectives, respectively, the struggle over livelihoods as the central thrust of a politically charged agrarian question of labour, which is increasingly divorced from transnational capital. Teubal operates at a tangent within this terrain. AQ6 also sees the global struggle between transnational capital and transnational peasant movements as reconfiguring the content of the agrarian question. For its part, AQ5 is critical of the conception of struggle offered by the contributors; O'Laughlin stresses that these struggles need to be gendered.

A concluding comment

This book offers a historical and contemporary examination of these alternative perspectives on the continued salience or otherwise of the agrarian question as classically understood. It is worth stressing that, in terms of accumulation, production and politics agriculture has had, in developed capitalist economies, the capacity to facilitate structural transformation and capitalist development. Thus the agrarian question and the process of agrarian transition is, in this light, one of continued historical significance. This historical significance is principally explored in chapters 2–6 of this book. The more pressing, salient issue, in terms of the global agrarian crisis, is whether, in an era of globalization, agriculture continues to have, in contemporary developing and transition economies, the capacity to contribute to or constrain structural transformation and the emergence of capital in ecologically sustainable ways. The relevance or otherwise of the agrarian question is, in this light, a pressing contemporary issue, and is explored principally, but not exclusively, in chapters 7–12, wherein contemporary perspectives on the continued relevance of the agrarian question will be elaborated at length, along with some critical commentaries. This is neither the time nor the place to weigh up the evidence for and against each of these contemporary perspectives. Rather, we invite readers to weigh up the evidence for themselves, in the pages that follow, and to judge our own evaluation of these perspectives in Chapter 13, the conclusion to this book.

What can be said at this time is that the diversity of perspectives offered within this book is testimony to the continuing power of the issues raised by the agrarian question, and agrarian political economy more generally, in contemporary capitalism. In this sense, this book will not conclude the debate; rather, we hope it will contribute to an ongoing dialogue within political economy concerning the interaction between peasants and globalization and thus the place of the agrarian question in contemporary capitalism.

Notes

1 There are a variety of definitions of the peasantry. For a classic analysis of the characteristics of the peasantry, see Wolf (1966). The two editions of *Peasants and Peasant Societies*, which are very different, in a substantive sense, edited by Shanin (1971, 1988), were very widely read. Ellis (1993) offers an exceedingly clear exposition of the economic characteristics of the peasantry. For a reconceptualization of the peasantry as 'polybians', see Kearney (1996), a position that is heavily critiqued by Michael J. Watts in this volume (chapter 11).

2 For excellent, critical overviews of globalization, see Hirst and Thompson (1996); Weiss (1997); and Chernomas and Sepehri (2005).

3 Hobsbawm's (1994: 289) obituary of the peasantry has been contested by, among others, Otero (1999); Bernstein (2000); Bryceson *et al.* (2000); Watts (2002); Johnson (2004); McMichael (2006a, 2006b).

4 As Bernstein (2006) reminds us, the phrase 'agrarian question' is derived from the title of Kautsky's book.

5 As evidenced by, for example, the continued relevance of the *Journal of Agrarian Change*, the *Journal of Peasant Studies*, and the attention paid to agrarian issues in a range of internationally recognized peer-reviewed international development journals, best exemplified by the recent special thematic section of the *Canadian Journal of Development Studies* (Veltmeyer 2006) on 'Development and the agrarian question', to which two contributors to this book also contribute. Two excellent and highly readable books, Patel (2007) and Weis (2007), also seek to resituate agrarian issues at the heart of global political economy.

6 A useful analysis of the discussion by the German Social Democrats and the Russian Marxists on the agrarian question and the peasantry is given by Hussain and Tribe (1981). For an analysis of Kautsky's agrarian question, see Banaji (1990). Some of Lenin's writings on the agrarian question, largely written at the turn of the 19th century, have been collected in Lenin (1976).

7 The remainder of this section plunders material from Akram-Lodhi (1992).

8 The issue of the comparative merits of small- versus large-scale agricultural production or peasant versus capitalist agriculture was intensely debated by Kautsky

and other members of the German Social Democratic party at the turn of the nineteenth century, and is discussed in Hussain and Tribe (1984). This is an ongoing debate, as can be gauged by the recent debate between Griffin *et al.* (2002, 2004), Byres (2004a) and others (Byres 2004b). The World Bank (2007) has also recently re-entered this debate, apparently arguing, in a remarkable shift, about the advantages of large-scale farming in an era of globalization.

9 There is a huge literature on the political economy of the agrarian transition from feudalism to capitalism. Key contributions include Dobb (1964); Hilton (1976); Sweezy (1976); Sweezy *et al.* (1976); Brenner (1977, 1985); Aston and Philpin (1985); and, more recently, Byres (1991a, 1996).

10 For a review essay on the classic book by T.J. Byres (1996) that influenced the writing of this chapter, see Akram-Lodhi (1998).

11 In an even earlier (albeit more limited) attempt, Byres (1977) tackled the agrarian question in a comparative and contemporary context. For a comparative analysis of the transition to agrarian capitalism between Europe and Latin America, see Kay (1974).

12 Many authors have made important contributions to the analysis and debate on the agrarian question. In addition to those already mentioned, see Harris (1978); Harriss (1980); de Janvry (1981); Murray and Post (1983); Cox and Littlejohn (1984); Pearce (1985); Saith (1985); Mamdani (1987); Levin and Neocosmos (1989); Watts (1989, 2002); Brass (1990); van der Ploeg (1993); Roseberry (1993); Byres (1995); Drew (1996); McLaughlin (1998); and Bernstein (2003, 2004), among others. Our own perspective is contained in chapter 13, the conclusion to this book.

References

Akram-Lodhi, A.H. (1992) 'Women's work and peasant class differentiation: a methodological and empirical study in political economy, with reference to Pakistan', PhD thesis, Winnipeg, Canada: University of Manitoba.

—— (1998) 'The agrarian question, past and present', *Journal of Peasant Studies*, 25 (4): 134–149.

Aston, T.H. and C.H.E. Philpin (eds) (1985) *The Brenner Debate: Agrarian Class Structure and Economic Development in Pre-Industrial Europe*, Cambridge: Cambridge University Press.

Banaji, J. (1980) 'Summary of selected parts of Kautsky's *The Agrarian Question*', in H. Wolpe (ed.), *The Articulation of Modes of Production: Essays from Economy and Society*, London: Routledge and Kegan Paul.

—— (1990) 'Illusions about the peasantry: Karl Kautsky and the agrarian question', *Journal of Peasant Studies*, 17 (2): 288–307.

Bernstein, H. (1994) 'Agrarian classes in capitalist development', in L. Sklair (ed.), *Capitalism and Development*, London: Routledge.

—— (1996/97) 'Agrarian questions then and now', *Journal of Peasant Studies*, 24 (1/2): 22–59.

—— (2000) 'The peasantry in global capitalism', in L. Panitch and C. Leys (eds), *Socialist Register 2001: Working Classes, Global Realities*, London: Merlin Press/ New York: Monthly Review Press/Halifax: Fernwood.

—— (2003) 'Land reform in southern Africa in world-historical perspective', *Review of African Political Economy*, 96: 203–226.

—— (2004) '"Changing before our very eyes": agrarian questions and the politics of land in capitalism today', *Journal of Agrarian Change*, 4 (1/2): 190–225.

—— (2006) 'Is there an agrarian question in the 21st century?', *Canadian Journal of Development Studies*, 27 (4): 449–460.

Bonanno, A., L. Busch, W. Friedland, L. Gouveia and E. Mingione (1994) *From Columbus to ConAgra: The Globalization of Agriculture and Food*, Lawrence, KS: University Press of Kansas.

Borras, S., Jr (2004) *La Vía Campesina: An Evolving Transnational Social Movement*, Transnational Institute Briefing Series No. 6, Amsterdam: Transnational Institute.

Brenner, R. (1977) 'The origins of capitalist development: a critique of neo-Smithian Marxism', *New Left Review*, 104: 25–92

—— (1985) 'The agrarian roots of European capitalism', in T.H. Aston and C.H.E. Philpin (eds), *The Brenner Debate: Agrarian Class Structure and Economic Development in Pre-Industrial Europe*, Cambridge: Cambridge University Press.

Buckland, J. (2004) *Ploughing Up The Farm: Neoliberalism, Modern Technology and the State of The World's Farmers*, Black Point, Nova Scotia/Winnipeg, Manitoba: Fernwood.

Brass, T. (1990) 'Peasant essentialism and the agrarian question in the Colombian Andes', *Journal of Peasant Studies*, 17 (3): 444–456.

Bryceson, D. F., C. Kay and J. Mooij (eds) (2000) *Disappearing Peasantries? Rural Labour in Africa, Asia and Latin America*, London: ITDG Publishing.

Byres, T. J. (1977) 'Agrarian transition and the agrarian question', *Journal of Peasant Studies*, 4 (3): 258–274.

—— (1986) 'The agrarian question, forms of capitalist agrarian transition and the state: an essay with reference to Asia', *Social Scientist*, 14(11–12): 3–67.

—— (1991a) 'The agrarian question and differing forms of capitalist transition: an essay with reference to Asia', in J. Breman and S. Mundle (eds), *Rural Transformation in Asia*, Delhi: Oxford University Press.

—— (1991b) 'Agrarian question' and 'peasantry', in T. Bottomore (ed.), *A Dictionary of Marxist Thought*, Oxford: Blackwell.

—— (1995) 'Political economy, the agrarian question and the comparative method', *Journal of Peasant Studies*, 22 (4): 561–581.

—— (1996) *Capitalism from Above and Capitalism from Below: An Essay in Comparative Political Economy*, London: Macmillan.

—— (2003) 'Paths of capitalist agrarian transition in the past and in the contemporary world', in V. K. Ramachandran and M. Swaminathan (eds), *Agrarian Studies: Essays on Agrarian Relations in Less-Developed Countries*, London: Zed Books.

—— (2004a) 'Neo-classical neo-populism 25 years on: *déjà vu* and *déjà passé* – towards a critique', *Journal of Agrarian Change*, 4 (1/2): 17–44.

—— (ed) (2004b) 'Special Issue on "Redistributive Land Reform Today"', *Journal of Agrarian Change*, 4 (1/2).

Chattopadhyay, P. (2006) 'Passages to socialism: the dialectic of progress in Marx', *Historical Materialism*, 14 (3): 45–84.

Chernomas, R. and A. Sepehri (2005) 'Is globalization and its success a myth?', in A. H. Akram-Lodhi, R. Chernomas and A. Sepehri (eds), *Globalization, Neo-Conservative Policies and Democratic Alternatives: Essays in Honour of John Loxley*, Winnipeg: Arbeiter Ring.

Cox, T. and G. Littlejohn (eds) (1984). *Kritsman and the Agrarian Marxists*, London: Frank Cass.

Davis, M. (2006) *Planet of Slums*, London: Verso.

Dobb, M. (1964) *Studies in the Development of Capitalism*, New York: International Publishers.

Drew, A. (1996) 'The theory and practice of the agrarian question in South African socialism', *Journal of Peasant Studies*, 23 (2/3): 53–92.

Ellis, F. (1993) *Peasant Economics* (2nd edn), Cambridge: Cambridge University Press.

Engels, F. (1950) 'The peasant question in France and Germany', in *K. Marx and F. Engels: Selected Works*, Vol. 2, London: Lawrence and Wishart (first published in 1894).

FAO (2005) *The State of Food Insecurity in the World 2005*, Rome: Food and Agriculture Organization of the United Nations.

Friedmann, H. (1993) 'The political economy of food', *New Left Review*, 197: 29–57.

—— (2004) 'Feeding the empire: the pathologies of globalized agriculture', in L. Panitch and C. Leys (eds), *The Socialist Register 2005: The Empire Reloaded.*, London: Merlin Press/New York: Monthly Review Press/Halifax: Fernwood.

Goodman, D. and M.J. Watts (1997) *Globalising Food: Agrarian Questions and Global Restructuring*, London/New York: Routledge.

Griffin, K., A. R. Khan and A. Ickowitz (2002) 'Poverty and the distribution of land', *Journal of Agrarian Change*, 2 (3): 279–330.

—— (2004) 'In defence of neo-classical neo-populism', *Journal of Agrarian Change*, 4 (3): 361–386.

Harris, R. (1978) 'Marxism and the agrarian question in Latin America', *Latin American Perspectives*, 5 (4): 2–26.

Harriss, J. (1980) *Contemporary Marxist Analysis of the Agrarian Question in India*, Working Paper No. 14, Madras: Institute of Development Studies.

Hilton, R.H. (1976) 'Introduction', in P. Sweezy, M. Dobb, K. Takahashi, R. Hilton, C. Hill, G. Lefebvre, G. Procacci, E. Hobsbawm and J. Merrington (eds), *The Transition from Feudalism to Capitalism*, London: Verso.

Hirst, P. and G. Thompson (1996) *Globalization in Question: The International Economy and the Possibilities of Governance*, Cambridge: Polity Press.

Hobsbawm, E.J. (1994) *Age of Extremes: The Short Twentieth Century, 1914–1991*, London: Michael Joseph.

Hussain, A. and K. Tribe (1981) *Marxism and the Agrarian Question*, London/Basingstoke: Macmillan.

—— (eds) (1984) *Paths of Development in Capitalist Agriculture*, London/Basingstoke: Macmillan.

IFAD (2001) *Rural Poverty Report 2001: The Challenge of Ending Rural Poverty*, Oxford: Oxford University Press for the International Fund for Agricultural Development.

IFPRI (2007) *The World's Most Deprived: Characteristics and Causes of Extreme Poverty and Hunger*, Washington, DC: International Food Policy Research Institute.

de Janvry, A. (1981) *The Agrarian Question and Reformism in Latin America*, Baltimore, MD: Johns Hopkins University Press.

Johnson, H. (2004) 'Subsistence and control: the persistence of the peasantry in the developing world', *Undercurrent*, 1 (1): 55–65.

Kautsky, K. (1988). *The Agrarian Question*, London: Zwan Publications (first published in 1899).

Kay, C. (1974) 'Comparative analysis of the European manorial system and the Latin American hacienda system', *Journal of Peasant Studies*, 2 (1): 69–98.

Kearney, M. (1996) *Reconceptualizing the Peasantry: Anthropology in Global Perspective*, Boulder, CO: Westview Press.

Lenin, V.I. (1964) *The Development of Capitalism in Russia*, Moscow: Progress Publishers (first published in 1899).

——— (1966) 'Preliminary draft theses on the agrarian question', in *Collected Works Volume XXXI* (4th edn), Moscow: Progress Publishers (first published in 1920).

——— (1976) *The Agrarian Question and the 'Critics of Marx'*, Moscow: Progress Publishers.

Levin, R. and M. Neocosmos (1989) 'The agrarian question and class contradictions in South Africa: some theoretical considerations', *Journal of Peasant Studies*, 16 (2): 230–259.

McLaughlin, P. (1998) 'Rethinking the agrarian question: the limits of essentialism and the promise of evolutionism', *Research in Human Ecology*, 5 (2): 25–39.

McMichael, P. (ed.) (1994) *The Global Restructuring of Agro-Food Systems*, Ithaca, NY: Cornell University Press.

——— (1997) 'Rethinking globalization: the agrarian question revisited', *Review of International Political Economy*, 4 (4) 630–662.

——— (2006a) 'Peasant prospects in the neoliberal age', *New Political Economy*, 11 (3): 407–418.

——— (2006b) 'Reframing development: global peasant movements and the new agrarian question', *Canadian Journal of Development Studies*, 27 (4): 470–483.

Magdoff, F., F.H. Buttel and J. Bellamy Foster (2000) *Hungry for Profit: The Agribusiness Threat to Farmers, Food, and the Environment*, New York: Monthly Review Press.

Mamdani, M. (1987) 'Extreme but not exceptional: towards an analysis of the agrarian question in Uganda', *Journal of Peasant Studies*, 14 (2): 191–225.

Marx, K. (1967) *The Eighteenth Brumaire of Louis Bonaparte*, Moscow: Progress Publishers (first published in 1852).

——— (1973a) 'The class strugles in France', in *Surveys From Exile: Political Writings, Volume 2*, Harmondsworth: Penguin (first published in 1850).

——— (1973b) *Grundrisse*, Harmondsworth: Penguin (first published 1939–41).

——— (1976) *Capital*, Vol. I, Harmondsworth: Penguin (first published in 1867).

——— (1981) *Capital*, Vol. III, Harmondsworth: Penguin (first published in 1894).

——— (1983) 'Marx–Zasulich correspondence: letters and drafts', in T. Shanin (ed.), *Late Marx and the Russian Road: Marx and 'the Peripheries of Capitalism'*, London: Routledge & Kegan Paul (first published in 1925).

Murray, M.J. and C. Post (1983) 'The "agrarian question", class struggle and the capitalist state in the United States and South Africa', *The Insurgent Sociologist*, 9 (4): 37–56.

Otero, G. (1999) *Farewell to the Peasantry? Political Class Formation in Rural Mexico*, Boulder, CO: Westview Press.

Patel, R. (2007) *Stuffed and Starved: Markets, Power and the Hidden Battle for the World's Food System*, London: Portobello.

Pearce, R. (1985) 'The agrarian question', in Z.G. Baranski and J.R. Short (eds), *Developing Contemporary Marxism*, London/Basingstoke: Macmillan.

Petras, J. (1997) 'Latin America: the resurgence of the left', *New Left Review* (first series), 223: 17–47.

van der Ploeg, J.D. (1993) 'Rural sociology and the new agrarian question', *Sociologia Ruralis*, 33 (2): 240–260.

Preobrazhensky, E. (1965), *The New Economics*, Oxford: Clarendon Press (first published in 1926).

Ripple, K. (2007) *A Moveable Feast: Ten Millennia of Food Globalization*, Cambridge: Cambridge University Press.

Roseberry, W.W. (1993) 'Beyond the agrarian question in Latin America', in F. Cooper, A.F. Issacman, F.E. Mallon, W. Roseberry and S.J. Stern (eds), *Confronting Historical Paradigms: Peasants, Labor, and the Capitalist World System in Africa and Latin America*, Madison, WI: University of Wisconsin Press.

Tribe, K. (1981) *Genealogies of Capitalism*, London/Basingstoke: Macmillan.

Saith, A. (ed.) (1985) *The Agrarian Question in Socialist Transitions*, London: Frank Cass.

Shanin, T. (ed.) (1971) *Peasants and Peasant Societies* (1st edn), London: Penguin.

—— (1983) 'Late Marx: gods and craftsmen', in T. Shanin (ed.), *Late Marx and the Russian Road: Marx and 'the Peripheries of Capitalism'*, London: Routledge and Kegan Paul.

—— (ed.) (1988) *Peasants and Peasant Societies* (2nd edn), London: Penguin.

Sweezy, P. (1976) 'A critique', in P. Sweezy, M. Dobb, K. Takahashi, R. Hilton, C. Hill, G. Lefebvre, G. Procacci, E. Hobsbawm and J. Merrington (eds), *The Transition from Feudalism to Capitalism*, London: Verso.

Sweezy, P., M. Dobb, K. Takahashi, R. Hilton, C. Hill, G. Lefebvre, G. Procacci, E. Hobsbawm and J. Merrington (eds) (1976) *The Transition from Feudalism to Capitalism*, London: Verso.

Veltmeyer, H. (2006) 'Introduction: development and the agrarian question', *Canadian Journal of Development Studies*, 27 (4): 445–448.

Watts, M.J. (1989) 'The agrarian question in Africa: debating the crisis', *Progress in Human Geography*, 13 (1): 1–41.

—— (1998) 'Recombinant capitalism: state, de-collectivization and the agrarian question in Vietnam', in J. Pickles and A. Smith (eds), *Theorising Transition: The Political Economy of Post-Communist Transformations*, London: Routledge.

—— (2002) 'Chronicle of a death foretold: some thought on peasants and the agrarian question', *Österreichische Zeitschrift für Geschichtswissenschaften*, 13 (4): 22–50.

Weis, T. (2007) *The Global Food Economy: The Battle for the Future of Farming*, London: Zed Press.

Weiss, L. (1997) 'Globalization and the myth of the powerless state', *New Left Review* (first series), 225: 3–27.

Wolf, E.R. (1966) *Peasants*, Englewood Cliffs, NJ: Prentice Hall.

World Bank (2007) *World Development Report 2008: Agriculture for Development*, Oxford: Oxford University Press.

Part 2

Historical Perspectives on Agrarian Change

2 Peasants and the market imperative

The origins of capitalism

Ellen Meiksins Wood

Introduction

The idea that capitalism was born in the city is conventional wisdom.[1] On the face of it, this is an eminently plausible notion. If we think of capitalism as just more and better trade and commerce, nothing seems more natural than to assume that the birthplace of capitalism must have been in cities, where merchants and traders were most at home and where commercial interests flourished. This assumption also tends to be associated with a conviction that capitalism is fundamentally natural: if not an outgrowth of some basic human nature – such as what Adam Smith called the inclination 'to truck, barter and exchange', or perhaps an incurable greed and competitiveness – then at the very least a natural extension of the acts of exchange on which human communities have relied since time immemorial to supply the necessities they cannot produce for themselves. All that is needed to bring about capitalism, apparently, is for such processes of exchange to expand, in conditions that permit an accumulation of wealth sufficient to encourage investment.

Yet, looked at more closely, capitalism, as a particular way of organizing the production and allocation of life's basic necessities, is a very specific social form, quite different in fundamental ways from other modes of organizing the supply of material needs; and it has a relatively short history, marked by deep and painful social transformations, which belie the easy assumption that it emerged naturally out of basic human inclinations, or out of the most rudimentary acts of exchange. Moreover, as we shall see, once its specificities are acknowledged, it may seem far less obvious that it must have been born in the city, and much more convincing to situate its origins in the countryside.

What is capitalism?

Capitalism is a system in which virtually all goods and services are produced for, and obtained from, the market. More fundamentally, it is a system in which those who produce and those who appropriate the surplus labour of direct producers are dependent on the market for the basic conditions of their survival and self-reproduction. The direct producer's access to the means of production, to the means of labour itself, is mediated by the market. In mature capitalism, workers can gain access only by selling their labour-power in exchange for a wage; but the dynamics of capitalism were already set in motion when direct producers, without being completely dispossessed, lost non-market access to the land, gaining access only by means of economic leases subject to the market. The capitalist appropriator also depends on the market for the conditions of survival and the self-expansion of capital, being obliged to enter the market both for access to labour and for the means of realizing the profits derived from it.

This market dependence has substantial consequences. The fact that capitalists can make profit only if they succeed in selling their goods and services on the market, and selling them for more than the costs of producing them, means that making profit is uncertain. Capitalists must compete with other capitalists in the same market. Competition is, in fact, the driving force of capitalism – even if capitalists often do their best to avoid it, for example by means of monopolies. It is the social average of productivity that, in any given market, determines success in price competition, and this is beyond the control of individual capitalists. They cannot command the prices at which their products will sell successfully, nor do they even know in advance what conditions are necessary to guarantee a sale at all, let alone a profitable one.

The one thing capitalists can control to a significant extent is their costs. So, as their profits depend on a favourable cost/price ratio, they will do everything possible to cut their costs to ensure profit. This means, above all, cutting the costs of labour; and this requires constant improvements in labour productivity, to find the organizational and technical means of extracting as much surplus as possible from workers within a fixed time period, at the lowest possible cost.

To keep this process going requires regular investment, the reinvestment of surpluses, and constant capital accumulation. This requirement is imposed on capitalists regardless of their own personal needs and wants. Even the most modest and socially responsible capitalist is subject to these pressures, and is compelled to accumulate by maximizing profit, just to stay in business. The need to adopt 'maximizing' strategies is a basic feature of the system, and not just a function of greed – although it is certainly true that a system based on market principles will inevitably place a premium on wealth and encourage a culture of greed.

What should immediately be clear from this account of how capitalism operates is that the system is driven by certain inescapable imperatives – of competition, profit maximization, constant accumulation, and the endless need to improve labour productivity. The effect has been, among other things, to drive a process of self-sustaining economic growth without parallel in history. In its constant drive for accumulation and profit maximization, it has also given rise to a uniquely wasteful and destructive exploitation of natural resources – to say nothing of the social inequities in the relations between capital and labour. These capitalist imperatives are historically specific, emerging fairly late in human history, and quite distinct from any other mode of organizing social life and supplying its basic necessities. More particularly, such imperatives did not affect relations of exchange and distribution before the advent of capitalism, not even in the most advanced and prosperous commercial systems.

The simplest acts of exchange, which can take place within a single community or among adjacent communities, do not by themselves require competitive production or profit maximization. This may be reasonably obvious, for instance, in cases of barter, where no money changes hands. However, even more complex commercial transactions that do involve substantial profit-taking create no inherent compulsion to produce competitively. Great commercial wealth before capitalism was generally based on long-distance trade. The typical trading arrangements that characterized the wealthiest commercial centres – whether in antiquity, in the commercial city-states of Renaissance Europe, or in the vast trading empires of Asia – involved transactions between separate markets, in which profits were made by buying cheaply in one and selling expensively in another, in the process of conveyance from one market to another or arbitrage between them. Profit by means of carrying trade or arbitrage did not depend on transforming production, and commercial interests even tended to resist the integration of markets that imposed competitive imperatives. Precapitalist merchants thrived on fragmented markets and movement between them, rather than on competition within a single market; and the links between production and exchange were generally very tenuous.

If capitalist markets are driven by imperatives, non-capitalist markets typically responded not to imperatives, but to opportunities. Even producers who sold their products in the market, whether local markets or through middlemen for long-distance trade, would typically respond to market conditions in ways very different from those of capitalist producers. So, for instance, where declining demand or falling prices typically compel a capitalist producer to cut the costs of production in order to survive in a competitive market, the producer responding to market opportunities would tend to reduce or even withdraw from production when opportunities declined, increasing production again only when it became possible to take advantage of increasing demand or rising prices. Such producers may have been price-sensitive in their motivations to produce for the market or withdraw from production, but they were not subject to the cost/price pressures of capitalist competition.

The conventional wisdom that treats capitalism as little more than the quantitative growth of commerce tends to perceive the market as opportunity rather than imperative. This means that, if the birth of capitalism requires any explanation at all, it is an explanation of growing opportunities and the removal of obstacles to the expansion of commerce. Once we identify capitalism with market imperatives, however, the search for its origins must take a different form. The question then becomes not how commercial opportunities expanded and economies were freed to take advantage of them, but rather how social arrangements and the production of basic human needs were so fundamentally transformed as to impose compulsions and necessities unlike any that had governed human social life before. Seen from this perspective, the capitalist system appears more likely to have originated in a transformation of agrarian relations, the source of life's most basic necessity, food. This, as we shall see, is not to say that production of food for the market is always and necessarily subject to capitalist imperatives. Nor does it mean that capitalist production would always begin in agriculture: after the origin of capitalism in the English countryside, even in other parts of Western Europe, capitalist development could be led by the industrial sector. However, the fact remains that capitalist imperatives first imposed themselves on production when agricultural producers became market dependent; and until the production of food was subject to market imperatives, there was no capitalist system. The imperatives of capitalism preceded industrialization and were set in motion as soon as agriculture became subject to them. The question, then, is how the production of food came to be driven by the imperatives of competition, profit maximization and the compulsion constantly to improve the forces of production.

Markets and the production of food

Throughout history there have existed many kinds of markets, and agricultural producers have entered them in diverse ways, with various different purposes and consequences. There are, of course, huge differences between, on the one hand, a 'market system', in which virtually all commodities are produced for the market and where all factors of production, including land and labour, are treated as commodities; and, on the other hand, peasant markets in which producers own, or securely possess, the means of production – in particular, land – and sell their surpluses as an adjunct or supplement to their own production for subsistence. In the latter category, there has been a wide range of conditions in which agricultural producers, producing for their own subsistence, have at the same time sold surplus produce in the market, to obtain necessities they could not produce for themselves; to meet the obligations imposed on them by landlords and states in the form of rent and tax; or even sometimes to acquire luxuries. Even production for the market can continue essentially to follow peasant rules for reproduction, dictated by their own immediate consumption needs rather than requirements of competitive production, profit maximization or capital accumulation.

The essential question is this: in what specific conditions do competitive production and profit maximization themselves become survival strategies, the basic condition of subsistence itself? Strategies for survival are identical with strategies for maximizing profit, at least for producers, only in capitalism. The conditions of capitalist competition, as we have already observed, require maximizing strategies because capitalists have no guarantee of 'realization' in advance. They cannot know whether their commodities will sell, or even what conditions and production costs would ensure sale at all, let alone profit. Lacking the capacity to control prices in a competitive market, they must adopt strategies that will optimize the price/cost ratio, and their only available strategy is to reduce costs by enhancing labour productivity, to achieve the maximization of surplus value. So, in what conditions do agricultural producers enter the market in such a way as to subject them to these pressures?

We cannot take it for granted that producers will pursue the maximization of profit in exchange simply on the grounds that it would give them the best return for their labour and other inputs. We cannot presume the kind of calculation of returns to factors specific to capitalism, which may be quite alien to non-capitalist peasant economies, where all kinds of other considerations enter into the calculation of the value of labour and land. Even when peasants do respond to the market with some kind of economic rationality, it may be in ways very different from capitalist responses to market imperatives.

We have remarked on how farmers may respond to rising prices for their particular commodities – typically in cases of growing demand – by increasing their output of those commodities as much as possible, perhaps by bringing more land under cultivation or even by employing more (cheap) labour, in order to take advantage of the opportunities for increased profits. The typical response to falling prices would, in such cases, be to reduce or withdraw from production, which might then have the effect of causing prices to rise again. However, this kind of price sensitivity is very different from the cost sensitivity of a capitalist producer who strives for increasing labour productivity at lower cost, especially by transforming the methods of production, in a competitive market with many producers.

The latter kind of market response presupposes conditions that have not prevailed in most societies, throughout most of human history. There must, of course, be the material possibility of systematic innovation in the methods of production, which is seldom present in peasant communities with limited resources. We cannot simply assume, though, that peasants would, if only they could, systematically improve the forces of production and that nothing but their poverty prevents them from doing so. There are also social constraints, the requirements and regulations of the peasant community, which may themselves be essential to survival; and there can even be legal and institutional barriers to agricultural innovation.

Yet even such constraints, with or without the material limits of peasant property, are not enough to account for the absence of the systematic development of the productive forces that we associate with capitalism. On the whole, it is a mistake to think in terms of blockages. The self-sustaining development unique to capitalism requires not just the removal of obstacles to development, but a positive compulsion to transform the forces of production; and this comes only in competitive conditions, where economic actors are both free to move in response to those conditions, and obliged to do so.

Even the need to produce surpluses for exploiting classes or states has not, throughout most of history, by itself transformed the methods of production in that way, including production for exchange. Where exploiters – whether rent-taking landlords or tax-hungry states – have had at their disposal the extra-economic means of surplus extraction, the direct military, political and judicial powers of coercion to squeeze more surpluses from peasants, there has been no systematic compulsion to enhance labour productivity. Indeed, the effect of exploitation has typically been to impede such transformations of the productive forces. Coercive 'extra-economic' modes of surplus extraction have both lacked the incentive to promote the development of the productive forces, and positively hindered it by draining the resources of direct producers. What capitalist development requires is a mode of appropriation that must extract maximum surplus from direct producers, but can do so only by encouraging or compelling producers to increase their labour productivity and by enhancing rather than impeding the development of the productive forces. That kind of appropriation is a rare and contradictory formation, with very specific and stringent conditions of existence.

We can, then, reformulate our basic questions: first, why, and in what highly unusual conditions, did agricultural producers abandon their old survival strategies, producing for their own subsistence and for the market only as an adjunct? How did it happen that they abandoned strategies that were not based on profit maximization by means of 'efficient' production and began pursuing a strategy that did take this form? Or, to put it another way, how did survival strategies come to be united with profit-maximizing strategies; and, for that matter, how did profit maximization and 'efficiency' come to be joined? Second, how did appropriators come to depend for their wealth on competitive production, profit maximization in the sphere of production and the constant improvement of productive forces?

From feudalism to capitalism

The critical turning point occurred when producers lost non-market access to the means of production – to the land itself. The emphasis here is on non-market access, not complete dispossession, because market imperatives were set in motion well before the complete dispossession of direct producers or the complete commodification of labour-power. Indeed, if anything, the complete dispossession of direct producers was a result, more than a cause, of these market imperatives. This critical turning point appeared in very specific historical conditions, and in one specific place – the English countryside – where there developed a new relationship between landlords and peasants, which generated an unprecedented dynamic of competition and self-sustaining growth and gave birth to a new, capitalist mode of exploitation. On the one hand, tenant producers increasingly held their land (*de jure* or *de facto*) on 'economic' leases and paid 'economic' rents in cash or kind, not dictated by law or custom, but responsive instead to market conditions. On the other hand, landlords who lacked extra-economic powers of surplus extraction (that is to say, the powers of direct coercion to squeeze more surplus from producers) depended for their wealth on the productivity, competitiveness and profitability of their tenants.

When the direct producers' possession of land is directly market-dependent, and when they are responding to pressures from appropriators who rely on economic, rather than extra-economic, appropriation, the market truly becomes an imperative. The prosperous yeoman tenant in England, for instance, did not have even the kind of room for manoeuvre that a poorer peasant owner-occupier in a non-capitalist economy had. It is a truism that peasants throughout history have continued to produce for their own subsistence, even in the most constrained conditions, cutting their own domestic consumption to the bone rather than abandoning the land. Even if they have engaged in production for the market, they have adjusted production not only to changing commercial demand, but to their own consumption, which can itself be adjusted, in ways and degrees ruled out by capitalist competition, where profit maximization is a condition of survival. Their room for manoeuvre has, of course, been that much greater when they have not been subject to surplus extraction by landlords or states.

By contrast, tenants who possessed the land itself on market principles had no such flexibility. They were subject to competitive pressures and the need for maximizing strategies, even if they were more than capable of producing for their own subsistence, and no adjustment in their own consumption would obviate the need for producing competitively. Their possession of land itself was dependent on competitive production. It was in these circumstances that, for the first time in history, both producers and appropriators came to depend on the market for access to the conditions of their self-reproduction, and the relationship between them was mediated by the market. That is the story of the so-called transition from feudalism to capitalism.[2]

How, then, did this transition take place, and did it happen throughout feudal Europe, or only in very specific conditions? The concept of feudalism is often said to be of questionable value, and there has certainly been much variation in its usage. Yet there can be little doubt that developments in the medieval West produced distinctive social forms without which the later history of Europe is inexplicable, and some kind of shorthand designation seems all but indispensable. For the sake of convenience, if for no other reason, we can apply the term 'feudalism', or perhaps feudal society, to these social forms, while acknowledging that there was no single feudal order unvarying throughout the West.

There is much debate about when, or even whether, 'feudalism' emerged. For our purposes here, it is enough to say that the Roman Empire and its imperial state apparatus were replaced in the remnants of the Western empire by what has been called 'parcelized sovereignty', a patchwork of jurisdictions in which state functions were vertically and horizontally fragmented. Domination by an overarching imperial state was replaced by geographical fragmentation and organization by means of local or regional administration, in which various kinds of aristocracy held sway.

The Empire had left another powerful legacy, which was no less important, and far more lasting, than the political and administrative forms of imperial rule. This was the regime of private property, which had developed in Rome in ways unequalled in any other ancient civilization. A kind of property more private and exclusive than ever before was not only recognized in law, but coexisted with the state in a historically unprecedented partnership, in contrast to all other known civilizations where a powerful state tended to mean a relatively weak regime of private property. More particularly, the Roman state not only coexisted with, but strengthened, a landed aristocracy. The Empire was governed through, and sustained by, a widespread coalition of local propertied elites rather than a massive bureaucracy. Even when, in later years, the imperial bureaucracy grew, above all for the purpose of extracting more taxes – as always, largely to maintain the Empire's military power – that growth was as much a sign of weakness as of strength. The Roman army was overstretched in keeping control of the existing empire, while the bureaucracy and the tax-hungry state grew in order to sustain the army. At the same time, the state continued to sustain the system of property and a landed elite. When the imperial state apparatus crumbled, it left behind a legacy of landed aristocracies. In that sense, the Roman imperial state always had a tendency to fragmentation rooted in a powerful system of private property; and without this very specific configuration of property and state, it is hard to imagine the emergence of Western 'feudalism', where the jurisdictional and military functions of the state took the form of a hierarchical system of property. As the imperial state disappeared, there would be much oscillation between fragmentation and attempts at centralization by successor kingdoms in the West; but, although the process took place in different ways and at different rates in different parts of the Western empire, by the eleventh century the forces of parcelization had more-or-less prevailed. This is what is commonly called feudalism.

Here, then, is a working model of feudalism, which should suffice for our purposes: feudal lordship, which constituted a personal relationship to property and command of the peasants who worked it, took over many of the functions performed in other times and places by the state. The corollary of feudal lordship was a juridically dependent peasantry. The most obvious form of dependence was serfdom, although this more-or-less transparently dependent legal status could shade into other forms of peasant obligation, involving not personal lack of freedom, but possession of land conditional on one or another kind of service to the lord. The effect of feudal lordship was to combine the private exploitation of labour with the public role of administration, jurisdiction and enforcement, in what we have called the parcelization of sovereignty. Appropriation, although it occurred by 'extra-economic' means – by the exercise of political, jurisdictional and military power – took the form of rent instead of state taxation; and lordship thus combined the power of individual appropriation with possession of a fragment of state power.

The parcelization of sovereignty was present even in kingdoms that were effective, at least for a while, in their attempts to recentralize state power. Monarchies typically depended, to varying degrees but always unavoidably, on territorial aristocracies that exercised functions – judicial, administrative and military – formerly belonging to the state. The disintegration of such monarchical rule in the tenth century left local castle lords in command, while the east, particularly Germany, was controlled by powerful duchies. By the early eleventh century, there was a more-or-less complete breakdown of legal and political order, while the peasantry remained under the control of individual lords.

Here we come to a paradox: the particular case of European feudalism that gave rise to capitalism did not entirely conform to our model of parcelized sovereignty. The Roman imperial apparatus, and even the system of property, broke down more completely in Britain than it did elsewhere. Yet in the Anglo-Saxon period, state functions were restored to a degree unmatched in other parts of the former Western Empire, with kings, landlords and church hierarchy working in tandem to produce an unusually centralized authority. England would prove to be the most notable exception to the feudal breakdown of state order in the West. While France was disintegrating, the English forged a unified kingdom, with a national system of justice and the most effective administration in the Western world. It is certainly true that lords of the manor in England had their own kinds of rights and jurisdictional powers over their tenants, and England too had serfdom. Nonetheless, this was something quite different from the parcelized sovereignty of continental feudalism, and these aristocratic rights coexisted with a centralized state power. Although, in the eleventh century, the Normans would bring with them elements of continental feudalism – and with it, a legacy of Roman property and aristocracy – feudal parcelization never took hold in England as it did elsewhere. The Norman ruling class arrived, and imposed itself on English society, as an already well organized and unified military force, and consolidated the power of its newly established monarchical state by adapting Anglo-Saxon traditions of rule against Norman traditions of aristocratic freedom. A national system of law and jurisdiction also emerged very early, in the shape of the common law.

It is true that property law in England was, on the face of it, the most 'feudal' in Europe, in the sense that here, more than anywhere else, the dominant principle was 'no land without its lord', and there was no allodial land. The paradox of English 'feudalism', however, is that the condition for the complete feudalization of property was the centralized monarchy – not parcelized sovereignty but, on the contrary, the relative weakness of parcelization. If all land had its lord, it was because the monarch was conceived as the supreme landlord.

Nonetheless, the relative strength of the centralized state did not mean the weakness of the landed aristocracy. In significant ways, the contrary is true. The important point to remember is that the development of the English monarchy, despite the moments of conflict between king and aristocracy, was, and continued to be, at bottom a cooperative project between monarchs and landlords (Brenner 1985: 236). There emerged a cooperative division of labour between the landed class and the central monarchical state.

Moreover, even (or especially) tenements held directly, in common law, under the jurisdiction of the king – including certain types of humble property held by tillers and freeholders, who owed no service to the king and were free of lordly jurisdiction – constituted private property more exclusive and less subject to obligations to an overlord than anything that existed on the continent. For all the feudal trappings of English property, and the departures of the common law from the legal traditions of Rome, the Roman legacy of private and exclusive property would be carried forward more completely in England than in any of the continental states where Roman law survived.

While legislation and jurisdiction were increasingly centralized in England, land was concentrated in the hands of the aristocracy to a degree unusual in continental states, such as France, where peasant possession was more widespread. The English aristocracy may not have enjoyed the degree of parcelized sovereignty that existed elsewhere, in which jurisdictional and political powers were used by dominant classes as a primary extra-economic means of direct appropriation, or what Brenner has called 'politically constituted property'. Lords in England, however, remained in control of the best land and would increasingly depend on that control for their wealth. The particular configuration of central state and landed class in England would lead to a wholly new pattern of development, with no historical precedent.

We have already observed how the combination of peasant production and extra-economic modes of surplus extraction can impede the improvement of productive forces, not only because there is no incentive to promote their development, but because this mode of exploitation tends to drain the resources of direct producers. In feudal Europe, this pattern of development, which kept coming up against its own inherent barriers of productivity, inevitably produced increasing burdens on peasants and revenue crises for landlords. The tensions between appropriators and producers gave rise to class conflict between them, as peasants struggled to liberate themselves, or even fled the land, while landlords sought ways to reimpose their dominance in various modes of seigneurial reaction. The demographic crisis of the late fourteenth and fifteenth centuries aggravated these tensions, not least by making available more land as an object of struggle between landlords and peasants. How various European feudalisms responded to this crisis depended on existing social property relations. The English had the advantage of an already more effective central state; and English landlords, already reliant on their dominant control of landed property, rather than on extra-economic powers of surplus extraction, were in a uniquely favourable position to exploit the purely economic powers that they still enjoyed.

The decline of serfdom certainly meant a loss of extra-economic dominance of landlords over peasants, but the concentration of land in the hands of large landholders gave them greater economic powers over tenants. The nature of English tenancies underwent changes that distinguished agricultural producers in England from their continental counterparts in ways that set off a new pattern of self-sustaining economic growth. Before we explore the effects of these English economic tenancies, we can get some measure of England's distinctive agrarian relations by contrasting it with France.[3]

In France, the ruling class responded to the feudal crisis in a different way, which eventually produced a different kind of state and a different kind of state centralization, together with different forms of appropriation. The monarchy emerged out of feudal rivalry, as one patrimonial power established itself over others in the context of parcelized sovereignty. This meant that the monarchical state continued to confront the challenge of feudal parcelization, the independent powers and privileges of aristocracy and various corporate entities. The monarchy certainly did pursue a centralizing strategy with some success, and royal courts did emerge, which, among other things, could be used to protect peasants from lords – not least in order to preserve the peasantry as a source of state taxes. However, the dominant class continued to depend to a great extent on politically constituted property, on powers of appropriation dependent on political, military and judicial powers, or extra-economic status and privilege. The state developed, as a competing form of politically constituted property, a primary resource, a mode of direct appropriation for state office-holders by means of taxation, which some historians have called a kind of centralized rent. If the absolutist state was able to undermine the independent powers of the aristocracy, it did so in large part by replacing those powers with the lucrative resource of state office for a segment of the aristocracy; and the centralizing project of the state proceeded by replacing autonomous aristocratic powers with prerequisites and privileges deriving from the state – for instance, by granting privileged exemption from royal taxation in place of seigneurial jurisdiction. The elaborate bureaucracy, which distinguished France from England, developed not just for political and administrative purposes, but as an economic resource, proliferating offices as a means of private appropriation through taxation. Throughout the *ancien régime* and beyond, state office would be the favoured career not only for the aristocracy, but for the bourgeoisie. When the Revolution came, the revolutionary bourgeoisie – consisting typically of office-holders, professionals and intellectuals – was less concerned with breaking the shackles impeding the development of capitalism than with preserving and enhancing their access to the highest state office, 'careers open to talent'.

The peasantry, which remained in possession of most land in France, continued to be exploited by extra-economic means, increasingly by the state in the form of tax. This would continue to be true even after the Revolution. Although private property in office was abolished, state office remained a lucrative career, in which office-holders appropriated the surplus labour of peasants through taxation; and the state apparatus, which provided the bourgeoisie with their favoured careers, remained, as Marx called it in *The Eighteenth Brumaire of Louis Bonaparte* (Marx 1967), a huge parasitic body, feeding on the peasantry. So even the Revolution did not transform the social property relations between the state and peasants that had prevailed in absolutist France.

It should, then, already be clear that not all transitions from European feudalism led to capitalism. In France, it was rather a transition from feudalism to absolutism – not just absolutism as a political form, but the absolutist state as a form of politically constituted property, a social property relation, a means of exploiting the peasantry. Elsewhere in Europe, feudalism gave way to different political and economic forms. Even the highly successful commercial city-states of northern Italy did not produce capitalism. The commerce practised by these city-states was not, in our sense, capitalist. Instead, it exemplified precisely the kind of non-capitalist commerce described above, in which the market acted more as opportunity than imperative. The only case in which a transition from feudalism to capitalism may be said to have occurred is that of England – and that was in large part due to the specific ways in which English feudalism differed fundamentally from other forms, in particular the relative weakness of parcelized sovereignty and the modes of exploitation that went with it.

Transition debates

Explanations of the transition from feudalism to capitalism have traditionally emphasized the effects of growing commercialization. While there have been different versions of the 'commercialization model', they have generally had in common the view that feudalism represented a hiatus in the development of commerce as, for one reason or another, trade routes were blocked or commercial exchanges hindered, whether by 'barbarian' invasions and the collapse of the Roman Empire, or by Muslim conquests. This view is not incompatible with the assumption that some vestiges of a commercial economy remained within what Marx called the 'interstices' of feudalism, waiting for release and the opportunity to flourish. When, according to this view, trade did resume and grow, it undermined the 'natural' economy of feudalism and the dominant relations between landlords and peasants, especially where peasant producers could escape rural exploitation by moving to increasingly prosperous towns.

The first real challenge to such explanations came from Marx himself, although not before he and Engels had elaborated their own variations on the old explanations. In early works such as the *German Ideology* and the *Communist Manifesto*, they certainly adopted a more critical stance and gave a greater role to class struggle than did the conventional versions; but they painted a historical picture not essentially different from the prevailing accounts offered by classical political economy and Enlightenment conceptions of progress. Taken together with shorthand formulations such as the famous passages about the contradictions between the forces and relations of production in the 1859 Preface (Marx 1977) – according to which history moves forward as inevitably developing forces come into conflict with inhibiting relations and compel them to change – the emergence of capitalism appears to result from a transhistorical process of technological development and the division of labour, in which the emergence of capitalism is the hitherto highest stage. Capitalism even seems to exist already, without the need for explanation, in the 'interstices' of feudalism; and all that is needed is to free the burgher classes, the bearers of capitalism, from the shackles of the feudal system. The origin of capitalism, in other words, is not so much explained as presupposed.

Marx would move far beyond conventional accounts of capitalist development in *Capital* (Marx 1971). He did this firstly by transforming the definition of capitalism itself, so that it was no longer simply 'commercial society', or a bigger and better system of trade. Instead, it was an essentially new social form, with distinctive social property relations and unique laws of motion, not the universal laws of markets and economic rationality, but imperatives arising from historically specific social relations and a distinctive mode of exploitation. Having explicated the specific logic of the system, he then sketched out a history of its emergence, which was not a narrative of technological development or commercialization, but the story of a historically specific social transformation.

In his historical account, Marx sets himself apart from classical political economy by dissecting its notion of 'primitive accumulation', which suggested that capitalism or 'commercial society' matured when the accumulation of commercial wealth had reached a critical mass that permitted reinvestment. For Marx, this represents an evasion, which fails to explain the origin of capitalism, because capital, in his terms, is not simply wealth for reinvestment but rather a specific social relation; and what brought about capitalism was not simply the accumulation of wealth, but the transformation of social property relations. No amount of accumulation, however it is achieved, can by itself produce capitalism. 'The so-called primitive accumulation', he argued, 'is nothing else than the historical process of divorcing the producer from the means of production' (Marx 1971: Ch. 26). This process occurred in its first and 'classic' form with the expropriation of direct producers in the English countryside (as discussed by Akram-Lodhi and Kay in Chapter 1), establishing a new system of relations between landlords, tenants and wage labourers in which landlords – unlike their counterparts else-where – increasingly derived their rents from the profits of capitalist tenants, while many small producers became propertyless wage labourers. That social transformation was, for Marx, the real 'primitive accumulation'.

It would, however, be a long time before Marx's promising departure from convention led to serious historical debate on the origin of capitalism. In 1950, an exchange took place between two Marxists, the British economic historian Maurice Dobb, and the American economist Paul Sweezy, who had criticized Dobb's book *Studies in the Development of Capitalism*, published in 1946. Their exchange launched an important debate among largely Marxist historians about the 'transition' from feudalism to capitalism, which would remain a major reference point in discussions of capitalist history.[4]

The main issue between Dobb and Sweezy concerned the 'prime mover' in the transition from feudalism to capitalism. Dobb had argued that, contrary to many historical conventions, the growth of trade was not the principal solvent of feudalism. Feudalism was not dissolved by trade and towns, which were not essentially inimical to feudalism, but by developments within the constitutive relations of feudalism itself, the relations between lords and peasants. Sweezy countered with an argument that feudalism was tenacious and intrinsically resistant to change, and that the prime mover had to be found outside the feudal system. He thus renewed the case for the expansion of trade as the solvent of feudalism, responsible for the system's dissolution as it increased production for exchange at the expense of production for use. At the same time, this did not immediately give rise to capitalism: 'it was the growth of commodity production which first undermined feudalism and then *somewhat later*, after this work of destruction had been substantially completed, prepared the ground for the growth of capitalism' (Sweezy 1976: 50). However, there were, he pointed out, cases of highly developed commodity production that did not give birth to capitalism, so the development of capitalism remained to be explained. Although he did not go on to offer a systematic explanation, he did cast doubt on Dobb's contention that capitalists rose from the ranks of petty producers. In the 'transition debate' that followed, Dobb reiterated his argument that capitalism emerged out of the relations of feudalism, as class struggle between lords and peasants served to

> modify the dependence of the petty mode of production upon feudal overlordship and eventually to shake loose the small producer from feudal exploitation. It is then from the petty mode of production (in the degree to which it secures independence of action, and social differentiation in turn develops within it) that capitalism is born.
>
> (Dobb 1976: 59)

The case for the internal dissolution of feudalism was greatly strengthened by the Marxist medieval historian R.H. Hilton, who, having forcefully argued that towns and trade did not dissolve feudalism, elaborated on the relations and struggles between lords and peasants that drove the transition from feudalism to capitalism. He suggested, for example, that the pressure to improve techniques of production, and with it the growth of simple commodity production, came from within, from the lords' demands on peasants, while peasant resistance was central to the transition to capitalism:

> peasant resistance was of crucial importance in the development of the rural communes, the extension of free tenure and status, the freeing of peasant and artisan economies for the development of commodity production and eventually the emergence of the capitalist entrepreneur.
>
> (Hilton 1976: 27)

Both Dobb and Hilton seemed to suggest that capitalism emerged when, and because, petty commodity producers were released, largely by means of struggle, from the feudal fetters that had obstructed their development and hindered the expansion of commodity production.

The arguments of Dobb and Hilton were major advances beyond the old commercialization model, and important elaborations of Marx's sketchy historical narrative in *Capital*. Their focus on relations between appropriating and producing classes, instead of on the expansion of trade, and their shift of the 'prime mover' from city to countryside, represented major challenges to old conventions. Nonetheless, in one essential respect they remained within the old paradigm: in their arguments that the transition occurred when and because the fetters of feudalism were removed and commodity production was free to grow into capitalism, they still proceeded as if a capitalist logic were already present, just waiting for release. Again, the origin of capitalism was assumed rather than explained.

In 1976, a quarter century after the first Dobb–Sweezy debate, another Marxist historian, Robert Brenner, published a groundbreaking article that sought to fill the gap left open by his predecessors (Brenner 1976). In it he systematically explored the process by which feudal social property relations gave rise to new, capitalist social property relations. This, too, launched a heated controversy, which came to be known as the Brenner Debate. After a series of criticisms by distinguished historians, Marxist and non-Marxist, Brenner produced an extended reply; and this, taken together with the original article, constituted a comprehensive challenge to both the commercialization model in all its forms, and the influential demographic arguments that had sought to replace the old model. In the process, Brenner challenged quite a few Marxist orthodoxies too.

Influenced by Dobb, Brenner nonetheless remained dissatisfied with the assumption that some kind of embryonic capitalism was already present in feudalism, which only needed to be liberated from its chains. He did not accept that trade, or even petty commodity production, was a kind of protocapitalism, which would naturally develop into a full-blown capitalist system if only it was given free rein. Like Sweezy, Brenner argued that the tenacity of feudalism should not be underestimated; but unlike Sweezy, he agreed with Dobb and Hilton that the dynamic of change had to be found not in some external intervention, but within the constitutive relations of feudalism. He went on to construct a powerful argument about how the distinctive property relations of the English countryside – which Marx had identified in *Capital* – set in train a new historical dynamic leading to capitalism.

Capitalism, according to this argument, did not emerge from the release of already present capitalist impulses; nor was it the outcome of a bourgeois revolution that had as its objective the liberation of capital or capitalist classes; nor was it the result of a relentless transhistorical drive for technological improvement. There was no embryonic capitalism in the interstices of feudalism that only needed to be freed of extraneous obstacles, nor was there any law of history that required one mode of production to be replaced by a more productive one. The relentless need for maximizing strategies, endless accumulation and reinvestment, profit maximization, and improvements in labour productivity were not transhistorical causes, but historically specific consequences of specifically capitalist imperatives.

Capitalism, in this argument, was the unintended consequence of relations between appropriating and producing classes seeking to reproduce themselves as they were, not trying to transform themselves into capitalists. On one side were landlords whose extra-economic powers were relatively weak or non-existent, but whose control of the best land could be exploited productively. On the other side were free tenants on essentially economic leases, or on customary leases vulnerable to conversion into *de facto* economic leases. Neither landlord nor tenant was seeking a transformation of social property relations in a capitalist direction, but as both pursued the strategies for reproduction that suited their existing conditions, both came to rely increasingly on competitive success in the market and increasing productivity – tenants, in order to keep their land and perhaps to gain more; landlords, to secure and increase their rents. Unsuccessful producers were driven off the land – not simply by direct coercion but by the force of market pressures – and the result was the distinctive 'triad' of English agrarian capitalism: landlord, capitalist tenant and wage labourer.

Agrarian capitalism

It is not possible to identify one specific moment when capitalism was born, nor is it particularly useful to try. What we can do is recognize a new historical dynamic when we see it, and it is clearly visible by the seventeenth century. While we can trace the processes that created this dynamic further back, it is clear that, by then, market imperatives were already well established. This dynamic had been set in motion once landlords and tenants became dependent on the market for the conditions of their own self-reproduction – tenants because their possession of land was mediated by the market, through economic rents responsive to market conditions; and landlords because their wealth depended on the competitive production of their tenants. By this time, producers who had lost non-market access to the means of their self-reproduction were not only free to enter the market, but obliged to obey its imperatives, simply in order to survive and maintain access to the land. The new dynamic was already at work even though wage labour still constituted only a minority of the labour force in England. It is certainly true that market imperatives came fully into their own when labour-power was generally commodified; but, even if we choose to reserve the term 'capitalist' for this mature form, it remains important to acknowledge that a wholly new dynamic was already in train before the complete proletarianization of the workforce and, indeed, as a precondition to it.

By the seventeenth century, there were clear differences between this dynamic of market imperatives and the patterns of development in societies with different social property relations, where direct producers continued to pursue their old survival strategies, resorting to the market only as a supplement or opportunity. These differences are visible in various ways: in attitudes toward rents, in the organization of production, and in what might be called the general culture of the economy; and the contrasts between England and its neighbours, like France, are especially revealing.

Already in the sixteenth century, English landlords were preoccupied with the notion of competitive rents. Where they could do so, they would lease land at the highest rent the market would bear. Where customary rents resisted these market conditions, landlords were conscious of the difference between them and some putative market rent, and landlords' surveyors might even calculate the rental value on the basis of some more-or-less abstract principle of market value, measuring the shortfall of actual rents and treating them as an unearned increment obtained by the tenant. There was great pressure to convert such customary rents into at least *de facto* economic rents, and landlords would use every available means to achieve such conversion. In sixteenth- and seventeenth-century France, by contrast, at a time when peasants were consolidating their rights of inheritance – with the help of a growing absolutist state anxious to preserve its revenue base in the form of peasant taxes – French surveyors, unlike their English counterparts, searched the records to find grounds for restoring or inventing seigneurial rights and peasant obligations, using their specialist skills not to calculate market values but to promote a revival of feudalism.

These differences were reflected in the organization of production. English landlords did everything possible, increasingly with the help of the courts, to redefine property rights in order to make property more exclusive, especially by barring customary rights – notably, for instance, by means of enclosure – that intruded on their profitable utilization of land. This would permit various innovations in land use that might be obstructed by commoners' use rights or interference by village communities. In France, production continued to be regulated in substantial ways by the village community, even in those regions where there were concentrated landholdings and tenancies

(Comninel 1987). In England, in the seventeenth century there was a flour-ishing culture of 'improvement' – the enhancement of productivity for profit – both in practice and in theory, spawning not only a body of legal decisions citing 'improvement' as a criterion for determining property rights, but also a body of scientific improvement literature in which even members of the Royal Society played a significant role in promoting agricultural practices conducive to productivity and profit. In France there was no such body of literature, and only after the mid-eighteenth century – when English agriculture was held up as a model – did anything like it appear. Even rural grievances and conflicts differed in England and France, as commoners in England defended their customary rights against new definitions of property rights, while French peasants were preoccupied with the growing burden of taxation.

The consequences of the new social property relations and the imperatives that drove the new economy were visible, above all, in the productivity of English agriculture, which was able to sustain a large and growing popula-tion not engaged in agricultural production. Some historians have estimated that the urban population of England had already reached close to a quarter of the total by the late seventeenth century, while the rural population of France remained steady at about 85–90 per cent of the total until the Revolution and beyond. It is sometimes said that there was nothing remarkable about agricultural productivity in England, and that it was equalled by the French. However, this means, at best, that output per unit of land in France and England was roughly the same. Their divergent demo-graphic patterns alone make it clear that output per unit of work was sub-stantially different, and that in France a significantly larger workforce was engaged in producing the same output per unit of land.

This was not, in the first instance, a matter of more advanced technologi-cal development in England, but rather a different pattern of land use, responding to different imperatives. Nor, for that matter, was the emergence of this new historical dynamic dependent on a particularly advanced tech-nological development. England's productive forces were, at the outset, no more developed than the French; and Europe in general was less advanced in many respects than the great empires of Asia. The operation of market imperatives certainly presupposed productive forces sufficient to produce surpluses beyond the conditions of subsistence and self-reproduction; but we should not exaggerate the required technological capacities, and we should keep in mind the relative modesty of England's material culture when it embarked on its distinctive historical path.

The English pattern bespeaks a society in which increasing numbers of agricultural producers were leaving the land, while those that remained were producing for an ever-growing number of consumers dependent on the market for the most basic necessities of life. It was also a society with an increasingly integrated national market, with a huge hub in London, which became the largest city in the West. Its immense population included not only many prosperous 'bourgeois' consumers of luxury goods of a kind that existed in other European cities, but also a distinctive concentration of relatively poor consumers, including many dispossessed migrants from the countryside. This population, supported by an unusually productive agriculture, constituted a large potential labour force and, equally important, a large consumer market for cheap ordinary goods such as food, clothing and basic kitchen utensils.

The transformations in property relations, together with the size and nature of the domestic home market, to say nothing of the nature and extent of British trade and British imperialism, built on the foundation of agrarian capitalism, all led in the direction of industrial capitalism. The so-called 'Industrial Revolution' was less the product of any prior technological advances than of an integrated market providing cheap necessities of life for mass consumers, in an economy already driven by imperatives of competition. Industrialization of one kind or another occurred elsewhere too – not least in France, where it was driven, above all, by the pressures of war. The social revolution of industrial capitalism, however, and the relentless imperatives of self-sustaining growth, happened organically only in Britain, the home of agrarian capitalism. When its principal rivals embarked on their own state-led development in a capitalist direction, they were responding not to imperatives generated by domestic social property relations, but to external military, geopolitical and commercial pressures. Here, in a sense, industrialization preceded the transformation of social property relations. Thereafter, capitalism would continue to spread throughout the world both by means of colonial expansion (as discussed by Bagchi in Chapter 4) and, increasingly, by imposing its relentless economic imperatives.

Conclusions

Capitalism, then, had its origin in agriculture. To stress the agrarian origin of capitalism, however, is not only to make a historical observation about how the system came into being. It is also to recognize something fundamentally important about the nature of capitalism: that it is not a sphere of choice and freedom, but a system of coercion, imposing its imperatives on the provision of life's most basic necessities. At the same time, to acknowledge the transformations that brought the system into being is also to recognize its essential historicity, as a very particular form with a relatively short history, with a beginning and, presumably, an end, which leaves open the possibility of organizing human subsistence in more socially equitable and ecologically less destructive ways.

Notes

1 Parts of this chapter are drawn from my articles 'The question of market dependence' (Wood 2002a) and 'The origin of capitalism' (Wood 2008). I have developed my arguments on the origin of capitalism at greater length in *The Origin of*

Capitalism: A Longer View (Wood 2002b), and it is in this book that readers will find the more extensive references necessary to substantiate my arguments.

2 See Chapter 1, endnote 9 for a partial selection of references.
3 For a discussion of the specificities of English feudalism, especially in contrast to France, see George Comninel's (2000) important article.
4 See Chapter 1, endnote 9.

References

Brenner, R. (1976) 'Agrarian class structure and economic development in pre-industrial Europe', *Past and Present*, (70): 30–75.

—— (1985) 'The agrarian roots of European capitalism', in T.H. Aston and C.H.E. Philpin (eds), *The Brenner Debate: Agrarian Class Structure and Economic Development in Pre-Industrial Europe*, Cambridge: Cambridge University Press.

Comninel, G. (1987) *Rethinking the French Revolution: Marxism and the Revisionist Challenge*, London: Verso.

—— (2000) 'English feudalism and the origins of capitalism', *Journal of Peasant Studies*, 27 (4): 1–53.

Dobb, M. (1976) 'A reply' in P. Sweezy *et al.* (eds), *The Transition from Feudalism to Capitalism*, London: Verso.

Hilton, R.H. (1976) 'Introduction' in Paul Sweezy *et al.* (eds), *The Transition from Feudalism to Capitalism*, London: Verso.

Marx, K. (1967) *The Eighteenth Brumaire of Louis Bonaparte*, Moscow: Progress Publishers (first published in 1852).

—— (1971) *Capital, Volume 1*, Moscow: Progress Publishers.

—— (1977) Preface to *A Contribution to the Critique of Political Economy*, Moscow: Progress Publishers.

Sweezy, P. (1976) 'A critique' in Paul Sweezy *et al.* (eds), *The Transition from Feudalism to Capitalism*, London: Verso.

Wood, E.M. (2002a) 'The question of market dependence', *Journal of Agrarian Change*, 2 (1): 50–87.

—— (2002b) *The Origin of Capitalism: A Longer View*, London: Verso.

—— (2008) 'The origin of capitalism', in W. Fritz Haug (ed.), *Historico-critical Dictionary of Marxism*, Vol. 7, Berlin: Berliner Institut für Kritische Theorie.

3 The landlord class, peasant differentiation, class struggle and the transition to capitalism

England, France and Prussia compared

Terence J. Byres

Introduction

The three examples I have chosen to consider are all very important instances of agrarian transformation. They illustrate, moreover, strikingly different experiences of transformation: differing paths of agrarian transition.

England, the first historical example of such transformation, of 'capitalism triumphant', one might describe as landlord-mediated capitalism from below – that, at least, is how I would choose to describe it. As Wood discusses in Chapter 2 of this book, the former feudal landlord class became a capitalist landlord class, letting its land to capitalist tenant farmers on fixed-term leases at 'competitive' rents, and 'English farming came to be dominated by the triple division into landlords, (capitalist) tenant farmers and hired labourers' (Hobsbawm and Rudé 1973: 6). The transition to capitalist agriculture proceeded vigorously in Tudor England in the sixteenth century, and was completed during the seventeenth. Not everyone would accept such a characterization. Robert Brenner (2001), for example, would dispute both its historical priority, arguing that this, in fact, belongs to the Low Countries, or any suggestion of its representing capitalism from below.

In Prussia, by contrast with England, the class of feudal landlords – the Junkers – had ceased, by the beginning of the nineteenth century, to be feudal landlords. Prussian feudalism gave way to a distinctive form of agrarian capitalism, in the wake of the 'freeing' of Prussian serfs in 1807: a transition to capitalism that came some three centuries after the English transition. Prussian feudal landlords ceased to be a landlord class and became a class of capitalist farmers, working the land with an oppressed force of wage labour, who had formerly been serfs. Here was Lenin's celebrated 'capitalism from above': the impulse was an exclusively landlord one, accompanied by 'the degradation of the peasant masses' (Lenin 1964: 33, first published 1899). There was no question of capitalism from below.

France embodies, one might say, 'capitalism delayed'. Here, the capitalist impulse in the countryside was frustrated, or at least significantly delayed, as noted previously by Wood (Chapter 2). At the end of the nineteenth century, France could still be portrayed as 'the classical land of small peasant economy' (Engels 1970: 460, first published 1894) – a land, one might say, dominated by poor and middle peasants. Here, we have a stubbornly endur- ing peasantry: a peasantry that refused to go. Sharecropping was still wide- spread, and persisted well into the twentieth century. At no point had the French landlord class, either before or after 1789, shown any significant move of either the English kind or the Prussian. There was no dominant 'capitalism from above' and no broad progressive landlord role; and there was no 'capitalism from below', from within the ranks of the peasantry.

In this chapter, I offer an explanation of how these different outcomes came to pass and of why there was such a marked divergence in the nature of agrarian transition. I do so in terms of the kind of landlord class, the kind of class struggle and the kind of peasant differentiation that was integral to 'agrarian transformation'; thus, I do so within the terrain of the agrarian question, as discussed by Akram-Lodhi and Kay in Chapter 1 of this book. I argue that the character of the landlord class and of class struggle has determined both the timing of each transition and the nature of the transition. Both the quality of the landlord class and the manner and outcome of the class struggle have sometimes delayed, perhaps for prolonged periods, and sometimes hastened, transition, and have had profound implications for the nature and quality of the transformation and how reactionary or progressive it has been. In this the state has always played a prominent part. I further argue that differentiation of the peasantry is central to transformation: it is not an outcome but a determining variable, a *causa causans* rather than a *causa causata*. My argument is that differentiation of the peasantry feeds into and interacts with the landlord class and class struggle, these being critical to the eventual outcome. Such, then, is the theme of the present chapter. Differentiation is no mere outcome. The dis- tinctly varying trajectories in the three crucial instances are explained in these terms.

Some preliminary analytical observations

In each instance, I consider a transition from feudalism to agrarian capital- ism. I start with some preliminary observations concerning feudal social formations, to help to clear our analytical path. I will then proceed to take each of the cases separately.

Contra many social historians, conflict, rather than harmony, was the principal underlying feature of the relationship between the main classes of feudal society in Europe. As Marc Bloch (1961a, 1961b), the great historian of European feudalism and of the French countryside, stressed of European feudalism: 'agrarian revolt is as natural to the seigneurial regime as strikes, let us say, are to large-scale capitalism' (Bloch 1966: 170). Rodney Hilton, the outstanding Marxist historian of medieval England, and a formidable comparativist, also emphasized the importance of conflict – class conflict – in feudal Europe 'between peasants and ruling groups over the disposal of the surplus (disputes about rents and services) and over the sanctions used to enforce its appropriation (serfdom, private jurisdiction)' (Hilton 1974: 207).[1] Indeed, the nature, manifestations and implications of this lord/peasant class conflict is a recurring theme in all his work: 'the conflict between the peasants as a whole on the one hand and the landowning class and its institutions on the other' (1974: 210). This was true of each of my three examples.

Peasant resistance in medieval Europe falls into different subgenres. First, 'some movements were obviously direct confrontations between lords and peasants over the proportion of the surplus product of peasant labour which should go in rents, services and taxes' (1973: 62). Very broadly, 'on the whole, the(se) more elemental movements with the simplest demands were at the village level' (1973: 64). The demands in question may have been the 'simplest', but they were quite fundamental. They occurred at the points of production and of distribution. These existed throughout the medieval period. They may be subdivided into those that proceeded via individuals or groups of individuals within a village and those that involved whole peasant communities seeking village enfranchisement. Second, there were those that appear as 'movements of social, religious or political protest' (1973: 62). These were a feature of the later medieval epoch. By contrast, 'the movements affected by the new developments in medieval society tended to be regional in scope, and generally to have wide horizons, which were extended not merely beyond the village but beyond purely social aspirations' (1973: 62). They may have sought religious goals, or attempted to confront and moderate the increasing encroachments of the state. Both of the subgenres were obvious in England and France. It is the direct confrontation over surplus that interests me most here. It is clearly visible in feudal Prussia.

Under feudalism, the peasantry is to be viewed as a single class. Kosminsky (1956: 198), the author of the classic Marxist treatment of thirteenth century England's agrarian history, insists:

> And yet whatever distinctions and contradictions may have existed within the peasantry, they do not preclude our seeing in the peasantry of the epoch a single class, occupying a definite place in the feudal mode of production, and characterized by the anti-feudal direction of its interests and its class struggle.

Hilton takes the same position, with respect to the final era of English feudalism, 1350–1450, as he does for the whole of the feudal era in Europe (1975: 3–19). What all sections of the peasantry had in common was, as emphasized by Wood, their servile condition: tied to the land, subject to an array of feudal restrictions, with surplus appropriated via extra-economic coercion – in Chris Wickham's (1985: 170) incisively reductive phrase, feudalism is 'coercive rent-taking'. Moreover, as the feudal era proceeded, they were subject to attempts at increased exploitation and seigneurial onslaught. That bound them together in hostile conflict against feudal lords.

Despite seeing the peasantry as a class, it is crucial to note that these peasantries were socially differentiated. In Europe, 'the peasant community was not a community of equals' and 'the stratification of peasant communities, moreover, was at least as old as the earliest records which we have of them' (1973: 32). In analysing the differentiation of the peasantry, it is common to refer to three strata: a rich peasantry, a middle peasantry and a poor peasantry. It is appropriate to do so with respect to medieval Europe, and historians such as Kosminsky and Hilton proceed thus (see, for example, 1978: 272, 280; Kosminsky 1956: 354). Hilton stresses that 'the internal stratification of the peasantry, during the medieval period, was strictly limited' (1973: 34). Rich peasants hired wage labour, especially at peak seasons, whether from the ranks of poor peasants or from a class of completely landless labourers. That this might generate conflict seems possible. Yet there was remarkably little conflict of this kind (1966: 166; 1975: 53). Nor was there a social gulf, or a 'competitive element', between rich and poor peasant: 'The social gulf that was still the most important was that between the peasant and the lord' (1975: 53). Certainly, the conflict between peasant and lord was far more important than conflict within peasant communities. There was a clear absence of struggle within the feudal peasantry. Yet differentiation might deepen, within feudal limits. Such deepening needs close attention. These observations are valid for all three of my case studies.

I have posited a servile feudal peasantry. Yet there was the possibility of a relatively free peasantry under feudalism. From the eleventh century onwards there was, in different parts of Europe, land hunger and the possibility of alleviating it through the settling of uncultivated land (1973: 43, 92). This proceeded as 'the consequence of increasing population, increased production for the market, and firmer and more ambitious political organization by the aristocracy and the ruling kings and princes'; and 'it involved a response by landowners to the search by peasants for more land, which took the form of attempts to direct this land hunger towards the colonization of forest, scrubland and marsh' (1973: 43). Hilton distinguishes two distinct movements in this respect. The first was in western Germany, France, England and Italy, where unsettled areas of such land 'were filled up by the overflow from crowded villages in old settled areas' (1973: 43). The 'best-known' (1973: 43) and most important historically was, however, the second, which involved the settlement of empty lands to the east, in Slav territories. Peasants needed inducements to cultivate such land, and so a free peasantry was created in Prussia: a peasantry that remained among the most free in Europe until the sixteenth century. That was not so in any general way in England and France. This Hilton describes as 'the expansion of German colonization in central and Eastern Europe' (1973: 43). It included, most importantly, Prussia east of the Elbe.

England

Differentiation and the emergence of a stratum of powerful rich peasants

Differentiation of the English peasantry existed from earliest times. It was a structural feature of feudalism at its very inception (let us say, by the sixth century CE). Hilton (1978: 272) cites Kosminsky (1956: 207) to the effect that 'the deep-seated causes of peasant differentiation probably lie as far back as the disintegration of the pre-feudal lands into the ownership of single families'.[2] Hilton stresses that 'the contours of a peasantry divided between a wealthy minority, a solid middle peasantry and a significant proportion of smallholders can easily be seen in the Domesday Book, 1086' (1978: 272; cf. 1973: 33). That it developed and deepened, in the wake of the Norman Conquest, as the medieval era proceeded, is also clear. We have a superb treatment for the thirteenth century and for the century 1350–1450 by Hilton (1949, 1978), Hilton and Fagan (1950), as well as valuable accounts of the thirteenth century by non-Marxist historians (Postan 1966: 617–632; Miller and Hatcher 1978: 149). I have considered this in detail elsewhere (Byres 2006: 32–53). Here, with the transition to capitalism in mind, I would note the following of the rich peasantry.

In the thirteenth century, a lower stratum of rich peasants held more than 30 acres, while a select few worked more than 60. Hilton (1949: 130) stresses 'the growth of a rich upper stratum among the peasants'. Thus,

> whether we look at peasant life in the south-east, in the Thames valley, in East Anglia or in the Midlands, we find standing out from the ordinary run of tenants with their fifteen or twenty-acre holdings, a small group of families sometimes free, more often serf, holding a hundred acres or more.

These were 'the village aristocrats', some of whom 'were climbing towards yeoman status' (Miller and Hatcher 1978: 149). The rich peasants 'controlled the commons, declared local custom, and maintained order' (1978: 278). Here, then, was clear space within which rich peasants could operate. That they took advantage of this, to maintain and further their interests, is clear. Motivated by the existence of a sizeable market for agricultural products, that they wanted to accumulate more land is also clear. However, there were strict limits on such accumulation (1978: 278).

In the century 1350–1450, 'the village community was dominated by the richer peasant families, who ran the manorial court in its jurisdictional, punitive and land-registration functions' (1978: 281). Rich peasants strengthened their position, and did accumulate more land in the shape of 'the abandoned demesnes of the aristocracy' (1978: 282), although, within the village community, limits on the accumulation of land continued. Thus, 'by the end of the fourteenth century an upper class of peasants (was clearly in evidence)' and 'four or five families in the village were now cultivating sixty or a hundred acres of arable land, and tending several hundred head of livestock' (Hilton and Fagan 1950: 29–30). This should not tempt one into seeing the rich peasantry of this era as being stronger than it actually was. To be sure, 60 to 100 acres of arable land and several hundred head of livestock represented a sizeable, and unprecedented, holding and considerable village standing. 'But if the upper peasants were able to take advantage of the economic embarrassment of both nobles and poorer peasants, they still remained socially and politically a subject group in society' (Hilton and Fagan 1950: 30). Here, indeed, was a class in the making, 'chafing at ... (the) feudal restrictions on ... (its) economic enterprise' (Hilton and Fagan 1950: 31), without the class autonomy that would ensure the accumulation it sought to pursue. Here was a stratum of 'capitalist farmers in embryo', and the rich peasant constituted, in this sense, a 'revolutionary ... figure' (Hilton and Fagan 1950: 31). Hilton identifies this era as a '"marking time" phase' (1978: 281). This notion represents 'the natural tendency to focus on the minority or rich peasants, the "yeomen", because they seemed to be the group which would evolve into the capitalist tenant farmers of a later period' (1978: 281). They would so evolve, but were still constrained in this respect; were still, to use Ellen Wood's phrase, in the grip of 'a precapitalist logic taken to its absolute limits' (Wood 2002: 59). The era of vigorous transition would come in the sixteenth century. What is crucial is that a long process of 'prior differentiation' had yielded a strong class of rich peasants, with the desire, the means and the capacity to accumulate and expand, if the opportunity presented itself.

Peasant resistance in the feudal era: class struggle, peasant victory and the demise of feudalism

Prior to the thirteenth century, peasant resistance was limited and was 'defensive rather than aggressive' (1973: 85). In the thirteenth century, however, as the intensification of exploitation of peasants by their lords increased significantly (1949: 122–123), this changed. In England, it was landlords who took the initiative: they expanded and reorganized their demesnes, 'in order to sell agricultural produce on the market' (1949: 123), and employed professional agents to supervise them. These bailiffs, 'in order to make as much profit as possible, had to pay special attention to labour requirements' (1973: 87). In the absence of sufficient wage labour (1949: 123), they sought to increase peasant labour services via 'legally sanctioned coercive powers' (1973: 87). The outcome was that 'labour services were increased, even doubled', an 'increase in services (that) appears to have been almost universal'; this made 'it ... inevitable that there would be resistance by those of whom more was being demanded' (1949: 123–124). Nor was it increased services alone that were a source of discontent and social tension. How this was achieved, along with several other surplus-appropriating impositions, further stoked resentment. Here was a formidable array of feudal impositions, all of them deeply resented. The era of peasant quiescence was over.

The 'earliest signs of resistance' came in the royal courts: individual rather than collective disputes about increased services initiated by villeins (1949: 124). However, 'individual clashes such as these were but the heralds of the storm' (1949: 125). Then came collective action, 'which was to be most disturbing to the social order and which was the training ground for revolt on a large scale' (1949: 125). Groups of tenants now sought 'a legal basis for resistance to claims by the lords for increased services by denying that they were of ordinary villein status and so subject to the lord's arbitrary will' (1949: 125). There was resistance, too, over, for example, the collection of tallage, the right to buy and sell land, the payment of merchet, and the attempt to extract labour rents fully; there was also collective refusal to perform services (1949: 125–7). Hilton stresses: 'behind this litigation we become conscious of a continuous day-to-day struggle between lords and villein' (1949: 126).

The aforementioned were activities conducted legally. There were also, in the thirteenth and fourteenth centuries, those that were illegal and were pursued violently. We find peasants breaking into manor houses and carrying away charters, threats to burn houses, and threats to physically harm the occupants of manor houses. There are many instances of assault, and of 'violent defiance of both private and public authority'; in one case we find tenants being excommunicated 'for laying violent hands on the abbot and his brethren' (on this and more see 1949: 127–130).

Then, at the end of the 1340s, these social conflicts were intensified dramatically by the savage impact of the Black Death, which cut the population by as much as 50 per cent. It induced a seigneurial reaction to control tenants and labour, on top of the seigneurial offensive we have considered, and so generated further class struggle between lords and peasants. The English Rising of 1381 was, in part, the outcome. The 1381 rebels were defeated, and did not secure their goals. What, then, of the effect of the rebellion on long-term social and economic development? Hilton argues that, seen in the context of the popular discontent that preceded it in the thirteenth and fourteenth centuries, and not in isolation as a one-off, it did, surely, have an effect. It probably kept in check quite markedly the post-Black Death seigneurial reaction (1973: 230–232). More generally, as a result of the peasant resistance we have identified, some fundamental peasant aims were secured. These included: an altering of 'the level and nature of rents and services owed by peasants to their lords ... (and) a long-term, though occasionally reversed, trend away from labour rent toward money rent' (1973: 234).

Critically, with respect to the outcome of class struggle, one notes the effect on rents and wages, and the implications this had for the viability of feudal estates. Rents fell more or less universally between the early fourteenth and the early sixteenth century (1973: 153). This made the renting out of manorial land for money rent, at a time when services became far less common, decreasingly profitable. The critical element was pervasive customary rent, which was protected from increase. By the early fifteenth century, a crisis situation had arisen. Wages, too, rose over the long term: 'whereas between the beginning of the thirteenth century and the middle of the fifteenth century agricultural prices had fallen by ten per cent, real wages had multiplied by nearly two-and-a-half times and cash wages had nearly doubled' (1973: 154). For landlords whose demesne cultivation was increasingly done by wage labour, such 'rising wage cost' (1973: 154) was of great significance. Landlords increasingly let out their demesne land for money rent, often on short leases, at competitive rents. Hilton refers to the 'collapsed seigneurial economy' of the fifteenth century (1957, republished 1975: 161). The course of rents and of wages indicates something of the nature of the collapse. Many of the nobility were bankrupt. By the middle of the fifteenth century, there was a crisis, which was certainly at least partly the result of a successful class struggle waged by the peasantry. Feudalism was no longer workable. What would take its place?

Transition: class struggle and the victory of a reconstituted landlord class and the class of capitalist tenant farmers[3]

Elsewhere in Europe – in Eastern Europe – feudalism received a new lease of life in the so-called 'second serfdom'. That was the case in Prussia. Not so in England, or, indeed, France. In England, the sixteenth century was the era of 'the transition to capitalist agriculture' (Tawney 1912: 175). With a revitalized feudalism off the agenda, what followed depended on how the former feudal landlord class, now in crisis but still owning the vast preponderance of land in England, responded to that crisis. It might itself have sought to work the land as capitalist farmers, as, eventually, the Prussian Junkers would do. It did not. It opted, rather, to continue as a landlord class, and that required a reversal of the decline in rental income and a dramatic increase in that income. The English outcome depended also on how the relationship between the rich peasantry, or at least its most powerful representatives, and the landlord class developed, and on whether the shackles on its urge to accumulate might be broken. The great bulk of its land was rented. The rental form would be critical.

Until the mid-fifteenth century, it was an antagonistic relationship, with rich peasant pitted against lord in the social conflicts waged in the English countryside. Hilton argues that if, up to 1450, the peasantry achieved a victory, those who gained most were the rich peasants (the 'villein sokemen'), who were often the leaders in collective action (1973: 89). Here, then, was a significant stratum of rich peasants, some of whom were truly substantial: before 1450, not yet detached as a class from the rest of the peasantry; still powerfully constrained, in myriad ways, in its urge towards accumulation and sharing feudal restrictions with other segments of the peasantry; and sharing common enemies, along with those other segments of the peasantry, in the landlord class and the state. However, its economic interests were very different from those of other strata of the peasantry. Here was a class of rich peasants ripe for transformation into a class of capitalist farmers. The English transition to capitalist agriculture would not have been possible without that. The fifteenth century saw the end of feudalism in England. This ushered in the possibility of the formerly antagonistic relationship between rich peasant and feudal landlord being transformed into one of mutual advantage, although this was not so for the rest of the peasantry. Their antagonism increased, and with that came bitter class struggle, now with a transformed landlord class, or at least with one whose transformation was under way. The sixteenth century was an era of 'fierce agrarian struggles' (Hilton and Fagan 1950: 192).

Already, by the middle of the fifteenth century, landlords had rented out most of their demesne land, largely on leasehold, at competitive rents (Tawney 1912: 202–203). That was not sufficient to secure the rental income they sought. What we now see is their transformation from a feudal into a capitalist landlord class. The former feudal landlord class responded vigorously and ruthlessly to its predicament. At the end of the feudal era, the landlord class was determined to renew its fortunes and was reconstituted as a capitalist landlord class. This entailed a concerted effort to let land already let on copyhold, that is to say, customary, terms, and protected by custom from increase, as leasehold land, with the new capitalist tenants paying competitive rents. Landlords, in search of far higher rents, sought to dispossess small, customary tenants of their rented land, which was farmed in strips, and let it out in large units on 'economic' leases rather than customary copyhold; they also appropriated part of the commons and similarly let it out. Such land, to be suitable for capitalist farming, whether arable or pasture, had to be enclosed. It might be enclosed either by the landlord himself or by the new capitalist tenant, usually the latter. This was bitterly resisted.

Tawney (1912) gives a detailed account of peasant resistance. The rich peasantry, or its most powerful stratum, had been detached from the peasantry, and no longer provided strength and leadership in its struggle. He analyses at length the deeply felt grievances that 'at one time or another in the sixteenth century, set half the English counties ablaze' (Tawney 1912: 304). Thus: 'sometimes the discontent swelled to a small civil war, as it did in Lincolnshire and Yorkshire in 1536, and in the eastern and southern counties in 1549' (Tawney 1912: 318). Between 1547 and 1549 there was 'violent agitation and … drastic expedients' (Tawney 1912: 362). Tawney draws attention to disturbances and sometimes violent unrest – induced by high rents, seizing of land for pasture, enclosure, and the taking of the commons – in 1550, 1552, 1554, 1569, 1595 and 1607 (Tawney 1912: 319–320). The riots in the Midlands in 1607, a reaction to a preceding decade of enclosure and depopulation, were the 'last serious agrarian uprising in England' (Tawney 1912: 320).[4] By then, the peasantry had been defeated. By the end of the Tudor era the transition had been completed, the new class structure was in place, and the way was set for the stark opposition, in the countryside, of agricultural proletariat and capitalist employer in alliance with a powerful capitalist landlord class.

France

Differentiation, the rich peasantry and the absence of a clear movement towards capitalism

As in England, a differentiated peasantry was a feature of the French countryside from the very dawn of feudalism. This was so at least as early as the ninth century, sometimes 'with immense differences in the sizes of peasant holdings' (1973: 33). Hilton cites evidence for the Paris region (Perrin 1945) and Picardy (Coopland 1914). Likewise, Bloch points to 'marked differences in size' of the manse and 'glaring inequalities' 'in the early Middle Ages', the earliest he notes also being in the ninth century: these inequalities indicate clear social stratification, the critical dividing line being 'the possession or lack of a plough team' (Bloch 1966: 190–191 and 152–153). He argues that 'the indications seem to be that these small rural groups were at all periods divided into quite well-defined classes' (Bloch 1966: 190). Such social stratification continued 'in later centuries' (1973: 33). Bloch further notes considerable stratification in the twelfth and thirteenth centuries (Bloch 1966: 191). When, by the end of the fifteenth century, serfdom had collapsed, as it had in England, a differentiated peasantry continued, but there were 'no clear movements in the direction of agrarian capitalism' (1978: 282). A differentiated peasantry continued to be reproduced thereafter. We have an illuminating account of its nature in the seventeenth century, by Goubert, first for the last quarter of that century for the region of Beauvaisis (Goubert 1956) and subsequently for all of France for the whole century (Goubert 1986). Soboul (1956) provides an incisive treatment for the eighteenth century up to 1789, and thereafter until the end of the nineteenth century.

Goubert (1956: 57) tells us that 'were we to erect a social pyramid of peasant property, it would have a very broad base and an absurdly slender apex'. At the base was 'a swollen mass of dwarf peasants and labourers' (Soboul 1956: 87). This 'host of *manouvriers* constituted, in nearly every village, the majority – the overwhelming majority – of the inhabitants' (Goubert 1956: 59; 1986: 98): the *manouvrier* typically owning a few acres, a cottage and a small garden; half without a cow, rarely keeping a pig, and without horses (Goubert 1956: 58–60; 1986: 98–99); and 'forced to hire himself out to *laboureurs* and big farmers and, perhaps, to try and take up a secondary occupation (cooper, wheelwright, tailor, weaver)' (Goubert 1956:

60; cf. 1986: 100–105). In the eighteenth century, the indebtedness of small peasants to larger ones increased, there was an increasing tendency towards hiring small peasants as wage-labourers, and there emerged a growing category of landless day labourers, who worked for wages (Soboul 1956: 87).

Above them were differing categories of rich peasant. At 'the very peak of the peasant social pyramid' (Goubert 1956: 58) was a tiny group of very rich peasants. These were the large and enterprising tenants in areas of large-scale farming: either the *laboureurs-fermiers*, the substantial tenant farmers; or the *receveurs de seigneurie*, the receivers for the lords of the manors or *fermiers-receveurs* (Goubert 1956: 58, 64–65). These tenants leased lands concentrated in large units, from 80 to 150 hectares and more, especially church land (Goubert 1956: 548); they employed wage labour; they produced large surpluses; and they were extremely important as creditors. However, they existed only where land was 'owned (as) a large compact domain', which was by no means common (Goubert 1956: 64); and, other than in the north around Paris and Lille, 'they were only to be found in the villages in ones or twos; in some villages they were not to be found at all' (Goubert 1956: 58; 1986: 111–114).

There were, secondly, wealthier *laboureurs*. These were rich peasants. A *laboureur* 'was, almost by definition, a man who owned a plough and a pair of horses' (Goubert 1956: 63); who was not a sharecropper, but owned land; 'ploughing ... his own land with his own horses' (Goubert 1956: 63); perhaps taking in other land on lease; using his horses for carting; hiring his horses out to peasants who owned no horses; the *laboureurs* becoming 'the creditors of the mass of small peasants and, when occasion demanded, their employers at low wages' (Goubert 1956: 63; 1986: 114–116). They had considerable reserves and produced regular surpluses. Some *laboureurs* 'farmed no more than 35-40 acres' (Goubert 1956: 64). However, the larger ones – the truly rich peasants – farmed up to 100 acres (Goubert 1956: 64). Like the previous category, though, their significance in the total social formation should not be exaggerated: 'the *laboureur* is a fairly rare social specimen' (Goubert 1956: 4; cf. 1986: 114–116).

In France, however, by 1789, no transition to capitalism had taken place. Soboul (1956: 84) insists that at the end of the Old Régime the differences within the French peasantry 'were in no sense fundamental'. Differentiation of the peasantry there assuredly was, but it was still quantitative rather than qualitative in nature (Soboul 1956: 88). Thus, while 'mere quantitative differentiation between those possessing more or less real or movable property, land or money' had always existed, this 'did not entail a modification of the relations of production' (Soboul 1956: 88). For Soboul (1956: 84), 'the structure of landed property ... remained feudal' and 'social differences within the (peasant) community were much less important than the antagonism between the peasantry as a whole and the landed aristocracy'. A rich peasantry had yet to detach itself.

Contenders for a capitalist **primum mobile** *role*

The full capitalist transformation of the French countryside was not finally effected until the very end of the nineteenth century. Eugen Weber (1979: 117–118) suggests that a critical juncture can be located in the 1840s, but only for the areas of large-scale farming found in the north. There, capitalist transformation had already proceeded, largely via rich tenant farmers. For the great bulk of France – the centre, south and west, areas of small peasant farming where sharecropping was often prevalent – a turning point may be found in the 1890s or 1900s, and not before (Weber 1979: 118-129). Part of the explanation for this may be sought in the nature of the class struggle fought in the French countryside. Before considering that, however, it is instructive to consider the possible contenders for a *primum mobile* role in securing such a transition before 1789.

In England, the landlord class played a critical role: transforming itself into a capitalist landlord class, letting the land as leasehold at competitive rents to rich peasants who became capitalist tenants, and ensuring that the land was enclosed, as stressed earlier by Wood. No such role was played by the French landlord class. As Lefebvre (1977: 34) noted, 'the most important feature of France's rural physiognomy, the one characteristic whose underlying influence may well have had the most profound consequences' was that 'priests, nobles, and bourgeois almost never managed their properties directly; their domains were extremely fragmented and rented out as middle-sized farms, even as individual fields'. As Meek observes in his classic work on physiocracy, in France of the mid-eighteenth century:

> the main feature which distinguished French agriculture from that of England at this time was the relative lack of enclosures and the consequent survival of very large numbers of small peasant proprietors, who, although they were normally subject to heavy seigneurial dues, had the right to transfer their property or pass it on to their heirs.
>
> (Meek 1962: 23)

The French landlord class was, in this respect, thoroughly unprogressive.

If the French landlord class was thus defective, what of those who administered its estates? These were the *fermiers-généraux*. Here was a particular form of agrarian concentration, that of estate administration, which gave access to the marketable surplus. Crucially, 'numerous *fermiers-généraux* also traded in agricultural produce' (Soboul 1956: 86). They would usually take the form of 'a businessman, a notary, a large shopkeeper' (Soboul 1956: 86). They stood between proprietor and sharecropper: leasing in sharecropping units (the *métairies*) from one or perhaps more than one proprietor and subletting them; perhaps assigned by the proprietor, if the proprietor were a lord, to collect seigneurial revenues; and possibly entrusted with feudal rights of usage. The surplus they acquired from their sharecropping tenants enabled them to pursue a lucrative business as traders. They might, presumably, have been transformed ultimately into large capitalist farmers. Soboul (1956: 87) rejects them, however, as a likely destroyer or transformer of 'the old mode of production'. The *fermier-général* represented 'the application of commercial capital to agricultural production', and was caught in the contradictions characteristic of merchant's capital: that is to say, 'being integrated into the old system and profiting from it, generally himself the receiver of seigneurial revenues, the *fermier-général* had a vested interest in the maintenance of the old system which guaranteed his own position' (Soboul 1956: 86). That logic is powerful. They were a possible, but not the most likely, agent of agrarian transition.

Soboul argues that the large tenant farmers had to be discounted. They 'were indeed active agents in the evolution of agriculture inasmuch as they combined small farms into large ones and strove for a scientific and intensive form of agriculture' (Soboul 1956: 86–87). However, their potential revolutionary role was limited. Soboul insists that 'they brought into agriculture capital of commercial origin … (so that) their productive activity was subordinate to their commercial function' (Soboul 1956: 86–87). Moreover, they had deep involvement 'in the old productive system', as they were often 'receivers of seigneurial revenues and ecclesiastical tithes' (Soboul 1956: 87).

It is to the *laboureurs* that Soboul attributes the potential revolutionary role. It was they, certainly, who proved to be so in the north. They had no binding commitment to 'the old productive system'. It was they who 'tended to destroy and not to preserve feudal production' (Soboul 1956: 87). If there were signs of the rural community beginning to disintegrate, this was 'because of the progress of capitalist production, which involved both the creation of a market for commodities and a market for labour … (which) took place within the community essentially through the action of the *laboureurs*' (Soboul 1956: 88). It would be a transition, if it were to proceed, via the agency of the rich peasantry: not the aforementioned very rich peasantry, as represented by the substantial tenants, but the *laboureurs*. Their capacity to accumulate was, however, constrained by the siphoning off of much of their surplus. From the seventeenth century they, along with the rest of the peasantry, were taxed very heavily by the state: in Richelieu's phrase, the peasantry became the 'donkey of the state' (Goubert 1986: 189). Royal taxes, along with others – those of the church, the seigneur and sometimes the peasant community itself – which, for the first time, they now outstripped, constituted a heavy burden (Goubert 1986: Ch. 15).

Peasant resistance: class struggle and the frustrating of the capitalist impulse

While in England in the thirteenth century it was landlords who took the initiative, to which peasants then responded, in France participation in wider economic activity in the twelfth and thirteenth centuries enabled peasant communities – whole villages – to take aggressive action (1973: 87). This was the major form taken by peasant movements in France in the period from the late twelfth to the mid-fourteenth century (1973: 83). There was a powerful movement for village enfranchisement (1973: 74–85), with demands very similar to those made on an individual basis in England; for example, for fixed judicial fines, abolition or regularization of the *taille* (the seigneurial tax), eradication of *mainmorte* (death duty), a fixed rather than arbitrary marriage tax, and fixed payments to the lord on alienation of property (1973: 80–81). Thus:

> on the whole these were movements which aimed to obtain from the lord of the village a charter granting, at least, exemption from various exaction and fixed rather than arbitrary obligations, and at most an element of autonomy in the running of the village community.
>
> (1973: 75)

The demands also included 'freedom of personal status' (1973: 75). The struggle was often prolonged, violent and bitter (1973: 81–83). The peasants were often defeated by a combination of the nobility and royal power; and where they made gains, they often paid heavily (1973: 85). Achievements were tangible but partial, and gained at considerable cost (1973: 84–85). Yet there was some success: chartered privileges were enjoyed and there was abolition of certain tolls and certain services. (1973: 81–85).

Within such communities, it was rich peasants who were the driving force and the major beneficiaries:

> The struggle for village charters in the earlier period was part of the peasant reaction to the economic expansion of the period when the development of production for the market made the wealthy peasants who benefited from it socially and politically ambitious, and their demands and achievements were a straightforward reflection of the potentialities of the situation, primarily economic.
>
> (1973: 74)

However, if rich peasants gained most, by the end of the fifteenth century, as we have seen, they did not constitute a presence comparable with that of the English rich peasantry. Nor, thereafter, were they a force sufficient to spearhead capitalist transformation. Moreover, if serfdom had collapsed by then, the French peasantry continued to be subject to a host of feudal restrictions.

A prolonged struggle was pursued, which often erupted into violence, against the *seigneurie* (the feudal lords) until the end of the Old Régime: a struggle punctuated by peasant uprisings and agrarian revolt, by riots, disturbances and *jacqueries*. The 'great insurrections were altogether too disorganised to achieve any lasting result' and 'almost invariably doomed to defeat and eventual massacre' (Bloch 1966: 170).[5] At another level, 'the patient, silent struggles stubbornly carried out by rural communities over the years would accomplish more than these flashes in the pan (Bloch 1966: 170). The more-or-less cohesive 'French rural community' was unsuccessful in ridding itself of feudal obligations before 1789. However, united around struggles against the *seigneurie* for communal land and involved in a 'constant struggle for its economic existence and administrative autonomy' (Soboul 1956: 80), it did succeed in maintaining 'an economic and social system founded on the interplay of communal pressures, the limitation of private property and the existence of collectively exploited lands' (Soboul 1956: 80). The rich peasantry, the *laboureurs*, had not detached itself from the peasantry. By 1789 there had been no transition to capitalism, spearheaded by the rich peasantry or any other rural class.

The French Revolution cleared the ground for a possible unleashing of capitalism. It removed the massive barrier inherent in the feudal relationships that had persisted despite an apparently 'free' peasantry – free inasmuch as they were not serfs. It 'destroyed the seigneurial regime and abolished feudal rights. It proclaimed the total right to property; hence the freedom to enclose and cultivate and the restriction of collective rights' (Soboul 1956: 88). It modified the distribution of land and proprietary rights in land, as church land and the land of *émigré* nobles were sold. The major beneficiaries were the urban middle class and the rich peasantry (Soboul 1956: 88). Indeed, 'the French rural community' was destroyed. Nonetheless, the attempt to secure a compulsory division of communal lands failed (Soboul 1956: 89). On the one hand, 'the *laboureurs* ... finally constituted themselves (as) a class', and clearly became the 'dominant class in the countryside' (Soboul 1956: 89). With the changes, moreover, 'the hitherto latent antagonism between the *laboureurs* ... and the mass of peasants ... became overt' (Soboul 1956: 89). On the other hand, the 'mass of peasants' – a poor and middle peasantry – 'clung desperately to the traditional forms of production and stubbornly called for the maintenance of the limitations which collective constraint imposed on private property' (Soboul 1956: 89). From the very early post-1789 years, they demanded the retention of gleaning and stubble rights, of common grazing land, of the requirement to reap with sickles, of the communal herd, and opposed attempts to enclose lands and meadows (Soboul 1956: 91–92), and a bitter struggle lasted throughout the nineteenth century. The resistance was most marked in the south-east, south-west and centre of France, while in the countryside of the north, capitalist transformation did not meet such opposition (Soboul 1956: 93). This prolonged resistance 'considerably inhibited the capitalist transformation of French agriculture' (Soboul 1956: 91). It was sufficient to continue to stifle the capitalist impulse and prevent the unleashing of capitalism throughout the French countryside until the very end of the nineteenth century.

Prussia

From the 'free peasants east of the Elbe' to subjugation as serfs: class struggle red in tooth and claw

Engels (1965: 156, first published 1885) refers, for the period up to the sixteenth century, to 'the free peasants east of the Elbe', and Brenner (1976: 43) to 'what had been, until then, one of Europe's freest peasantries'. Here was a relatively free peasantry within feudalism, or as an outpost of feudalism. This arose as follows. From the eleventh and twelfth centuries 'lay and church magnates obtained grants of land, or took part in movements of conquest in sparsely settled wooded areas', and 'they put into the hands of special agents the recruitment of peasants from the Rhineland and the Low Countries to take up new holdings and, in effect, to create new village settlements' (1973: 43). These

> colonizing German and Polish landowners, in the eastern territories beyond the Elbe, deliberately created villages whose inhabitants were offered, as bait, freer terms and conditions of life than in the western ones. The landlords' agents were authorized to offer holdings on free and heritable terms, to be held often for no more than money rents and church tithes. Superior jurisdictions and fiscal pressures were avoided and the agent himself, provided with a holding three or four time the size of the peasants', became in effect the immediate lord, presiding over the village court and taking a proportion of the fines.
>
> (1973: 92)

These peasant colonists had tenure on free status, with 'low fixed money rents and with no labour services, together with a degree of local autonomy' (1973: 44). It was a peasantry in which the seeds of differentiation were planted, and differentiation must have proceeded to a not insubstantial extent, remaining so until the sixteenth century (Byres 1996: 54–55, 67). Hilton stresses: 'although such villages might to some extent reflect the peasant ideal, they came into existence as a result of seigneurial, not peasant initiative' (1973: 92). This had nothing to do with class struggle waged by peasants.[6]

However, class struggle between Prussian lords and this relatively free peasantry would come red in tooth and claw. In the wake of the Black Death and other later visitations of the fourteenth century came widespread flight from the land and, as the fifteenth century wore on, depopulation, totally deserted villages, and a serious shortage of labour brought an ominous seigneurial offensive. The Junkers themselves began to acquire and to farm deserted peasant land. This, at first, was something of an emergency measure until new peasants might be found. In the sixteenth century, however, when corn prices began to rise, it became more permanent. The Junkers confronted a serious labour shortage, whether in the form of the free wage labourers employed hitherto, or of labour supplied via labour services. They reacted: with increasing curtailment of peasants' freedom to move, the imposition of mandatory maximum wages, an assault on fixed money rents and, finally, a concerted move to extend mandatory labour services. In the sixteenth century, the latter multiplied and became the norm and a free peasantry disappeared completely. In Prussia 'the peasants did not accept the deterioration of their rights and conditions without resistance' (Carsten 1989: 13–14): that is to say, there was class struggle between peasants and lords. They appealed to princely authority through the judicial process, and there were peasant uprisings. Whatever the apparent judicial victories, they were a very limited deflection of the powerful forces engulfing the peasantry, and peasant uprisings were cruelly suppressed with no great difficulty.[7] The tide of enserfment would not be stemmed. In this class struggle, the Junkers won a crushing victory. Where, in England, the peasantry had successfully resisted the seigneurial reaction, and so sounded feudalism's death knell, in Prussia the opposite was true. There, 'the "manorial reaction" shattered the free institutions of East Elbia and wrought a radical shift in class relationships' (Rosenberg 1958: 29). By the end of the sixteenth century, the Prussian Junkers had succeeded, with the aid of state power, in enserfing to themselves 'the formerly free peasants of the German East ... (in) an almost complete subjugation of large segments of the peasantry' (Gerschenkron 1966: viii). It was the case that:

> Everywhere in north-east Germany, and equally in neighbouring Poland, there developed in the course of the sixteenth century the system of *Gutsherrschaft* consisting of demesne farming and serf labour, which was entirely different from the agrarian system of central, western, and southern Germany (*Grundherrschaft*).
>
> (Carsten 1989: 19)

The outcome was 'the classic Junker estate economy ... as a form of seigneurial market production (*Teilbetrieb*) in which, by means of extra-economic coercion, the landlords forced the peasantry to shoulder the cost of the labour, horsepower and tools necessary to demesne farming' (Hagen 1985: 111). When serfdom had broken down irretrievably in England and France, in Prussia it was established with a vengeance. It would remain in place until the early nineteenth century.[8]

Peasant differentiation in late feudal Prussia and the unlikelihood of capitalism from below[9]

As Prussian junkerdom mounted a feudal offensive that changed fundamentally agrarian relationships east of the Elbe, processes of peasant differentiation first would be brought to a severe halt, then would be reversed and would have a tight rein placed upon them. Between the sixteenth and the early nineteenth centuries, the Junkers expanded their demesne at the expense of the peasantry, and imposed ever new burdens on an enserfed peasantry. Yet, by the second half of the eighteenth century, the east Elbian peasantry was by no means homogeneous.

There was, first, a line of division between an overwhelming majority of unfree peasants and a tiny minority of free peasants. The free peasants were 'large peasants with especially favourable conditions' (Harnisch 1986: 41). They were analogous to the very rich peasants identified in France by Goubert (the *laboureurs-fermiers* and the *fermiers-receveurs*). They were 'completely free of obligations or subservience to the noble estates' (Berdhal 1988: 29); and frequently served the Junkers' interests, working closely with the Junkers, serving as chief administrative and police officers and directing the village's labour force. Like their French counterparts, they may be discounted as likely candidates for a capitalist transforming role. Their relationship with the Junkers was close, so that a possible independent role was unlikely. Any transformation would be likely to be in concert with, rather than in competition with, the Junkers. Conceivably, that might have been as capitalist tenant farmers renting from a transformed feudal landlord class. However, they 'comprised a very small percentage of the rural population' (Berdhal 1988: 29), and alone could not have become a class of capitalist farmers. In terms of sheer control of a sufficient quantum of resources within the village, their transforming significance was very limited. As Harnisch observes, 'we can more or less discount the comparatively small number of free peasants' (Harnisch 1986: 41).

The unfree peasantry were divided into 'true *Bauern*', described by Harnisch (1986: 56) as 'the middle and large peasants' and those who were not 'true *Bauern*'. The class of peasantry beneath the Bauern – the great majority of the rural population – had far less favourable property rights (if they had any at all), seldom had strips of land on the estate, and were unable to support a team of animals. They were divided into a stratum of smallholders (*Kossaten*), with 5–10 and at most 15 hectares, but without teams of draught animals; cottagers with small plots (*Büdner*); garden cottagers (*Häusler*); and a multitude of day labourers (*Tagelöhner*). For the purposes of this chapter, I concentrate on the true *Bauern*.

The true *Bauern* had property, inheritance and contractual rights; were able to support a team, or teams, of draught animals; and had holdings of between 20 and 70 hectares. They might be subdivided into full *Bauern*, with at least four teams (*Spannen*) of two horses or oxen each; half *Bauern* (*Halbbauern*), with two teams; and quarter *Bauern* (*Viertelbauern*), with one team. Their ownership of draught animals needs to be qualified by the reality that 'the labor obligation required peasants to keep far more draft animals than they needed for their own operation' (Blum 1978: 150). A full peasant, for example, with heavy labour obligations, and with 12 horses, might need eight for his labour obligations and four for his own needs (Blum

1978: 150). By way of contrast, a peasant with two teams would have one of the teams to meet his labour services. Such peasants 'had to maintain one team, with a farm servant (*Knecht*) and quite often also a maid, merely to be able to meet their dues' (Blum 1978: 150). They were a feudal rich peasantry, heavily constrained by feudal obligations. Surplus appropriation was heavy and stripped them bare. Labour rent varied regionally. It might be two to three days per week, but the lighter the burden of labour obligations, the heavier the feudal dues in kind, with instances of dues in grain constituting 20 per cent of an average harvest where there was only one day of service. They did participate in production for the market, but their marketed surplus was not a true commercial surplus of the kind that market-oriented rich peasants in a non-feudal situation might set out to sell regularly. The outcome was not a growing source of accumulation. Rather, it was one in which 'their net proceeds were minimal, which meant that they could only keep their farmsteads going through the utmost exertions' (Harnisch 1986: 47). A class of rich peasants with the size, strength and resources of the English rich peasantry simply did not exist. There was, certainly, peasant resistance – clear class struggle – centring on the need for the abolition of feudal dues, especially labour services, increasing in intensity, and with a growing determination and resilience, in the second half of the eighteenth century.[10] The most prominent proponents of such struggle were rich and substantial peasants – the full and half *Bauern* – who were particularly irked by labour services, and from whom the Junkers were seeking to extract even heavier services. This now posed a threat to the feudal order.

The agrarian traverse in Prussia in the nineteenth century: capitalism from above[11]

By the end of the eighteenth century, increasingly aware of peasant pressure and fearful of revolutionary activity such as had erupted in France, 'an influential group among the Prussian leaders of state now realised that (abolition of feudal dues) ... had become an urgent necessity' (Harnisch 1986: 64). This led to reforms in 1799, on the royal demesnes, and that action was surely induced, in part, by peasant pressure – class struggle – over previous decades. Then, in 1807, in the wake of crushing defeat by Napoleon's armies in 1806, feudalism was abolished with the emancipation of the serfs – some 350 years after its demise in England. There followed a period of transition. If the sixteenth century was the era of the transition to capitalist agriculture in England, the nineteenth century was so for Prussia. However, in Prussia it was the erstwhile feudal landlords who became capitalist farmers. It was 'capitalism from above'. It was the first such agrarian traverse in history.

As Harnisch (1986: 37) points out, 'the landowning families stayed in full possession of their large estates as well as their often extensive forests', just as the English landlord class retained ownership of their land. The Junkers took over and enclosed, in the teeth of opposition, the land of both poor and rich peasants – the land they worked and common land. However, a change took place in the composition of Prussian landowners. By the late eighteenth century, the Prussian nobility had accumulated much debt. In the 1820s there was a severe depression and the market for grains virtually collapsed. It was then that decisive changes took place. A large number of noble estates were sold to commoners. The new estate owners, equipped with fresh capital, 'led the way in the transformation of Prussian agriculture' (Berdhal 1988: 282). By the 1850s, the proportion of Junker estates owned by those without title – commoners – had tripled or quadrupled since 1807, and in 1856 the figure was 56 per cent more. It was not, though, only the new owners who took to capitalist farming. The old were similarly receptive to new ways.

The Prussian landlord class retained ownership of most of the land, engrossing large quantities of peasant land. However, unlike English land-lords, they ceased to be landlords. We note a particular characteristic of this dominant landlord class, which was important to their transformation – or those of them who had been feudal landlords. Of critical importance was their character as takers of labour rent, which meant that they took decisions with respect to the form production would take (such as which crops would be grown, among others); and that, therefore, before 1807 they were not totally divorced from the process of production. Such a landlord class is more likely to be poised for possible transformation to hirers of wage labour than is one that appropriates surplus via kind or money rent. The transition to kind and, even more, money rent, as was the case in England, constitutes an important change for a landlord class. Such a transition represents a severing of links with production. It is not inconceivable that such a landlord class might be transformed into a class of capitalist farmers: hiring wage labour, and appropriating surplus thus. However, such a transformation is more likely where the landlord class has a direct relationship with labour, through labour rent, and has links with the process of production.

With the disappearance of obligatory labour services, Prussian landlords had lost their captive labour supply. Former serfs were unwilling to work on Junker holdings. The relationship with the new forms of labour, however, was not immediately fully capitalist. It involved, initially and for some time, transitional forms. The Junkers, then, did not spring fully caparisoned as capitalist farmers from the belly of feudalism. They would take time to slough off their feudal skins. At first, 'peasant labour services and the com-pulsory farm service of peasant youth on Junker farms were replaced by contractually hired farm servants and the cottager system … the latter (involving) the exchange of labour for an allocation of the land' (Perkins 1984: 5). While farm servants were technically free, there were restrictions on their movement. This was followed by the system of confined labourers, hired on written short-term contracts. In each case, there was an absence of the money wage. Living standards were pitifully low. Ultimately, the Junkers were forced to employ day labourers, or 'free labourers' (*frei Arbeiter*), paid a money wage. It was wage labour, 'free' in Marx's double sense, but not without the vestigial traces of feudalism. By 1871 the transition was complete. By then the Junkers were, in every useful sense, fully capitalist. It was a capitalism marked deeply by Prussia's immediate feudal past and the powerful subjugation of the peasantry that it entailed.

Some rich peasants did emerge – from the suggested sources of free peasants and true *Bauern* – to be transformed, eventually, into capitalist farmers. However, they were exceptional, 'a small minority of *Grossbauern* ("big peasants")' (Lenin 1962: 239, first published 1908) in close alliance with Junker capitalist farmers. The dominant class in the Prussian countryside, the 'masters of the countryside', were the latter.

Conclusions

In England a feudal landlord class, rendered obsolete by class struggle waged by a united peasantry, was transformed into a progressive, capitalist landlord class that let its land (which was enclosed) in leases at 'competitive' rents; and a rich peasantry (or at least its upper stratum), emerging from prior feudal differentiation, was metamorphosed into a class of capitalist tenant farmers able to pay 'competitive' rents and earn the average rate of profit. Integral to that outcome was the victory of the reconstituted landlord class over the peasantry during the sixteenth century, the era of transition. In France, a clearly unprogressive landlord class displayed no evidence of either transformation into a capitalist landlord class or a class of capitalist farmers; while the rich peasantry, the *laboureurs*, a potential class of capitalists, was constrained, in part, by its surplus being effectively appropriated by the state and by landlords. This continued until 1789, while capitalist transformation was further postponed until the end of the nineteenth century by a relentless struggle waged by poor and middle peasants. In Prussia, a powerful feudal landlord class, the Junkers, having in the sixteenth century crushed the free peasantry that existed east of the Elbe and enserfed it comprehensively eventually was transformed in the nineteenth century into a class of capitalist farmers; while the possibility of capitalism from below, via a rich peasantry, was wholly pre-empted by the absence of a rich peasantry of sufficient strength. The Junkers' decisive victory over the 'free' peasantry in the sixteenth century, which ushered in Prussian feudalism, was repeated in the nineteenth century over the formerly enserfed peasantry in an equally crushing conquest, which was the prelude to a capitalism from above.

I have sought elsewhere to consider something of the relevance of the historical experience of the agrarian question and paths of capitalist agrarian transition for contemporary developing countries (Byres 2002). I do not wish to repeat that here, or seek to draw any detailed conclusions. Clearly, however, one must proceed with the utmost caution.

I can do no better, perhaps, than quote the late Rodney Hilton, the outstanding Marxist historian of feudal England, who had a formidable knowledge, too, of medieval Europe and a keen interest in the contemporary world:

> ... historians and sociologists are engaged in comparative studies of peasant societies in different epochs. It would be very risky to transfer any generalizations about peasant societies of medieval Europe to any other time. For example, the capitalist farmers who were to be an important element in the history of early European capitalism emerged in a general environment of small-scale enterprise. What could the fate of peasant societies in the present world of almost world-wide commercial and industrial monopoly capitalism have in common with that of peasant societies of the late medieval world? Clearly, the tasks of leadership in contemporary peasant society have nothing in common with the tasks of the past, except in the recognition that conflict is part of existence and that nothing is gained without struggle.
>
> (1973: 236)

To that I might add that, when dealing with peasantries in the past or the present, and however different the one is from the other, it is always important to consider the nature, the extent and the progress of the social differentiation that characterizes such peasantries, and the nature of the landlord class.

Notes

1 From this point on, where a reference appears with a date but no name it refers to 'Hilton'. Many of Hilton's writings cited in this chapter can be found in Hilton (1975, 1990).
2 Kosminsky (1956: 225–6) also observes:

> The formation of an upper layer among the free peasantry may be partially connected with processes taking place even in pre-feudal society, with the advance of early property differentiation and may represent, as it were, certain elements of incompleteness in the feudalization of English society.

Significant aspects of this may be seen in Rosamond Faith's (1997) book *The English Peasantry and the Growth of Lordship*. She notes: 'differentiation begins to appear in the sixth century' (Faith 1997: 5).
3 The sixteenth century experience is told at length and most eloquently in R.H. Tawney's (1912) classic *The Agrarian Problem in the Sixteenth Century*. Among more recent work, see the excellent book by Jane Whittle (2000), *The Development of Agrarian Capitalism: Land and Labour in Norfolk 1440–1580*.
4 The fascinating Kett's Rebellion of 1549, in Norfolk, which was directed against enclosure, has given rise to a particularly large body of scholarship. Russell (1859) has become something of a *locus classicus*. Later scholars include, for example, Bindoff (1949); Land (1977); Cornwall (1977, 1981); MacCulloch (1979, 1981); Fletcher and MacCulloch (2004); and Walter (2004). For them, the focus is not on the kind of questions addressed here – questions of class struggle, the transition to capitalism and the agrarian question. Among writers who do have such a focus,

see Tawney (1912: 149, 326, 331–337); Hilton and Fagan (1950: 193); and Whittle (2000: 1, 45, 69, 76, 287, 312–313, 329). Whittle points to the complex nature of the rebellion, which took place in a region that was in the vanguard of agrarian capitalism, in the era of transition. Kett's Rebellion bore the contradictions of transition at a time when those contradictions had yet to work themselves out fully.

5 Ladurie (1987), in his *The French Peasantry 1450–1660*, provides a cogent account of peasant revolts over the two centuries from 1450 to 1660 (Ladurie 1987: Ch. 5, 359–99), with particular stress on the capacity of 'taxation … to arouse the resentments of the peasants' (Ladurie 1987: 359). In view of what has been said already about the increased burden of taxation, this is not, perhaps, surprising. The seventeenth century, indeed, the *grande siècle*, has attracted detailed treatment of peasant revolts and uprisings by, for example, the Soviet scholar Boris Porchnev (2002), in a meticulously researched and exciting work first published in 1963; and by Foisil (1970); Mousnier (1971); Mollat and Wolff (1973); Goubert (1986: Ch. 16, 205–219); and Bercé (1990). We cannot consider here that rich literature and the considerable debate embodied in it.

6 I have cited Hilton to maintain comparative perspective. I have considered the creation of a free peasantry in Prussia in my book (Byres 1996: 48–52). In addition, on this see Rosenberg (1943: 2; 1944: 228; 1958: 30); Carsten (1954: 80–81, 111; 1989: 3); Engels (1965: 154–155); Leyser *et al.* (1978: 75–76); and Hagen (1985: 3–4).

7 For a brief treatment of peasant resistance, see Byres (1996: 60–61). It has been suggested by Rosenberg (1944: 233) that 1525 – the German Peasant War – was a probable turning point: that 'a long period of peasant unrest had come to an end with the crushing defeat suffered by the rebellious Prussian peasants in the uprising of 1525'. In fact, as Rosenberg himself suggests (1944: 233), the peasants east of the Elbe were 'relatively docile'. Engels (1965: 156) points out that in only one region of east Elbia was there an active peasant movement in 1525 – in Eastern Prussia. That is where they were crushingly defeated. Elsewhere, east of the Elbe, the peasants 'left their insurgent brethren in the lurch, and were served their just desserts' (Engels 1965: 156). If that was the case, they paid a harsh penalty.

8 This I consider at length in my book (Byres 1996: 53–68). Here I simply state the barest of outlines.

9 This is treated in detail in Byres (1996: 81–90), of which the following is a highly condensed version. There I draw especially on the unerringly excellent Harnisch (1986) and the valuable Berdhal (1988); as well as Blum (1978) and Hagen (1985).

10 On 'peasant struggle: its nature and implications' see Byres (1996: 90–96).

11 I consider the Prussian transition in detail in my book (Byres 1996: Ch. 4, 104–158).

References

Bercé, Y.-M. (1990) *History of Peasant Revolts* (translated by A. Whitmore), Ithaca, NY: Cornell University Press (first published in French in 1986).

Berdhal, R.M. (1988) *The Politics of the Prussian Nobility: The Development of a Conservative Ideology*, Princeton, NJ: Princeton University Press.

Bindoff, S.T. (1949) *Kett's Rebellion 1549*, London: George Philip and Son for the Historical Association.

Bloch, M. (1961a) *Feudal Society, Volume 1: The Growth of Ties of Dependence* (translated by L.A. Manyon), London: Routledge and Kegan Paul (first published in French in 1939).

—— (1961b) *Feudal Society, Volume 2: Social Classes and Political Organization* (translated by L.A. Manyon), London: Routledge and Kegan Paul (first published in French in 1940).

—— (1966) *French Rural History: An Essay on its Basic Characteristics* (translated by J. Sondheimer), London: Routledge and Kegan Paul (first published in French in 1931).

Blum, J. (1978) *The End of the Old Order in Rural Europe*, Princeton, NJ: Princeton University Press.

Brenner, R. (1976) 'Agrarian class structure and economic development in pre-industrial Europe', *Past and Present*, (70): 30–75.

—— (2001) 'The Low Countries in the transition to capitalism', *Journal of Agrarian Change*, 1 (2): 169–242.

Byres, T.J. (1996) *Capitalism from Above and Capitalism from Below: An Essay in Comparative Political Economy*, Basingstoke/London: Macmillan/New York: St Martin's Press.

—— (2002) 'Paths of capitalist agrarian transition in the past and in the contemporary world', in V.K. Ramachandran and M. Swaminathan (eds), *Agrarian Studies: Essays on Agrarian Relations in Less-Developed Countries*, New Delhi: Tulika Books.

—— (2006) 'Differentiation of the peasantry under feudalism and the transition to capitalism: in defence of Rodney Hilton', *Journal of Agrarian Change*, 6 (1): 17–68.

Carsten, F.L. (1954) *The Origins of Prussia*, London: Oxford University Press.

—— (1989) *A History of the Prussian Junker*, Aldershot: Scolar Press.

Coopland, W.G. (1914) 'The Abbey of Saint-Bertin and its Neighbourhood, 900–1350', in P. Vinogradoff (ed.), *Oxford Studies in Social and Legal History, Volume 4*, Oxford: Clarendon Press.

Cornwall, J. (1977) *Revolt of the Peasantry 1549*, London: Routledge and Kegan Paul.

—— (1981) 'Kett's Rebellion in context', *Past and Present*, (93): 160–164.

Engels, F. (1965) 'On the history of the Prussian peasantry', in *The Peasant War in Germany*, Moscow: Progress Publishers (first published in 1885).

—— (1970) 'The peasant question in France and Germany', in *Selected Works of Karl Marx and Frederick Engels, Vol. 3*, Moscow: Progress Publishers (first published in 1894-95).

Faith, R. (1997) *The English Peasantry and the Growth of Lordship*, London/Washington: Leicester University Press.

Fletcher, A. and D. MacCulloch (2004) *Tudor Rebellions* (5th edn), Harlow: Pearson Education (Longman).

Foisil, M. (1970) *La Révolte des Nu-Pieds et les révoltes normandes de 1639*, Paris: Presses Universitaires du France.

Gerschenkron, A. (1966) *Bread and Democracy in Germany* (new edition), New York: Howard Fertig.

Goubert, P. (1956) 'The French peasantry of the seventeenth century: a regional example', *Past and Present*, (10): 55–77.

—— (1986) *The French Peasantry in the Seventeenth Century* (translated by Ian Patterson), Cambridge: Cambridge University Press (first published in French in 1982).

Hagen, W. (1985) 'How mighty the Junkers? Peasant rents and seigneurial profits in sixteenth-century Brandenburg', *Past and Present*, (108): 80–116.

Harnisch, H. (1986) 'Peasants and markets: the background to the agrarian reforms in feudal Prussia east of the Elbe, 1760–1807', in R. Evans and W.R. Lee (eds), *The German Peasantry*, London: Croom Helm.

Hilton, R. (1949) 'Peasant movements in England before 1381', *Economic History Review* (2nd series), 2(2): 117–136.

—— (1957) 'A Study in the pre-history of English enclosure in the fifteenth century', in *Studi in onore di Armando Sapori*, Milan: Istituto Editoriale Cisalpino.

—— (1966) *A Medieval Society: The West Midlands at the End of the Thirteenth Century*, London: Weidenfeld and Nicolson.

—— (1973) *Bond Men Made Free: Medieval Peasant Movements and the English Rising of 1381*, London: Temple Smith.

—— (1974) 'Medieval peasants: any lessons?', *Journal of Peasant Studies*, 1 (2): 207–219.

—— (1975) *The English Peasantry in the Later Middle Ages*, London: Oxford University Press.

—— (1978) 'Reasons for inequality among medieval peasants', *Journal of Peasant Studies*, 5 (3): 271–284.

—— (1980) '*Feodalité* and *seigneurie* in France and England', in D.F. Johnson, F. Bedarida and F. Crouzet (eds), *Britain and France: Ten Centuries*, Folkestone: W. Dawson and Son.

—— (1990) *Class Conflict and the Crisis of Feudalism*, Verso: London.

Hilton, R. and H. Fagan (1950) *The English Rising of 1381*, London: Lawrence and Wishart.

Hobsbawm, E.J. and G. Rude (1973) *Captain Swing*, Harmondsworth: Penguin Books.

Kosminsky, E.A. (1956) *Studies in the Agrarian History of England in the Thirteenth Century* (translated by Ruth Kisch, with an editor's introduction by R. Hilton), Oxford: Basil Blackwell (first published in Russian in 1947).

Ladurie, E.L. (1987) *The French Peasantry 1450–1660* (translated by Alan Sheridan), Aldershot: Scolar Press (first published in French in 1977).

Land, S.K. (1977) *Kett's Rebellion: The Norfolk Rising of 1549*, Ipswich: The Boydell Press.

Lefebvre, G. (1977) 'The place of the revolution in the agrarian history of France', in R. Forster and O. Ranum (eds), *Rural Society in France: Selections from the Annales – Economies, Sociétés, Civilisations*, Baltimore/London: Johns Hopkins University Press.

Lenin, V.I. (1962) *The Agrarian Programme of Social Democracy in the First Russian Revolution, 1905-1907*, Vol. 13 of *Collected Works*, Moscow: Foreign Languages Publishing House (first published in 1908).

—— (1964) *The Development of Capitalism in Russia*, Vol. 3 of *Collected Works*, Moscow: Progress Publishers (first published in 1899).

Leyser, K.J., C.C. Bayley, T.S. Hamerow, H.D. Starke and editors (1978) 'Germany, history of', in *Encyclopaedia Britannica*, 15th edn, Vol. 8, Chicago: Encyclopaedia Britannica.

MacCulloch, D. (1979) 'Kett's Rebellion in context', *Past and Present*, (84): 36–59.

—— (1981) 'A rejoinder', *Past and Present*, (93): 165–173.

Meek, R.L. (1962) *The Economics of Physiocracy: Essays and Translations*, Cambridge, MA: Harvard University Press.

Miller, E. and J. Hatcher (1978) *Medieval England: Rural Society and Economic Change 1086–1348*, London and New York: Longman.

Mollat, M. and P. Wolff (1973) *Popular Revolutions of the Late Middle Ages*, London: Allen & Unwin.

Mousnier, R. (1971) *Peasant Uprisings in Seventeenth Century France, Russia and China* (translated by B. Pearce), London: Allen & Unwin (first published in French in 1967).

Perkins, J.A. (1984) 'The German agricultural worker, 1815-1914', *Journal of Peasant Studies*, 11 (3): 3–27.

Perrin, C.E. (1945) 'Observations sur le manse dans la région parisienne au début du IXe siècle', *Annales d'Histoire Sociale*, VII: 39–52.

Porchnev, B. (2002) *Les soulèvements populaires en France de 1623 à 1648*, Paris: Flammarion (first published in 1963).

Postan, M.M. (1966) 'England', in M.M. Postan (ed.), *The Cambridge Economic History of Europe, Vol. 1: The Agrarian Life of the Middle Ages* (2nd edn), Cambridge: Cambridge University Press.

Rosenberg, H. (1943) 'The rise of the Junkers in Brandenberg–Prussia 1410–1653, Part 1', *American Historical Review*, XLIX (1): 1–21.

—— (1944) 'The rise of the Junkers in Brandenberg–Prussia 1410–1653, Part 2', *American Historical Review*, XLIX (2): 228–242.

—— (1958) *Bureaucracy, Aristocracy and Autocracy: The Prussian Experience, 1660–1815*, Cambridge, MA: Harvard University Press.

Russell, F.W. (1859) *Kett's Rebellion in Norfolk*, London: Longman

Soboul, A. (1956) 'The French rural community in the eighteenth and nineteenth centuries', *Past and Present*, (10): 78–95.

Tawney, R.H. (1912) *The Agrarian Problem in the Sixteenth Century*, London: Longmans, Green & Co.

Walter, J. (2004) 'Kett, Robert (*c.* 1492–1549)', in H.C.G. Matthew and B. Harrison (eds), *Oxford Dictionary of National Biography*, Oxford: Oxford University Press, online: www.oxforddnb.com/view/article/15485.

Weber, E. (1979) *Peasants into Frenchmen: The Modernisation of Rural France, 1870-1914*, London: Chatto & Windus.

Whittle, J. (2000) *The Development of Agrarian Capitalism: Land and Labour in Norfolk 1440–1580*, Oxford: Clarendon Press.

Wickham, C. (1985) 'The uniqueness of the East', *Journal of Peasant Studies*, 12 (2–3): 166–196.

Wood, E. (2002) 'The question of market dependence', *Journal of Agrarian Change*, 2 (1): 50–87.

4 Nineteenth century imperialism and structural transformation in colonized countries

Amiya Kumar Bagchi

Introduction[1]

The advent of industrialization in Europe in the eighteenth century transformed the economic structures of the early industrializers, so that secondary industry and services came to provide increasingly larger proportions of output and employment. As an integral part of this process of industrialization, the pioneering capitalist countries conquered territories in Asia, Africa, Latin America and the Caribbean, ushering in the era of imperialism. Private property rights and free labour were the central features of a liberal ideology that, as discussed by Farshad Araghi in Chapter 5, was propagated by the imperial powers in the nineteenth century to justify their formal and informal control of much of the world. However, despite such promises, in most colonized countries the objective of imperialism was to reshape land and labour regimes so as to facilitate a transfer of resources to the metropolitan country, a process that I have called 'export-led exploitation' (Bagchi 1982: Ch. 2).

Imperial conquests began in the sixteenth century and reached their apogee in the last quarter of the nineteenth century (Bagchi 1982: Ch. 3–4, 2005). European conquest was followed in most of the larger colonies by the greater insinuation of commercial markets into economic activities and even the growth of some large-scale industry. Nonetheless, these colonies failed to industrialize under imperialism. The imperial powers reconfigured prevailing social and economic mechanisms governing the control of labour and land, using violence and rigged market transactions so as to favour metropolitan capital and the imperial state, extracting surplus from the colonies and semicolonies that was largely reinvested in the imperialist countries.

The imperialist countries therefore ruled their domain not with the objective of creating institutions that would usher in capitalism, as they knew it in their own countries, but with that of consolidating their rule and extracting tribute for the metropolitan country. The structures of control in the colonies in most areas of economic and social life were shaped by imperialism so as to impede the transformation of the economy away from the predominantly rural primary sector and the growth of free markets. Of course, imperial objectives were contested by the ruled, and their resistance and movements also greatly influenced the outcomes that were witnessed.

This chapter explores the main reasons for the lack of structural transformation in the colonial and semicolonial countries in the era in which the North-Western European countries and their overseas offshoots were experiencing industrialization and high rates of economic growth. It does this, firstly, by examining some prevailing myths in the understanding of rural social structures under imperialism. Next, it summarizes the main processes that were witnessed in the colonized countries in the nineteenth century under imperialism, before reviewing these processes in somewhat more detail in Africa, Latin America and Asia. Cumulatively, it is demonstrated that global capitalism and capitalist colonialism were born together, and that colonialism was the most important factor preventing the upward movement of incomes and the rural and social transformation of colonies in Africa and Asia and the newly independent semicolonial states of Latin America.

Rural social structures of colonies: myths and realities

In the analysis of social change involving rural people in the colonies, the initial obstacle is the choice of terms by which to describe them. The aggregative categories themselves carry the baggage of particular ideologies. For example, in the title of George Dalton's anthology on social change across the world (Dalton 1971), there is the assumption that all precapitalist rural societies must have been 'village communities', with no element of private or individual appropriation of resources, an assumption that has been falsified by empirical evidence in the three most populous countries of Asia and the world, namely China, India and Indonesia (Breman 1988; Boomgaard 1989). The title also assumes that these communities must have been undergoing 'modernization' in the sense understood by US political scientists such as Gabriel Almond. The point is not, as Boomgaard (1991) has cogently argued, that there was no period in which village corporate entities existed, or even that something resembling a village community, with a minimum amount of exposure to the outside world, ever existed in precolonial Asia or Latin America, but that in many cases 'village communities' were constructed by the colonial authorities for purposes of taxation and the exploitation of the land and labour of the concerned areas. Such constructed communities, of course, had little autonomy, with the village head generally being an official appointed by the government.

However, communities were also formed in the course of struggle, as in the case of the great peasant-army revolt in India in 1857, when Hindus and Muslims fought side by side against the British. Moreover, community identities, whether constructed or otherwise, were used in many peasant struggles all over the colonial and semicolonial countries. At the same time in Latin America, in countries such as Bolivia, Ecuador and Peru, there was a large degree of overlap between peasant or landless labour and Amerindian identities; elite racism bore heavily on the fortunes of the underprivileged in all these countries (Guerrero 1997; Otero 2003).

Another idea, prevalent mainly among certain Marxist scholars, was that many of these precapitalist societies must have been 'feudal' in a sense analogous to that found in Western Europe from around the tenth or eleventh centuries (discussed by Wood in Chapter 2). However, even among Western European countries, there were major differences in the political and juridical structures in the feudal epoch (Bloch 1962). The application of the concept of feudalism to Africa or India in the period immediately preceding European conquest has been severely criticized by such scholars as Thorner (1971) and Goody (1971) (cf. Beattie 1967; Leach *et al.* 1985). Beyond the very general idea that magnates in such societies often used non-market coercion, no major analytical advantage accrues from treating the societies involved as feudal just before colonial subjugation. Indeed, imperialist grabbers of the land of colonized people often created and perpetuated the myth either that the latter had no conception of private property of any kind, or that the land in precolonial societies belonged to the sovereign (Bagchi 1992, 2005: Ch. 9–10). Curiously enough, though, in precapitalist societies stretching from the Americas to many lands of Africa, much of pre-British India and Tokugawa Japan, the right to the occupation of land, or rather to the various use values it yielded, approximated the fiction that John Locke used to build up his theory of private property: namely, the idea that a person acquired rights in land when they mixed their labour with it (Macpherson 1962: Ch. 5; Ryan 1984: Ch. 1).[2]

Therefore I shall avoid using terms like feudalism, village communities, or 'Asiatic' or 'African' modes of production. Colonialism profoundly reshaped the nature of pre-existing structures of power or action, and the nature of this colonial hybrid is the focus of my attention here.

Imperialism and colonized countries: violence, law, land and labour

The pioneering industrializing countries advanced techniques of manufacture of arms and ammunition and of civilian production at the same time, leading to the rise of large factories run on water power, followed by steam (Headrick 1981; McNeill 1982: Ch. 6–8; Brewer 1989). That advance in the means of coercion and the means of production, for example, converted India and China, which were until the middle of the eighteenth century the two biggest economies in the world, into direct or indirect dependencies that were increasingly rural. However, the use of violence and aggressive economic infiltration was reinforced by changes that were imposed on and reshaped previously prevailing social rules and norms. These changes were based on an ideological onslaught that claimed, among other things, to bring into existence the 'rule of law' among predominantly rural 'lawless peoples' or the subjects of 'Oriental despots'.

Thus, in regions without established state structures and with fluid social hierarchies, colonialism defined land rights by denying that peoples without codified systems of law had any rights at all. The conquerors used the right of conquest to take over all land as the sovereign, and excluded all local peoples from exercising their uncodified but generally recognized rights. Land laws, whether under the British or French imperium, thus almost invariably gave more restricted rights of ownership and control to the local subjects of imperialism than to the colonial state and the citizens and firms of the ruling country, and sometimes of other imperialist nations (Meek 1949). The natural resources of the conquered territory were thereby usurped and subsistence farming by local people was massively expanded, while at the same time a class of predominantly rural, landless workers was created. Granted, many regions with exploitable resources, such as many parts of Sub-Saharan Africa, were thinly populated. In these cases, the colonial rulers used *corvée* labour or coercive taxes, such as the hut tax – as exemplified in the infamous Congo Free State created by King Leopold, but also witnessed in most of the French and British colonies in Sub-Saharan Africa (Iliffe 1995: 196–202; Hochschild 1998) – to force rural people into labouring for the colonial state or European private enterprise.

Regions without established state structures and with fluid social hierarchies can be set beside those areas that before the impact of imperialism had developed state structures, had commercialized agriculture and craft production, and had regulated private property in most assets, often including land. Thus China, India and many parts of Southeast Asia, as well as much of North Africa, had undergone what has been characterized by Wong (1997) as 'Smithian growth'. A good deal of peasant differentiation had occurred in these regions, just as it had in feudal Europe in its last stages and in early modern Europe (Bagchi 2005: Ch. 9–10; Byres 2006a, 2006b, Byers this volume). Concomitantly, a stratum of landless workers, or workers without rights to the use of land for subsistence or even habitation, had also emerged. Some of these workers were unfree in most areas of life; some might be servants of communities and might be paid partly or wholly in kind; some approximated the condition of serfs in medieval Western Europe or early modern Eastern Europe; some, though very rarely, approximated the condition of chattel slaves typical of Caribbean and North American plantations. However, many were also free wage labourers, working in farms, mines or craft occupations.

Despite this diversity of circumstances, imperialism undertook legal and regulatory changes designed to reinforce further the capacity of the citizens and firms of the metropolitan country, and sometimes of other imperialist nations, to control labour. Thus the colonial period, across Asia and Africa, ushered in a reshaping of prevailing rural land and labour regimes, and hence social structures, in a manner that commonly sought to be complicit with older structures of power.

arose at the same time as the proletariat (Atieno-Odhiambo 1977). However, as men were compelled to work for colonial state projects or for private European interests in plantations and mines, women, traditionally the main cultivators, had to work far harder to provide family subsistence. It is thus more than merely ironic that when the colonial rulers introduced legislation to give their subjects limited private property rights in land, it was, following the general European pattern, the men who were endowed with those rights and women who lost their traditional rights in a generally patriarchal society.

Estate or large-scale agriculture did not, however, always prevail over peasant production, petty trade or local credit networks. In Kenya, much of the production of European estate-owners was outsourced to Arab or Kikuyu smallholders. Following a similar pattern, in the Copperbelt 'Luba cultivators defeated Shaba's white settlers in competition for the food market in copper towns, while peasant cotton growers drove European planters out of business in Nyasaland and Uganda' (Iliffe 1995: 206). Such successes were, however, relative: in East-Central Africa, as in Southern Africa, imperial rulers used imperially regulated markets and coercion to sustain their racist regimes. Thus, just as African pastoralists had been forcibly displaced from their land in Kenya to make way for European settlers, when Indian traders prospered in the fast-commercializing economy, the imperial rulers stepped in to deny them any right to purchase land, especially in the so-called 'White Highlands' (Meek 1949). Similarly, legislation was introduced along the lines of the Masters and Servants Ordinance, which criminalized breach of contract by employees, long after it had been given a quietus in England in 1875 (Anderson 2000; Hay and Craven 2004). Thus 'law was the cutting edge of colonialism, an instrument of the power of an alien state and part of the process of coercion' (Chanock 1991: 4).

Latin America

The colonial heritage

Under Iberian imperium – supplemented by French, British and Dutch rule in the Caribbean and Northern South America – Latin America had been the biggest importer of enslaved Africans in the world. As a consequence, slavery and the displacement of Amerindian populations strongly shaped emerging agrarian relations around land and labour. For example, in Brazil, wherever freemen had a real choice they opted to become cultivating peasants on their own, or to engage in other occupations, as they did in Bahia, where the sugar estates (*fazendas*) were principally worked by slaves. Where they did not have such choice, they became subject to the authority of the landlord (*fazendeiro*) for whom they worked (Barickman 1996).

Similarly, in Spanish America, the typical units of production were *haciendas*, which grew on the basis of the *encomienda* system under which whole communities of Amerindians were entrusted to the designated *encomenderos* of Spanish origin. The tradition of entrusting communities to the *encomenderos* was predicated on the idea that the *encomenderos* would 'protect' the communities on behalf of the Spanish crown and thus demonstrate the beneficence of imperial royalty; in reality, such protection facilitated the control of essentially captive agrarian labour. The *encomenderos* created huge agricultural estates, often measuring hundreds of square miles, and the Amerindians became essentially their serfs, paying taxes in labour and providing *corvée* labour to the landlords (Bagchi 1982: Ch. 3; Mörner 1987). *Haciendas* produced for the commercial market, although many of the production inputs, such as the labour of Amerindians or their subsistence costs, did not pass through the market. Over time, the *encomenderos* and other estate-owners were freed from the royal requirement that they protect Amerindian populations and they 'progressively became masters, legislators, judges, and magistrates over the *hacienda* residents' (Florescano 1987: 264).

As already noted, most of Latin America became independent in the 1820s. In most countries, except in Chile, Argentina and Uruguay, the majority of people were of Amerindian origin, but the *criollos* claiming European descent became the ruling class. These countries had strongly imprinted structures of Spanish and Portuguese colonialism. Brazil, for example, was one of the last countries in the world formally to abolish slavery, in 1888. The new states were also subjected to the influence of the informal colonialism of the British, accompanied by US expansionism towards Mexico and then followed by explicit US imperialism in Cuba.

Agrarian structure in the nineteenth century

In the mid-nineteenth century, the vastly variegated countryside of Latin America could be classified into four categories of rural social structure (Bauer 1989). First there were the *haciendas*, with a dependent peasantry in the former territory of Spanish America. In Mexico, for example, huge *haciendas*, measuring anywhere from 400 to 25,000 square miles, dominated even remote areas (Bauer 1989: 121–122). Brazilian *fazendas* and sugar *engenhos*, while formally similar, were worked by slaves until 1888, as well as by seasonal workers who came in as casual labour (Bagchi 1982: 154). Second, there were the Amerindian communities with *criollo* landlords still extracting tribute from them in the form of labour and product surpluses. In a third category were a few areas with smallholding peasants, often migrating from other parts of the state or, as settlers, from Europe. Finally, there were Amerindian communities in remote areas that remained to some extent immune to attacks by the aggrandizing elites.

The colonial tradition of royal protection – at a considerable price – of communities of Amerindians, and the spatial fragmentation of imperial control characteristic of 'old-style' colonialism, impeded the post-independence liberal project of converting all assets, including land and labour, into commodities under the patronage of a centralized state. For example, in the

Amerindian communities subjugated to *criollo* landlords extracting labour and product surpluses, liberal projects of breaking up communal land-holdings were resisted in many cases, both by the landed elite because they might lose their captive labour force and the tribute paid by it, and by the Amerindian communities because they might lose their remaining, minimal guarantee of employment and subsistence, which was so important given the appalling conditions under which they had to construct their livelihood. Thus the liberal project of constructing a polity on the basis of private property rights did not include the right to civil freedom of the Amerindians. As a consequence, attempts to carry out the liberal project, discussed by Farshad Araghi in Chapter 5, provoked peasant protests on a large scale. In Mexico, peasant insurrection ignited the first sparks of movement for inde-pendence until a frightened *criollo* oligarchy took charge and brought the political apparatus under their control (Knight 1992). Thus rural and national class structures were shaped by structural factors and by the nature and intensity of resistance to elite rule by peasants and workers.

Independent countries such as Peru and Bolivia functioned as *criollo*-controlled, agrarian, semi-feudal polities during the nineteenth century. For example, in Peru the ruling classes were able to repress most of the incipient rural movements and build a state based on the racist and seigniorial exclu-sion of the socially subordinated (Knight 1992; Mallon 1995). In this con-text, imperialist influence tended to consolidate seigniorial power rather than weaken it. Mexico, for example, had more than its share of the onslaught of US imperialism from the 1830s, losing first Texas and then half of its territory to its powerful northern neighbour in the 1840s. As a consequence, the Porfirian regime attracted foreign capital, and its 'crony capitalist' auto-cracy was blessed by both domestic and foreign capital. However, the 'cred-ible commitment' (Wasserman 2005) of the Mexican autocracy to nascent domestic and foreign capital, at the expense of a subordinate rural population, plunged Mexico into the biggest peasant war in Latin American history.

In many ways, Argentina stands apart in nineteenth century Latin America. In Argentina most of the Amerindians had been killed, leaving vast plains suitable for commercial agriculture. As a consequence, in the 1830s the Argentine rulers aggrandized vast quantities of land and created a polity of *ranchero* rentier oligarchs who used land as the basis of political and economic control (Bagchi 1982: Ch. 3). Consequently, as immigrants from Italy, Spain and other European countries flooded into Argentina from the 1870s onwards, few could become property-owning farmers; most became insecure tenants, rendering the income distribution highly unequal. The Argentine oligarchy was notable for its rapaciousness; it depended entirely on foreign capital for new investment in railways and other infra-structure, and for much of the agro-processing industry that grew up before the First World War. The foreign investors exacted a high price – for exam-ple, guaranteed interest rates for railroads of 15 per cent or even higher, along with grants of hundreds of square miles of land on both sides of rail-way tracks (Bagchi 1982: 54–59).[4] Argentine policy in the 1880s and 1890s was biased towards depreciating the paper peso: this policy increased land-lords' incomes from exports while the wages of immigrant labour, fixed in pesos, declined in real terms. A depreciation of the peso also lowered the oligarchs' real indebtedness to local banks as domestic prices rose. However, a major crisis of confidence among foreign investors occurred in 1890, when it appeared that the Argentine government would be unable to honour its foreign debt. Argentina had to undergo a painful adjustment process, which took the form of a decline in the prices of its exportables: the major importers brought down their inventories as export demand for primary products declined, and as the credit situation in the metropolitan countries became more stringent. The result was that Argentine per capita income, which exceeded that of Southern Europe in 1913, was nonetheless falling behind Canada and Australia by the end of the 1890s (Sanz-Villarroya 2005). Further erosion of its prosperity was caused by remittances abroad as a consequence of Argentina's foreign borrowing. Thus resources flowed from Argentina to imperial Britain even as the landed oligarchy sustained their social privileges and the bulk of the country's population witnessed declining living standards.

In Latin America, then, just as Byres emphasizes in the previous chapter, rural social structure and the nature of the ruling class determined the pro-cess or lack of development and change. Social structure was rooted in con-trol of land, labour and the surpluses generated from their use. Surpluses that were generated either were used for conspicuous consumption by the dominant classes, or were remitted to the metropolitan countries through forms of export-led exploitation, profit remittances or debt repayments.

Asia

China and nineteenth century imperialism

China has had the largest population from at least the second millennium of the Common Era. In the eighteenth century, China was one of the largest, most prosperous societies in the world. In 1700, China was responsible for around 23.1 per cent of global gross domestic product (GDP) (Maddison 1998: Table 2.2a),[5] and until about 1750 China was producing around 33 per cent of global manufacture (Simmons 1985).

In this light, it is not surprising that the European companies that started trading with Asian countries such as China in the mid-eighteenth century had little to offer except firearms and bullion. By way of contrast, English demand for tea, an agricultural product of China, increased dramatically from the late eighteenth century, partly to supplement the beverage con-sumption of urban workers who could not afford beer. The result was that Britain developed an adverse commodity balance of trade with China in the early nineteenth century. The British conquest of Bengal and later major parts of India by 1818 eased this problem by providing bullion as tribute from India and, more importantly, by increasing exports of cotton and opium from India to China. Both offset Britain's trade deficit with China, demonstrating the ways in which global agricultural flows could be mediated by an imperial power to its benefit, and to the detriment of an agricultural producer that became, as I will show, increasingly subjugated to the imperial power.

Opium was initially produced under the supervision of the English East India Company, one of a number of Crown-designated trading houses with monopoly privileges in specific geographical regions, and smuggled into China by British private traders. After the British Parliament in 1833 abolished the monopoly rights of trade to China hitherto enjoyed by the East India Company, British private traders became far more aggressive in smuggling opium into China. In the name of freedom of trade, the British government went to war with China in 1841 (Headrick 1981: Ch. 1–2). In 1842 the Chinese emperor sued for peace, ceding Hong Kong to Britain and opening five treaty ports, including Canton and Shanghai, to trade by foreign merchants. The French and US governments soon exacted similar privileges.

Defeat in the first Opium War, and the resulting opening of China to foreign merchants, led to the Taiping Revolt and a number of other revolts spanning most of China. These revolts could be defeated only by the Qing rulers by taking help from the same imperial powers that had despoiled China in a series of counterinsurgency operations in the second Opium War, which had the effect of rendering Qing rule increasingly illegitimate to the Chinese population (Bagchi 2005). The result was the increasing subjugation of the Chinese state to the imperial powers during the latter part of the nineteenth century.

In Qing China, commercialization had already led to the diversification of crops and occupations in villages, with sericulture, the weaving of textiles, the production of sugarcane and indigo, and sugar refining being combined with the cultivation of rice, especially in central and south China. The opening up of China as a result of the first Opium War led to a direct influence of the world market on the Chinese rural economy. Emblematic of this were the entry of foreign enterprises into sugar refining, and the impact of the European silkworm blight on Chinese production, which induced a further intensification of specialization for export (Mazumdar 1998: Ch. 7). The growth in exports was also caused by China's obligations to pay large indemnities after its defeat in a series of wars with foreign powers, from the first Opium War, through the Sino-Japanese war of 1894–95, to the sacking of Beijing in 1901 by armies of the imperialist countries. The imperialist nations, for example, in 1901 exacted an indemnity of roughly US$330 million. Thus China was subjected, as a direct consequence of imperialist war, to export-led exploitation as product surpluses flowed out of China as a result of trade and indemnities through markets controlled by the imperial powers, to the detriment of the Chinese rural population (Bagchi 1982: Ch. 2).

The decline of Qing imperial rule and military-led imperial entry into China led to retrogression in most aspects of the country's economic and social structure. Globally competitive craft industries went into decline. Irrigation works and canals often became disabled because of lack of maintenance by an enfeebled state apparatus, with a consequent impact on rice, sugarcane and indigo production, all of which were important exports. Thus between 1850 and 1952, the proportion of land irrigated fell from 29.4 to 18.5 per cent (Maddison 1998: Table 1.5b). In this light, it is clear that imperialist wars, the revolts against the Qing, imperial-led counterinsurgency operations, the El Niño famines that followed these imperial incursions, and the increasing use of exports and indemnities to transfer surpluses into imperial control were extremely destructive of lives, the means of production, and the means of subsistence in rural China (Maddison 1998: Ch. 2; Bagchi 2005). By 1913, China's output of manufactures had fallen to 3.6 per cent of world manufacturing output (Simmons 1985), while the share of world GDP produced by China fell to 5.2 per cent by 1952 (Maddison 1998: Table 2.2a). This well nigh disastrous outcome in one of the most prosperous countries in the world was a direct result of the onslaught of imperialism empowered by the industrial revolution in the lands of the North Atlantic seaboard, using sophisticated means of coercion to reinforce processes of export-led exploitation to the detriment of the Chinese population.

Southeast Asia

Burma, Vietnam, Siam and the Philippines have been regarded as cases *par excellence* of development through international commerce providing a vent for their surpluses. The British first occupied lower Burma in 1852 by defeating the Burmese king in the second Anglo–Burmese war, and conquered upper Burma in 1885 (Bagchi 1997: Ch. 10). The French first conquered north Vietnam and then the south of the country in the 1860s. In both cases, the imperial rulers set about developing an infrastructure within which foreign merchants could operate, and for immigrants from other parts of the country to come in as agricultural workers. In Burma land was given out to smallholders, many of whom migrated from the north of the country. In Vietnam, land confiscated from local people was given out in large blocks to Europeans and some wealthy Vietnamese. Immigrants worked as tenants, and thus 'by 1930 2.5 per cent of the landholders (in the Mekong delta) held 45 per cent of the land, while one peasant household in four did not possess any land at all' (Elson 1999: 142). Moreover, neither in Burma nor in Vietnam did the peasants have access to cheap credit or to foreign markets, except through foreign merchants. In Burma, they became highly indebted to Indian moneylenders – the Chettiars from south India – and in Vietnam to Chinese moneylenders. The Bank of Bengal, the biggest of the state-backed banks, carried on a highly profitable business by lending to European rice millers, timber merchants, and so on. However, it would lend to the Burmese or other non-Europeans mainly through intermediaries such as the Chettiars (Bagchi 1997: Ch. 10). Naturally, most of the benefits resulting from the vent for surplus accrued to European capitalists and groups of Asian bankers and landlords as debt-induced export-led exploitation was facilitated.

In the Philippines, following the pattern witnessed in Spanish Latin America, a *hacienda* system grew up. After defeat in the Filipino war of independence in 1898, first against the Spaniards and then against the US government, *haciendas* continued. The Chinese *mestizos* and the other members of the Filipino elite in control of the *haciendas* moved into the cultivation of rice, tobacco and sugar. Immigrants from around Manila moved into the plains in the interior. They set up first as smallholders, but soon became embroiled in a debt nexus and either lost their land or became tenants on their own land. Thus, as in Vietnam, tenancy became the predominant mode of cultivation in the Philippines (Aguilar 1994; Elson 1999: 146–147), with tenant farmers producing cash crops for export through imperially structured international markets. After US occupation commenced, sugar plantations modernized their methods of production, in large part because there was privileged access of sugar to the US market, but an ongoing struggle for shares of the surplus between *hacendados* and the sharecroppers was witnessed. Only in some cases, such as the island of Negros, did wage labour become the predominant method of exploitation in the sugar *haciendas* (Aguilar 1994).

Interestingly enough, Siam, although bound by the British into a relation of dependence in foreign economic and political relations, by the Bowring Treaty of 1855, provides an example of the development of rice cultivation for export under the auspices of reasonably independent peasants. The availability of local credit and the efforts of the local ruling aristocratic class to keep formal imperial control at bay were pivotal in this development (Baker and Phongpaichit 2005). However, even though Siam did not become a formal colony, imperial control of trade resulted in significant flows of product surpluses out of the country as export-led exploitation allowed Europeans to reap the benefits of the rice trade.

Indonesia in the nineteenth century

The great staples of the Indonesian archipelago were spices, which had a huge market in Europe. Therefore the Portuguese set up a number of major trading outposts in Indonesia from the first decade of the sixteenth century. In the beginning of the seventeenth century, the Dutch ousted them from Indonesia and proceeded to establish a more thoroughgoing dominion over the islands (Bagchi 1982: Ch. 4, 2005: Ch. 11), subjecting the archipelago to a thoroughgoing regime of export-led exploitation organized by the Dutch East India Company. Its policies decisively altered the economic structure of many of the most affected islands, and hampered their demographic and economic growth.

Export-led exploitation became systematized when van den Bosch, governor of the Dutch East Indies, introduced the so-called *kulturstelsel* or Cultivation System in 1830 in a bid to make the colony generate a much larger remittable tribute than before (Geertz 1963; Aass 1980; Bagchi 1982: Ch. 4, 2005: Ch. 7, 11, 16). Under this system, in theory, the cultivator was supposed to devote one-fifth of their fields to the cultivation of commercial export crops such as coffee, sugar and indigo, as designated by the colonial state. A peasant delivering the crop according to government stipulation was also supposed to be exempt from taxation. In practice, not only did the peasant have to continue paying the tax, but the government might commandeer as much as the whole of a peasant's plot (Aass 1980: 226–227).

The destructive impact of the *kulturstelsel* can easily be illustrated. When sugar initially became the favoured commercial export commodity 'about one half of the village's land, now one-third, now two-thirds, was in sugar cane, and half in peasant crops ... either rice, or dry season second crops such as soya or peanuts' (Geertz 1963: 86–87). However, when the *kulturstelsel* was introduced, the result was what has famously been styled by Geertz (1963) as 'agricultural involution', a situation in which the intensification of labour led to increased agricultural productivity of a few crops – in this case, sugar – but crop diversification was reversed and villagers were yoked to a low-income agriculture because of imperial economic structures that resulted in the benefits of specialization accruing to the Dutch through processes of export-led exploitation.

How did this retrograde pattern come about? First, typical Javanese villagers had earlier devoted some of their time in the lean season to the production of handicrafts. The Cultivation System took away the villagers' time for non-agricultural production activity. Second, the free import of manufactures decimated Indonesian industry, exactly as in India around the same period. As a result of British pressure, the Dutch had imposed a duty of 12.5 per cent on all cotton goods. However, under a secret arrangement with the *Nederlandsche Handelsmaatschappij*, the company that was given the monopoly of Dutch trade with Indonesia, duties were refunded to the company by the colonial state. As a consequence, imports of cotton goods into Indonesia increased from (in Dutch guilders) *f*1,696,000 in 1825 to *f*13,100,000 in 1840 and *f*96,274,000 in 1913 (Aass 1980: Table III). Third, because of the forced concentration on the production of sugarcane and other commercial crops, Indonesia had to import increasing quantities of rice from the latter part of the nineteenth century onwards (Bagchi 1982: Ch. 4). In fact, the Cultivation System, since it adversely affected the production of rice, led to repeated famines and population decline in Java in the 1840s: 'in one regency the population fell from 336,000 to 120,000 and in another from 89,500 to 9,000' (Furnivall 1939: 138).

This intrusive intervention in agriculture in the nineteenth century by the colonial state had a profound effect on rural social structure and agrarian relations. Van den Bosch justified his policies by appealing to the fiction of Javanese 'custom' and to that of a 'village community'. However, Javanese customs were moulded by the previous two centuries of Dutch suzerainty. The village headmen and the regents derived their authority from the colonial government, not from independent village institutions. As in many other parts of the world, in Java villagers had the right to cultivate a piece of land on condition of long residence or membership of a lineage that claimed to be the original founders of the village. The collectivity of the village could dispose of this right if the villager died without heirs or left the village permanently. The collectivity also would occasionally redistribute some of the land in order to maintain a kind of equity. The access to uncultivated land or forests and their produce would be regulated by local custom (Aass 1980: 229–231). However, this still did not make up a self-sufficient village community (Breman 1988; Boomgaard 1989, 1991). The beneficiaries of the system were the local elite, *priyayi*, who the Dutch used as intermediaries for controlling the ordinary cultivators, and the mainly Chinese and Arab businessmen who supplied them with capital (Ricklefs 2001: Ch. 11). This structure continued through the period when private European capital started to transform rural Indonesia, in that Europeans became the chief plantation owners. Indonesia entered the twentieth century with a predominantly agrarian economy, an all-powerful imperial bureaucratic state that heavily regulated rural land, labour and products in order to look after the interests of Dutch businessmen and bureaucrats, and a weak Asian business community dominated by Chinese settlers in the archipelago.

British India

The British conquered Bengal in 1757. However, as in China, the imperial power operated at a disadvantage. Thus in 1700 India produced 22.6 per cent of world GDP, and around 1750 India was responsible for around 25 per cent of global manufactures (Maddison 1998: Table 2.2a). In South Asia the British found a developed state system that extracted tribute in money in a commercialized economy. The British imperial rulers therefore, over the course of a century, turned that tributary system towards a mechanism of remittance to the metropolitan country, come hail, drought, flood or famine, and moreover sought to intensify the extraction. However, the method of extraction of the surplus as well as its quantum mattered in shaping the trajectory of evolution of the social structure in colonized India (Bagchi 1992; Washbrook 1994). Myths of origin were constructed to justify the colonial dispensation, while other myths, such as the immemorially surviving village community or the *jajmani* system, were built up as the regime endured (Mayer 1993).

The conquest and 'pacification' of South Asia (which I will designate as India from now on) between 1757 and 1848 involved transformations in colonial ideology, long and drawn-out depressions, effective demonetization of large parts of the interior, repeated demographic disasters, and the erection of localized coercive monopolies with new types of bondage for workers and peasants around the production of indigo, sugar, and tea and coffee plantations, as land and labour regimes were reorganized around the priority of export. However, the fundamental objectives and imperatives of those imperial policies remained basically unchanged from the time Clive defeated the army of Sirajuddaula in 1757 to the last days of the British Raj. What began as the necessity of paying the dividends of a royally chartered company – the East India Company – that could not pay dividends by any semblance of free trade because of the productive superiority of the colonized, continued as the imperial imperative was established of remitting an ever-growing tribute to London for maintaining a huge self-financing state apparatus of coercion that would, coincidentally, further the interests of the British empire east of the Cape of Good Hope.

Thus, during the days of the Company Raj, the British realized the tribute as a land tax augmented by what has been called a coercive monopoly of trade – or what I have called export-led exploitation – run by the East India Company, a clique of British businessmen. When the business of governing India was taken over by the British parliament, the land tax was still the major avenue of extracting the surplus, but to that was added a debt process that included not only the interest and dividends on the construction and operation of railways, ports and irrigation works, but also on the expenditure for reconquering northern India when the anti-imperialist war of 1857 broke out. In other words, as in other parts of the world, the British imperial state made those who had been conquered responsible for paying for being conquered.

Such phrases as 'colonial capitalism', a 'colonial mode of production', or 'imperialism as the harbinger of capitalism' are thus thoroughly inappropriate for what happened to India. The British did not try to construct a social structure that rendered all markets free, with non-market coercion being exercised only by the state. Precolonial India had had a thriving exchange economy moving along a path of what was earlier in this chapter called 'Smithian growth', although it harboured many varieties of non-market power exercised by the ruling classes. In these circumstances, the British created rather insecure forms of market dependence as labour and land regimes were reconfigured. Thus, apart from the dependence that was induced by endemic unemployment and the insecurity of subsistence, the British curbed the freedom of workers by specific legislation. Similarly, in place of a free market in land, they made landholding conditional on the prompt payment of an often exorbitant land tax (Bagchi 1992). At most, they created a market in 'revenue farming rights'. The British introduced the *zamindari* system under which the land tax was collected by a set of 'tax farmers'; in south and west India they collected the tax directly from recognized individual owners; in north-west India they conjured up a non-existent village community and introduced a system under which the village as a whole was assessed for tax. As Marx (1966: 333–334, first published 1894) put it, 'in Bengal they created a caricature of large-scale English landed estates; in south-eastern India a caricature of small parceled property; in the north-west they did all they could to transform the Indian economic community with common ownership of the soil into a caricature of itself'. The majority of peasants were kept at near-starvation levels, while possible avenues of advance for emerging capitalist strata were blocked by explicit imperial policy and implicit racial discrimination.

Thus, and paradoxically enough, the British rulers, with all their stress on the freedom of the individual, helped consolidate a situation of agrestic serfdom suffered by the so-called 'untouchable' castes, termed Dalits in modern India. It was in the interest of securing their land revenue that the British were unwilling to disturb the servile relations between upper caste Indian landholders and their farm servants, many of whom were Dalits (Sarkar 1985). As in other imperial possessions, British rulers shored up extreme forms of bondage in the interest of preserving the stability of their rule, which was erected on the consent of the property- and power-holders in the colony (Lovejoy and Hogendorn 1993).

By the end of the nineteenth century, India had become a largely agrarian economy, in which 75 per cent of the workforce was engaged in agriculture earning 62 per cent of GDP (Sivasubramonian 2000: Tables 7.16, 7.18). The very high rates of taxation in rural areas where direct tax extraction prevailed led to the pauperization of the peasantry and frequent famines, especially in drought-prone areas (Visaria and Visaria 1983; Lardinois 1989), which directly killed between 15 million and 17 million people over the period between 1866 and 1906 alone (Bagchi 2005: Ch. 10, 18). With continued depression of the economy, and increasing numbers of people becoming dependent on an agriculture that received little productive investment, parasitical tax farmers were also greatly impoverished, especially through a process of subdivision of their patrimony as their numbers grew. In the district of Monghyr in central Bihar, for instance, it was found that 901 estates had been partitioned into no less than 5899 shares, with the smallest recorded subdivision of proprietary rights being 1/39,680,000,000 (Bagchi 1975). India had gone through a process of deindustrialization in which many regions, such as Bihar, had seen a decline in the proportion of industrial workers from around 20 per cent to fewer than 10 per cent of the labour force, reducing wages and security even as the capacity to produce local manufactures was decimated. Thus by 1913 India's output of world manufactures had fallen to 1.4 per cent of the global total (Simmons 1985), while India's share in the world GDP fell to 3.8 per cent by 1952 (Maddison 1998: Table 2.2a).

The resurgence of a neocolonial view that somehow India thrived under British rule (Roy 2007) is thus based on wilful illiteracy and total insensitivity to the direct deaths of tens of millions of Indians in famines; the indirect deaths of several hundred million in avoidable malnutrition and epidemic diseases; and a structural retrogression of the economy that squeezed both the base of, and incentives for, domestic investment in industry and, even more, in agriculture, as land and labour regimes were reconfigured to support the interests of the imperial power. It was a disastrous outcome in one of the most populous and prosperous countries in the world, and was a direct result of the onslaught of an imperialism that was predicated upon export-led exploitation.

Conclusions: liberal ideology, economic development and imperialism in the nineteenth century

Economic growth, in Kuznets's sense, is denoted by a sustained rise in productivity and income per head, accompanied by a shift in incomes and employment from agriculture to industry and services as structural transformation occurs (Chenery and Syrquin 1986). However, in the two most populous countries of the world in the nineteenth century, China and India, there was an actual retrogression in the economic structure, with a larger proportion of the workforce being dependent on agriculture in 1900 than before the onslaught of imperialism on and in those countries, as a consequence of widespread de-industrialization resulting from the export-led remittance of surpluses to the metropolitan countries. Structural transformation was also halting in the semicolonial countries of Latin America. In Mexico, for example, under 30 years of Porfiriato, more than 70 per cent of the capital invested was foreign, and 75 per cent of Mexican workers remained engaged in highly insecure agriculture despite the fact that the distribution of land had, as elsewhere in Latin America, become more unequal during the period between the 1870s and 1910s (Coatsworth 2005).

Landlord domination cannot be seen only as a matter of the distribution of land. Even if a large number of peasants in China under the late Qing period owned their land, there were others, especially in southern China, who were insecure sharecroppers (Gray 1990: Ch. 7). Such insecurity was common throughout the world of nineteenth century imperialism. At the same time, even with a stagnating economy, and very large payments to the imperialist powers for indemnity and coercive railway construction, China, like many other colonized countries in the nineteenth century, produced an agricultural surplus that was largely wasted in elite consumption, including the maintenance of retainers (Riskin 1975), or which was remitted, in various forms, back with the imperial centres of the global economy through export-led exploitation. Thus the structure of social relations governing access to land, a structure that in many parts of the imperial world favoured either landlords or European settlers, led to the blocking of investment and rural structural transformation in colonies or semicolonies, which had severe implications for ordinary people. In every imperially dominated country, people in the countryside were faced with endemic unemployment, under-employment and other kinds of insecurity, and were thus denied substantive freedom, and indeed often had to choose voluntary bondage (Bagchi 1973; Breman 1974).

Granted, in India a Dalit leader such as Jotirao Phule might welcome British rule because it promised to get rid of the oppressive, Brahman-dominated caste system (Phule 2002), or a Brahman woman such as Pandita Ramabai might convert to Christianity because of her experience of Brahmanical tyranny (Ramabai 2000), or a Muslim woman such as Rokeya Sakhawat Hossain would dream of a women's utopia where women would live in freedom (Hossain 2005). However, the imperatives of imperial rule would not allow the alien rulers to disturb the existing hierarchical order unless it interfered with the process of realizing a large remittable tribute from the colony. Similar processes that denied substantive freedom worked throughout the colonial and semicolonial world of the nineteenth century. In the voluntary colonies or semicolonies of Latin America, the racist and seigneurial ideology of the ruling class fitted snugly with the landlord oligarchy's determination to hold on to power, while in Southern and East-Central Africa imperial restrictions on landownership and capital formation effectively created classes of landless workers and near-subsistence peasants as the reconfiguration of land and labour regimes failed to bring substantive freedom.

Capitalist colonialism demonstrated the contradiction between its promise of civil freedom and its actual imposition of bondage on peasants and workers. Thus, while private property rights and free labour were central features of a liberal ideology propogated by the imperial powers in the nineteenth century, in most colonized countries force was used extensively to dispossess earlier occupiers or users of land, and coercion and slavery remained major instruments for the control and exploitation of labour. The alien rulers, despite their liberal ideology, did not seriously undermine many pre-existing systems of bondage, and in many cases imperial property rights established by the colonial state increased systems of inequality, including gender discrimination (Coquery-Vidrovitch 1997: 65). These processes are explored further by Araghi in Chapter 5. However, what is clear at this point is that export-led exploitation and the competition for markets and resources backed by force was not the only means by which the structural transformation of the colonies and semicolonies was set back. Law, racial discrimination and inegalitarian ideologies were used to sustain imperialist domination and defeat the promises of freedom propagated by the classic thinkers of the European Enlightenment or the democratic thinkers of the colonized and semicolonized countries.

Notes

1 I am indebted to Cris Kay and Haroon Akram-Lodhi for their penetrating comments. The usual non-incriminating disclaimer applies.

2 I am indebted to Barnita Bagchi for suggesting this formulation.
3 For a vivid account of the dispossession of the native people by colonists and *con-cessionaires* from France, including Fourierists and Saint Simonians, and the wanton destruction of forests in that ecologically fragile region, see Prochaska (1990: Ch. 3).
4 The distorting effect of Argentina's social structure on land and industrial investment policies is readily seen by contrasting its policies with those of the USA, Canada and Australia. In those nations, cultivators' right to land was recognized, and an expanding home market and a regime of protection and government patronage promoted learning, technological development and competitive import substitution (Solberg 1987; Korol 1991; and Morris 1992).
5 I have reason to believe that Maddison's figure for China in 1700 is an underestimate, because Maddison underestimates the population of China in that period. On the other hand, Maddison's figures for India in 1820 and 1890 are both overestimates because Maddison has underestimated the damage caused by the British occupation of India from the 1760s down to independence.

References

Aass, S. (1980) 'The relevance of Chayanov's macro theory to the case of Java', in E. J. Hobsbawm, W. Kula, A. Mitra, K.N. Raj and I. Sachs (eds), *Peasants in History: Essays in Honour of Daniel Thorner*, Calcutta: Oxford University Press.

Aguilar Jr, F.V. (1994) 'Sugar-planter state relations and labour processes in colonial Philippine *haciendas*', *Journal of Peasant Studies*, 22 (1): 50–80.

Allman, J. and V. Tashjian (2000) *'I Will Not Eat Stone': A Women's History of Colonial Asante*, Oxford: James Currey.

Anderson, D.M. (2000) 'Master and servant in colonial Kenya, 1895–1939', *Journal of African History*, 41 (3): 459–485.

Atieno-Odhiambo, E.S. (1977) 'The rise and decline of the Kenya peasant', in P.C.W. Gutkind and P. Waterman (eds), *African Social Studies: A Radical Reader*, London: Heinemann.

Austen, R. (1987) *African Economic History: Internal Development and External Dependency*, London: James Currey.

Bagchi, A.K. (1972) *Private Investment in India 1900–1939*, Cambridge: Cambridge University Press.

—— (1973) 'Some implications of unemployment in underdeveloped areas', *Economic and Political Weekly*, 8 (31–33): 1500–1510.

—— (1975) 'Relation of agriculture and industry in the context of South Asia', *Frontier*, 8 (22–24): 12–27.

—— (1982) *The Political Economy of Underdevelopment*, Cambridge: Cambridge University Press.

—— (1992) 'Land tax, property rights and peasant insecurity in colonial India', *Journal of Peasant Studies*, 20 (1): 1–50.

—— (1997) *The Evolution of the State Bank of India, Volume 2: The Era of the Presidency Banks 1876–1920*, New Delhi: Sage.

—— (2005) *Perilous Passage: Mankind and the Global Ascendancy of Capital*, Lanham, MD, USA: Rowman and Littlefield.

Baker, C. and P. Phongpaichit (2005) *A History of Thailand*, Cambridge: Cambridge University Press.

Barickman, B.J. (1996) 'Persistence and decline: slave labour and sugar production in the Bahian Reconcavo, 1850–1888', *Journal of Latin American Studies*, 28 (3): 581–633.

Bauer, A. (1989) 'Rural society', in L. Bethell (ed.), *Colonial Spanish America*, Cambridge: Cambridge University Press.

Beattie, J.H.M. (1967) 'Bunyoro: an African feudality?' in George Dalton (ed.), *Tribal and Peasant Economies: Readings in Economic Anthropology*, Garden City, NY: Natural History Press.

Bloch, M. (1962) *Feudal Society, Vols. 1 and 2*, translated by L.A. Manyon, London: Routledge and Kegan Paul.

Boomgaard, P. (1989) *Between Sovereign Domain and Servile Tenure: The Development of Rights to Land in Java, 1780–1870*, Amsterdam: Free University Press.

—— (1991) 'The Javanese village as a Cheshire cat: the Java debate against a European and Latin American background', *Journal of Peasant Studies*, 18 (2): 288–304.

Breman, J. (1974) *Patronage and Exploitation: Changing Agrarian Relations in South Gujarat, India*, Berkeley, CA, USA: University of California Press.

—— (1988) *The Shattered Image: Construction and Deconstruction of the Village in Colonial Asia*, Dordrecht, the Netherlands: Foris.

Brewer, J. (1989) *The Sinews of Power: War, Money and the English State, 1688–1783*, London: Unwin Hyman.

Byres, T.J. (2006a) 'Rodney Hilton (1916–2002)', *Journal of Agrarian Change*, 6 (1): 1–16.

—— (2006b) 'Differentiation of the peasantry and the transition to capitalism: in defence of Rodney Hilton', *Journal of Agrarian Change*, 6 (1): 17–68.

Chanock, M. (1991) 'A peculiar sharpness: an essay on property in the history of customary law in colonial Africa', *Journal of African History*, 32 (1): 65–88.

Chenery, H. and M. Syrquin (1986) 'The semi-industrial countries' in H. Chenery, M. Syrquin and S. Robinson (eds), *Industrialization and Growth: A Comparative Study*, Oxford: Oxford University Press.

Coatsworth, J.H. (2005) 'Structures, endowments, and institutions in the economic history of Latin America', *Latin American Research Review*, 40 (3): 126–144.

Colson, E. (1971) 'The impact of the colonial system on the definition of land rights' in V. Turner (ed.), *Colonialism in Africa 1870–1960, Vol. 3: Profiles of Change – African Society and Colonial Rule*, Cambridge: Cambridge University Press.

Coquery-Vidrovitch, C. (1997) *African Women: A Modern History*, translated by B. G. Raps, Boulder, CO: Westview Press.

Curtin, P.D. (1969) *The Atlantic Slave Trade: A Census*, Madison, WI: University of Wisconsin Press.

Dalton, G. (ed.) (1971) *Economic Development and Social Change: The Modernization of Village Communities*, Garden City, NY: Natural History Press.

Elson, R.E. (1999) 'International commerce, the state and society: economic and social change', in Nicholas Tarling (ed.), *The Cambridge History of Southeast Asia, Vol. 3: From c. 1800 to 1930s*, Cambridge: Cambridge University Press.

Florescano, E. (1987) 'The hacienda in New Spain', in L. Bethell (ed.), *Latin America Economy and Society, 1870–1930*, Cambridge: Cambridge University Press.

Freund, B. (1984) *The Making of Contemporary Africa: The Development of African Society since 1800*, Bloomington, IN: Indiana University Press.

—— (1991) 'The rise and decline of an Indian peasantry in Natal', *Journal of Peasant Studies*, 18 (2): 263–287.

Furnivall, J.S. (1939) *Netherlands India: A Study of Plural Economy*, Cambridge: Cambridge University Press.

Geertz, C. (1963) *Agricultural Involution: The Process of Ecological Change in Indonesia*, Berkeley, CA, USA: University of California Press.

Goody, J. (1971) 'Feudalism in Africa?', in George Dalton (ed.), *Economic Development and Social Change: The Modernization of Village Communities*, Garden City, NY: Natural History Press.

Gray, J. (1990) *Rebellions and Revolutions: China from the 1800s to the 1980s*, Oxford: Oxford University Press.

Guerrero, A. (1997) 'The construction of a ventriloquist's image: liberal discourse and the "Miserable Indian Race" in late nineteenth-century Ecuador', *Journal of Latin American Studies*, 29 (3): 555–590.

Hay, D. and P. Craven (eds) (2004) *Masters, Servants, and Magistrates in Britain and the Empire, 1562–1955*, Chapel Hill, NC and London: University of North Carolina Press.

Headrick, D.R. (1981) *The Tools of Empire: Technology and European Imperialism in the Nineteenth Century*, New York: Oxford University Press.

Hochschild, A. (1998) *King Leopold's Ghost*, New York: Houghton Mifflin.

Hossain, R.S. (2005) *Sultana's Dream and Padmarag: Two Feminist Utopias*, translated and introduced by B. Bagchi, New Delhi: Penguin.

Howard, R. (1980) 'Formation and stratification of the peasantry in colonial Ghana', *Journal of Peasant Studies*, 8 (1): 61–80.

Iliffe, J. (1995) *Africans: The History of a Continent*, Cambridge: Cambridge University Press.

Isichei, E. (1997) *A History of African Societies to 1870*, Cambridge: Cambridge University Press.

Knight, A. (1992) 'The peculiarities of Mexican history: Mexico compared with Latin America', *Journal of Latin American Studies*, 24 (Quincentenary Supplement): 99–144.

Korol, J.C. (1991) 'Argentine development in a comparative perspective', *Latin American Research Review*, 26 (3): 201–212.

Lardinois, R. (1989) 'Deserted villages and depopulation in rural Tamil Nadu *c.* 1780–*c.* 1830', in T. Dyson (ed.), *India's Historical Demography: Studies in Famine, Disease and Society*, London: Curzon Press.

Leach, E., S.N. Mukherjee and J. Ward (eds) (1985) *Feudalism: Comparative Studies*, Sydney, Australia: Sydney Association for Studies in Society and Culture.

Lester, A. (1997) 'The margins of order: strategies of segregation on the eastern Cape frontier, 1806–*c.*1850', *Journal of Southern African Studies*, 23 (4): 635–653.

Lovejoy, P.E. (1983) *Transformations in Slavery: A History of Slavery in Africa*, Cambridge: Cambridge University Press.

Lovejoy, P.E. and J.S. Hogendorn (1993) *Slow Death for Slavery: The Course of Abolition in Northern Nigeria*, Cambridge: Cambridge University Press.

Macpherson, C.B. (1962) *The Political Theory of Possessive Individualism*, Oxford: Oxford University Press.

Maddison, A. (1998) *Chinese Economic Performance in the Long Run*, Paris: Organisation for Economic Co-operation and Development Development Centre.

Mallon, F.M. (1995) *Peasant and Nation: The Making of Postcolonial Mexico and Peru*, London: University of California Press.

Marx, K. 1966. *Capital, Vol. III*, Moscow: Progress Publishers (first published in 1894).

Mayer, P. (1993) 'Inventing village tradition: the late 19th century origins of the North Indian Jajmani system', *Modern Asian Studies*, 27 (1): 357–395.

Mazumdar, S. (1998) *Sugar and Society in China: Peasants, Technology and the World Market*, Cambridge, MA: Harvard University Asia Centre.

McNeill, W.H. (1982) *The Pursuit of Power: Technology, Armed Force, and Society since A.D. 1900*, Oxford: Blackwell.

Meek, C.K. (1949) *Land Law and Custom in the Colonies* (2nd edn), London: Frank Cass.

Mörner, M. (1987) 'Rural economy and society in Spanish South America', in L. Bethell (ed.), *Colonial Spanish America*, Cambridge: Cambridge University Press.

Morris, C.T. (1992) 'Politics, development and equity in five land-rich countries in the latter nineteenth century', *Research in Economic History*, 14: 1–68.

Oliver, R. and A. Atmore (1981) *Africa since 1800* (3rd edn), Cambridge: Cambridge University Press.

Otero, G. (2003) 'The "Indian question" in Latin America: class, state and ethnic identity construction', *Latin American Research Review*, 38 (1): 248–267.

Phule, J. (2002) *Selected Writings of Jotirao Phule*, edited and introduced by G. P. Deshpande, New Delhi: LeftWord.

Prochaska, D. (1990) *Making Algeria French: Colonialism in Bộne, 1870–1920*, Cambridge: Cambridge University Press.

Ramabai, P. (2000) *Pandita Ramabai Through Her Own Words*, edited with translations by M. Kosambi, Delhi: Oxford University Press.

Riskin, C. (1975) 'Surplus and stagnation in modern China', in D. Perkins (ed.), *China's Modern Economy in Historical Perspective*, Stanford, CA: Stanford University Press.

Ricklefs, M.C. (2001) *A History of Modern Indonesia since c. 1200* (3rd edn), Basingstoke: Palgrave.

Roy, T. (2007) 'Industrialization', in K. Basu (ed.), *The Oxford Companion to Economics in India*, Delhi: Oxford University Press.

Ryan, A. (1984) *Property and Political Theory*, Oxford: Blackwell.

Sanz-Villarroya, I. (2005) 'The convergence process of Argentina with Australia and Canada: 1875–2000', *Explorations in Economic History*, 42: 439–458.

Sarkar, T. (1985) 'Bondage in the colonial text', in M. Dingwaney and U. Patnaik (eds), *Chains of Servitude: Bondage and Slavery in India*, Madras: Sangam Books.

Simmons, C. (1985) ' "De-industrialization", industrialization and the Indian economy, ca.1850–1947', *Modern Asian Studies*, 19 (3): 593–622.

Sivasubramonian, S. (2000) *The National Income of India in the Twentieth Century*, Delhi: Oxford University Press.

Smith, M.G. (1954) 'Slavery and emancipation in two societies', *Social and Economic Studies*, 3 (3–4): 239–280.

Solberg, C.E. (1987) *The Prairies and the Pampas: Agrarian Policy in Canada and Argentina, 1880–1930*, Stanford, CA: Stanford University Press.

Sparks, A. (1991) *The Mind of South Africa: The Story of the Rise and Fall of Apartheid*, London: Mandarin Books.

Thompson, V. and R. Adloff (1975) 'French economic policy in tropical Africa', in L. H. Gann and P. Duignan (eds), *Colonialism in Africa 1870–1960, Vol. 4: The Economics of Colonialism*, Cambridge: Cambridge University Press.

Thorner, D. (1971) *The Shaping of Modern India*, New Delhi: Allied Publishers.

Visaria, P. and L. Visaria (1983) 'Population (1757–1947)', in D. Kumar and M. Desai (eds), *The Cambridge Economic History of India, Vol. 2: c. 1757–c. 1970*, Cambridge: Cambridge University Press.

Washbrook, D. (1994) 'The commercialization of agriculture in colonial India: production, subsistence and reproduction in the "Dry South", *c.* 1870–1930', *Modern Asian Studies*, 28 (1): 129–164.

Wasserman, M. (2005) ' "It's not personal … it's strictly business": the operation of economic enterprise in Mexico during the nineteenth and twentieth centuries', *Latin American Research Review*, 40 (3): 335–345.

Wong, R.B. (1997) *China Transformed: Historical Change and the Limits of European Experience*, London: Cornell University Press.

Worden, N. (1995) *The Making of Modern South Africa* (2nd edn), Oxford: Blackwell.

5 The invisible hand and the visible foot
Peasants, dispossession and globalization

Farshad Araghi

I saw innumerable hosts, foredoomed to darkness, dirt, pestilence, obscenity, misery and early death.

Charles Dickens, A December Vision (1986, first published 1850)

The odor in the air could be a bit sweeter actually, a lot sweeter. And the flies and rats could be, well, less numerous ... 'We came here to make money,' said Mr He, 26, who moved to this trash lot on the south side of Beijing three years ago from a hopelessly overcrowded patch of Sichuan province ... Mr He and his wife are part of a remarkable legion of some 82,000 rural migrants in Beijing – nearly half of them from a single county in Sichuan – who rummage through the waste of this burgeoning city, extracting everything of conceivable value and selling it to recycling factories in a neighboring province ... The migrants have a more direct saying: 'Beijingers wouldn't bend their waists to pick up five grains of rice'.

The New York Times, 11 February 2000

... we are aggrieved by the appropriation by individuals of meadows and fields which at one time belonged to a community. These we will take again into our own hands.

The Twelve Articles of the Peasants, 1525 (Engels 2000: 87–91,
first published 1850)

Global peasantries and the storm of globalization

Markets and movies have one thing in common: the hands that create them are not to be seen (Polanyi 2001).[1] They both mask the very processes that bring them into being; in both, the illusion of a self-generating reality requires masking the reality that generates them. Hence, I use the metaphor of the visible foot to step outside the theatre, as it were. The visible foot is a Brechtian device to show that the invisible hand is not a reality *sui generis*; it is rooted in political power, and its power is to make its politics invisible.

Here, the visible foot is a metaphor for the 'global push factors' (Araghi 1991, 1995) that are derived from politically constructed global agrarian relations, the postwar food order, food aid and dumping, which cumulatively

lay the preconditions for the massive transfer of the world's peasant populations to camps of surplus labour in urban locations. The invisible hand, the
theory would tell us, plays a necessary role in eliminating inefficient producers – indeed, this is a central message of the World Bank's (2007) *World
Development Report 2008: Agriculture for Development*. However, we can
very widely see the visible foot, in state policies that dismantle social welfare
systems; deregulate land markets; remove import controls and food subsidies; impose agro-exporting regimes; and expose millions of agrarian petty
producers in the South to competition with heavily subsidized food transnational corporations and highly capitalized agricultural producers in the
North. We also see the visible foot in the population movements that I call
'enclosure-induced displacement', which have been well documented in the
literature. Two documentations are typical: a World Bank Environment
Department (1994) study of the Bank's own 'development projects' in the
South, which concluded in the early 1990s that an estimated 4 million people
would have to be forced off their lands each year; as well as Cernea's (1996)
study of World Bank-assisted and other development projects, which concluded that in one decade at least 80 to 90 million people had been forcibly
displaced, almost four times the number of people worldwide displaced as a
result of war and conflict (McDowell 1996; Van Hear 1998). The visible foot
is also reflected in the extensive policy advice that will shape Bank lending,
and which is offered in the *World Development Report 2008*. Global peasantries, to borrow the unforgettable words of Walter Benjamin (2006), are
caught in a storm of violent forces that uproot, dispossess, and propel them
into emerging vast spaces of informal labour in the global slums, spaces
outside the traditionally rural but not even past the margins of urbanity;
what Mike Davis (2006) calls 'existential ground zero'. These existential
ground zeroes are, as we will see, expanding: Wednesday 23 May 2007
marked a demographic milestone of world-historical significance, in that the
earth's population, for the first time in human history, became more urban
than rural (Population Reference Bureau 2007; Kulikowski 2007). The storm
that is depeasantizing the Earth's population, as Benjamin might have said
today, is what we call globalization.

This chapter is an attempt to delineate the relationship between globalization and depeasantization from a world-historical perspective. I relate
peasant studies, food regime analysis, and human geography literatures to
specify the global spatiotemporal coordinates of the ongoing, massive process of 'dispossession by displacement' (Araghi 2000; Harvey 2006) of the
world's peasantries. This perspective allows a coherent linking of three central processes that can now be witnessed as everyday occurrences:

- global depeasantization as 'the great global enclosure of our times'
  (Araghi 1991, 1995, 2000); and the special component of this process
  reflected in
- global deruralization on the one hand; and

- global hyperurbanization on the other hand (Araghi 1995, 2000, 2003; Davis 2006).

Following Lefebvre (1979, 1991), spatial relations are here conceptualized as fundamentally social relations, and *vice versa* (Massey 1993, 1995; Harvey 1997; Ferguson 1999; Araghi and McMichael 2006). Theoretically, then, the space I am attempting to study is neither the binary, the fixed, or given rural or urban localities; nor is it the quantitative and flat space of the rural–urban continuum. Rather, I will attempt to survey the space of social relations in formation; that is, the relational, globally uneven and historical space associated with the dynamics of global depeasantization, defined as peasant dispossession through displacement, which is now very widely seen. It is within this theoretical space that one can see the profound interconnectedness of phenomena that are otherwise disparately studied as the agrarian question, environmental devastation, informalization and deproletarianization, hyperurbanization and slumization, and dispossession and displacement, among others. The political context of this space is the global countermobilization of capital (Hopkins 1978, 1979; O'Connor 1984), which interrelates diverse phenomenal forms and heterogeneous times and places without resorting to metaphysical monism and world-system functionalism (McMichael and Buttel 1990; Tomich 1990, 2004; McMichael 1994, 1995; Burawoy 2000; Stoler 2001; Collins 2003; Araghi and McMichael 2006).

In the following, I first review and critique the debate on the agrarian question, offering an alternative interpretation that, in turn, paves the way for a world-historical framing of the peasant question of our times. Distinguishing between two forms of peasant dispossession – dispossession by rural differentiation and dispossession by displacement – I consider the fortune of the world's peasantries under:

- colonial–liberal globalism up to the end of the nineteenth century;
- what I call 'long national developmentalism' between 1917 and 1973; and
- postcolonial neoliberal globalism, commonly known as globalization, since the 1970s.

In doing so, I offer an alternative periodization of 'political capitalism', which should, as argued in the following section, be distinguished from 'theoretical capitalism' (Araghi 2003).

I argue that the period of national developmentalism was an exceptionally reformist phase of world capitalism. While national developmentalism proper, or what McMichael (2008) has called the 'development project', is conventionally dated between 1945 and 1973, I trace the political origins of 'long' national developmentalism to the aftermath of the October Revolution of 1917. The period between 1917 and 1973 witnessed colonial liberalism's retreat from globalism, in response to the challenges posed by various forms of socialism and anticolonial nationalism. Unwilling to accept fascism as its possible future, liberalism sided, through the use of the theories of Keynes and his accommodationist ideas, with reformism and, especially in the postwar period, it compromised with various strands of third world nationalism on the content of the development project; a 'development compromise' engineered by the United Nations (UN) Economic Council for Latin America under the leadership of Raul Prebisch (1950), for which the UN provided an institutional structure.[2] Thus, and this is critical to my argument, the two globalisms of political capitalism, which were colonial–liberal globalism between 1834 and the late nineteenth century, and post-colonial neoliberal globalism from 1973 to the present, have more in common than is usually assumed: economic liberalism, antiwelfarism, free-market fetishism, and designs for constructing a truly global division of labour, as witnessed in the 'workshop of the world' project shared by both.

The point I would like to make is that current processes of globalization are a continuation of colonial–liberal globalism, and not of national devel-opmentalism. That is, while from a chronological and linear point of view the postcolonial neoliberal globalism of the late twentieth century is a con-tinuation of national developmentalism, from a world-historical viewpoint it is a continuation of nineteenth century colonial–liberal globalism.[3]

History, theory and the peasant question

The agrarian question

Posed in late nineteenth century Europe the agrarian question – originally termed 'the peasant question' by Engels (1977, first published 1894) – was (as discussed by Akram-Lodhi and Kay in Chapter 1) about the future pro-spects for the peasantries of the continent. In the context of the rise of *laissez faire* in the 1840s and its deleterious consequences following the Poor Law Amendment Act of 1834, the Irish Poor Laws of 1838, and the Anti-Corn Law bill of 1846, and drawing on Marx's analysis of capital accumulation, the theoretical expectation was that European peasantries, like artisans, journeymen and other petty commodity producers, had no economic future under capitalism. Thus, in Engels' words in *The Peasant Question in France and Germany*, written in 1894: 'it is precisely the individual farming condi-tioned by individual ownership that drives the peasants to their doom ... they will inevitably be driven from house and home and their antiquated mode of production superseded by capitalist large-scale production' (Engels 1977: 466). This perspective is reflected in the critical consideration offered by Ray Kiely on the work and followers of Bill Warren in Chapter 7 of this book.

However, with British hegemony beginning to fracture into crisis, and its project of colonial–liberal globalism in the last decades of the nineteenth century starting to show signs of failure; and in the context of rising rivalries between   emerging   nation-states   and,   as   a   consequence,   growing protectionism for national agricultures (Polanyi 2001), the peasant question had a concrete political component that was inconsistent with abstract theoretical expectations. This political component was that in reality, and especially in continental Europe, peasantries had not – yet? – disappeared. It was precisely this lack of correspondence between abstract theory and political history, or what Byres (1996) terms 'historical puzzles', that gave rise to the peasant question.

Logically, the peasant question could have been resolved in favour of either economic evolutionism or political activism. The latter was adopted by Engels and later Lenin and the Bolsheviks; the former was adopted by Plekhanov (1961, first published 1885) and later the Mensheviks and the Second International. Hence, as Engels (1977) put it, while 'small-holding ownership' was 'destined to disappear', the European peasantry was still 'a very essential factor of the population, production, and political power'. More directly, Engels argued 'it will serve us naught to wait with transformation until capitalist production has developed everywhere to its utmost consequences, until the last small handicraftsman and the last small peasant have fallen victim to capitalist large-scale production' (Engels 1977: 457–466).

Five years later, in 1899, the peasant question was further developed by two influential analyses, Lenin's (1960, first published 1899) *The Development of Capitalism in Russia* and Kautsky's (1988, first published 1899) *The Agrarian Question*, works that are assessed extensively in this book. Both works intended to bridge the apparent gap between theory and history, although from opposite directions. Kautsky sought to refine the theory of the disappearing peasantry by recasting it as a tendency subject to countervailing influences. Lenin's intent was to show empirically that history, or least Russian history, contrary to Narodnik populism,[4] was in fact in line with the theory: capitalism, Lenin showed, was indeed developing in the Russian countryside, and the Russian peasantry was a differentiated and differentiating entity. Thus,

> the old peasantry (was) not only 'differentiating', it (was) being completely dissolved, it (was) ceasing to exist, it (was) being ousted by absolutely new types of rural inhabitants ... a class of commodity producers in agriculture and a class of agricultural wageworkers.
>
> (Lenin 1960: 174)

Based on this analysis, Lenin addressed the politics of the peasant question, later arguing forcefully for a reconceptualization of the role of the peasantry in the making of a Russian revolution. In particular, he argued that a revolution in Russia was not possible without building an 'alliance of the working class and the peasantry' (Lenin 1971a: 12, first published 1901), and this required building 'political consciousness into the peasant movement' (Lenin 1971b: 89, first published 1905), in part by offering vigorous support for the peasant movement and its demands.

Both Lenin's and Kautsky's analyses were more historically nuanced than later adaptations, but the history they were preoccupied with was bounded by the conjunctural reality of the late nineteenth century nation-state and the formation of a home market. Following Engels, Lenin's solution to the peasant question became a cornerstone of Bolshevik political and revolutionary strategy. By way of contrast, Mensheviks such as Maslov and Martov carried the economic and evolutionary logic behind the theory of a disappearing peasantry to its final conclusion, and argued that a socialist revolution had to wait until capitalism had done its work on the peasantry.[5] Instead of changing history, the Mensheviks would wait for history to catch up with theory.

Neopopulism

In contradistinction to these Marxist answers to the peasant question which, despite variations in emphasis, saw peasant differentiation as the destiny of every nation-state's countryside under capitalist transformation, there was a second orientation that closed the apparent gap between theory and history by correcting the theory. Peasant societies, according to this perspective, had a logic of their own that defied the disintegrative forces of modern capitalism (Chayanov 1986). Thus, for this orientation, non-differentiation was destiny: peasants would never disappear.

The origin of this position was, in part, rooted in the rise of theoretical romanticism, which was itself a response to the crisis of capitalist modernity in the closing decades of the nineteenth century (Löwy and Sayre 2001). Inspired by the thoughts of Chernyshevskii and Herzen, Russian populists such as Nicolai Danielson agreed with one side of Marx's critique of capitalism: that it was a destructive force (Walicki 1989). At the same time, however, the populists did not accept that capitalism was, simultaneously, a progressive force. Instead, they argued that it was neither possible nor desirable for capitalism to develop in Russia. The refutation of this thesis was at the heart of Plekhanov's evolutionist critique of populism in the mid-1880s and later influenced a generation of Russian Marxists.

In 1925, theoretical romanticism found its most original advocate, Alexander Chayanov, who, in his *The Theory of Peasant Economy*, formulated a specific theory of what may be called a 'peasant mode of production' (Chayanov 1986). Drawing on marginalist economics to address the problems of developmentalist Marxism, Chayanov's aim was to show that Marx's list of modes of production (Marx 1970, first published 1859) could be expanded to include the peasant economy. Diametrically opposed to the prognosis of modernist Marxism, which stated that peasant production was but a transitory form of petty commodity production, Chayanov treated peasant production as an economic system in its own right, with laws of production and reproduction that enabled it to outcompete agrarian capitalism. However, while Chayanov and his 'organization and production school' reached conclusions that were diametrically opposed to those of Russian Marxists, what both had in common was a teleological interpretation of history and an empiricist understanding of the relationship between abstract theory and history (McMichael and Buttel 1990; Araghi 2003).

Third world extensions

With the hegemony of national developmentalism in the period following the Second World War, the early twentieth century debate on the peasant question was extended to the third world. Marxian interpretations in general argued that peasants were differentiating or, in more qualified accounts inspired by Kautsky's work, they were not differentiating for theoretical reasons, including:

- the sluggish pace of capitalist accumulation in agriculture;
- non-differentiation being functional to the needs of capital;
- peasant differentiation occurring in a disguised form.

For Marxian interpretations, theoretical innovations were thus necessary to reduce the gap between history and a theory suggesting that peasants were destined to disappear.[6]

By way of contrast, Chayanovian arguments for permanent peasantries required less theoretical innovation, as in the third world context, peasantries were numerous and showed weak signs of rapid class differentiation in national countrysides. Therefore, for Chayanovians, history for the most part happened to correspond to theory.[7] Thus, as late as 1988, Arturo Warman (1988: 499) argued that 'peasants make up the majority of humanity, a proportion that will remain the same indefinitely'.

Such arguments today, in my view, show the clear limits of the debate on the peasant question. Indeed, one could say that the postwar literature on the peasant question was even more problematic than its late nineteenth century original, for the following reasons.

1 The late nineteenth and early twentieth century debate was meant to analyse an altogether different ensemble of world-historical phenomena. While an interpretation of the peasant question based on the nation-state in the age of colonial–liberal globalism may have made phenomenal and even apparent sense, the adaptation of the terms of that debate in an era of national developmentalism, not to say postcolonial neoliberal globalism, would seem to be phenomenally irrelevant.

2 More importantly, the original peasant question, whatever problems there were with its premises, was in its origins a socialist problematic rooted in a political concern about how to conduct socialist revolutions when a

substantial majority of the population consisted of peasants. However, the postwar peasant question in the main became a developmentalist problematic rooted in a theoretical concern about how to understand the lack of development – or the persistence of 'backwardness' – in third world countrysides. Byres (1991: 7), for example, noted that 'a central distinguishing characteristic of economic backwardness is an unresolved agrarian question', which exists because capitalist development has not 'yet rooted out and destroyed … non-capitalist (agrarian) relations'.

Thus, not only did the postwar debate on the peasant question share the nation-state and the teleological orientation of the original debate; it applied the lessons of the original debate to an altogether different purpose, turning the political peasant question into a developmentalist peasant question focused on third world development.[8]

Moving beyond the limitations of the original and subsequent debates on the peasant question therefore requires a critique of:

1 the positivist and problematical understanding of the relationship between theory and history; which would lead to
2 a rejection of the determinist, evolutionist and teleological assumptions of both the disappearance thesis espoused by orthodox Marxists and the permanence thesis espoused by Chayanovians; and
3 moving beyond the nation-state and the home market as the unit of analysis.[9]

As I have argued elsewhere in more detail (Araghi 1995; 2000), an alternative world-historical interpretation of the peasant question would lead us in an altogether different direction. Utilizing a world-historical perspective, I have, in particular, argued that the postwar debate on the peasant question, limited as it was to the space of the nation-state, could not conceptualize the spatial dimensions of class formation and value relations as a global process, and it is precisely the global spatial dimensions of the peasant question that must be interrogated if it is to be understood world-historically as the social question of our times.

In considering the global spatial dimensions of the peasant question in general, my earlier work distinguished between two world-historical forms of the dispossession of the peasantry:

1 peasant dispossession by differentiation in eras of national protectionism of the home market; and
2 peasant dispossession by displacement in eras of world market hegemony.

I argue here that the specific character of the peasant question of our times is, simultaneously, dispossession by displacement and deproletarianization on a world scale. These are spatial dimensions of historical value relations and global class formation that lead to:

1 global deruralization, which is witnessed in the constriction of global
   rural space via depopulation, an expansion of enclosed suburbias and
   exurbias, and the increasing encroachment of industrial, agro-commercial,
   information and service economies into what was formerly rural space;
2 global hyperurbanization, demonstrated by the peripheral expansion of
   global urban space via the amassment of deproletarianized and homeless
   surplus labour populations;
3 the emergence of a global food regime – what I shall call the 'enclosure
   food regime' – characterized by a structure of forced underconsumption
   for the surplus populations of the world's hyperurbanized cities; which is
   witnessed alongside
4 sustained subsidized consumption and overconsumption on a world scale,
   but among an urbanized minority.

The concept of forced underconsumption is important to my argument, in
that it is an 'underreproduction' strategy of global capital. It is witnessed, in
its classic form, in absolute hunger, or what can be thought of as 'positive
starvation', which is increasingly an urban as well as a rural phenomenon.
However, and crucially, it is also witnessed in the form of relative hunger and
'negative' starvation; that is to say, it can be witnessed in the form of the
cheap food and cheap calories in the North, both of which can be seen to
have given rise to increasing global obesity among overconsuming poor
people in the North (Mintz 1985; Dixon 2007).

Although I use the phrase 'food regime' here, I use it differently from
its usual meaning (Araghi 2007; Pritchard 2008). I have previously suggested
that the theoretical omission of global value relations from food regime
analysis[10] has served to blur world-historical analysis of the peasant
question, and specifically of forms of peasant dispossession grounded in the
social and political relations of extant world capitalism (Araghi 2003). Here,
the global food regime of capital is conceptualized as a regime that produces,
transfers and distributes value. Global value relations are of central
importance because they provide

1 a theoretical basis for bringing agriculture and food into the analysis of
   capital accumulation on a world scale; and
2 a relational framework in which the underreproduction strategies of
   capital, witnessed in the creation of mobile surplus populations, are seen
   as the basis of forms of subsidized consumption and overconsumption.

While Marx's analysis of the production of value is theoretically based on
the assumption that labour-power is exchanged at its value, historically,
under both colonial–liberal globalism and postcolonial neoliberal globalism,
the global supplies of dispossessed, racialized, undocumented, gendered and
rightless surplus populations have given rise to highly uneven geographies of
consumption. Moreover, the emergence and consolidation of the global food

regime of capital is a unified, but historically interrupted, process. Thus colonial–liberal globalism gave birth to the global food regime of capital, national developmentalism forced it into retreat, and postcolonial neoliberal globalism has been attempting to resurrect it in the form of what I call the enclosure food regime. As a consequence, the global food regime of capital is, through its impact on the value of labour-power and thus the production of surplus value, a historically specific constituent element of global value relations.

The character of the global food regime of capital, as a regime that produces, transfers and distributes value, is thus fundamental to understanding the relationship between what can now be seen as forced underconsumption on the one hand, and subsidized consumption and overconsumption on the other: the peasant question of our times. Thus, by situating my argument within a specified world-historical context, I do not ahistorically transfer research questions from one historical and social complex to another, as is done in much current study of the agrarian question.[11] This strategy further allows me to uncover the abstract similarities and continuities, as well as the concrete differences and discontinuities across space and time. Therefore, considering the political history of capital relative to dispossession and displacement in the *longue duree*, I distinguish three periods, which are now discussed in turn.

Colonialism and dispossession

In world-historical terms, what I have called 'the great global enclosures of our times' is both old and new (Friedmann 2006: 462). It is old in the sense that the formation of labour-power free from spatially fixed ties to specific localities and free from self-reproduction alternatives is theoretically the defining component of capitalism. It is new in the sense that the capital accumulation process, as an intrinsically expropriating, privatizing and commodifying process, is historically inclusive of ever-expanding forms of enclosures, defined as historical forms of private appropriation by social exclusion. Capital came to life via enclosures, and it continues to live through enclosures (De Angelis 2004; Akram-Lodhi 2007). This explains its unending need and insatiable appetite for the privatization, through dispossession, repossession or commodification of public use values, of labour, of knowledge systems – or what is now called intellectual property rights – of land, of the environment and other resources, of housing, of food and social provisioning systems, of spatial, civil and political rights, of plant and human genotypes, of ecology, biology and, in the end, of life itself.

The long colonial period extends from the fifteenth to the twentieth century, and can be subdivided into two periods: 1492–1834 and 1834–1917. The period between 1492 and 1834 was the era of colonial enclosures and the original primitive accumulation of capital in England, as discussed by Wood (Chapter 2). The year 1492 marks the beginning of systematic systemic colonial and racialized enclosures in the Americas as well as in Castilian Spain. It was marked, on the one hand, by massive peasant dispossession and displacement via the Tudor enclosures of the sixteenth century, and continued with the parliamentary enclosures of the eighteenth and nineteenth centuries. On the other hand it was marked, as discussed at length by Bagchi (Chapter 4), by the dispossession and extermination of the indigenous peoples of the Americas and the enslavement of African labour; the violent confiscation of non-European lands and resources; the appropriation and subjugation of native crafts and industries; and the forced specialization of labour and trade in primary agricultural products. The colonial and English enclosures together constituted a necessary condition for the rise of industrial capital in the nineteenth century. They were not, however, a result of the invisible hand; rather, they were clearly an outcome of the visible foot.

The second period begins in the year 1834, which marks the passage of the Poor Law Amendment Act and the beginning of a systematic attempt by the English liberal industrial bourgeoisie to dismantle the traditional and rudimentary welfare system that had developed piecemeal from the sixteenth century. The food regime of capital originated in this second period, in that the agrarian programme of emerging industrial capital sought to construct a value-based global division of labour, a project that expressed the coming of age of industrial capital in the nineteenth century.

The early political expression of the food regime of capital came in 1839 with the formation of the Anti-Corn Law League and in 1846 with the abolition of the Corn Laws. It is also demonstrated in Latin American constitutional processes discussed by Teubal (Chapter 6). However, it is the Great Irish Famine of 1845–49 that particularly illustrates the relational character of the emerging global food regime of capital: one in which forced underconsumption, witnessed in the stark form of starvation and death, followed by evictions, dispossessions, rural depopulation, depeasantization and massive global migration, became the corollary of a growing English taste among the ruling class for beef consumption. As Rifkin (1992: 57) notes,

> the Irish food crisis only served to help the British … Between 1846 and 1874 the number of cattle exported from Ireland to England more than doubled, from 202000 to 5558000 head. By 1880 Ireland had been virtually transformed into a giant cattle pasture to accommodate the English palate.

India repeated the same experience: by the late nineteenth century it had become a major exporter of rice and wheat, and during the famine of 1881 it exported much of its surplus to England:

> Londoners were in effect eating India's bread. 'It seems an anomaly,' wrote a troubled observer, 'that, with her famines on hand, India is able to supply food for other parts of the world' … Grain merchants, in fact,

preferred to export a record 6.4 million cwt. of wheat to Europe in 1877–78 rather than relieve starvation in India.

(Davis 2001: 26–32)

In the settler colonies, the continued extermination of indigenous populations and the seizure of extremely productive lands, along with continuing plantation slavery (Tomich 1990, 2004) and unpaid family labour, provided the consumption needs of urban industrial capital, its workers, and urban consumers. In this way, an increasingly globally organized system of forced underconsumption lowered food costs, which in turn lowered the value of labour-power and enhanced the rate of surplus value. Peace and profit were, as a result, maintained in the Europe.

The agrarian policy of the colonial–liberal globalism of this period was thus depeasantization, proletarianization and urbanization at home, and peasantization, ruralization and the superexploitation of coerced labour in the colonies (the latter is discussed by Bagchi, Chapter 4, using the concept of export-led exploitation). This was done by reorganizing trade with the colonies in accordance with the initial formation and solidification of global value relations, and hence the emergence of the operation of the law of value on a world scale (Araghi 2003). Trade in luxuries, which had characterized the first part of the long colonial period, thus gave way to trade in agricultural commodities that eradicated the need for wage supports and non-market subsistence alternatives in the North, and in so doing subsidized the reproductive needs of European labour and capital (Mintz 1985). A global division of labour led, as a direct consequence, to the emergence of a global food regime (Friedmann and McMichael 1989) based on the international integration of peasant and coerced labour and formally free urban wage labour. However, the emergence of socialist movements at home and of global peasant and anticolonialist movements in the colonies on the one hand, and the rise of European nationalisms and global warfare on the other hand, marked the political end of this, beginning in the late nineteenth century.

Developmentalism and dispossession

Two victories in two world-historical revolutions during the twentieth century, the Russian Revolution of 1917 and the Vietnamese Revolution of 1975, mark the beginning and the end of what I term 'long national developmentalism'. The first revolution, along with both the emergence of a powerful wave of peasant, nationalist, and anticolonialist movements, as well as inter-capitalist rivalry, militarism, war, and the rise of an unmanageable fascist alternative, forced a global reformist retreat from classical liberalism. The economic content of the retreat came from Keynesianism, in the form of abandoning *laissez faire* for a mixed economy model. The social and the political content of this model took the form of adapting three innovations drawn from the Russian Revolution: the bureaucratic welfare state; the recognition of postcolonial peoples' nationalist and developmentalist aspirations – excepting socialist nationalisms, as the Vietnam War confirmed; and the acknowledgment of postcolonial peasantries as a political force and the resulting necessity – if reluctantly and through a tortured path – of adopting an agrarian reform platform to accommodate the demands of revolutionary and/or nationalist peasantries. This reformism, which at the same time formed the foundation of US hegemony in the three decades or so following the Second World War, was a practical retreat from classical liberalism, as can be seen in the dominant discourse of state officials, politicians and economists.

The origins of national developmentalism may be traced back to Wilsonian reformism, which was itself in part a response to socialist and fascist alternatives offered to the deepening crisis of colonial–liberal globalism, a crisis that was demonstrated by imperial rivalry, nationalism, protectionism, the scramble for colonies, rebellions in those colonies, the First World War, and the developing alliance between the socialist and anticolonialist movements. Thus, during the height of the First World War and prior to the October Revolution, Woodrow Wilson sent his advisor and confidant, Edward House, to Europe to advocate a negotiated peace and a new postwar order. As House put it to the British,

> my plan is that if England, the United States, Germany and France will come to an understanding concerning investment by their citizens in underdeveloped countries, much good and profit will come to their citizens as well as to the countries needing development.
>
> (cited by Levin 1968: 24)

The October Revolution changed the course of events for the rest of the world. World-historically, the emergence of the Soviet Union as the first major national developmental state facilitated the later rise of the welfare state in the West – the latter cannot be understood without reference to the former – and later still, the era of national developmental states in the third world after the conclusion of the Second World War, when fascism was dead and colonialism was dying. By participating in the war against fascism, colonial peoples had learned how to defeat colonialism. There followed a powerful wave of national liberation movements leading to the final break-up of the old colonial blocks.

For the emerging postcolonial states, the economic content of political independence quickly came to be defined as inward-oriented, nationally based industrial growth, or what I call national developmentalism. However, in the Cold War context there were soon two distinguishable kinds of national developmentalisms: socialist, or state-led, national developmentalisms; and Western-oriented, market-led national developmentalisms. As regards the latter, while the New Dealers in the USA had a clear programme for the reconstruction of Europe and Japan in the aftermath of the Second World

War, they were ambivalent about the place of postcolonial nationalisms in the emerging international order. In particular, unlike European colonialists in the era of colonial–liberal globalism, US policy-makers had yet to learn what to do with peasant societies in the expanding international economy.

Quite the reverse was true for the Soviet Union, which, based on its own revolutionary heritage, had a ready-made formula stipulating the correct attitude towards anticolonial nationalist movements. This formula was to link the national and colonial question with the peasant question by carrying anticolonial and nationalist struggle into the countryside and actively supporting the demands of an insurgent peasantry. It was clearly the success of this formula, and the rapid expansion of state and socialist nationalisms, that put the third world and its development on the agenda of the USA. The urge to respond on the part of the USA came from the fact that the expansion of state and socialist nationalisms would have restricted the political and commercial space of the global free trade and free enterprise regime, the implementation of which was being sponsored by the USA. Ultranationalists – that is to say, state or socialist nationalists – had to be either contained by military force or incorporated by more peaceful, commercial and political, means.

Incorporation, however, meant that the USA had to compromise its internationalism with third world nationalism; this meant acknowledging the demands of third world urban bourgeoisies and insurgent peasantries. The main components of this compromise were embodied in the market-led national developmentalisms promoted by the USA: import-substituting industrialization policies and US-sponsored land reform programmes. The first component was to promote a managed nationalism that recognized the yearnings of the urban populations of the postcolonial nations for modernity and national industrialization; the second component was to placate their peasantries. Neither represented the invisible hand; rather, both represented the visible foot. As to the need to placate peasantries, after decades of peasant unrest and mobilization for socialist and nationalist revolutions in Asia and Latin America, the USA developed its first programmatic solution to the peasant question in the 1950s and 1960s.

That solution was land reform, American-style. The development of the American discourse on land reform is an interesting case of what I have called 'discourse formation in world-historical context'. This discourse had four elements:

1 it expressed itself emphatically in individualistic and explicitly anti-communist terms; along with having
2 insistent ideological references to America's own past experience with family farming, as embodied in the free land movement and the 1862 Homestead Laws, as its model; while in fact
3 borrowing its *raisons d'être* and content from Leninist agrarian programmes; and, at the same time

4   radically altering the political goal of those programmes.

In terms of the latter two points, as we have seen, Lenin had turned orthodox Marxism's identification of the peasantry as a reactionary force upside down. The crux of Lenin's approach was to take full advantage of peasant demands, especially those around the confiscation of land, in order to mobilize the countryside in support of revolution. Indeed, it can be strongly argued that it was based on this strategy that the October Revolution was won, and that from then on the slogans derived from this formula became the refrain of revolutionary movements around the world.

The USA was able to borrow this Leninist formula because national developmentalism, with the regime of colonial liberalism in retreat, was, in relative terms, a regime of accommodation in the Gramscian sense of the concept (Gramsci 1971; Sassoon 1982). Land reformism, as the emerging agrarian programme of the USA in the third world, was thus designed to placate postcolonial peasant movements by accommodating their land hunger within a market-led framework. As such, it turned the Leninist agrarian strategy on its head: if the Leninist agrarian programme was intended to build broad-based political alliances by linking the peasant question to the national question, the purpose of US agrarian policy was precisely the reverse – to demobilize third world peasant movements and, more particularly, to unlink them from urban nationalist and/or socialist movements.

That this was the political impulse behind US third world agrarian programmes can be seen from the discourse on land reform articulated by US policy-makers in the 1950s and 1960s. Thus, as Dean Acheson (1951: 660) warned in 1951,

> (for) millions of people in the world, there is no more urgent problem than the impoverishment resulting from primitive methods of cultivation of the land under antiquated systems of landownership. Soviet propagandists have dangled promises of great change to those impoverished and hungry people, and to many, in such a state, it may have seemed that any change must be an improvement.

That same year a US representative to the Economic and Social Council of the UN said that 'land reform is important not only because of its potential effect on incentives to production. It has a far larger significance. It can mean the difference between explosive tensions and stability' (Lubin 1951: 468). This was reinforced by views such as those of Lester Mallory, the Deputy Assistant Secretary for Inter-American Affairs, who stressed that 'land reforms ... will arm its millions of subsistence farmers, tenants, and squatters against the blandishments of communism by giving them pride of possession and the kind of incentive that every human being has a right to have' (Mallory 1960: 821). Indeed, the importance of land reform as an

American global political imperative was earlier captured by Acheson's (1952: 202) comment before the Food and Agriculture Organization (FAO) of the UN that 'the subject of land reform ... is a matter which we in the Department of State have believed is absolutely foremost in our whole international relations'.

By 1960, a year after the Cuban revolution and the land redistribution that followed, land reform had become such an integrated component of US development discourse that John F. Kennedy (1961) could argue that

> the leaders of Latin America, the industrialists and the landowners are, I am sure, also ready to admit past mistakes and accept new responsibilities. For unless all of us are willing to contribute our resources to national development, unless all of us are prepared not merely to accept, but initiate, basic land and tax reforms, unless all of us take the lead in improving the welfare of our people, then that leadership will be taken from us and the heritage of centuries of Western civilization will be consumed in a few months of violence.

There were, then, two questions regarding US-led agrarian reformism as it spread in the 1960s: first, why land reform? As just argued, the answer came from the Leninist tradition, but with an American anticommunist twist. The second question was: land reform how? The answer to this came from persistent ideological references to US history. Ideologically, the creation of family-sized farms – as opposed to collectivization – was seen as a way of creating a stable and highly conservative social base on which to construct US agrarian policy. Thus Dean Acheson, in offering the US Draft Resolution on Land Reform submitted to the UN Economic and Social Council, had noted that

> the peasants of Eastern Europe, like the peasants of Russia, have learned that Soviet 'collectivization', or land reform imposed from the top, brings worse oppression than before ... we have regarded our family-sized farms ... being of fundamental importance to the prosperity and stability of the entire nation. Our democracy has its roots in a sound land policy.
> (Acheson 1951:660)

As a result, the US concept of agrarian reform, according to the US Delegate to the FAO Conference on World Land Tenure Problems, was

> based on the thought that men everywhere cherish that which is their own, and that there are few human instincts stronger than the desire of men and women to possess a little spot of earth which they can call their own. Farm and home ownership in any nation makes for stability of government.
> (Hope 1951: 999)

This was only in part because, as Oliver Freeman, the US Secretary of Agriculture later noted, 'efficiency and progress is stimulated by individual ownership and personal incentive' (Freeman 1964: 387). It was more fundamentally tied to the relationship between land ownership and the character of political regimes emphasized by both Acheson and Hope: as Charles Brannan, another US Secretary of Agriculture, put it, '(the) American pattern of family farming has long been accepted as one of the basic strengths of our democracy ... The love of freedom is deeply rooted in the family farm ... This love of freedom is the real backbone of democracy' (Brannan 1951: I–V).

Rhetorical references to freedom, democracy, efficiency and family farming to one side, the ideological and political impulse behind US third world agrarian programmes can be easily inferred from the land reforms that the American military government implemented immediately following the Second World War in Japan, and thereafter in South Korea and Taiwan. These reforms were a direct response to powerful peasant movements and communist-inspired tenant unions, and were explicitly designed to undercut the political and ideological orientation of these movements. Cumulatively, the reforms reduced tenancy in Japan from 49 per cent in 1945 to 9 per cent in 1950, with peasant land ownership increasing from 31 to 70 per cent during the same period (Ogura 1968: 17). In Taiwan, between 1948 and 1959 tenancy decreased from 36 to 14 per cent, while peasant ownership increased from 33 to 59 per cent (Chen 1961: 312). In South Korea, peasant ownership increased from 14 per cent in 1945 to 70 per cent in 1965, while tenancy reduced from 49 to 7 per cent (Morrow and Sherper 1970: 38–41).

In a similar fashion, land reforms were carried out in Germany and Italy with the same objective: to prevent the growth of communist tendencies. southern Italy, in particular, was the scene of demonstrations, strikes and land occupation in the early postwar period (Tarrow 1967). Thus in Sicily, Calabria and Lazxlo between 1944 and 1949, peasant cooperatives with a total membership of a quarter of a million took over more than 165,000 hectares of land, displacing the former owners of the land (Ginsborg 1984: 94).

While the consequences of the many land distribution programmes in the third world that were implemented under national developmentalism differed according to local geographies, ecologies, the kind of crops cultivated, prior political histories, existing land tenure systems, strength of the landholding classes, geopolitics, and the local balance of forces, they had far-reaching impacts for the future of third world peasantries. For some, the visible foot of land reforms carried out in this era successfully transformed extant landlord–peasant relations, which were based on various historical forms of direct domination, and led to a proliferation of near-subsistence family-sized farm units, some of which were capable of accumulation. Thus, as Llambi (1989) and Katzmann (1978) have shown, in some regions such as northern Ecuador, the Argentine Pampas, southern Brazil, western Venezuela and northern India, the reforms, when combined with privileged access to credit and marketing (Edelman 1980) or labour markets (Lehmann 1982), led to the emergence of capital-accumulating family farms producing overwhelmingly for the market and worked by owners with some hired labour.

However, this occurred in only a minority of cases. The majority of near-subsistence family-sized farm units were petty commodity producers, and depended heavily for their production and subsistence needs on state subsidies. The benefits of agrarian reform to such farm households were minimal, even given the visible foot of state intervention. Even where land was in theory available for smallholders, the reforms in general left most of the productive land in the possession of large owners. In Latin America, for example, the number of family farms with an average of about two hectares increased by 92 per cent between 1950 and 1980. However, in 1980 20 per cent of large commercial holders continued to occupy 80 per cent of the land area, while about 80 per cent of petty land owners occupied a mere 20 per cent of the cultivated area (de Janvry *et al.* 1989). During the period of national developmentalism, many who had the potential to benefit from land and agrarian reform did not, while others saw their situation deteriorate, in particular the landless, whose numbers increased.

In sum, the political and ideological character of land reforms during the national developmentalist era led to the creation of masses of potentially mobile peasantries. Ironically, a global agrarian programme that, in Stolypin's fashion, had sought to create a class of peasant proprietors as a stable social base for postcolonial states *ipso facto* created the conditions for a process of depeasantization at a world scale. In this connection, two important dynamics should be noted. First, state credit and subsidies promoted the expansion of monetized and commodity relations into the countryside and increasingly exposed the emerging small farms to market forces. Second, while formally nation-state-based divisions of labour and national home markets were promoted as a way of accommodating the demands of the postcolonial bourgeoisies in the third world, the emerging world market and global division of labour substantively undercut and derailed home market formation and nation-based divisions of labour.

The politics of world market formation in this period are brilliantly captured by Harriet Friedmann's (1982) historical analysis of the postwar international food order between 1945 and 1972. Sponsored by the USA in order to dispose of its mounting grain surpluses as food aid or concessional sales, the postwar food order depressed world prices of grain and encouraged third world food imports and food import dependency. As Oliver Freeman, the aforementioned US Secretary of Agriculture, put it in 1964,

> ... American agriculture is proportionally more concerned with expanding exports than is American industry. Production from one acre out of every four harvested in 1963 was exported. Our agricultural exports have been increasing rapidly in recent years. In the 1963–64 fiscal year US agricultural exports reached a new record high level of

$6.1 billion – $1 billion larger than the previous year. All of this increase was in commercial sales for dollars. In the year just ended our exports were 35 per cent larger than in 1959.

(Freeman 1964: 384-5)

Between the 1950 and 1970, the US share of world exports had increased by 90 per cent for soybean, 50 per cent for maize and 35 per cent for wheat (Tubiana 1989: 25). As American diets were adopted on a world scale, local food production declined in Latin America, Asia, the Middle East and Africa, and by the early 1970s Asia and Latin America, formerly surplus-producing regions, became dependent on food imports. In the third world as a whole, the ratio of food imports to food exports increased from 50 per cent in the period between 1955 and 1960 to 80 per cent in 1980 (Manfredi 1978: 16). In other words, the reorganization of world agriculture to the advantage of American farmers contradicted the political rhetoric that stressed balanced national development and expanding petty capitalist ownership on the third world countryside.

The global food order in the postwar period should be seen not only as a response to farm politics in the USA (Friedmann 1982), but also as a way of containing socialist nationalisms in the postwar period (Cleaver 1977; Wallerstein 1980; Ross 1998; Dowie 2001). Thus the public financing of US agricultural exports as food aid was motivated by the ongoing politics of the reformist accommodation of the period rather than by the narrow economics of mercantilist capital accumulation. Indeed, even though in practice the Green Revolution led to increased technological and input dependency, and even though in practice food aid led to depeasantization and food dependency in the third world, both programmes were ideologically reformist components of national developmentalism.

Increased dependence on food imports spatially reconfigured populations in the third world. Thus between 1960 and 1980, in all regions of the South, both the rural population as a percentage of the total population and the agricultural labour force as a percentage of the total labour force declined significantly (United Nations 1980; World Bank 1984; UN Economic Commission for Latin America 1988). As independence became synonymous with modernization, and the latter was equated to urban industrialization, postcolonial national developmentalist states welcomed the availability of cheap food in the form of food aid or credit-financed concessional food sales such as US Public Law 480, with attendant low interest rates and long repayment periods. The resulting poverty among the new small landowners, who were now free from bondage, combined with the postcolonial state's urban bias in terms of state resource allocations (Lipton 1974), led to a substantial draining-off of rural population growth through out-migration. Thus, the number of third world rural migrants increased by 230 per cent between 1950 and 1975, compared with the previous 25 years (United Nations 1980; World Bank 1984; UN Economic Commission for Latin America 1988).

Hence third world peasantries were being located in national markets and at the same time being exposed, through cheap food imports, to world market competition with capitalized and heavily subsidized farms in the North. Nation-based peasantization and global depeasantization thus expressed the contradictions of national developmentalism and the postwar national developmentalist compromise.

To relate this to the debate between the advocates of the permanence versus the disappearance of the peasantry, discussed in an earlier section, it is apparent from a close examination of the national developmentalist period that peasantization and depeasantization are neither unilinear nor mutually exclusive national processes. Both the metaphysical 'peasants-for-ever' theses, and the teleological or functional theses on the 'destiny' or function of the peasantries within capitalism, as espoused by some orthodox Marxists, miss Marx's methodological caveat that 'the concrete is concrete because it is the concentration of many determinations, hence unity of the diverse' (Marx 1973: 100, first published 1939–41). As a world-historically concrete account of peasantries under national developmentalism, analysed as a historical regime of political capitalism, this analysis offers an alternative conclusion: that peasant dispossession in the form of nation-based rural class differentiation in this period occurred at a sluggish rate and was in the end subordinated to peasant dispossession via urban displacement.

Therefore, if we redefine from a global perspective the nation-state-based demographic concepts of push and pull migration factors (Harris and Todaro 1970), global push factors can be witnessed in the postwar food order, food aid and dumping, and global pull factors can be witnessed in the postcolonial equation of national independence with industrialization and urbanization. In other words, and crucially, it was the historical mix of both that explains what I call relative depeasantization, which was a defining character of global dispossession under national developmentalism. The relative depeasantization witnessed in the period between the 1950s and the 1970s was a reflection of simultaneous peasantization and depeasantization processes, and the relative protection of national agricultures through subsidies, price supports and state financing of agricultural inputs, which slowed down the rate at which millions of newly created small peasant landowners were exposed to global push factors. If we define the rate of deruralization as the contribution of rural out-migration to rural population decline, it appears that all developing countries for which data are available experienced accelerating declines in their rural populations due to net rural out-migration; in Latin America and in the Middle East this decline was by more than 50 per cent (United Nations 1980).

Globalization and dispossession

By the early 1970s, the contradictions of national developmentalism (i.e. demands for more independence and control over national resources by the

South) and the contradictions of Keynesianism (i.e. the accommodation of Northern working classes through full employment policies leading to wage inflation, stagflation, a profit squeeze, and increasing global competitive pressures) along with the inability of the North to either suppress or accommodate the South, had created a major systemic crisis (Armstrong *et al.* 1991). Neither Keynesianism at home nor national developmentalism abroad seemed compatible with the requirements of capital accumulation; hence, capital withdrew from both reformist social compacts (Akram-Lodhi 2005, 2006). The retreat from development was a component of a systemic counteroffensive that emerged in the 1970s and 1980s and sought to reverse the protection of society from the market (Polanyi 2001). As this project evolved, it came to include the following features:

1 withdrawal from the postwar Keynesian social compact with labour in the North through flexibilization, casualization, deproletarianization and the spatial mobility of capital;
2 withdrawal from the agrarian welfare state, with a resulting deepening of depeasantization;
3 dismantling of nation-state-based agricultural versus industrial divisions of labour that had come to symbolize independence and nationhood for postcolonial states as the socioeconomic content of national developmentalism;
4 reconstruction of global value relations (Araghi 2003) that had been undercut during the period of national developmentalism to accommodate the project of home market construction;
5 dismantling of the postwar aid-based food order as a component of the agrarian welfare state;
6 reconstruction of a global food regime modelled on the colonial–liberal food regime of the late nineteenth century, but where the British workshop of the world is replaced by consumption hubs in the North; and
7 the socialization of finance as a means of subsidizing aggregate demand (Araghi *et al.* 2008) and the deployment of a global debt regime as a means of restructuring the world's division of labour.

The last component, that is the creation of the debt regime, was, from an instrumental point of view, central to the counteroffensive strategy of reshaping the world's many home markets to fit the needs of an emergent world market. Without it the only alternative was a strategy of militarization and a reversion to the colonial–liberal globalism of the late nineteenth century. That this was unthinkable in the post-Vietnam era was a point well understood by Robert McNamara who, as the Secretary of Defense between 1961 and 1968, was responsible for the massive, but in the end ineffective, use of military violence during Vietnam's war for national unification. Thus McNamara's strategy during his long World Bank presidency between 1968 and 1981 was dubbed by Bank staff as 'pushing money out the door'

(George and Sabelli 1994); during his presidency the Bank's lending increased 13-fold, from $953 million in 1968 to $12.4 billion in 1981 and, in a sense, debt became the continuation of war by other means. Commercial banks followed suit as their petrodollar lending to the South increased by 4400 per cent between 1972 and 1981 (George and Sabelli 1994). It was thus in this era that policy lending under the rubric of rural development and poverty reduction paved the way for the rise of agro-industrial export model.

The bestowal of the Nobel Prize in Economics on Friedrich Hayek in 1974 and on Milton Friedman in 1976 presaged the coming of the neoliberal age, and with it postcolonial neoliberal globalism. With *détente* the communist 'threat' was relaxed for the moment in order to deal with more serious threats of internal wage inflation and the external unruliness of postcolonial nationalisms. There then followed major realignments in established political parties, particularly in the UK and the USA, the creation of new institutions such as the Trilateral Commission, the World Economic Forum and the G-7, and the activation of existing interstate institutions such as the World Bank and the International Monetary Fund in the service of a programmatic withdrawal from national developmentalism, Keynesianism and public welfare institutions.

As part of this process of realignment, the political use of food as a coercive way of dealing with the third world was refined by the US state during the Nixon Administration. Of course, food aid had always had a broadly defined political dimension, as demonstrated by the Egyptian experience under Nasser in 1966 (Dethier and Funk 1978) and the US withholding food aid from Bangladesh at the height of the 1974 famine until the newly born state abandoned plans to try Pakistani war criminals (Sharma 2002). From 1973 onwards, however, food in the service of national developmentalism clearly gave way to commercial and subsidized exports as a mechanism of dismantling nation-state-based divisions of labour in the third world. In this light it is not surprising that as early as 1974 commercial food exports by the US had increased to $20 billion, while food aid shipments had declined to $1 billion (Rosenfeld 1974: 21; Hopkins 1984). Moreover, between 1973 and 1986 the European Community matched the commercial, export-oriented and nationally protectionist policies of the USA; thus a food regime that managed the disposal of food surpluses in a manner that was divorced from price regulation gave way to the need for markets for commercial agrarian dumping. As a direct consequence, between 1980 and 1987 the rate of increase in agricultural production in the USA and Europe together exceeded the rate of increase in domestic consumer demand by 100 per cent (Srinivasan 1989: 40; Watkins 1991). The contradictions of this 'structural overproduction' (Watkins 1991), due in no small measure to the use of export subsidies, was, at least in part, as we will see, the impetus behind the transformation of the General Agreement on Tariffs and Trade (GATT) into the World Trade Organization (WTO).

The 'new' free market economics, or what we may call the second *laissez faire*, while fiercely anti-institutionalist in rhetoric, in fact actively developed its own interventionist institutions. Thus by the late 1980s the latter were enforcing a comprehensive set of antireformist economic policies that came to be known as the Washington Consensus, which included the following elements: the privatization of the state and state functions, and hence the privatization of the public sphere; the privatization of welfare, law and a vast expansion of the legal dominion of property rights, tax reform and upward income redistribution; the deregulation of labour markets and deproletarianization policies; trade and market liberalization; and currency devaluations. Hence, while national developmentalism was characterized by mixed economies and the formal subsumption of capital, both colonial–liberal globalism and postcolonial neoliberal globalism were characterized by attempts to construct a global division of labour based on the real subsumption of capital.

The privatization of the agrarian welfare state created in the national developmentalist era, to the advantage of Northern agribusiness transnational corporations and capitalist farms, forms the context in which the relative depeasantization and displacement of the postwar period gave way to absolute depeasantization and displacement under postcolonial neoliberal globalism. It was in this period that the invisible hand of the debt regime – currently standing at $2.5 trillion – functioned as the visible foot of the global enclosures of our times (Akram-Lodhi 2007). Policy lending of the McNamara era evolved into debt-enforced structural adjustment in the global agrarian sector, leading to

1 the deregulation of land markets and the reversal of land reform policies originating in the national developmentalist era;
2 drastic cuts in farm subsidies and price supports and the disengagement of both postcolonial states and the World Bank from irrigation support;
3 the expanded use of agrarian biotechnologies and the expanded commodification of seeds and seed reproduction;
4 a marked, and growing, dependence on chemical, biological and hydrocarbon farm inputs;
5 the promotion of agro-exports at the expense of food crops through an expansion of livestock agro-exports, expanded cash crop production for export as animal feed, and the export of niche luxury foods, fresh fruits, vegetables and ornamental flowers for the global centres of over-consumption, as argued by Watts (Chapter 11).

The power relations that guided the subsumption of formerly protected home markets by the world market created a world division of labour marked by unmediated exchange relations. These unmediated exchange relations brought together formally equal but substantively unequal participants, thereby forcing millions of petty producers in the South to compete with heavily subsidized agro-industrial food transnational corporations in the North (McMichael 2008). The inability to compete led, in turn, to massive peasant dispossessions by displacement. Thus the global enclosures of postcolonial neoliberal globalism, which are similar to the enclosures of colonial–liberal globalism, have led to the creation of a massive reserve army of migratory labour.

I distinguish between two forms of the reserve army of migratory labour: actual and potential. This distinction is based on the theoretical difference between the ownership of means of production and the ownership of the means of subsistence. The distinction is relevant to historical conditions under which peasant differentiation through capital accumulation in national countrysides is subordinated to global urban capital accumulation and corporate agro-food capital accumulation processes. More specifically, the sluggish rate of peasant differentiation in national countrysides has led to the creation of masses of semi-dispossessed peasantries, those who have lost their non-market access to their means of subsistence but still hold formal and/or legal ownership to some of their means of production. While corporate capital and its chain of subcontractors appropriate their surplus labour via the provision of credit, seeds and other inputs, and market access, it leaves the labour process and partial ownership of means of production in the hands of the direct producers. As I develop the argument elsewhere (Araghi 2003), this is a form of production of absolute surplus value by commodity-producing labour-power. Hence, while the loss of ownership of the means of production is at the same time the loss of non-market access to the means of subsistence, the reverse is not always the case in the historical context under consideration. Partially dispossessed peasantries of the South today are part of the potentially or partially mobile reserve army of migratory labour. The latter comprises a major proportion of the world slum population, recently estimated at 1 billion (United Nations 2006), and a concrete analysis of their conditions, needs and demands is crucial for understanding the emerging mass movements of resistance among the peasantries of the South.

The agrarian programme of capital in the era of postcolonial neoliberal globalism has thus intensified depeasantization via displacement across the global space. In other words, if simultaneous peasantization and depeasantization was the distinguishing character of the agrarian programme of national developmentalism, simultaneous depeasantization and deproletarianization is the defining feature of the agrarian programme of postcolonial neoliberal globalism. However, in order to understand the profound consequences of postcolonial neoliberal globalism's agrarian programme for the world's peasantries in the present period, it is necessary to consider the transformation of the food regime of the postwar era into what I call the 'enclosure food regime' (McMichael 2005; Friedmann 2005).

I use the concept of an enclosure food regime to emphasize the exclusionist and violent character of the agrarian programme of postcolonial neoliberal globalism. This programme has the double aim of

1 finally dismantling postcolonial nation-based divisions of labour that were at the core of national developmentalism; and
2 reorganizing world production and exchange relations on the basis of global value relations.

The enclosure food regime of our times is a historical form of the food regime of capital, the emergence of which marks a radical departure from the reformist-based food order of the era of national developmentalism. Theoretically, the construction of truly global value relations requires the construction of a global division of labour at the expense of home markets, national divisions of labour and national food security. In this sense, the postwar food regime represented a political retreat from colonial–liberal globalism's project of constructing value relations on a global basis. The enclosure food regime, as the agrarian programme of a re-energized, reglobalizing capital, represents a reversal of the suspension of global value relations, with drastic consequences for the masses of agrarian direct producers who become redundant on a daily basis, and who are thrown out of collapsing national divisions of labour into the vortex of globalization as masses of surplus labour in motion.

Thus the specific character of the enclosure food regime is the enclosure of the spaces of existence of the world's peasantries. As a spatial regime of dispossession, it devours national agricultures, land and means of subsistence, and frees labour-power for global consumption. Key to this project was the transformation of the GATT into the WTO, and the latter's enforcement of the Agreement on Agriculture that had been negotiated by the former.

It is not in a figurative sense that I characterize the Agreement on Agriculture as the agrarian programme of capital in the era of postcolonial neoliberal globalism: Daniel Amstutz, a former Chief Executive Officer of the futures trading and commodities division at Cargill, the world's largest global grain trading company, was the US Chief Negotiator for Agriculture and led the negotiations on agriculture in the Uruguay Round, thus playing a critical role in drafting the Agreement on Agriculture (Ritchie 1993). Following the completion of the negotiations he returned to Cargill, and later was again charged with drafting food and agricultural policies for the Iraqi constitution (Choudry 2006: 3).

At its core, the Agreement on Agriculture was an agreement between the USA and Europe to resolve their overproduction crisis by expanding the space of commercial dumping in the South. This required

1 an international legal framework for the purpose of eradicating the legacies of the national developmentism, most particularly nation-based divisions of labour; and
2 a discursive system that delegitimized agrarian nationalism and, in its place, rationalized the commodification of food security.

However, there is a central contradiction here. As noted presciently by Kevin Watkins (1991: 40) in his early critique of the GATT Uruguay Round, doing away with formal and informal export subsidies in the USA and the European Union (EU) has not been on the agenda; the 2007 US Farm Bill makes this quite clear. The invisible hand is not going to supplant the visible foot; it cannot, as it would be tantamount to a major transfer of payments and differential advantage from the North to the South. It would also result in a massive reduction in the size of the mobile surplus labour population which, as undocumented and under reproduced labour-power, serves as the basis for metropolitan agricultures. Thus, in the USA and Europe, agro-food transnational corporations are the primary recipients of depeasantized Southern migrant labour who are now increasingly living in enclosed forced and indeed slave labour camps in the heartlands of metropolitan agriculture (Brass 1999).[12]

What a *New York Times* editorial (Anon. 2003) calls 'hypocrisy' and 'the one way street of globalization' are in fact systemic aspects of the agrarian programme of capital under the enclosure food regime. Subsidies to agriculture by the Organization for Economic Cooperation and Development member states increased by 65 per cent between 1995 and 2005, and the total amount of subsidies paid by the USA and EU is at least $1 billion a day. The 2007 US Farm Bill proposed to increase these subsidies by $2 billion a year. These subsidies are, moreover, notable in that they are so inequitably distributed: the top 10 per cent of recipients receive more than 70 per cent of all farm subsidies, with allocations going to agro-food transnational corporations (Environmental Working Group 2007). This can be contrasted with the situation facing the marginalized surplus labour population: according to Green and Griffith (2002), 3 billion of the world's poor earn less than the subsidies received by the average dairy cow in the EU, which amounts to $2.20 per day.

Accounts of agricultural subsidies often focus attention on the direct corporate recipients and the costs to taxpayers. However, it is important to note that from a value-theoretic viewpoint, the subsidization of agro-food capital functions to

1   overproduce food commodities and drive down the price of domestic food and wage costs, thereby benefiting not only the direct corporate agro-food recipients of subsidies, but also all fractions of capital;
2   subsidize overconsumption in the North;
3   depress the price of food commodities in the world market to the advantage of urban consumers and all fractions of non-agrarian capital in the South;
4   rapidly and massively displace agrarian petty commodity producers;
5   forcibly deflate wages through coerced underconsumption, the under-reproduction of labour, and deproletarianization strategies; and
6   vastly expand a globally mobile population of agricultural refugees.

Thus, from a value-theoretic viewpoint, the subsidization of agro-food capital is wholly consistent with the solidification of a global food regime of capital that deepens value relations on a world scale.

Conclusions

According to a former World Bank official, the number of dispossessed and displaced peasants in India who will 'migrate from rural to urban India by the year 2015 is expected to be equal to twice the combined population of UK, France, and Germany' (Sharma 2007). The Indian state is using the Land Acquisition Act of 1894 to acquire land for 500 planned special economic zones: 125,000 hectares of agricultural land is being enclosed in the first stage of these clearances, with about the same amount to be acquired in the second stage. Here, then, deruralization means the state-sponsored substitution of rural space by enclosed economic zones. The scale and pace of change in farmer bankruptcies and peasant dispossession led to a 52 per cent increase in the rate of farmer suicide in four major states between 1997 and 2005, compared with 23 per cent increase among the non-farmers. Sainath (2007a, 2007b) thus notes that these states 'might be termed ... [a] Special Elimination Zone for farmers this past decade'.

Similar to the scale of peasant dispossession and displacement in India is China, whose different political history until the 1980s makes for a revealing comparison. From 1949 to 1978, China's rapid industrialization, in a striking contrast with the rest of the world, was accompanied by sluggish and politically managed rural–urban migration. By the early 1980s, China still had only 2 million peasant migrants. However, in the postreform period, in an astonishing reversal, China's migrant peasant population increased to about 71 million in 1994, and from there to around 115 million at present (Chan 1988; Wu 1994; Guang 2001). By 1994, farmland had declined by 20 per cent from that recorded in the 1950s (Shenon 1995). Following its entry into the WTO, China began drastically reducing its tariffs and use of agricultural subsidies. As a consequence, peasants, particularly cotton and soybean farmers, are leaving the countryside *en masse*:

> Anyone who has visited China's ballooning, chaotic cities cannot help but notice the construction cranes ... Less obvious are the armies of migrant workers toiling below ... the farmers arriving at bus or train stations, often hundreds at a time with possessions bundled in nylon sacks; the girls flooding out of thousands of dying villages to fill the humming factories along China's southern coast ... Government experts predict the number will rise to 300 million by 2020, eventually to 500 million. Today, Shanghai alone has 3 million migrant workers; by comparison, the entire Irish migration to America from 1820 to 1930 is thought to have involved perhaps 4.5 million people.
>
> Yardley (2004)

In Mexico, enclosures took the form of privatization of the *ejido* following the signing of the North American Free Trade Agreement (Barros Nock 2000; Akram-Lodhi 2007: 1446). According to an analysis by Oxfam (Fanjul and Fraser 2003), the threefold increase in US corn exports since the early 1990s has led to a 70 per cent fall in the price of domestically produced corn. Particularly affected are 3 million peasant corn producers. Nearly 50 per cent of the Mexican rural population, and fully 70 per cent of those living in the corn-producing states of Chiapas, Oaxaca and Guerrero, now live in extreme poverty. As a result, many leave their villages to urban centres or, of course, to the USA – every year at least 300,000 displaced Mexicans migrate to the USA.

I use these examples not to show a uniform experience, nor to assert what is going to be the destiny of the peasantry, but to bring out the world-historical meaning of the peasant question of our times: dispossession by displacement, differentiation at the level of global space, enclosures and deruralization, hyperurbanization and deproletarianization. The analysis in this chapter has thus intentionally stood the agrarian question on its head: historically, the agrarian question was to be resolved in its peripheral and subordinate relationship to a national urban question. In this chapter, by way of contrast, the conceptual focus on the global context of the uneven reproduction of labour-power has brought agriculture and food to the centre of analysis, and a world-historical investigation of the agrarian question is, in my view, the key to understanding the global transformations of our times.

From this standpoint, depeasantization is not synonymous with proletarianization, nor are peasantization and depeasantization mutually exclusive phenomena. My analysis of postwar agrarian reform instead demonstrates that peasantization under national developmentalism was the precondition of global depeasantization under postcolonial neoliberal globalism. Thus global depeasantization is not a completed or self-completing process leading to the death of the peasantry. Social classes do not simply end or die; they live and are transformed through social struggles. The era of long national developmentalism has important lessons for the peasant question of our times: it shows that global social movements have successfully imposed severe limitations[13] on unbounded capital accumulation. In so doing, global social movements forced into retreat the agrarian programme of colonial–liberal globalism for six decades. Moreover, although postcolonial neoliberal globalism is a desocializing project, this is its Achilles heel: the peasant question of our times is being answered by global social movements, which, through a variety of social demands and clashes, is emerging and coalescing as a 'movement of movements', and in so doing constitutes an epochal and world-historical counter-enclosure struggle (Borras, Edelman and Kay 2008). It is the outcome of this struggle that will resolve not only the peasant question, but indeed all our questions.

Notes

1 I am grateful for the helpful comments of Haroon Akram-Lodhi and Cristóbal Kay. I also wish to thank Srabana Gupta for her helpful suggestions.
2 Prebisch drew heavily on the experience of Eastern Europe (Love 1980); his work heavily influenced W.W. Rostow, who reinvented the development compromise as the 'nationalization of take-off' (1963) and as a stage of development (Rostow 1971). In the 1980s the crisis of the development compromise was central to the crisis of the UN.
3 This point will also be made, albeit somewhat differently, by Miguel Teubal in Chapter 6.
4 As espoused, for example, by Narodnik economists such as Nikolai Danielson and Vasily Vorontsov (Perelman 2000).
5 As Kingston-Mann (1983: 102) argued, 'from the Menshevik point of view, the egalitarian demands of revolutionary peasants ... were hopelessly at odds with the capitalist requirements of economic development'.
6 A very select listing of those that might be included here could include Wolpe (1972); Rey (1975); Banaji (1977, 1990); de Janvry and Garramon (1977); Meillassoux (1981); de Janvry (1981); and Mann (1990). Preobrazhensky (1965, first published 1926) could be said to have been the earliest proponent of what might, in this regard, be called a 'functional dualism' thesis, although he envisaged one planned by the state in the service of 'socialist' – for which read 'industrial' – transition. For a critical review see McMichael and Buttel (1990); Araghi (1995); and Bryceson *et al.* (2000).
7 Two tendencies can be observed within what might be called 'post-Chayanovian' analysis. The first is the more abstract and determinist tendency, whose essentialist interpretation of Chayanov promotes a *sui generis* conception of national peasantries. Examples include Vergopoulos (1978); Taussig (1978); Reinhardt (1988); Glavanis and Glavanis (1990); and Attwood (1992). The second are those more historical Chayanovian accounts, some of which blend Chayanov and Marx (Lehmann 1986), and which include Friedmann (1978); Harriss (1982); Thorner (1987); Shanin (1990); and Llambi (2000). For a critical discussion of these see Kitching (1989) and Araghi (1995).
8 See, for example, Richards (1982) on Egypt; Rahman (1986) on Bangladesh; Patnaik (1987, 1990) on India; and Mamdani (1987) on Uganda. The Editors of this book have, from their earliest work, consistently adopted this approach (Kay 1974; Akram-Lodhi 1993).
9 There have been a number of recent studies of the impact of globalization on the peasantry – indeed, this book could be seen in that vein. In this light, I think it is important to distinguish the arguments in this chapter both from the generalist macronarratives that deduce the end of the peasantry from the logic of globalization, exemplified by Elson (1997), and from the particularist micronarratives that critique modernist essentialism but, somewhat ironically, then invent and attribute a new essence to a postpeasant 'transnational person'. Kearney (1996) exemplifies the latter. For a critique of Kearney's work in particular see, in addition to Michael J. Watts (Chapter 11 in this volume), Edelman (1998); Djürfeldt (1999); Otero (2000); Brass (2000); and Owen (2005).
10 For an exception see McMichael's concept of the 'corporate food regime'. In the absence of explicit value analysis, the food regime approach risks losing theoretical coherence as supposedly 'new' food regimes are 'discovered' and phenomenally specified from various points of departure. Conversely, the use of global value relations within food regime analysis makes it possible to specify the historically unique character of a food regime within overarching processes of historical continuity.

11 This perspective is, in my view, witnessed in the work of several contributors to this volume – including, notably, that of the Editors.

12 '[M]odern day slavery around the world is ongoing and systematic, including within the United States. In Florida, significant numbers of workers are in slavery and/or forced labour at any given moment within the agriculture industry. Indeed, in the last decade there have been six successful federal government criminal prosecutions in Florida for forced labour and slavery resulting in up to 15 year prison terms and the freeing over 1000 workers ... Forced labour and slavery are driven by the economic and legal context in which farm workers find themselves. These violations are enabled by 1) discriminatory and inadequate labour laws; 2) failure to ensure basic economic and social rights; and 3) economic structures enabling slavery through concentrated buying power, which has driven down wages and fueled inhumane working conditions ... Farm workers are among the poorest labourers in the United States economy ... Undocumented workers earn less than half (that of farm workers with legal status)' (NESRI 2005; cf. Maxwell 2002; Albisa 2007).

13 Haroon Akram-Lodhi (2007) develops De Angelis's (2004) concept of 'counter-enclosure' in a similar sense. National developmentalism and the postwar food regime were, in this sense, world-historical forms of counter-enclosure.

References

Acheson, D. (1951) 'Conference on world land tenure problems', *Department of State Bulletin*, 25 (643): 660–664.

—— (1952) 'Statement by Secretary Acheson before FAO meeting at Rome', *Department of State Bulletin*, 26 (659): 200–202.

Akram-Lodhi, A.H. (1993) 'Agrarian classes in Pakistan: an empirical test of Patnaik's labour-exploitation criterion', *Journal of Peasant Studies*, 20 (4): 557–589.

—— (2005) 'Neoconservative economic policy, governance and alternative budgets', in A.H. Akram-Lodhi, R. Chernomas and A. Sepehri (eds), *Globalization, Neoconservative Policies and Democratic Alternatives*, Winnipeg: Arbeiter Ring Publishing.

—— (2006) 'What's in a name? Neo-conservative ideology, neoliberalism and globalisation', in R. Robison (ed.), *The Neoliberal Revolution: Forging the Market State*, London: Palgrave.

—— (2007) 'Land, markets and neoliberal enclosure: an agrarian political economy perspective', *Third World Quarterly*, 28 (8): 1437–1456.

Albisa, C. (2007) 'What does Burger King have to do with modern day slavery in U.S. agriculture?', New York: Drum Major Institute for Public Policy, online: www.dmiblog.com/archives/2007/12/what_does_burger_king_have_to_1.html

Araghi, F. (1991) *Depeasantization*, Working Paper No. 1, Binghamton, NY: Fernand Braudel Center, Binghamton University.

—— (1995) 'Global depeasantization, 1945–1990', *Sociological Quarterly*, 36 (2): 337–368.

—— (2000) 'The great global enclosure of our times: peasants and the agrarian question at the end of the twentieth century', in F. Magdoff, F.H. Buttel and J. Bellamy Foster (eds), *Hungry for Profit: The Agribusiness Threat to Farmers, Food, and the Environment*, New York: Monthly Review Press.

—— (2003) 'Food regimes and the production of value: some methodological issues', *Journal of Peasant Studies*, 30 (2): 41–70.

—— (2007) 'Food regimes in *longue durée*', paper delivered at the Joint Annual Meetings of the Agriculture, Food and Human Values Society and the Association for the Study of Food and Society, University of Victoria, Victoria, BC, 30 May–3 June.

Araghi, F. and P. McMichael (2006) 'Trayendo lo histórico mundial de regreso: crítica del retroceso postmoderno en los estudios agrarios', *Revista ALASRU: Asociación Latinoamericana de Sociología Rural*, 3 (September): 2–38.

Araghi, F., M. Frezzo and M. Karides (2008) 'Fracturing the consensus: popular unrest and the decline of neoliberalism', in J. Misra and A. Lao-Montes (eds), *Contested Futures: The World-System in Crisis*, Boulder, CO: Paradigm Publishers.

Armstrong, P., A. Glyn and J. Harrison (1991) *Capitalism since 1945*, Oxford: Basil Blackwell.

Attwood, D.W. (1992) *Raising Cane: The Political Economy of Sugar in Western India*, Boulder, CO, USA: Westview Press.

Banaji, J. (1977) 'Modes of production in a materialist conception of history', *Capital & Class*, 1: 1–44.

—— (1990) 'Illusions about the peasantry: Karl Kautsky and the agrarian question', *Journal of Peasant Studies*, 17 (2): 288–307.

Barros Nock, M. (2000) 'The Mexican peasantry and the *ejido* in the neo-liberal period', in D.F. Bryceson, C. Kay and J.E. Mooij (eds), *Disappearing Peasantries? Rural Labour in Africa, Asia and Latin America*, London: Intermediate Technology Publications.

Benjamin, W. (2006) *Walter Benjamin: Selected Writings Volume 3, 1935–1938*, Cambridge, MA: Harvard University Press.

Borras Jr, S.M., M. Edelman and C. Kay (eds) (2008) *Transnational Agrarian Movements Confronting Globalization*, Oxford: Blackwell Publishing

Brannan, C.F. (1951) 'Preserving the family farm', *Family Farm Policy Review*, 11 June.

Brass, T. (1999) *Towards a Comparative Political Economy of Unfree Labour: Case Studies and Debates*, London: Frank Cass.

—— (2000) *Peasants, Populism and Postmodernism: The Return of the Agrarian Myth*, London: Frank Cass.

Bryceson, D.F., C. Kay and J.E. Mooij (eds) (2000) *Disappearing Peasantries? Rural Labour in Africa, Asia and Latin America*, London: Intermediate Technology Publications.

Burawoy, M. (2000) *Global Ethnography: Forces, Connections, and Imaginations in a Postmodern World*, Berkeley, CA, USA: University of California Press.

Byres, T.J. (1991) 'The agrarian question and differing forms of capitalist agrarian transitions: an essay in reference to Asia', in J. Breman and M. Sudipto (eds), *Rural Transformation in Asia*, Delhi: Oxford University Press.

—— (1996) *Capitalism From Above and Capitalism From Below: An Essay in Comparative Political Economy*, New York: Macmillan.

Cernea, M. (1996) 'Bridging the research divide: studying development oustees', in T. Allen (ed.), *In Search of Cool Ground: War, Flight and Homecoming in Northeast Africa*, London: UN Research Institute for Social Development.

Chan, K.W. (1988) 'Rural–urban migration in China, 1950–1982: estimates and analysis', *Urban Geography*, 9 (1): 53–84.

Chayanov, A.V. (1986) *The Theory of Peasant Economy*, Madison, WI: University of Wisconsin Press.

Chen, C. (1961) *Land Reform in Taiwan*, Taipei: China Publishing Company.

Choudry, A. (2006) 'Bilateral free trade and investment agreements and the US corporate biotech agenda', online: http://www.bilaterals.org/article.php3?id_article=4861

Cleaver, H. (1977) 'Food, famine and the international crisis', *Zerowork*, 2: 1–47.

Collins, J.L. (2003) *Threads: Gender, Labor, and Power in the Global Apparel Industry*, Chicago, IL, USA: University of Chicago Press.

Davis, M. (2001) *Late Victorian Holocausts: El Niño Famines and the Making of the Third World*, London: Verso.

Davis, M. (2006) *Planet of Slums*, New York: Verso.

De Angelis, M. (2004) 'Separating the doing and the deed: capital and the continuous character of enclosures', *Historical Materialism*, 12 (2): 57–87.

Dethier, J.J. and K. Funk (1978) 'The language of food: PL 480 in Egypt', *Middle East Report*, 145: 22–28.

Dickens, C. (1986) *A December Vision*, New York: HarperCollins (First published in 1850).

Dixon, J. (2007) 'From the imperial to the empty calorie, onto the anti-oxidant and beyond: can the nutrition crisis shed light on a third food regime?', paper delivered at the Joint Annual Meetings of the Agriculture, Food and Human Values Society and the Association for the Study of Food and Society, University of Victoria, Victoria, BC, 30 May–3 June.

Djürfeldt, G. (1999) 'Essentially non-peasant? Some critical comments on post-modernist discourse on the peasantry', *Sociologia Ruralis*, 39 (2): 207–208.

Dowie, M. (2001) *American Foundations: An Investigative History*, Cambridge: MIT Press.

Edelman, M. (1980) 'Agricultural modernization in small-holding areas of Mexico: a case study in the Sierra Norte de Puebla', *Latin American Perspectives*, 27 (4): 29–49.

—— (1998) 'Transnational peasant politics in Central America', *Latin American Research Review*, 33 (3): 49–87.

Elson, R. (1977) *The End of the Peasantry in Southeast Asia: A Social and Economic History of Peasant Livelihoods, 1800–1900s*, New York: St Martin's Press.

Engels, F. (1977) *The Peasant Question in France and Germany*, in K. Marx and F. Engels, *Selected Works, Vol. 3*, Moscow: Progress Publishers (first published in 1894).

Engels, F. (2000) *The Peasant War in Germany*, New York: International Publishers (first published in 1850).

EWG (2007) 'What's the plan? U.S. farm subsidies, 1995 through 2003'. Environmental Working Group, online: http://farm.ewg.org/farm/whatstheplan.php

Fanjul, G. and A. Fraser (2003) 'Dumping without borders: how US agricultural policies are destroying the livelihoods of Mexican corn farmers', Oxfam America, online: www.oxfamamerica.org/newsandpublications/publications/briefing_papers/art5912.html

Ferguson, J. (1999) *Expectations of Modernity: Myths and Meanings of Urban Life on the Zambian Copper Belt*, Berkeley, CA, USA: University of California Press.

Freeman, O.L. (1964) 'Improving the effectiveness of U.S. assistance to international rural development', *Department of State Bulletin*, 14 September: 376–388.

Friedmann, H. (1978) 'World market, state, and family farm: social bases of household production in the era of wage labor', *Comparative Studies in Society and History* 20 (4): 545–586.

—— (1982) 'The political economy of food: the rise and fall of the post war international food order', *American Journal of Sociology*, 88: 248–286.

—— (2005) 'From colonialism to green capitalism: social movements and the emergence of food regimes', in F.H. Buttel and P. McMichael (eds), *New Directions in the Sociology of Global Development: Research in Rural Sociology and Development, Vol. 11*, Oxford: Elsevier.

—— (2006) 'Focusing on agriculture: a comment on Henry Bernstein's "Is there an agrarian question in the 21st century?"', *Canadian Journal of Development Studies*, 27 (4): 461–464.

Friedmann, H. and P. McMichael (1989) 'Agriculture and the state system: the rise and fall of national agriculture, 1870 to the present', *Sociologia Ruralis*, 29 (2): 93–117.

George, S. and F. Sabelli. (1994) *Faith and Credit: The World Bank's Secular Empire*, Boulder, CO, USA: Westview Press.

Ginsborg, P. (1984) 'The communist party and the agrarian question in southern Italy, 1943–48', *History Workshop Journal*, 17: 81–101.

Glavanis, K. and P. Glavanis (eds) (1990) *The Rural Middle East: Peasant Lives and Modes of Production*, London: Zed Books.

Gramsci, A. (1971) *Selections from Prison Notebooks*, London: Lawrence and Wishart.

Green, D. and M. Griffith (2002) 'Dumping on the poor: the Common Agricultural Policy, the WTO and International Development', London: Catholic Agency for Overseas Development, online: www.eldis.org/go/topics/resource-guides/trade-policy/agriculture&id = 19957&type = Document

Guang, L. (2001) 'Reconstituting the rural–urban divide: peasant migration and the rise of "orderly migration" in contemporary China', *Journal of Contemporary China*, 10 (28): 471–493.

Harris, J. and M. Todaro (1970) 'Migration, unemployment and development: a two-sector analysis', *American Economic Review*, 60 (1): 126–142.

Harriss, J. (1982) *Rural Development: Theories of Peasant Economy and Agrarian Change*, London: Hutchinson.

Harvey, D. (1997) 'Contested cities: social process and spatial form', in N. Jewson and S. MacGregor (eds), *Transforming Cities: Contested Governance and New Spatial Divisions*, New York: Routledge.

—— (2006) *Spaces of Global Capitalism*, New York: Verso.

Hope, C.R. (1951) 'The U.S. concept of agrarian reform as a foundation for world peace', *Department of State Bulletin*, 25 (651): 988–1000.

Hopkins, R. (1984) 'The evolution of food aid', *Food Policy*, 9 (4): 345–363.

Hopkins, T.K. (1978) 'World-system analysis: methodological issues', in B.H. Kaplan (ed.), *Social Change in the Capitalist World-Economy*, Beverly Hills, CA: Sage.

—— (1979) 'The study of the capitalist world-economy: some introductory considerations', in W.L. Goldfrank (ed.), *The World-System of Capitalism: Past and Present*, Beverly Hills, CA: Sage.

de Janvry, A. (1981) *The Agrarian Question and Reformism in Latin America*, Baltimore, MD: Johns Hopkins University Press.

de Janvry, A. and C. Garramon (1977) 'The dynamics of rural poverty in Latin America: an interpretation', *Journal of Peasant Studies*, 4 (3): 206–216.

de Janvry, A., E. Sadoulet and L.W. Young (1989) 'Land and labour in Latin American agriculture from the 1950s', *Journal of Peasant Studies*, 16 (3): 369–424.

Katzmann, M.T. (1978) 'Colonization as an approach to regional development: northern Parana, Brazil', *Economic Development and Cultural Change*, 26 (4): 797–724.

Kautsky, K. (1988) *The Agrarian Question*, London: Zwan Publications (first published in 1899).

Kay, C. (1974) 'Comparative development of the European manorial system and the Latin American hacienda system', *Journal of Peasant Studies*, 2 (1): 69–98.

Kearney, M. (1996) *Reconceptualizing the Peasantry: Anthropology in Global Perspective*, Boulder, CO, USA: Westview Press.

Kennedy, J.F. (1961) 'Address at a dinner at the San Carlos Palace in Bogota', The American Presidency Project, online: www.presidency.ucsb.edu/ws/index.php?pid = 8495

Kingston-Mann, E. (1983) *Lenin and the Problem of Marxist Peasant Revolution*, New York: Oxford University Press.

Kitching, G. (1989) *Development and Underdevelopment in Historical Perspective*, New York: Routledge.

Kulikowski, M. (2007) 'Mayday 23: World Population Becomes More Urban Than Rural', North Carolina State University Newsroom, online: http://news.ncsu.edu/releases/2007/may/104.html

Lefebvre, H. (1979) 'Space: social product and use value', in J.W. Freiberg (ed.), *Critical Sociology: European Perspectives*, New York: Irvington.

—— (1991) *The Production of Space*, Cambridge, MA: Blackwell.

Lehmann, D. (1982) 'Peasantisation and proletarianisation in Brazil and Mexico', in S. Jones *et al.* (eds), *Rural Poverty and Agrarian Reform*, New Delhi: Allied Publishers.

—— (1986) 'Two paths of agrarian capitalism, or a critique of Chayanovian Marxism', *Comparative Studies in Society and History*, 28 (5): 601–627.

Lenin, V.I. (1960) *The Development if Capitalism in Russia: The Process of the Formation of a Home Market for Large-Scale Industry*, Moscow: Foreign Languages Publishing House (first published in 1899).

—— (1971a) 'The workers' party and the peasantry', in *Alliance of the Working Class and the Peasantry*, Moscow: Progress Publishers (first published in 1901).

—— (1971b) 'Report on the resolution of the support of the peasant movement', in *Alliance of the Working Class and the Peasantry*, Moscow: Progress Publishers (first published in 1905).

Levin, N.G. (1968) *Woodrow Wilson and World Politics: America's Response to War and Revolution*, New York: Oxford University Press.

Lipton, M. (1974) *Why Poor People Stay Poor: A Study of Urban Bias in World Development*, London: Temple Smith.

Llambi, L. (1989) 'Emergence of capitalized family farms in Latin America', *Comparative Studies in Society and History*, 31 (4): 745–774.

—— (2000) 'Global–local links in Latin America's new ruralities', in D.F. Bryceson, C. Kay and J.E. Mooij (eds), *Disappearing Peasantries? Rural Labour in Africa, Asia and Latin America*, London: Intermediate Technology Publications.

Love, J. (1980) 'Raul Prebisch and the origins of the doctrine of unequal exchange', *Latin American Research Review*, 15 (3): 45–72.

Löwy, M. and R. Sayre. (2001) *Romanticism Against the Tide of Modernity*, Durham, NC: Duke University Press.

Lubin, I. (1951) 'Land reform problem challenges free world', *Department of State Bulletin*, 25 (638): 467–474.

Mallory, L.D. (1960) 'The land problem in the Americas', *Department of State Bulletin*, 28 November: 815–822.

Mamdani, M. (1987) 'Extreme but not exceptional: towards an analysis of the agrarian question in Uganda', *Journal of Peasant Studies*, 14 (2): 191–225.

Manfredi, E.M. (1978) *World Economic Conditions in Relation to Agricultural Trade*, Washington, DC: US Department of Agriculture.

Mann, S. (1990) *Agrarian Capitalism in Theory and Practice*, Chapel Hill, NC: University of North Carolina Press.

Marx, K. (1970) *A Contribution to the Critique of Political Economy*, Moscow: Progress Publishers (first published in 1859).

—— (1973) *Grundrisse: Foundations of a Critique of Political Economy*, New York: Vintage Books (first published in 1939–41).

Massey, D.B. (1993) 'Power-geometry and a progressive sense of place', in J. Bird (ed.), *Mapping the Futures: Local Cultures, Global Change*, London: Routledge.

—— (1995) *Spatial Divisions of Labor: Social Structures and the Geography of Production*, New York: Routledge.

Maxwell, B. (2002) 'Slavery alive in Florida agriculture industry', *St Petersburg Times*, 3 July.

McDowell, C. (1996) *Understanding Impoverishment: The Consequences of Development-Induced Displacement*, Providence, RI: Berghahn Books.

McMichael, P. (ed.) (1994) *The Global Restructuring of Agro-Food Systems,* Ithaca, NY: Cornell University Press.

—— (ed.) (1995) *Food and Agrarian Orders in the World-Economy*, Westport, CT: Greenwood Press.

—— (2005) 'Global development and the corporate food regime', in F.H. Buttel and P. McMichael (eds), *New Directions in the Sociology of Global Development: Research in Rural Sociology and Development, Vol. 11*, Oxford: Elsevier.

—— (2008) *Development and Social Change: A Global Perspective* (4th edn), Thousand Oaks, CA: Pine Forge Press.

McMichael, P. and F. Buttel (1990) 'New directions in the political economy of agriculture', *Sociological Perspectives*, 33 (1): 89–109.

Meillassoux, C. (1981) *Maidens, Meal and Money: Capitalism and the Domestic Community*, Cambridge: Cambridge University Press.

Mintz, S. W. (1985) *Sweetness and Power: The Place of Sugar in Modern History*, New York: Viking.

Morrow, R.B. and K.H. Sherper (1970) 'Land reform in South Korea', US Department of State, *Spring Review of Land Reform*, 3: 1–6.

NESRI (2005) 'Modern day slavery in U.S. agriculture: legal failure and corporate complicity', Corporate Accountability Issue Brief, New York: National Economic and Social Rights Initiative, online: www.nesri.org/fact_sheets_pubs/index.html

O'Connor, J. (1984) *Accumulation Crisis*, New York: Basil Blackwell.

Ogura, T. (1968) 'The economic impact of postwar land reform in Japan', *Land Reform, Land Settlement and Cooperatives*, 2: 14–43.

Otero, G. (2000) 'Neoliberal reform in rural Mexico: social structural and political dimensions', *Latin American Research Review*, 35 (1): 187–207.

Owen, J.R. (2005) 'In defense of the "peasant"', *Journal of Contemporary Asia*, 35 (3): 368–385.

Patnaik, U. (1987) *Peasant Class Differentiation: A Study in Method with Reference to Haryana*, Delhi: Oxford University Press.

—— (1990) *Agrarian Relations and Accumulation: The 'Mode of Production' Debate in India*, Bombay: Oxford University Press.

Perelman, M. (2000) *The Invention Of Capitalism: Classical Political Economy and the Secret History of Primitive Accumulation*, Durham, NC, USA: Duke University Press.

Plekhanov, G.V. (1961) 'Our differences', in *Selected Philosophical Works, Vol. 1*, London: Lawrence and Wishart (first published in 1885).

Polanyi, K. (2001) *The Great Transformation: The Political and Economic Origins of Our Time*, Boston, MA: Beacon Press.

Population Reference Bureau (2007) 'World population highlights: key findings from PRB's 2007 world population data sheet', *Population Bulletin*, 62 (3): 1–12.

Prebisch, R. (1950) *The Economic Development of Latin America and the Principal Problems*, New York: UN Economic Commission for Latin America.

Preobrazhensky, E. (1965) *The New Economics*, Clarendon: Oxford (first published in 1926).

Pritchard, B. (2008) 'Food regimes', in R. Kitchin and N. Thrift (eds), *International Encyclopedia of Human Geography*, London: Elsevier.

Rahman, A. (1986) *Peasants and Classes: A Study in Differentiation in Bangladesh*, Atlantic Highlands, NJ, USA: Zed Books.

Rey, P.P. (1975) 'The lineage mode of production', *Critique of Anthropology* 3: 17–79.

Reinhardt, N. (1988) *Our Daily Bread: The Peasant Question and Family Farming in the Colombian Andes*, Berkeley, CA, USA: University of California Press.

Richards, A. (1982) *Egypt's Agricultural Development*, Boulder, CO: Westview Press.

Rifkin, J. (1992) *Beyond Beef: The Rise and Fall of the Cattle Culture*, New York: Dutton.

Ritchie, M. (1993) 'Breaking the deadlock: the United States and agriculture policy in the Uruguay Round', online: www.iatp.org/iatp/publications.cfm?accountID = 258&refID = 29768

Rosenfeld, S.S. (1974) 'The politics of food', *Foreign Policy*, 14: 17–29.

Ross, E.B. (1998) *The Malthus Factor: Population, Poverty, and Politics in Capitalist Development*, London: Zed Books.

Rostow, W.W. (1963) 'The nationalization of takeoff', *Department of State Bulletin*, 27 May: 824–829.

—— (1971) *The Stages of Economic Growth: A Non-Communist Manifesto*, Cambridge: Cambridge University Press.

Sainath, P. (2007a) 'Nearly 1.5 lakh farm suicides from 1997 to 2005', *The Hindu*, 12 November, online: www.thehindu.com/2007/11/12/stories/2007111257790100.htm

Sainath, P. (2007b) 'Suicides rising, most intense in 4 states', *The Hindu*, 12 November, online: www.thehindu.com/2007/11/12/stories/2007111253911100.htm

Sassoon, A.S. (ed.) (1982) *Approaches to Gramsci*, London: Writers and Readers Publishing Cooperative.

Shanin, T. (ed.) (1990) *Defining Peasants*, Cambridge: Basil Blackwell.

Sharma, D. (2002) 'Famine as commerce', *India Together*, August 2002, online: www.indiatogether.org/agriculture/opinions/dsharma/faminecommerce.htm

—— (2007) 'Displacing farmers: India will have 400 million agricultural refugees', Share The World's Resources, online: www.stwr.net/content/view/1999/37/

Shenon, P. (1995) 'Good earth is squandered: who'll feed China?' *The New York Times*, 21 September.

Srinivasan, T.N. (1989) 'Food aid: a cause of development failure or an instrument for success?', *World Bank Economic Review*, 38 (1): 39–65.

Stoler, A.L. (2001) 'Tense and tender ties: the politics of comparison in North American history and (post) colonial studies', *Journal of American History*, 88 (3): 829–865.

Tarrow, S. (1967) *Peasant Communism in Southern Italy*, New Haven, CT: Yale University Press.

Taussig, M. (1978) 'Peasant economics and the development of capitalist agriculture in the Cauca Valley, Colombia', *Latin American Perspectives*, 5 (3): 62–91.

Thorner, D. (1987) 'Peasant economy as a category in history', in T. Shanin (ed.), *Peasants and Peasant Societies* (2nd edn), New York: Basil Blackwell.

Tomich, D.W. (1990) *Slavery in the Circuit of Sugar: Martinique and the World Economy, 1830–1848*, Baltimore, MD: Johns Hopkins University Press.

—— (2004) *Through The Prism of Slavery: Labor, Capital, and World Economy*, Lanham, MD, USA: Rowman and Littlefield.

Tubiana, L. (1989) 'World trade in agricultural products: from global regulation to market fragmentation', in D. Goodman and M. Redclift (eds), *The International Farm Crisis*, London: Macmillan.

United Nations (1980) *Patterns of Urban and Rural Growth*, Population Studies No. 68, New York: United Nations.

—— (2006) *The Challenge of Slums: Global Report on Human Settlements 2003*, New York: Earthscan Publications.

UN Economic Commission for Latin America (1988) *Statistical Yearbook for Latin America*, New York: United Nations.

Van Hear, N. (1998) *New Diasporas: The Mass Exodus, Dispersal and Regrouping of Migrant Communities*, Seattle, WA: University of Washington Press.

Vergopoulos, K. (1978) 'Capitalism and peasant productivity', *Journal of Peasant Studies*, 5 (4): 446–465.

Walicki, A. (1989) *The Controversy over Capitalism: Studies in the Social Philosophy of the Russian Populists*, Notre Dame, IN, USA: University of Notre Dame Press.

Wallerstein, M.B. (1980) *Food For War–Food For Peace: United States Food Aid in a Global Context*, Cambridge, MA, USA: MIT Press.

Warman, A. (1988) 'The rural world and peasant studies', *International Social Science Journal*, 40 (4): 499–504.

Watkins, K. (1991) 'Agriculture and food security in the GATT Uruguay Round', *Review of African Political Economy*, 18: 38–50.

Wolpe, H. (1972) 'Capitalism and cheap labor-power in South Africa: from segregation to apartheid', *Economy and Society*, 1 (4): 425–456.

World Bank (1984) *World Development Report 1985*, Oxford: Oxford University Press.

—— (2007) *World Development Report 2008: Agriculture for Development*, Oxford: Oxford University Press.

World Bank Environment Department (1994) *Resettlement and Development: The Bankwide Review of Projects Involving Involuntary Resettlement, 1986–1993*, Washington, DC: The World Bank.

Wu, H.X. (1994) 'Rural to urban migration in the People's Republic of China', *China Quarterly*, 139: 669–698.

Yardley, J. (2004) 'In a tidal wave, China's masses pour from farm to city', *The New York Times*, 12 September.

6 Peasant struggles for land and agrarian reform in Latin America

Miguel Teubal

Preliminary observations[1]

The twentieth century was the century of peasant struggles for land and agrarian reform throughout Latin America, struggles that formed part of a set of important socioeconomic and political transformations. According to Cristóbal Kay, with the spread of neoliberalism across the region in the 1990s,

> the era of agrarian reforms seems to have come to a close ... This does not necessarily mean that the land question has been solved in Latin America, but that it no longer commands the political support that it did during the 1960s and 1970s, when cold war concerns arising from the Cuban revolution and an emergent peasant movement put agrarian reform firmly on the political agenda.
>
> (Kay 2000)

It is my contention in this chapter that despite the impact of neoliberalism, land questions continue to be important throughout Latin America, and indeed that they probably now have greater political significance than previously. The struggle for land is reflected in conflicts between proprietors and their employees, peasants and landlords, and different indigenous and peasant communities and social movements, on the one hand; and new investors and large companies that see the possibility of ejecting them from the land, on the other. Land has thus acquired new diverse meanings and significance, due precisely to the emergence of new agrarian movements of peasants, landless labourers and indigenous movements that are manifest throughout the continent. As Giarracca has put it, making reference to the case of Argentina in the 1990s,

> [t]he struggle for land was a claim made throughout the decade. In this heterogenous agrarian Argentina land has different meanings for different social actors. Land is an essential aspect of the world view of the *mapuche* or *kolla* indigenous population. For example, the *mapuche* or

kolla feel that they belong to the land. They seek basically historical reparation through laws that would permit them to recuperate the lands that belonged to their ancestors. For the peasant movements, for example, for the MOCASE (the *Movimiento Campesino de Santiago del Estero*) land is one of their main instruments of labour and they struggle to have (or maintain) access to it. In the meantime, for the *Mujeres Agropecuarias en Lucha*, that inherited the land from their fathers or grandfathers, on the whole European settlers, land forms part of their family heritage, and they struggle to not lose it. We can add to these multiple meanings that for the landowner land is simply a commodity, similar to any other commodity.

(Giarracca 2003: 204)

The agrarian question, including questions concerning the survival of the peasantry, is alive and well, although it assumes different characteristics from that which was the case for most of the twentieth century. This probably is so because it has become closely associated with important agrarian and social movements, as well as with environmental and alternative globalization movements. These agrarian social movements operate with greater force and autonomy than previously. In the following pages I intend to establish the basis for this argument. I compare aspects of the agrarian reforms of much of the twentieth century with trends that began to manifest themselves in the latter part of that century and the beginning of the new millennium.

In the new millennium, sociopolitical changes have begun to influence the agrarian and peasant questions in Latin America. New, important peasant movements have emerged, such as the *Ejército Zapatista de la Liberación Nacional* (Zapatista Army of National Liberation, EZLN) in Mexico, the *O Movimento dos Trabalhadores Rurais Sem-Terra* (Landless Rural Workers' Movement, MST) in Brazil, the *Confederación de Naciones Indígenas del Ecuador* (National Confederation of Indigenous Nations, CONAIE) in Ecuador, and other important movements around the continent. These movements approach land issues as essential aspects of the sociopolitical problems currently found in their societies. In this context, agrarian and peasant struggles that have emerged are not corporate struggles for control of the agricultural sector, but have more to do with broad world views or visions related to the overall problematic of society in general and rural world views in particular. For this reason, they tend to converge with the alternative globalization movements. Among other factors, they are against the spread of an industrial agriculture (Vallianatos 2001, 2003) led by large transnational agro-industrial corporations, that is, agribusiness.

At present, the struggle for land is not just a struggle of those that do not have access to it, but is part of the widespread struggle of the excluded, marginalized and unemployed, both urban and rural. More than a struggle for the conquest of state power and the application of top-down policies on the basis of occupying a place in the state, in general these movements emerge from below, and are oriented towards the transformation of society from below. Thus these struggles, as Anita Brumer and José Vicente dos Santos (1997) point out, are part of a struggle for citizenship, part of a worldwide democratic struggle for the fully fledged rights of citizenship.

Another difference from movements of the twentieth century is that these are not only movements that struggle against a traditional landowning oligarchy. In the present sociopolitical world context, the nature of dominant classes has changed substantially. In this new phase of the development of world capitalism, in which globalized dominant classes have emerged that are not necessarily landowners, the struggle for land has acquired other characteristics. The struggle is against a new agrarian or agro-industrial model which is hegemonic on a world scale and is led by large transnational corporations operating in the agricultural sector, or what is popularly known as agribusiness.

In this chapter I point out the new meanings that the struggle for land acquires for agrarian social movements in the context of a new globalized world. A new agrarianism, a new comunitarianism, appears be part of the debate, and of the present struggles for land. It is not a question of looking back, as Griffin *et al.* (2002: 280) point out when they argue that 'communal farming systems ... could in principle contribute to equity, efficiency, agricultural growth and a reduction in rural poverty, but their time has passed'. Rather, there is a need to develop a new perspective: new meanings for land and community that converge with the environmental, feminist and alternative globalization movements, but which are sustained mainly in the indigenous and peasant communities that have become some of the most exploited parts of humanity.

Land in Latin America: some historical precedents

Latin America was the continent of agrarian reform *par excellence*. This was, in part, due to the fact that the American continent was, as Amiya Bagchi notes in Chapter 4, a vast region of colonial rule and colonization. Five centuries of colonization and colonial domination, mostly by the Spanish and Portuguese, but assisted by the British, French and Dutch, caused havoc in pre-existing indigenous societies, whose institutions, productive relations and cultures were disarticulated, and their very existence put into question. The occupation and appropriation of land by the *conquistadores* subduing and exploiting the indigenous population, while at the same time massively enslaving the African labour that was taken to the Americas, had an enormous influence on succeeding developments. Throughout Latin America, the *latifundio* – or *latifundio–minifundio* complex – was established as part of colonial rule, and thereafter was consolidated with formal independence in the nineteenth century and, in particular, with the liberal reforms of the mid- and late-nineteenth and early twentieth centuries. The struggles for agrarian reform in the twentieth century were, in essence, struggles against agrarian regimes that had massively excluded indigenous and peasant populations in previous periods.

Liberal constitutions and reforms were created throughout the continent, and these documents had a major impact on the agrarian structure. The Mexican Constitution of 1857, the so-called *Lei de Terras* of the imperial Portuguese State of Brazil established in 1850, and the Argentine Constitution of 1853 were all documents that established the legal basis of private property regimes that contributed both to the rise of a class of large landowners and to the exclusion of peasants and indigenous communities – a point similar to that made by Farshad Araghi in Chapter 5. In El Salvador the *Ley de Extinción de Ejidos y Comunidades Indígenas* (Law of Extinction of *Ejidos* and Indigenous Communities) of 1882 made this quite explicit. Similar laws or measures were adopted by liberal regimes in Venezuela – the Law of 1904 – while in Bolivia throughout the nineteenth century peasant communities declined systematically due to a series of measures adopted by succeeding governments, most notably a decree of the Constitutional Assembly that both declared that indigenous land was the property of the state, and ordered its sale through public auction. Finally, Mexican reform laws and the Constitution of 1857 were directed initially against church property that was transferred to private landowners. However, the same occurred with indigenous communities, whose communal landholdings were declared illegal, with the result that communities were obliged to divide their land into individual holdings. As a result, the indigenous population lost most of its land as it fell into the hands of the *haciendas* and the companies that negotiated for control of these lands. It has been calculated that cumulatively more then 810,000 hectares of communal land was transferred to large landowners during the reign of Porfirio Diaz (Wolf 1973: 34). While the US agrarian model of small family farmers was usually indicated to be the ideal agrarian regime to be followed by many Latin American countries, the truth of the matter is that large-scale *latifundist* regimes prevailed in most of Latin America.

An important change in agrarian regimes came about towards the end of the nineteenth century when, under the guise of global liberalism, the integration of Latin American economies into the world economy was reshaped and new, so-called 'primary' or 'agro-export' sectors, developed. The *latifundista* system was consolidated through the fully fledged privatization of land throughout the continent, on the basis of just noted constitutional reforms, resulting in the widespread disarticulation or disintegration of peasant communities within the capitalist economy. As a consequence, multiple 'non-free' sets of social relations were established, including a system of debt peonage, a new agrarian regime that contributed to the consolidation of the *latifundio* despite the rhetoric of liberal reforms, and the establishment of constitutions in all the countries of the region. Large *haciendas* thus constituted the basis of the Latin American agrarian model by the late nineteenth century. In the case of Mexico, these large *haciendas* were sustained by indigenous populations subject to debt peonage, or indeed by the residents of the communities surrounding them, as the *hacienda* system tended to increase its importance as a source of living for these communities (Wolf 1973: 16).

It is not difficult to understand that these developments contributed to an intensification of the struggle for land and agrarian reform in many countries. Paradigmatic of this was the Mexican Revolution that appears

> above all as a violent eruption of the Mexican masses, outside the structure of state domination and against it, that disturbs, upsets and transforms from below all of the country's social relations during ten years of an intense revolutionary activity ... The revolution is presented as a *gigantic peasant war for land* [italics in the original] that by its own dynamic puts in question the power and structure of the State, controlled up to then by a power block in which the indisputable hegemony was held by the landowners.
>
> (Gilly 1979: 22)

The thrust of agrarian reforms in the twentieth century

The agrarian reforms of the twentieth century had three key characteristics. First, they were often part of a social and/or political movement struggling against the landowning oligarchic regime that controlled the state. The breadth and depth of these movements, however, varied enormously. Thus the more important agrarian reforms were the direct result of important revolutions that displaced a landowning oligarchy from power. For example, in the cases of Mexico, Nicaragua, Cuba and Bolivia, agrarian reform was part of an important political revolution that excluded from power a landowning oligarchy; in the case of Cuba the bourgeoisie was also excluded. More moderate reforms, predicated on a less broad social base, were carried out in the wake of the Alliance for Progress in Chile, Peru, Colombia and Ecuador. Some agrarian reforms were interrupted: that of Guatemala in 1954 and that of Brazil in 1964, in part because of the lack of ability on the part of the social movement struggling for reform to successfully confront the oligarchy, and, in the case of Guatemala, due to a military intervention driven by foreign interests. In Argentina, agrarian reform was totally absent.

Second, while the peasantry had an important part to play in some of these processes, they were not necessarily the main beneficiaries. While it is difficult to conceive of the struggle for land and agrarian reform in Latin America without considering the role of one of the main protagonists in these processes, the peasant movement, their interests did not always prevail, or did so in some cases after reform movements had been initiated. For example, the *comuneros* of Peru, who had initially been excluded from the agrarian reform, later managed to obtain access to land in the reformed sector. Similarly, in the Nicaraguan agrarian reform the Sandinistas initially privileged the constitution of large state farms, some of which were later transferred to cooperatives or peasant communities. Thus, in these cases, as well as in, say, Mexico and Bolivia, peasants managed to redirect reform movement in favour of their interests.

Third, despite the role of peasant movements struggling against oligarchic landowners in constructing the case for reform, very commonly agrarian reforms were instituted by the state on the basis of policies developed at the top which were then passed down the bureaucracy for implementation. Thus many Latin American governments implemented moderate agrarian reforms that were not really based on peasant movements or on the communities. The examples of Chile, Peru, Colombia and Ecuador come to mind. This was the case, for example, when the governments involved were too weak to be able to implement a substantial reform. It was also the case when the government was not intent on undertaking substantive reform, as they were implicitly promoting some sort of agrarian capitalism (Kay 1998).

One of the main paradigmatic agrarian reforms that emerged in the twentieth century was that of Mexico. It encapsulates each of the lessons: the role of a peasant movement struggling for reform, a state implementing a reform that is top-down, and consequentially the peasantry not being the main beneficiaries of land and agrarian reform. Thus, in this case

> the Revolution destroyed the old State based on landowners and an export bourgeoisie and that was sanctioned by the liberal Constitution of 1857. A new bourgeois State was created – the 1917 Constitution guaranteed private property – but eliminating its landowning classes, a unique case in all of Latin America until the Bolivian Revolution of 1952.
>
> (Aguilar Camín 1979: 17)

This would not have occurred but for the eruption of peasant struggles, carried out by Zapata in the south and Pancho Villa in the north, that time and again blocked the conciliatory proposals established by the Mexican state after the flight of Porfirio Díaz in 1911. Nevertheless, agrarian reform did not finally get under way until the Cárdenas years between 1934 and 1940. In this period, 18 million hectares were distributed to *ejidos* and communities, increasing the land available to this group to about 25 million hectares. While some large landholdings remained, it was during this period that the political and economic power base of the old landowning oligarchy was eliminated and the *ejidos* and communities became important components of Mexican agrarian structure. However, as Barkin (1994: 30) demonstrates,

> agricultural development over the half century following Cárdenas' reforms created a highly polarized rural society. Most *ejidatarios* were relegated to their traditional cultivation systems, producing maize and beans and a variety of other products for domestic consumption ...

Meanwhile a highly capitalized commercial agricultural sector emerged as a result of substantial public investments in irrigation, rural road networks, agricultural research, production of high-yielding varieties of seed, and new cropping systems.

Nonetheless, Barkin stresses the significance of the *ejido* and communitarian system:

> The stimulus of having their own land to work was sufficient, however, to encourage most farmers to dramatically improve their productive conditions. Contrary to what many experts predicted, these poor, unschooled peasants were able to increase the productivity of their lands at an average annual rate of more than 3 per cent following the redistribution of the 1930s, doubling their meager yields to more than 1.2 tons per hectare by 1960.
>
> (Barkin 1994: 30)

Further, the *ejido* system had lasting effects on Mexican society. Jessica Lewis, analysing certain changes occurring in the Mexican countryside in the 1980s and 1990s, and in particular reaction to the 1992 amendment to Article 27 of Mexico's Constitution, concludes that

> *ejidos* are deeply rooted in Mexican culture and rural identity. They serve as a continuing reminder to *campesinos* of the blood shed by their ancestors in the fight for equitable treatment. It is not surprising, then, that the legal and economic reforms of the 1990s and their impacts on *ejidos* are considered so significant in contemporary Mexican history, and thus will continue to be a topic of conflict and debate in Mexico for years to come.
>
> (Lewis 2002: 416)

The Mexican case demonstrates the contradictory character of land and agrarian reform as it was witnessed in much of Latin America in the twentieth century. Despite the struggles of peasants and indigenous communities for land and agrarian reform, that reform, when it occurred, was often imposed from the apex of the state and did not necessarily lead to a significant and sustained rise in the living standards of the intended beneficiaries, the peasantry and the indigenous communities. Nonetheless, peasants and indigenous communities attached great importance to the land they had obtained through reform, importance that was far broader than merely being a piece of soil to be used in production.

Agrarian reforms in the age of neoliberalism

In the 1970s, import substituting regimes of accumulation gave way to adjustment and then, in the 1980s, to structural adjustment throughout Latin

America, which formed part of the spread of the neoliberal policies given impulse by the International Monetary Fund and the World Bank. On the whole, these policies were applied in Latin America with probably much greater severity than in the advanced capitalist countries. Privatization, deregulation, an opening to the world economy, as well as the application of fiscal orthodoxy in budgetary policy, became central aspects of the policies of the 1980s and 1990s, introduced because of unmanageable amounts of foreign debt, and which gave primacy to the interests of finance capital.

In rural Latin America, in particular, new policies

> based on the privatization of the economy, on foreign investments and an opening to trade, together with reductions in subsidies and public expenditures in real terms, the withdrawal of the State in areas pertaining to the marketing and regulation of agricultural activities – were all measures tending to create the conditions that would contribute to transforming private national and foreign capital into the main agents for the reactivation of the (agricultural) sector.
>
> (Romero Polanco 1995: 69–70).

Thus policy changes in Latin America had important influences on agriculture, exerting effects on the institutional setting that had previously been established. In particular, new policies contributed to globalization processes that were shaped by the large agro-industrial transnational corporations that tended to proliferate throughout the continent, and which significantly influenced the development of Latin American agro-food systems (Teubal and Rodríguez 2002: 58). At the same time development programmes, including agrarian reform, were set aside, with the exception of the so-called market-led agrarian reforms promoted by the World Bank. These programmes were, in many cases, replaced by strategies designed to enhance agricultural exports, so as to facilitate the servicing of accumulated foreign debt (Huizer 1999: 1).

The end of systems of direct subsidies and of support prices for agricultural production resulted in an erosion of institutional structures that had presumably sustained small and medium-sized farm producers. Similarly, state-led credit systems were replaced by private sector-led credit systems, often in the form of microfinance, which became much more expensive and thus less accessible for many. There was a reduction of public resources for technical assistance in farming and for farm extension services, as well as cutbacks in funds for state scientific research and technologies associated with the agriculture sector. Throughout Latin America, many of the state organizations and institutions that had traditionally supported agriculture were either eliminated or privatized, resulting in large increases in farmer costs in the form of user fees, as well as cuts in investment. Finally, the aforementioned trade and tariff liberalization and the internationalization of economic processes and flows resulted in small and medium-sized farmers facing prices that were, as a consequence of opening up to international agro-food markets, much more variable and unstable. Cumulatively, structural adjustment in agriculture made it, in most cases, all but impossible for small and medium-sized farmers to compete with large transnational corporations that were, in any event, strongly subsidized in their home countries.

Mexico again offers a stark, near paradigmatic example. As Magdalena Barros Nock (2000) stresses, changes in the Mexican Constitution allowed the privatization of *ejido* land, giving private capital security and access to land. These changes were required in order for Mexico to accede to the North American Free Trade Area (NAFTA). Thus,

> in anticipation of NAFTA membership the Mexican government modified the Constitution in 1991 and permitted the privatization of the *ejido*. This change reversed the *ejido* principle of communally held land and brought an end to land redistribution. Members of each *ejido* could now decide in a general assembly whether they wanted to continue as they were or become private landowners. Other changes related to the right of *ejidos* to use their land as collateral for the purposes of obtaining credit, amongst other matters. The *ejido*, either as an *ejido* or as a number of private properties, was now allowed to engage in different forms of association with private national and international capital.
>
> (Barros Nock 2000: 166–167)

The implementation of these constitutional changes in Mexico led to major processes of social and economic differentiation within the *ejido* sector. The smaller *ejidos* fell below subsistence levels, and were often abandoned as their owners migrated. These lands were absorbed by farms with medium or large tracts of land, as part of a process of consolidation of *minifundia* into larger farms. These processes are also examined by Akram-Lodhi *et al.* in Chapter 9 of this volume. At the same time, communal pasture lands were reassigned for use as rainfed crop land. According to Barros Nock (2000: 167), 'the privatization of *ejido* land has paved the way to the alienation of the property rights of collectives and associations in favor of individual owners, and worsened the situation of the rural poor'. Nevertheless, the pace of change in land tenure patterns was slower then expected by some, due to a lack of stable non-farm income-generating opportunities outside the *ejido*, with the consequent result that farmers remained in farming even when operating at a sub-subsistence level.

Structural adjustment opened the way for globalization processes that affected agriculture and agro-food systems throughout Latin America. These processes were part of the consolidation of a world agro-food system under the command of large agro-food transnational corporations, as stressed by Philip McMichael (Chapter 12). In this new phase in the development of global capitalism, these firms control important segments of the agro-food systems of Latin American countries. In particular, global agribusiness dominates the seed industry and the provision of agrochemicals, as well as other inputs that are sold to farmers. Global agribusiness also dominates global food processing and distribution, as well as the sale of food by supermarkets to consumers in the advanced capitalist countries.

This neoliberal vision of agriculture prioritizes very large holdings that make extensive use of agrochemicals and pesticides, and that concentrate on capital-intensive monocultures of commodity crops for export. Brazil offers a clear example: in that country, 85 per cent of the farm area under cultivation is used for sugarcane, soybeans and coffee. Monocultures are produced on increasingly large farms, as landholdings continue to grow by absorbing smaller properties. Thus in the past few years, estates of over 1000 hectares have absorbed over 30 million additional hectares of land. One per cent of proprietors own more than 46 per cent of the land in *fazendas* of over 2000 hectares (Stédile 2002; Stédile and Mançano Fernándes 2005; Welch, 2006). Searching for higher rates of labour productivity, these large agro-food producers drive workers away from the countryside and exploit the few remaining, who earn the lowest wages in Brazil – the equivalent of about US $150 a month. Thus in 2005 almost 300,000 workers in the countryside lost their jobs and migrated to cities.

These processes are shaped and regulated by 10 transnational corporations that, through the provision of transgenic seeds, chemical pesticides and inorganic fertilizers, as well as through their dominance of global food trading, in effect control agrarian production in Brazil – Monsanto, Bunge, Cargill, ADM, BASF, Bayer, Syngenta, Norvartis, Nestlé and Danone. Production techniques attack the environment, destroy biodiversity and compromise natural resources through the large-scale use of pesticides, with a heavy cost to society and future generations. The road to global agro-food competitiveness is that of large estates producing on a large scale, combined with miserable wages and ecological devastation (Stédile 2002, 2007).

Needless to say, these elements contribute to a growing regressivity in the distribution of income within and across countries, and to a disarticulation of their economies with regard not only to agriculture and the agro-food system, but also to the economy as a whole. An increase in unemployment in all its forms, an increased degree of poverty and indigence, and the expulsion of vast segments of the peasantry and rural wage labour from agriculture can be construed to be a consequence of the application of these policies and, more generally, of globalization processes in the rural sector. Interestingly, these trends to some extent replicate those that were manifest towards the end of the nineteenth century in Latin America as a whole, under the impact of liberalism – a point also made by Araghi in Chapter 5.

However, in some countries a new 'agriculture without farmers' seems to be consolidating itself, shaped by the use of new technologies associated with the widespread production of transgenic crops and the massive expulsion of farmers and peasants from agriculture. For example, in Argentina a soybean explosion began in the 1970s in response to Europe's need to find substitute animal feeds. Then, during the mid-1990s, soybean farmers were encouraged to plant a genetically modified seed tolerant of glyphosate, a weed-eliminating herbicide commercially known as Roundup Ready. This was part of a new technological package designed and produced by Monsanto and developed to combine genetically modified seed, glyphosate and other agrochemicals in a path-breaking no-tillage system of farm production that did not require ploughing the land. During the course of the 1990s, this new no-tillage agrarian production complex was used in ever larger quantities in Argentina as soya expanded substantially in absolute and relative terms. As a consequence, farmers become increasingly dependent on agro-industrial transnational corporations such as Monsanto and the supplies of agro-chemical products that they provided, as well as – to a much greater extent than before – transgenic seeds. These developments in turn transformed Argentina's agriculture. The no-tillage system, Roundup Ready seeds and glyphosate tolerance reconfigured agriculture into an essentially extractive system not very different from mining, as resources are extracted from the soil without recompense. Moreover, this new technological package disproportionately benefited agrochemical transnational corporations in the form of cash payments, royalties and remittances.

A consensus currently prevails in Argentina: that this new model of industrialized agriculture has been successful; and that it will continue to be so in the future due to the new demand that is emerging across the world for the production of biofuels. Certainly, the new model brings Argentina closer to the frontier of rapidly emerging biotechnologies. Government officials also point out that the new model has been quite successful in that production has increased substantially, not just in national but in global terms.

However, the negative effects of the widespread diffusion of these technologies are not always considered, in particular the social, economic, environmental and health effects. Certainly, while the rapid expansion of soybean production has contributed to an expansion of fiscal and foreign trade surpluses, which are required for the servicing of foreign debt, there may in any event be an element of excess specialization in this commodity, which could denote a certain vulnerability of the external sector of the economy to global price movements and commodity demand. At the same time, there has been a disappearance of medium-sized and small farmers, peasants and farm labourers as agriculture has consolidated for global markets. There have also been tremendous environmental effects induced by this model, especially in northern Argentina, where the expansion of soya encroaches on the *yungas*, a natural setting that is about to disappear; the contamination caused by the massive fumigation, by air, of glyphosate has caused heath problems among the population; and a loss of local crops has caused protests of all sorts. The latter impact points to what is perhaps the greatest local effect of the new agricultural model: the loss of food sovereignty stressed by McMichael (Chapter 12). Thus, this new agricultural model can certainly lead one to ask: does the new agricultural model imply greater welfare for all, now and in the long run (Teubal *et al.* 2005; Teubal, 2006)?

The emergence of peasant and indigenous movements

Towards the end of the millennium, a series of important peasant, small farmer and rural labour movements, including the important indigenous movements noted by Watts (Chapter 11), emerged throughout Latin America, as a consequence of which the question of land and agrarian reform has acquired a new importance. The struggles and debates that have developed can be thought of as part of a reaction against the consolidation of neoliberalisn under the dominion of large transnational corporation agribusiness, although in many cases they are also related to resistance lasting 500 years since the conquest of the Americas. Finally, they can also be considered reactions against counter-reform movements and policies in many countries.

In some cases, for example in Mexico with the Zapatista EZLN, at least in its beginnings, and until recently in El Salvador and Guatemala, these were movements led by armed struggle as a reaction against the growing oppression of successive governments. In Mexico, the change in Article 27 of the Constitution and the country's entry into NAFTA was the spark that gave rise to the Zapatista movement, an explicit linking of local resistance to neoliberal globalization. In Guatemala, Bolivia, Mexico and Ecuador, important parts of these movements have reaffirmed the centrality of indigenous, ethnic and communitarian identities that have acquired a growing significance in rural Latin America. In some cases there has been a fusion between these and women's or ecological movements. The latter, for example, has developed action against large public works – such as hydroelectric projects – that displace millions from their lands and habitat, or the new mining projects that contaminate the health of innumerable numbers reliant on local subsistence agriculture. In general, these movements find their origin in the most exploited segments of rural society, although they also extend themselves to more prosperous farmers, the *chacarero*, family farmers who sustain themselves through some form of capitalization of agriculture, such as the *Movimiento de Mujeres en Lucha* of Argentina (Giarracca and Teubal 2001).

Operating outside state and quasi-state organizations established during previous episodes of agrarian reform, which were commonly used as instruments of social and political control, access to land has become one of the major demands of militant rural organizations in Brazil, Mexico, Colombia, Peru, Bolivia, Paraguay and elsewhere. The MST in Brazil offers the clearest, starkest, example. Since its inception in 1983, the MST has assumed a very important role in the political life of Brazil. Its strength lies in its social roots, its persistent strategy of mobilization, and the pressure it applies for the expropriation or occupation of *haciendas* that are either unproductive or whose owners have debts with the *Banco do Brazil* or the tax authority.

The MST began in three states of southern Brazil, but later acquired its important national role. The efficiency of its mobilizations is related to the strength of the land occupations it promotes, the occupations of the offices of the *Instituo Nacional de Colonizaçao e Reforma Agraria* (National Institute of Colonization and Agrarian Reform), its visible protests and its encampments. Like the EZLN in Mexico, the MST also managed to occupy an important space in the media. As a consequence, a large proportion of the population supports its struggle for agrarian reform and was in favour of having the government confiscate unproductive lands and redistribute them to the landless, admitting in the process that the occupation of land was a legitimate form of struggle (Poletto 1997).

According to João Stédile, one of the senior leaders of the MST,

> throughout 1983 and 1984 we held big debates about how to build an organization that would spread the struggle for land – and above all, one that could transform these localized conflicts into a major battle for agrarian reform. We knew it changed nothing just to bring a few families together, move onto unused land and think that was the end. We were well aware from the agrarian struggles of the past that if farmers don't organize themselves, don't fight for more than just a piece of land, they'll never reach a wider class of consciousness and be able to grapple with the underlying problems – because land in itself does not free the farmer from exploitation.
>
> (Stédile 2002: 80)

From its very beginnings, the organizers of the MST were convinced that agrarian reform in Brazil would move forward only if it was transformed into a mass struggle, involving as many people as possible. They were also convinced that they had to create a movement that was autonomous and independent of political parties. The size of the movement was and is reflected in the character of the occupations that are carried out and in the multiplicity of persons who participate: fathers, mothers, sons, daughters, old people and young people. The struggle for agrarian reform is part of a 'struggle for a different Brazil, a society without exploiters' (Stédile 2002: 81).

While the MST claims to have 20,000 activists, the struggle emerges from below, from the movement itself. This helps explain the central importance of occupations and the formation of *asentamientos*, settled communities that emerge from the occupation. According to MST sources, in the first 18 years of the movement 350,000 families occupied land, while as of June 2007 some 150,000 families were camping beside roads waiting for the possibility of occupying and creating *asentamientos*, thereby acquiring titling to the land (Stédile 2002: 91; Stédile and Mançano Fernándes 2005). These are families that have not solved their problems, and as a consequence are prepared to confront the government directly. It is a strategy that is not about taking the power of the state, but rather about giving impulse to an agrarian reform from below. In this respect, agrarian reform has been transformed into an important part of a movement for the democratization of Brazilian society.

Thus land has, once again, been transformed into the focus of attention, not only for those that work the land and have lost it, but also for the urban unemployed who see access to land as an important means whereby the problem of poverty and unemployment can be solved. This is particularly true in areas with a predominantly indigenous population. Thus the CONAIE in Ecuador, the *Consejo Regional Indígena del Cauca* (Regional Indigenous Council of the Cauca) in Colombia and the EZLN in Mexico, as well as the diverse rural and indigenous movements in Bolivia that support the present government led by Evo Morales, are all organizations that have assembled the indigenous peasantry under ethnic political identities in support of the struggle for land and social justice.

In this regard, João Stédile is very concrete when he argues that the need for agrarian reform is an international need. As he argues with reference to the participation of the MST in La Via Campesina,

> one plank on which we agree, at the international level, is that there must be the sort of agrarian reform that would democratize the land – both as the basis for political democracy, and for building an agriculture of another kind. This has major implications. From the time of Zapata in Mexico or of Juliao in Brazil, the inspiration for agrarian reform was the idea that the land belonged to those who worked it. Today we need to go beyond this. It's not enough to argue that if you work the land, you have proprietary rights to it ... We want an agrarian practice that transforms farmers into guardians of the land, and in a different way of farming, that ensures an ecological equilibrium and also guarantees that land is not seen as private property.
>
> (Stédile 2002: 100)

Thus the MST, other agrarian organizations in Brazil, and rural social and peasant movements in other parts of the world have tended to converge in their struggle against neoliberalism. While land occupations are carried out because they constitute the only way that many families have to solve their immediate problems – that is, the need for a place to work – the MST and other peasant and indigenous movements are conscious that, if they want to advance as a movement for agrarian reform, they must confront the neoliberal programme itself. Therefore alliances are created with other organizations that struggle against the neoliberal agro-food system, such as transnational corporations that control milk production and agro-chemical companies that dominate the production of genetically modified seeds. Indeed, the latter are the most extreme expression of the control of transnational corporations under the neoliberal economic model. Thus, according to Stédile (2002: 96, 100), at the present pace of development, in five years all the seed needed by Brazilian farmers to plant could be produced by big transnational corporations. The country's food sovereignty is, in this sense, in jeopardy. Transnational corporations also monopolize world agricultural trade and biotechnology research, and have been increasing their control over the property rights of living matter across the planet. Thus it is the current phase of global capitalism that has created the conditions whereby peasants and farmers can unite against the neoliberal model (Borras, Edelman and Kay 2008).

Final reflections

Agrarian reform movements in the twentieth century were part of the struggle against landowning oligarchies that controlled the national state and the agrarian regimes that sustained them. Within this perspective, and to counter the push for agro-export based economies, other *desarrollista* (developmental) perspectives were presented that promoted industrialization and the modernization of agrarian societies throughout the continent. Agrarian reform in this context was seen as instrumental to social transformation throughout the continent. While it is true that the implicit motto guiding these reforms was 'land to those that work it', a tension prevailed between the communitarian perspectives presented by the peasantry and indigenous communities, which was sometimes labelled 'populist', and those that sought a 'productivist' *desarrollista* large-scale agriculture that was either state-led or led by transnational firms. For the peasantry, including those from indigenous communities, land was and is seen as necessary for life itself, and therefore has a profound communitarian meaning. Needless to say, many of the agrarian reforms seeking the modernization of society were, and are, anathema to the interests of small farmers, peasants and indigenous communities.

Confronted with globalization processes, the struggle for land and agrarian reform presents new characteristics. In part, this is due to the changing nature of world capitalism, in which large agro-industrial transnational corporations acquire a leading role in world agriculture. In this context, the struggle for land and agrarian reform includes a struggle against the industrial agro-food system being shaped by the transnational corporations that tend to dominate food technology, food processing and distribution, as well as the production of transgenic seeds. In this sense, the struggle for land is also a struggle against a new establishment that has emerged worldwide and that influences multiple aspects of the issues pertaining to land questions and those of the agro-food system as a whole. As a consequence, according to Jose Bové of La Via Campesina, the agrarian movement defends the interests of peasants as workers:

> We're exploited too – by banks, by companies who buy our produce, by the firms who sell us equipment, fertilizers, seeds and animal feed ... it is a struggle against the whole intensive-farming system. The goal of the multinationals who run it are minimum employment and maximum,

export-oriented, production – with no regard for the environment or food quality.

(Bové 2001: 91–92)

Current agrarian reform movements tend to be more autonomous of political parties, trade unions and the state than was previously the case (Borras, Edelman and Kay 2008). They are based on the peasantry and on indigenous communities, and on the construction of their organizations from below. Furthermore, they are organizations that do not necessarily seek taking state power. The importance of these movements and the agrarian reforms they propose suggests that land and agrarian reform has acquired a new set of meanings that are not associated with the modernization movements that characterized previous reform movements.

Further, these peasant and agrarian movements tend to locate themselves within, and are related to, the alternative globalization movement. This is all the more so as the movements of Europe, Latin America, Asia and Africa converge. All adopt strategies that go beyond the traditional demand for land and agrarian reform. They also struggle against large transnational corporation agribusiness, free trade in agricultural production, and the use of hormones and genetically modified organisms, among others. They are in favour of a new form of food security, food sovereignty, on a world scale.

These movements thus go beyond a defence of specific corporate interests, presenting a global perspective that contains important democratizing elements, as noted by McMichael (Chapter 12). González Casanova, when he refers to the new agrarian social and political movements, and in particular the EZLN, points out that these movements struggle not only for land and territory, but also for a defence of culture, the rights of indigenous populations, respect for their autonomy and dignity, their culture and customs, and their participation and representation in the national state:

> What is involved is a democratic project that is opposed to any terrorist act and any relationship with narcotraffic; they are movements that do not struggle for the conquest of state power, yet they propose a profound transformation of juridical and social relations on the basis of a participative and non-excluding representative democracy that is to prevail in the civil society of the Indian and non Indian populations.
>
> (González Casanova 2001: 5)

These new agrarian movements assign great importance to their ability to converge with other diverse social movements. As Stédile of the MST puts it,

> If we are to move towards popular agrarian reform we have to confront the neoliberal programme itself, and that can't be done by land occupations alone ... Over the last eighteen years we've managed to build a social movement with a coherent ideology and a layer of activists. If we

had been the usual type of farmers' movement, they would have wiped us out. The avalanche of propaganda against the landless farmers in the media, the economic offensives against us, the attempts to suffocate us, to flatten us along with our settlements – all this has been impressive. ... What's saved us has been the support of the social forces that don't believe their propaganda, and protect us.

(Stédile 2002: 96)

The struggle for land and agrarian reform is part of the struggle for a new society on behalf of peasant and indigenous communities, based in large measure on communal values that, in essence, contradict the main tenets of capitalism. This struggle is also a struggle for autonomy on behalf of peasant and indigenous movements against the state, political parties and trade unions. Furthermore, it is a struggle based on social movements that do not necessarily seek taking state power as a means for the social transformation of society, but that stress the need for these transformations to be made from below. It is in these new social spaces that are being constructed where the seeds of a new society will probably be sown.

Notes

1 This chapter is based in part on an earlier paper in Spanish (Teubal 2003). A significantly different version will be published by *Latin American Perspectives*. I would like to thank Cristóbal Kay for inducing me to write this paper and for comments on a previous version, and Haroon Akram-Lodhi for his comments and excellent editing.

References

Aguilar Camín, H. (1979) 'Ovación, denostación y prólogo', in A. Gilly, A. Córdoba, A. Bartra, M. Aguilar Mora and E. Semo (eds), *Interpretaciones de la revolución mexicana*, Mexico City: Universidad Nacional Autónoma de México y Editorial Nueva Imagen.
Barkin, D. (1994) 'The spectre of rural development', *NACLA Report on the Americas*, 38 (1): 29–34.
Barros Nock, M. (2000) 'The Mexican peasantry and the *ejido* in the neo-liberal period',in D. Bryceson, C. Kay and J. Mooij (eds), *Disappearing Peasantries? Rural Labour in Africa, Asia and Latin America*, London: Intermediate Technology Publications.
Borras Jr, S.M., M. Edelman and C. Kay (eds) (2008) *Transnational Agrarian Movements Confronting Globalization*, Oxford: Blackwell Publishers.
Bové, J. (2001) 'A farmers' international?', *New Left Review* 12: 89–101.
Brumer, A. and J.V. Tavares dos Santos (1997) 'Tensoes agrícolas e agrárias na trasicao democrática brasileira', *Sao Paolo em Perspectiva*, 11 (2): 3–14.
Giarracca, N. (2003) 'La protesta agrorural en la Argentina', in J. Seoane (ed.), *Movimientos sociales y conflicto en América Latina,* Buenos Aires: Consejo Latinoamericano de Ciencias Sociales.

Giarracca, N. and M. Teubal (2001) 'Crisis and agrarian protest in Argentina: the *Movimiento Mujeres Agropecuarias en Lucha*', *Latin American Perspectives*, 28 (6): 38–53

Gilly, A. (1979) 'La guerra de clases en la revolución mexicana: revolución permanente y auto-organización de las masas', in A. Gilly, A. Córdoba, A. Bartra, M. Aguilar Mora and E. Semo (eds), *Interpretaciones de la revolución mexicana*, Mexico City: Universidad Nacional Autónoma de México y Editorial Nueva Imagen.

González Casanova, P. (2001) 'Los zapatistas del siglo XXI', *Observatorio Social de América Latina*, 4: 5–8.

Griffin, K., A. Rahman Khan and A. Ickowitz (2002) 'Poverty and the distribution of land', *Journal of Agrarian Change*, 2 (3): 279–330.

Huizer, G. (1999) *Peasant Mobilization for Land Reform: Historical Case Studies and Theoretical Considerations*, Discussion Paper No. 103, Geneva: UN Research Institute for Social Development.

Kay, C. (1998) 'Latin America's agrarian reform: lights and shadows', *Land Reform, Land Settlement and Cooperatives*, (2): 8–31, online: http://www.fao.org/sd/sda/sdaa/LR98_2/LR98_2.pdf

—— (2000) 'Latin America's agrarian transformation: peasantization and proletarianization', in D. Bryceson, C. Kay and J. Mooij (eds), *Disappearing Peasantries? Rural Labour in Africa, Asia and Latin America*, London: Intermediate Technology Publications.

Lewis, J. (2002) 'Agrarian change and privatization of *ejido* land in northern Mexico, *Journal of Agrarian Change* 2 (3): 401–419.

Poletto, I. (1997) 'Por caminhos nunca antes navegados o aprendizado político dos sem terra', *Sao Paolo em Perspectiva*, 11 (2): 79–85.

Romero Polanco, E. (1995) 'La modernización del campo mexicano: saldos y perspectivas', in A. Encinas, J. de la Fuente, H. Mackinlay and E. Romero Polanco, *El Campo Mexicano en el Umbral del Siglo XXI*, Mexico City: Espasa-Calpe.

Stédile, J.P. (2002) 'Landless battalions: the *Sem Terra* of Brazil', *New Left Review*, 15: 77–104.

—— (2007) 'Brasil: MST quer novo modelo para reforma agrária. Entrevista com João Pedro Stédile', *Biodiversidad en América Latina*, online: www.biodiversidadla.org/content/view/full/34278

Stédile, J.P. and B. Mançano Fernandez (2005) *Brava gente. La trayectoria del MST y de la lucha por la tierra en el Brasil*, entrevista a João Pedro Stédile realizada por Bernardo Mançano Fernandez, Buenos Aires: Ediciones América Libre.

Teubal, M. (2003) 'Tierra y reforma agraria en América Latina', *Realidad Económica* 200: 130–162.

—— (2006) 'Expansión del modelo sojero en la Argentina. De la producción de alimentos a los commodities', *Realidad Económica* 220: 71–96.

Teubal, M. and J. Rodríguez (2002) *Agro y alimentos en la globalización. Una perspectiva crítica*, Buenos Aires: La Colmena.

Teubal, M., D. Domínguez and P. Sabatino (2005) 'Transformaciones agrarias en la Argentina. Agricultura industrial y sistema agroalimentario', in N. Giarracca and M. Teubal (eds), *El campo argentino en la encrucijada. Estrategias y resistencias sociales, ecos en la ciudad*, Buenos Aires: Alianza Editorial.

Vallianatos, E.G. (2001) 'All of Africa's gods are weeping', *Race & Class*, 43 (1): 45–57.

—— (2003) 'American cataclysm', *Race & Class*, 44 (1): 40–57.

Welch, C. (2006) 'A preliminary historiography of Brazil's Landless Laborer's Movement (MST)', *Latin American Research Review*, 41 (1): 198–210.

Wolf, E.R. (1973) *Las luchas campesinas del siglo XX*, México City: Siglo XXI.

Part 3

Contemporary Perspectives on Agrarian Change

7 The globalization of manufacturing production

Warrenite fantasies and uneven and unequal realities

Ray Kiely

Bill Warren, exploitation and globalization

One of the most contentious contributions to debates over the agrarian question is derived from Bill Warren's (1973, 1980) controversial intervention into the once-thriving development theory debate. Warren's 'return' to an interpretation of Marx that was rooted in a stagist approach to history, in which he argued that imperialism was the pioneer of capitalism, paved the way for a number of contributions to the agrarian question, which broadly saw agrarian transitions as moving in a singular direction – or at least argued that this should be the case (Mueller 1980; Sender and Smith 1986, 1990). For these Marxists, progressive politics means supporting social processes and government policies that enabled the productive forces to develop, and that created a fully proletarianized wage labour force out of the peasantry, who presumably would later socialize these same productive forces and overthrow capitalism.

Much of this debate has disappeared as the discipline of development studies has concerned itself with more immediate, micro issues. At the same time, while there is considerable difference between the policies advocated by proponents of neoliberal globalization and Warrenite Marxism (Sender and Smith 1985; Sender 1999), much of the debate over the modernizing role of capitalism persists, albeit in a context in which capitalism – and indeed neoliberal capitalism – is taken for granted (Giddens 2000; World Bank 2002; Friedman 2005). This is most clear in the debates over whether globalization is promoting convergence or divergence in the world economy (Wolf and Wade 2002). It is also clearly – and related to this point – an undeniable fact that globalization has been associated with the rise of manufacturing in the developing world. At a superficial level, then, one could update Warren and argue that globalization is the pioneer of capitalism in the developing world. At the same time, the rise of manufacturing in the developing world begs a number of questions for agrarian transitions, be they interpreted in Warrenite or non-Warrenite ways, and the role of national accumulation in the current international order. These questions concerning globalization have in many respects repeated, albeit in new contexts, earlier debates concerning progressive alternatives to capitalism, and the rejection of reactionary populisms (Kitching 1989, 2001). For contemporary Warrenites, the so-called antiglobalization movement is simply the latest manifestation of such a backward-looking populism (Sender and Pincus 2006).

This chapter explores these themes, some in more depth than others, with a main focus on the similarities between the 1970s debate over Warrenism and the current debate over globalization. In particular, it draws a parallel between the prominent 1970s idea that the developing world is poor because it is insufficiently exploited, and the current argument that it is poor because it is insufficiently globalized. My contention is that the argument concerning insufficient exploitation is not necessarily incorrect, but it is one-sided, and more importantly, has been misinterpreted by the Warrenite position. It is precisely this misinterpretation which is repeated in the argument that poor countries are poor because they are insufficiently globalized. This is illustrated through an empirical account of the nature and direction of capital flows in manufacturing, which give rise to a far more cautious assessment of the globalization of manufacturing than that envisaged by both Warrenites and neoliberals. This has implications for understanding the agrarian question in the light of the supposed globalization of manufacturing production.

I proceed in the following way. First, I outline the Warrenite position on capitalist development and briefly show how this was applied to the agrarian question by his followers. Second, I relate these arguments to contemporary debates over globalization. Third, I question these contentions, through consideration of the question of dualism, and the links between different economic sectors. In doing so, I interpret the argument concerning insufficient exploitation in a way very different from the Warrenites. Finally, I illustrate the argument by examining the globalization of manufacturing production, and the ways in which this undermines, rather than upholds, both neoliberal and Warrenite contentions.

Warrenism, the agrarian question and agrarian transition

In the 1970s, when the study of development was far more concerned than it is now with theoretical debates, Bill Warren intervened in these debates in a particularly controversial way. Much of the debate in the 1970s was concerned with the nature and the viability of capital accumulation in the developing world. Various branches of dependency theory argued that capitalist development in the periphery was somehow hindered by Western domination of the world economy. At one extreme there was underdevelopment theory (Frank 1969a, 1969b), which suggested that capitalist development was impossible so long as the periphery remained part of the world economy. The logical solution of delinking from the world economy followed, although precisely what this meant was not always spelt out, and it often led to all kinds of dubious support for regimes on the grounds that these were antiwestern, and therefore progressive (Caldwell 1976). More nuanced analyses, less well known in the English-speaking world, suggested that the concepts of subordination or dependence could usefully be applied to understanding the concrete conditions of capitalist development in the so-called periphery, in the context of the uneven development of both international capitalism and specific national capitalisms (Palma 1978; Cardoso and Falletto 1979; Larrain 1989; Kay 1989). The latter approach was useful in that it could focus on the interaction between class relations on the one hand, and capital flows and trade on the other. Indeed, this approach has been used effectively by many writers in the context of neoliberalism in order to explain the continued hierarchies in the international order, based on the concentration of capital (Shaikh 2005; Saul and Leys 2006; Kiely 2007).

Warren, on the other hand, argued a position almost diametrically opposed to that of what some might label a 'crude' underdevelopment school. Where Frank saw integration into the world economy as leading to inevitable stagnation, Warren saw inevitable development. Where Frank argued that external factors were the main obstacles to development, Warren argued that the obstacles were overwhelmingly internal (Gulalp 1986). This either/or debate left little room for an analysis of mediating factors, or analysis of the specificity of capital accumulation in different parts of the so-called periphery (Jenkins 1984). Thus, for instance, the question of specific forms of integration, and whether or not or not such forms promoted accumulation, was not well answered by Frank or the Warrenite critique.

However, John Sender, the editor of Warren's notes (eventually published posthumously in 1980), developed Warren's position further, on the face of it providing a more grounded analysis that was more sensitive to specificity. Sender and Smith (1986, 1990) strongly argued the case for a focus on internal social relations, and how the development of capitalist social relations in Africa was leading to the rapid development of the productive forces in Africa (Sender and Smith 1986: 3, 67–68). While there were some important problems to be resolved, such as the promotion of a coherent trade strategy and the continued influence of a nationalist anti-imperialism that made a scapegoat of imperialism for Africa's ills, Sender and Smith's message was a fairly upbeat one: capitalist social relations and the development of the productive forces were moving in a progressive direction.

This was based on a unilinear account of the agrarian question, whereby capitalism developed through a process of primitive accumulation in which the direct producers, that is to say, principally petty commodity-producing peasant farmers, were successively separated from the means of production, and in particular land, as rural capital and rural capitalism emerged, thereby giving rise over time to generalized commodity production, and a resultant competitive accumulation of capital. The act of dispossession of peasant labour simultaneously served to provide industrial capital with a growing labour force, while the agrarian surplus produced under rural capitalism could be used to finance further industrial development. Productivity increases in agriculture – facilitated by the use of more advanced technologies provided by industry and the economies of scale provided by larger farms – would cheapen food costs, and thereby the costs of reproduction of labour, thus further increasing the rate of relative surplus value. For Warrenites, then, development is essentially concerned with replicating these processes associated with some interpretations of the classic agrarian question (Kitching 1989, 2001; Sender and Smith 1986; Sender 1999; Sender and Johnston 2004). Neoliberalism may have served to undermine some progress on this front (Sender 1999), but provided a more interventionist state could be revived to correct the policy errors associated with neoliberalism – unregulated free trade, too much focus on the informal sector, and/or a supposedly homogeneous peasantry as nascent small business classes – renewed progress could be made.

For Sender, there is plenty of evidence to back up this unilinear, path-dependent approach to the agrarian question, and he cites a great deal of evidence suggesting that capitalist social relations have developed vigorously in the countryside in Africa. This view has been questioned by many writers, not least some of those who have contributed to this volume. Critics have argued that the suggestion that there has been a significant development of high productivity agriculture employing wage labour, while at the same time there has also been migration to the towns and the significant development of industry also employing wage labour, is unconvincing. In constructing ahistorical models rather than examining concrete social processes of struggle in both countryside and town, it can be argued that Sender has one-sidedly looked for any signs of evidence that back up his path-dependent stagist views, and dismissed any counterevidence as residual elements, which will disappear with the inevitable development of advanced capitalism. On the other hand, however, there does remain the question of the rise of manufacturing in the developing world. We examine this question in detail in the final section of the chapter. First, though, we must consider a closely related debate concerning the rise of globalization.

Poverty through insufficient globalization?

At the height of the debates between Warrenites and some dependency theorists in the 1970s, it was clear that some of the most successful developers were progressing in terms of both economic and social development. In particular, in East Asia high rates of growth coincided with important advances in life expectancy, healthcare and education – although the treatment of organized labour had been very different, a major problem for those stagist Marxists who claimed to champion organized labour and trade unions. Moreover – and here the case was perhaps most compelling – for all the talk of the superexploitation of labour in world market factories (Frobel *et al.* 1980), usually located in export processing or free trade zones, the fact was that people were desperate to find work in these factories in preference to the drudgery and poverty of rural alternatives, a fact that Warrenites repeatedly emphasized. This seemed to back up their view that so-called superexploitation was merely an early stage of capitalism, to be transcended as rural labour was gradually proletarianized and urbanized. In short, primitive accumulation would eventually give rise to the real subsumption of labour and the extraction of relative surplus value.

This final point brings the argument up to date, for it is now various advocates of globalization who support the growth of industrialization, including world market factories. These views are far from identical to those of stagist Marxists following in the wake of Warren's untimely death, who have remained suspicious of rapid trade liberalization and neoliberal concerns with neoclassical, populist-inspired land reforms that champion small farmers (Sender and Smith 1985; Sender 2002, 2003; Sender and Johnston 2004). Where there is some convergence of views, however, is the way that both neoliberal and stagist Marxist analysis have provided answers to the question of whether or not to globalize (Seers 1979). Conventionally associated with a variation of neoliberal economics, the argument that the latter now makes is that the best route to development for the developing world is to promote open policies towards foreign investment, alongside trade – and perhaps financial – liberalization, and that this will allow labour surplus countries to absorb labour into factories producing labour-intensive goods. In this way, so-called new trade theory suggests (Krugman 1986; Grossman and Helpman 1991), the developed world can specialize in higher-value, skilled, high-technology goods, while labour abundant economies can focus on labour-intensive goods. Once labour is absorbed, wages will increase and upgrading will occur. In the short term there will be hardship, to be sure, but this is a necessary starting point – without these policies there will be hardship without any long-term development, and this is basically how economic and social development happened in the now-developed countries. Those who reject such a policy are simply condemning poorer countries to low growth and low development, and to a life in rural areas that is even worse than that which exists in factories. Just as 1970s Warrenite Marxists dismissed opposition to foreign investment as romantic populism, so too do today's globalization advocates dismiss antisweatshop, antiglobalization campaigns as backward looking, well meaning, but ultimately dangerous and counterproductive (Wolf 2003; Bhagwati 2004). This is a view also endorsed by some theorists of globalization otherwise highly critical of neoliberalism. Ulrich Beck (2000: 92–94, 2006: 108–109), for example, advocates such an international division of labour, in which low-skilled jobs are concentrated in poor countries, and skilled jobs concentrate in the developed world.

One of the key arguments of development economics in the 1950s onwards was that in the developing world there was a two-sector dual economy. On the one hand there was an advanced sector, on the other a backward or traditional sector. The former is characterized by high rates of productivity and growth of output; the latter, composed largely of subsistence farming, has low productivity and growth of output (Lewis 1954). Development is ultimately the growth of the former at the expense of the latter, in part through the absorption of the latter into the former. This dualist analysis also tends towards a unilinear account of social change, in which the processes of labour absorption and the shift from low-productivity agriculture to higher-productivity industry – which in turn would benefit agriculture – that occurred in the developed countries would repeat themselves in the developing countries. This view is most closely associated with Walt Rostow's (1971) stages of economic growth model, which (although it is often said to be hopelessly outdated) is still implicit in some mainstream accounts of globalization.

At the same time, and this is, for me, a key point, dualism remains influential among some Warrenite Marxists who see imperialism as promoting the diffusion of capitalism in the developing world so that the developed countries show to the less developed the image of their own future. For these Marxists, current antiglobalization protests are simply the latest reactionary response to the progressive spread of global capitalism (Sender and Pincus 2006). These criticisms are usually made without any effort to examine the actual content of debates among antiglobalizers. More importantly for the purposes of this chapter, however, although lip service is paid to the idea of uneven development, there is no attempt to concretize this concept, or to examine how this may manifest itself in a neoliberal era. Indeed, uneven development appears to be a residual effect of the existence of backward capitalisms, rather than a central feature of the workings of a mature international capitalist order. Furthermore, at times the current neoliberal context appears to be ignored; it is instead suggested that it is sufficient to recognize the fact that the state always play a role in processes of capitalist development – something with which few neoliberals would disagree. As a consequence, the continued progressive diffusion of capitalism in an era of neoliberal globalization is emphasized (Sender and Pincus 2006: 49; but cf. Sender 1999). Therefore, just as globalization's advocates stress the need for more globalization to resolve poverty, so Warrenites argue for more exploitation – a shift from absolute to relative surplus value – to do the same thing. Part and parcel of this process is, of course, the resolution of the classic agrarian question.

The fallacies of dualism: reinterpreting insufficient exploitation

This section interrogates Kay's (1975) statement, derived from Joan Robinson – and Marx – that capitalism created underdevelopment, not because it exploited the developing world, but because it did not exploit it enough. As we will see in the next section, a similar argument has been applied to globalization, but first we need to unpack the meaning of this statement. It could be interpreted in a Warrenite way, in order to suggest that the way forward for developing countries is to find new ways of being exploited – or, in Marxist terms, shifting from absolute to relative surplus value extraction – so that a process of catching up with the developed countries may take place. In neoliberal terms, this would mean opening up to foreign investment and exercising comparative advantage through trade liberalization. While for Marxists this would certainly constitute exploitation, the extraction of relative surplus value is also compatible with the increased consumption of goods (Bettelheim 1972), and therefore with the alleviation of absolute poverty.

However, an alternative interpretation of Kay's argument is possible, one that is closer to his original argument, and which in some respects is the polar opposite of the Warrenite position. The argument here is that, while it may be true that capital has not exploited the developing world in the same way that it carried out the exploitation of labour in the developed countries, it is unlikely to do so no, matter what state policies are adopted. Therefore a similar process of exploitation will not occur in the developing countries. In other words, capital may not have exploited the developing countries sufficiently, but equally it is unlikely to exploit them sufficiently. This is because the transition from absolute to relative surplus value extraction in the developed world has made it likely that capital will continue to concentrate in these already developed and thus established areas of accumulation. Related to this point, the process of absorbing unlimited supplies of labour in the developing world – including from agriculture – is bound to be hindered as capital flows from capital-poor to capital-rich areas. This has enormous implications, both for understanding the agrarian question in an era of globalization, and for labour, points I return to in the conclusion.

For now, though, we need to consider how this argument works in the context of the rise of manufacturing in the developing world. Does this mean convergence with the developed countries and the absorption of labour supplies in labour abundant areas? This is discussed in the next section.

Dualism and the globalization of production

In recent years, an increasing proportion of the value of exports from developing countries comes from manufacturing. In 1970, 18.5 per cent of the total exports from the developing world were manufactured goods; with the phenomenal rise of China since the early 1990s this figure had increased to over 80 per cent by the end of the 1990s (Baker *et al.* 1998: 7; UNCTAD 2002: 5). This is seen as good news, as the globalization of production is said to lead to the dispersal of manufacturing across the globe, thus fulfilling Warren's prediction that so-called imperialism is the pioneer of capitalism and/or the view that neoliberal globalization is good for development (Kitching 2001).

The globalization of production is often linked to the liberalization policies undertaken since the early 1980s, which are said to have rendered older
import-substitution industrialization policies redundant. Following earlier
neoliberal work that attacked state-guided development in the developing
world (Little *et al.* 1970; Krueger 1974; Lal 1983), a number of writers have
suggested that the promotion of manufactured exports has been a resound-
ing success, and this is often linked to the argument that global poverty has
been reduced in recent years (Krueger 1998; Ben-David and Loewy 1998;
Bhagwati and Srinivasan 1999). Following an argument consistently made,
albeit with some qualifications, by the World Bank since at least 1987, the
argument is that trade and investment – and perhaps capital account – liberalization allows developing countries to exercise their comparative advantage and attract foreign investment and savings (World Bank 1987, 1993,
1994, 2002). In contrast, those countries that have failed to develop are said
to be insufficiently globalized, as they have failed to capture the opportunities
presented by globalization, and instead continued with poor, globalization-
unfriendly policies (World Bank 2002).

This notion of insufficient globalization (Giddens 2002) closely parallels
Kay's contention, noted in the previous section, that countries are poor
because they are insufficiently exploited. However, as we saw in discussing
this statement, it is far from clear that Kay meant that states, regions or
workers can simply become more exploited by adopting appropriate policies.
Rather, this lack of exploitation in part reflects the greater opportunities for
exploitation through investment in established areas of accumulation, or in
Marxist terms, through the extraction of relative surplus value (Jenkins 1984;
Kiely 1994). This is the heart of the dualist fallacy discussed above. Much of
the mainstream literature on globalization, exemplified by Giddens' implicit
neoliberalism, assumes on an *a priori* basis that globalization is by its nature
inclusive. Therefore the problem for poor countries must be internal to those
countries. Giddens (2000: 129) suggests that the problems of underdevelopment

> don't come from the global economy itself, or from the self-seeking
> behaviour on the part of the richer nations. They lie mainly in the
> societies themselves – in authoritarian government, corruption, conflict,
> over-regulation and the low level of emancipation of women.

Many of the problems identified on this list would actually apply to the first-
tier East Asian newly industrializing countries, or indeed to China. Although
Sub-Saharan Africa may receive low levels of global foreign investment,
some of the main recipients have been conflict-ridden countries such as
Liberia, Sierra Leone and Congo (Reno 1999; Ferguson 2006: 41).
Furthermore, while this trend has been partly reversed in recent years, which
is attributable to the resurgence of populist developmentalist regimes in
Latin America, the unmistakable trend across the developing world since

1982 has been towards the liberalization of trade and investment, and thus away from 'overregulation' (UNCTAD 2006). Clearly, for all the talk of globalization's association with hybridity, difference and so on, there is also a narrative of 'undeveloped before and developed after' once countries are – and, crucially, choose to be – globalized. This linearity, like Rostowian modernization theory before it, bears no resemblance to the realities of globalization, and the uneven and unequal forms these take in different locations (Ferguson 2006: Ch.1). For the dominant discourse, globalization is an external reality to which nations must adapt; therefore, it cannot 'bear responsibility for its consequences' (Cameron and Palan 2004: 140). Globalization is regarded as a benign force that countries simply choose to accommodate. The reality is much murkier, however: as Ferguson (2006: 14) suggests for Africa, its participation in globalization 'has certainly not been a matter simply of "joining the world economy"; perversely, it has instead been a matter of highly selective and spatially encapsulated forms of global connection combined with widespread disconnection and exclusion'. In other words, rather than theorizing in terms of being sufficiently or insufficiently globalized, an approach that lies at the heart of dualist analyses, we need to understand better the forms of global integration and how these are unequally structured, and in so doing move beyond the renewed dualism of much of the mainstream globalization literature.

How, then, does this alternative understanding apply in an era where production has undoubtedly become increasingly globalized? The first point is that this varies across developing countries. Following the Organization for Economic Cooperation and Development (UNCTAD 2002: 65), we can divide exporters into at least five categories of goods exported: primary commodities, labour-intensive and resource-based industries, and products of low-to-medium, medium-to-high, and high levels of skill, technology and scale requirements. With this classification, on the face of it there is good news: developing countries' exports in the high-level category increased from 11.6 per cent of total developing country exports in 1980 to 31 per cent by 1998, and their share in this sector in total world exports increased from 20.2 to 30.2 per cent over the same period (UNCTAD 2002: 68).

However, if we break down these categories further, a rather different picture emerges. Based on a detailed study of 46 developing countries at different stages of industrial development, Shafaeddin (2005a, 2005b) suggests that around 20 of these countries, or 40 per cent of those studied, have experienced rapid export expansion, and 11 of these same countries have had high output growth. However, of these 20 success stories, two had moderate and seven had low output growth. The next 20 countries had moderate export growth, and the bottom six had low levels of export growth. Fifty per cent of the sample actually experienced a level of deindustrialization, which could not be attributed to industrial maturity and the diversification into services, but rather forced diversification based on the decline of some industries. Where new industries had emerged, these were often in resource-based or labour-intensive sectors, and where, on paper, developing countries did see a considerable increase in participation in medium-to-high-skill/-technology/-scale sectors, this was actually misleading as 'for the most part developing countries' involvement in skill and technology intensive products is confined to the labour intensive parts, frequently just assembly, of vertically integrated production systems', with the result that 'while developing countries are becoming increasingly similar to major industrial countries in the structure of their exports, this is not the case for the structure of their manufacturing value-added' (Kozul-Wright and Rayment 2004: 11–12).

By the end of the 1990s, the 15 fastest-growing exports from developed countries were all in the top 20 list of most dynamic global exports, while only eight of the top 20 exports from developing countries were among the top 20 most dynamic global exports – and in most of these cases (with the partial exception of East Asia) these were concentrated in the labour-intensive assembly stages of production (UNCTAD 2002: 71). Perhaps most tellingly, since the reform period started in the 1980s, while the developed countries' share of global manufacturing exports fell from 82.3 per cent in 1980 to 70.9 per cent by 1997, its share of manufacturing value-added actually increased over the same period, from 64.5 to 73.3 per cent. Over the same period, Latin America's share of world manufacturing exports increased from 1.5 to 3.5 per cent, but its share of manufacturing value-added fell from 7.1 to 6.7 per cent (Kozul-Wright and Rayment 2004: 14).

For developing countries as a whole, manufacturing output's contribution to gross domestic product (GDP) has barely changed since 1960: it stood at 21.5 per cent in 1960 and increased to just 22.7 per cent in 2000. There was significant regional variation: Sub-Saharan Africa saw a decline from 15.3 to 14.9 per cent; West Asia and North Africa increased from 10.9 to 14.2 per cent; Latin America saw a decline from 28.1 to 17.8 per cent, with the Southern cone declining from 32.2 to 17.3 per cent; South Asia increased from 13.8 to 15.7 per cent; East Asia (excluding China) increased from 14.6 to 27 per cent; and China increased from 23.7 to 34.5 per cent (Kozul-Wright and Rayment 2004: 32).

By the end of the 1990s, developing countries as a whole accounted for only 10 per cent of total world exports of goods with a high research and development, technological complexity and/or scale component (UNCTAD 2002: 56). In many cases, participation in global production networks is negatively correlated with manufacturing value-added, while some countries with substantial rates of manufacturing production but low rates of participation in global production networks have higher rates of manufacturing value-added (UNCTAD 2002: 78–80). Clearly, the empirical picture is a world away from the argument that countries are poor because they are insufficiently globalized, or the Warrenite argument that the development of industrial capitalism will gradually absorb labour from the countryside as the productive forces develop.

This analysis suggests that we could more fruitfully draw on the Prebsich–Singer thesis (Singer 1950; Prebisch 1959; Sarkar and Singer 1991; Maizels *et al.* 1998; Robbins 2003), which argued that there was a tendency for the terms of trade to decline for primary producers against manufacturing exporters – although it may need updating. The basic contention of this thesis was that primary goods exporters tended to suffer because of the low income elasticity of demand for their products, which essentially means that as average incomes increase, so consumers spend a decreasing proportion of their income on primary products. This argument was reinforced by the fact that there was intense competition between primary producers, where barriers to entry into the marketplace were low, and by the fact that industrialized countries had relatively fuller employment and higher wages, as against low wages and unlimited supplies of labour in the developing countries. With the rise of manufacturing exports from the developing world, this argument could be regarded as out of date, but in fact it can be used fruitfully to look at the terms of trade between different types of manufacturing exports (UNCTAD 2002: 118; Kaplinsky and Santos-Paulinho 2005). Based on a study of trade in manufacturing goods from 1970 to 1987, Sarkar and Singer (1991) have claimed that the price of manufacturing exports from developing countries fell by an average of 1 per cent a year. This has been challenged on methodological grounds, particularly the use of the category of non-ferrous metals when examining price movements (Athukorala 1993), but a further study has suggested that the price of this category made no difference to the overall movement of manufacturing prices (Rowthorn 2001). Other studies have supported the claim that the price of simple manufacturing exports from developing countries has tended to fall against more complex manufacturing and services from developed countries (Maizels *et al.* 1998). One study of Chinese exports suggests that the net barter terms of trade fell by 10 per cent against developed countries between 1993 and 2000, but improved against other developing countries (Zheng 2002).

The reason for these movements can easily be linked to the globalization of production. Essentially, as the evidence makes clear, developed countries still tend to dominate in high-value-added sectors, based on high barriers to entry, high start-up and running costs, and significant skill levels. In the developing world, where there are large amounts of surplus labour, barriers to entry, skills and wages are low. While this gives such countries considerable competitive advantages, at the same time the fact that those barriers to entry are low means that competition is particularly intense and largely determined by cost price, which also means low wages. Thus the clothing industry, where developing countries have achieved considerable increases in world export shares in recent years, has a very low degree of market concentration. In contrast, sectors such as machinery (non-electric engines, motors, steam engines) and transport equipment (aircraft, ships, boats, cars, motor bikes) have very high degrees of market concentration and are mainly located in the developed world (UNCTAD 2002: 120–123).

The dualist argument would be that production in these labour-intensive sectors is only a starting point, allowing countries to upgrade as more developed countries shift to higher-value production. This 'flying geese' model is seen as a useful starting point for developing countries.[1] However, it assumes that upgrading is a more or less inevitable, and indeed path-dependent, process that can be driven either by the resolution of the agrarian question or by the natural workings of the market. However, in practice upgrading has occurred by states deliberately protecting themselves from import competition from established producers, via a process of import-substituting industrialization. In the context of a global tendency towards freer trade, upgrading is far from inevitable and, faced with competition from established overseas producers, is unlikely to occur.

Developing country exporters still face considerable protectionism from developed countries. While there has been considerable liberalization, for instance in the textiles and clothing sectors, through the World Trade Organization (WTO), this has not eliminated practices such as the implementation of non-tariff restrictions, including subsidies and various product standards, some of which relate to safety issues, but some of which are open to abuse. In particular, developed countries have entered into bilateral agreements that bypass the WTO. For instance, the USA has recently entered an agreement with China that allows the USA to impose import quotas unilaterally on the grounds of market disruption after a 90-day consultation period, which led to China voluntarily agreeing to restrict textile exports until 2008. Similarly, the European Union's (EU) early warning system for monitoring Chinese imports has led to new quantitative restrictions and the much derided 'bra wars' of 2005, in which Chinese garments were left stranded in EU ports. While this eventually led to a renegotiation of China's quota ceiling, this increase was at the cost of a decrease in its quota for the following year (Heron 2006: 10–11). The continued existence of trade restrictions, both tariff and non-tariff in nature, discriminates particularly against some developing countries, as some of 'the products of export interest to developing countries face the highest barriers in developed country markets' (UNCTAD 2006: 75).

At the same time, import intensity within developing countries has grown, further encouraged by the high import content of global production networks, a shift to high-income luxury goods as liberalization has intensified inequality, and cheap imports fuelled by short-lived consumer booms on the back of financial flows entering a country encouraged by high interest and exchange rates (Santos-Paulino and Thirlwall 2004; Saad-Filho 2005). While encouraging imports, these inflows do little to stimulate investment in the context of high interest rates, so they eventually lead to deteriorating trade deficits, loss of confidence in local currencies, and a flight of capital out of the country. In this sense, then, the supposedly failed import-substitution policies of the 1950s and 1960s have been replaced by policies of production substitution, based on new, short-lived neoliberal models, rapidly replaced by financial crashes that are blamed on insufficient liberalization, when it is these very policies that contribute to and exacerbate financial crises.

Apart from East Asia, although foreign investment levels have increased, this has often reflected a shift in ownership from the state to the private sector rather than genuinely new greenfield investment. Investment/GDP ratios have been lower across the board since the reform process started in the early 1980s. Thus investment/GDP ratios for Sub-Saharan Africa fell from a peak of around 23 per cent in the early 1980s to around 15 per cent in 1985. By 2000, the figure stood at around 17 per cent. For Argentina, Brazil, Chile, Colombia and Mexico, the investment/GDP ratio peaked at close to 25 per cent in 1981 and then fell to 16 per cent by 1984. By 1989, just before the foreign investment boom, it stood at 19 per cent, and by 2000 it had increased only to 20 per cent (Kozul-Wright and Rayment 2004: 30).

The implications that follow are therefore different from the flying geese model, or Raymond Vernon's (1966) product cycle model, which both tended to imply that some form of convergence would eventually occur as early industrializers dispensed with earlier forms of industrialization and thus allowed later developers to follow. It also differs from new trade theory, which has influenced social democracy's current accommodation to neoliberalism, and particularly the strategy of progressive competitiveness, which supposedly encourages win–win situations through free trade and the exercise of comparative advantage (for a critique see Albo 2004).

However, the argument presented here suggests something else altogether. Even if we leave aside the limited development of skilled jobs in the developed countries, the fact is that an international division of labour of this kind is not one that is as mutually beneficial as this scenario suggests. The outcome may not be zero-sum, but it is highly unequal. Drawing on Schumpeter's theory of innovation, Arrighi *et al.* (2003; cf. Schumpeter 1954) suggest that early innovators have locked in advantages over later developers, so they tend to accrue a disproportionate amount of the benefits, for

> it is the residents of the countries where the innovation process starts who have the best chances to win (Schumpeter's) 'spectacular prizes', that is, profits that are 'much greater than would have been necessary to call forth the particular effort'. The process tends to begin in the wealthier countries because high incomes create a favorable environment for product innovations; high costs create a favorable environment for innovations in techniques; and cheap and abundant credit creates a favorable environment for financing these and all other kinds of innovations. Moreover, as innovators in wealthy countries reap abnormally high rewards relative to effort, over time the environment for innovations in these countries improves further, thereby generating a self-reinforcing virtuous circle of high incomes and innovations.
>
> (Arrighi *et al.* 2003: 17–18)

In other words, we can reinterpret the claims of the flying geese model, product cycle theory and new trade theory on the grounds that convergence does not occur, not only because the innovating country refuses to stand still and instead continues to innovate, but also because the earlier process of innovation makes further innovation more likely in these locations. Once the innovations are diffused, that is, 'by the time the "new" products and techniques are adopted by the poorer countries', such products 'tend to be subject to intense competition and no longer bring the high returns they did in the wealthier countries' (Arrighi *et al.* 2003: 17–18).

Thus, with the globalization of production, manufacturing in the developing world is overwhelmingly concentrated in lower-value production characterized by low barriers to entry, intense competition and diminishing returns. It is in these sectors – clothing, textiles, toys and so on – that developing countries have a cost advantage, particularly in low wages. However, precisely because they are characterized by low barriers to entry, they do not provide the basis for upgrading to sectors with higher barriers to entry, where rents can be accrued to the most dynamic producers (Kaplinsky 2005; Kiely 2007). Given the close connection between low wages and a reserve army of labour – with abundant supplies of under- and unemployed labour pushing down wages – neither does it provide much optimism concerning the resolution of the classic agrarian question, in which labour gradually moves out of the rural sector and is absorbed by industrial capitalism. The global context further intensifies these problems: thus since 1990 the growth of China's exports in absolute amounts has exceeded that of the rest of the top 10 leading manufacturing exporters from the developing world, and since 2000 the latter nine countries' combined export share has fallen while China's has risen (Eichengreen *et al.* 2004). This reflects the fact that competition in low-value sectors is particularly intense and not necessarily a springboard to further development. This is not lost on the Chinese Communist Party, which combines a policy designed to draw on foreign investment while at the same time trying to continue the promotion of industrial policy – import-substituting industrialization – in order to upgrade to higher-value activity (Nolan 2001). It is far from clear that this will be a successful process, as it is probably incompatible with membership of the WTO,[2] and China faces competition from established producers in these higher-value sectors, which presumably require full access to the Chinese domestic market.

In an otherwise very useful analysis of the impact of China in the world market, Glyn (2006: 84) has asserted that

> China will at some stage move up the 'value chain' in the same way as did Japan and the Asian NIEs [newly industrializing economies]; when wage levels grow industries can no longer compete so effectively in 'low value' markets where low wages for unskilled workers are the main source of competitive advantage.

This seems unconvincing. It downplays the difficulties of upgrading in a neoliberal context, and assumes that wages will increase as labour is progressively incorporated into formal employment. His own discussion of a growing reserve army of labour suggests that this is far from guaranteed, either globally or within China (Glyn 2006: Ch. 4 and 5). In opposition to earlier debates over the links between deindustrialization in the developed world and the rise of manufacturing in the developing world, one interesting development in the period between 1995 and 2002 was the decline in formal sector manufacturing employment, not only in the developed world, but also, it appears, in China and India. While there are certainly question marks over the reliability of the figures, especially for China, the likelihood is that the fall in formal manufacturing employment from around 98 million to 83 million is actually an underestimation, as many workers in the state sector and in township and village enterprises are effectively unemployed (Kaplinsky 2005: 214–215). The sustainability of a scenario in which deficit-led developed countries such as the USA and Britain continue to boom on the basis of debt-led growth and cheap imports from China, while workers are employed in the latter fuelled by demand in the former, is questionable to say the least. This adds weight to the argument of this chapter, which has shown a marked scepticism concerning both global integration and labour absorption in the developing world (Kiely 2007: Ch. 7 and 9).

Conclusions: dualism, the agrarian question and globalization

The previous section has strayed somewhat from the discussion of Warrenite interpretations of the agrarian question, but the implications for my argument should be clear. We have already seen that, just as globalization's advocates stress the need for more globalization to resolve poverty, so Warrenites have similarly argued for more exploitation to do the same thing and, as part of this process, the resolution of the agrarian question. However, globalization, rather than promoting convergence between developed and developing countries, whereby the latter catch up or at least follow similar stages of development through upgrading, demonstrates continued divergence based on a changing but unequal international division of labour. The question is thus not about choosing whether or not to globalize, but rather the uneven and unequal form taken by actually existing globalization. While the antiglobalization argument that there is a race to the bottom is problematic, in that it assumes convergence through a process of levelling down rather then neoliberal upgrading and levelling up, this argument does at least capture something of the intensity of competition within sectors characterized by low barriers to entry, and the pressure to reduce labour costs in order to remain competitive. The problem faced by developing countries competing in such sectors is that what works for one country cannot work for all.

For labour, this alternative analysis suggests that sweatshop production is not a sacrifice made now for a better future. Rather, it is an ongoing condition[3] that reflects not only labour's subordination to global capital, but continued North–South inequalities in the context of global uneven development. Thus, rather than an optimistic scenario for contemporary globalization, based on three closely related processes of convergence with developed countries, upgrading to higher-value production, and the gradual absorption of labour based on the shift from absolute to relative surplus value extraction, we have a far darker picture. As Arrighi and Moore (2001: 75) suggest,

> the underlying contradiction of a world capitalist system that promotes the formation of a world proletariat but cannot accommodate a generalized living wage (that is, the most basic of reproduction costs), far from being solved, has become more acute than ever.

Farshad Araghi makes the same point in Chapter 5 of this book. Crucially, and in contrast to the neoliberal and stagist Marxist dualist analyses criticized in this chapter, this has an impact on all forms of labour – formal and informal, free and unfree, rural and urban, organized and unorganized. Ultimately, it reflects the reality of the contemporary era of capitalism, in which neoliberal globalization ensures an intensification of the concentration of capital even as it simultaneously unequally incorporates other parts of the world through low-value production (Dicken 2007). These processes generate an intensification of the global fragmentation of labour, as discussed by Bernstein (Chapter 10), in the context of heightened uneven and unequal development. For these reasons, the search for a simple replication of the classic agrarian question, which was never resolved for capital by one singular process (Byres 1991), is no longer relevant (Bernstein 2004). The notion that agrarian transitions should be examined as part of the shift towards industrial capitalism, and specifically in terms of agricultural surpluses supporting industrialization, no longer retains the relevance it once did. In the context of the rise of transnational manufacturing, unequally and unevenly distributed, alongside falling formal employment in manufacturing in many parts of the developing world and massive rural and urban poverty, the central question must now be how this uneven development differentially affects global labour, both rural and urban.

In terms of development, upgrading is a far from inevitable process, not only because of the developmental lead established by earlier developers, but also because neoliberal policies of trade liberalization undermine the prospects for upgrading to higher-value production. Once such production processes are shed by developed countries, these processes are no longer high-value. This is the problem of the dualist fallacy operating at a global level. Furthermore, the existence of a global reserve army of labour reinforces these processes, as producers can continue to pay low wages and draw on the unemployed and underemployed. Therefore, to suggest that it is better to be exploited than not may be true, but it also rigidly separates those employed in the formal sector from those trying to make a living in the informal sector. The reality is that the high rate of exploitation that exists in the formal sector rests, in part, on the very existence of these high rates of unemployment and underemployment. This is the problem of the dualist fallacy at a local level. Perhaps most telling in this regard is that many trade unions have responded to the fragmentation of labour over the past 20–30 years by developing new strategies, sometimes described under the all-inclusive term of social movement unionism. This is an unwelcome development for those advocates of neoliberal globalization, but ironically it is one that should logically be dismissed as irredeemably populist by those still clinging to old stagist dogmas. However, their commitment to the cause of labour was always compromised by their support for a global diffusion of capitalism that flies in the face of reality, a reality denied by stagist Marxists in the 1970s and neoliberal globalization theorists in the early twenty-first century.

Notes

1 The flying geese model, based on the idea of East Asian states flying in unison, was first developed in the 1930s, but it was not until the 1960s that the main English language publication of its pioneer first came out (Akamatsu 1962). Balassa (1989) gave the idea a more explicitly neoliberal theoretical direction. For a critique, see Kasahara (2004).
2 This is growing source of concern to the USA. For instance, US Commerce Secretary Carlos Gutierrez claimed in 2006 that '[t]he bottom line is that our companies do not have their rightful access under the terms of China's WTO commitments', and suggested that this 'only strengthens those who want to build protectionist barriers around the US market' (see Breslin 2007: Ch. 3).
3 In rejecting linear accounts of the shift from primitive accumulation to expanded reproduction, this is the grain of truth that is associated with those autonomist accounts of the continued relevance of the primitive accumulation of capital (DeAngelis 2004; cf. Harvey 2003; Akram-Lodhi 2007). However, the problem with such accounts is that they tend to flatten out all forms of capital accumulation so that there is no distinction between different forms, and primitive accumulation is everywhere.

References

Akamatsu, K. (1962) 'A historical pattern of economic growth in developing countries', *Journal of Developing Economies*, 1 (1): 3–25

Akram-Lodhi, A.H. (2007) 'Land, markets and neoliberal enclosure: an agrarian political economy approach', *Third World Quarterly*, 28 (8): 1437–1456.

Albo, G. (2004) 'A world market of opportunities? Capitalist obstacles and left economic policy', in L. Panitch, C. Leys, A. Zuege and M. Konings (eds), *The Globalization Decade*, London: Merlin.

Arrighi, G. and J.W. Moore (2001) 'Capitalist development in world historical perspective', in R. Albritton, M. Itoh, R. Westra and A. Zuege (eds), *Phases of Capitalist Development: Booms, Crises and Globalizations*, Basingstoke: Palgrave.

Arrighi, G., B. Silver and B. Brewer (2003) 'Industrial convergence, globalization, and the persistence of the North–South divide', *Studies in Comparative International Development*, 38 (1): 3–31.

Athukorala, P. (1993) 'Manufactured exports from developing countries and their terms of trade: a re-examination of the Sarkar–Singer thesis', *World Development*, 21 (10): 1607–1613.

Baker, D., G. Epstein and R. Pollin (1998) 'Introduction', in D. Baker, G. Epstein and R. Pollin (eds), *Globalization and Progressive Economic Policy*, Cambridge: Cambridge University Press.

Balassa, B. (1989) *New Directions in the World Economy*, New York: New York University Press.

Beck, U. (2000) 'The cosmopolitan perspective: sociology of the second age of modernity', *British Journal of Sociology*, 51 (1): 79–105.

—— (2006) *Cosmopolitan Vision*, Cambridge: Polity.

Ben-David, D. and B. Loewy (1998) 'Free trade, growth and convergence', *Journal of Economic Growth*, 3 (1): 143–170.

Bernstein, H. (2004) ' "Changing before our very eyes": agrarian questions and the politics of land in capitalism today', *Journal of Agrarian Change*, 4 (1/2): 190–225.

Bettelheim, C. (1972) 'Appendix I: theoretical comments', in A. Emmanuel (ed.), *Unequal Exchange*, London: New Left Books.

Bhagwati, J. (2004) *In Defence of Globalization*, Oxford: Oxford University Press.

Bhagwati, J. and T. Srinivasan (1999) *Outward Orientation and Development: Are Revisionists Right?*, Discussion Paper No. 806, Economic Growth Center, New Haven, CT, USA: Yale University.

Breslin, S. (2007) *China in the Global Political Economy*, Basingstoke: Palgrave.

Byres, T. (1991) 'The agrarian question and differing forms of capitalist transition: an essay with reference to Asia', in J. Breman and S. Mundle (eds), *Rural Transformation in Asia*, Delhi: Oxford University Press.

Caldwell, M. (1976) *The Wealth of Some Nations*, London: Zed.

Cameron, A. and R. Palan (2004) *The Imagined Economies of Globalization*, London: Sage.

Cardoso, F. and E. Faletto (1979) *Dependency and Development in Latin America*, Berkeley, CA: University of California Press.

DeAngelis, M. (2004) 'Separating the doing and the deed: capital and the continuous character of enclosures', *Historical Materialism*, 12 (2): 57–87.

Dicken, P. (2007) *Global Shift* (5th edn), London: Sage.

Eichengreen, B., Y. Rhee and H. Tong (2004) *The Impact of China on the Exports of other Asian Countries*, Working Paper No. 10768, Cambridge, MA: National Bureau of Economic Research.

Ferguson, J. (2006) *Global Shadows: Africa in the Neo-liberal World Order*, Durham, NC: Duke University Press.

Frank, A.G. (1969a) *Capitalism and Underdevelopment in Latin America*, New York: Monthly Review Press.

—— (1969b) *Latin America: Underdevelopment or Revolution?*, New York: Monthly Review Press.

Friedman, T. (2005) *The World is Flat*, New York: Allen Lane.

Frobel, F., J. Heinrichs and O. Kreye (1980) *The New International Division of Labour: Structural Unemployment in Industrialised Countries and Industrialisation in Developing Countries*, Cambridge: Cambridge University Press.

Giddens, A. (2000) *The Third Way and Its Critics*, Cambridge: Polity.

—— (2002) *Which Way For New Labour?*, Cambridge: Polity.

Glyn, A. (2006) *Capitalism Unleashed*, Oxford: Oxford University Press.

Grossman, G. and E. Helpman (1991) *Innovation and Growth in the Global Economy*, Cambridge, MA: MIT Press.

Gulalp, H. (1986) 'Debate on capitalism and development: the theories of Samir Amin and Bill Warren', *Capital and Class*, 28: 135–59.

Harvey, D. (2003) *The New Imperialism*, Oxford: Oxford University Press.

Heron, T. (2006) 'The ending of the Multi-fibre Agreement: a development boon for the South?', *European Journal of Development Research*, 18 (1): 1–21.

Jenkins, R. (1984) 'Divisions over the international division of labour', *Capital and Class*, 22: 28–57.

Kaplinsky, R. (2005) *Globalization, Poverty and Inequality*, Cambridge: Polity.

Kaplinsky, R. and A. Santos-Paulinho (2005) 'Innovation and competitiveness: trends in unit prices in global trade', *Oxford Development Studies*, 33 (3/4): 333–355.

Kasahara, S. (2004) *The Flying Geese Paradigm: A Critical Study of its Application to East Asian Regional Development*, UNCTAD Discussion Paper No. 169, Geneva: UN Conference on Trade and Development.

Kay, C. (1989) *Latin American Theories of Development and Underdevelopment*, London: Routledge.

Kay, G. (1975) *Development and Underdevelopment*, London: Macmillan.

Kiely, R. (1994) 'Development theory and industrialisation: beyond the impasse', *Journal of Contemporary Asia*, 24 (2): 133–160.

—— (2007) *The New Political Economy of Development*, Basingstoke: Palgrave.

Kitching, G. (1989) *Development and Underdevelopment in Historical Perspective* (2nd edn), London: Methuen.

—— (2001) *Seeking Social Justice through Globalization*, Philadelphia, PA: Pennsylvania State University Press.

Kozul-Wright, R. and P. Rayment (2004) *Globalization Reloaded: An UNCTAD Perspective*, UNCTAD Discussion Paper No. 167, Geneva: UN Conference on Trade and Development.

Krueger, A. (1974) 'The political economy of the rent-seeking society', *American Economic Review*, 64 (3): 291–303.

—— (1998) 'Why trade liberalisation is good for growth', *Economic Journal*, 108: 1513–1522.

Krugman, P. (1986) *Strategic Trade Policy and the New International Economics*, Cambridge, MA, USA: MIT Press.

Lal, D. (1983) *The Poverty of 'Development Economics'*, London: Institute of Economic Affairs.

Larrain, J. (1989) *Theories of Development*, Cambridge: Polity.

Lewis, A. (1954) 'Economic development with unlimited supplies of labour', *Manchester School of Economic and Social Studies*, 22 (2): 139–191.

Little, I., T. Scitovsky and M. Scott (1970), *Industry and Trade in Some Developing Countries*, Oxford: Oxford University Press.

Maizels, A., T. Palaskas and T. Crowe (1998) 'The Prebisch–Singer hypothesis revisited', in D. Sapford and J. Chen (eds), *Development Economics and Policy*, Basingstoke: Palgrave Macmillan.

Mueller, S. (1980) 'Retarded capitalism in Tanzania', in R. Miliband and J. Savile (eds), *The Socialist Register 1980*, London: Merlin.

Nolan, P. (2001) *China and the Global Economy*, Basingstoke: Palgrave.

Palma, G. (1978) 'Dependency and development: a formal theory of under-development or a methodology for the analysis of concrete situations of under-development', *World Development*, 6 (8): 881–924.

Prebisch, R. (1959) 'Commercial policy in the underdeveloped countries', *American Economic Review* 44: 251–273.

Reno, W. (1999) *Warlord Politics and African States*, Boulder, CO: Lynne Rienner.

Robbins, P. (2003) *Stolen Fruit*, London: Zed.

Rostow, W.W. (1971) *The Stages of Economic Growth: A Non-Communist Manifesto*, Cambridge: Cambridge University Press.

Rowthorn, B. (2001) 'Replicating the experience of the NIEs on a large scale', in K.S. Jomo and S. Nagaraj (eds), *Globalization versus Development*, Basingstoke: Palgrave Macmillan.

Saad-Filho, A. (2005) 'The political economy of neoliberalism in Latin America', in A. Saad-Filho and D. Johnston (eds), *Neoliberalism: A Critical Reader*, London: Pluto.

Santos-Paulino A. and A. Thirlwall (2004) 'The impact of trade liberalisation on exports, imports and the balance of payments of developing countries', *Economic Journal*, 114: 50–72.

Sarkar, P. and H. Singer (1991) 'Manufactured exports of developing countries and their terms of trade', *World Development*, 19 (4): 333–340

Saul, J. and C. Leys (2006) 'Dependency', in D. Clark (ed.), *The Elgar Companion to Development Studies*, Cheltenham: Edward Elgar.

Schumpeter, J. (1954) *Capitalism, Socialism and Democracy*, London: Allen and Unwin.

Seers, D. (1979) 'The congruence of Marxism and other neo-classical doctrines', in A. Rothko (ed.), *Towards a New Strategy For Development*, New York: Pergamon Press.

Sender, J. (1999) 'Africa's economic performance: limitations of the current con-sensus', *Journal of Economic Perspectives*, 13 (3): 89–114.

—— (2002) 'Women's struggle to escape rural poverty in South Africa', *Journal of Agrarian Change*, 2 (1): 1–49.

—— (2003) 'Rural poverty and gender: analytical frameworks and policy proposals', in H.J. Chang (ed.), *Rethinking Development Economics*, London: Anthem.

Sender, J. and D. Johnston (2004) 'Searching for a weapon of mass production in rural Africa: unconvincing arguments for land reform', *Journal of Agrarian Change*, 4 (1/2): 142–164.

Sender, J. and J. Pincus (2006) 'Capitalism and development', in D. Clark (ed.), *The Elgar Companion to Development Studies*, Cheltenham: Edward Elgar.

Sender, J. and S. Smith (1985) 'What's right with the Berg Report and what's left of its critics', *Capital and Class*, 24: 125–146.

—— (1986) *The Development of Capitalism in Africa*, London: Methuen.

—— (1990) *Poverty, Class and Gender in Rural Africa*, London: Routledge.

Shafaeddin, S.M. (2005a) *Trade Liberalization and Economic Reform in Developing Countries*, UNCTAD Discussion Paper No. 179, Geneva: UN Conference on Trade and Development.

—— (2005b) *Trade Policy at the Crossroads*, Basingstoke: Palgrave Macmillan.

Shaikh, A. (2005) 'The economic mythology of neoliberalism', in A. Saad-Filho and D. Johnston (ed.), *Neoliberalism: A Critical Reader*, London: Pluto.

Singer, H. (1950) 'The distribution of gains from trade between investing and borrowing countries', *American Economic Review*, 40: 473–485

UNCTAD (2002) *Trade and Development Report 2002*, Geneva: UN Conference on Trade and Development.

—— (2006) *Trade and Development Report 2006*, Geneva: UN Conference on Trade and Development.

Vernon, R. (1966) 'International investment and international trade in the product cycle', *Quarterly Journal of Economics*, 80 (2): 190–207.

Warren, B. (1973) 'Imperialism and capitalist industrialisation', *New Left Review*, 813–844.

—— (1980) *Imperialism: Pioneer of Capitalism*, London: Verso.

Wolf, M. (2003) *Why Globalization Works*, New Haven, CT: Yale University Press.

Wolf, M. and R. Wade (2002) 'Are global poverty and inequality getting worse?', *Prospect* March: 16–21.

World Bank (1987) *World Development Report 1987*, Washington, DC: World Bank.

—— (1993) *The East Asian Miracle*, Oxford: Oxford University Press.

—— (1994) *Adjustment in Africa*, Oxford: Oxford University Press.

—— (2002) *Globalization, Growth and Poverty*, Oxford: Oxford University Press.

Zheng, Z. (2002) *China's Terms of Trade in World Manufactures, 1993–2000*, UNCTAD Discussion Paper No. 161, Geneva: UN Conference on Trade and Development.

8 Gender justice, land and the agrarian question in Southern Africa

Bridget O'Laughlin

Loveness ... is 20 years old and originally from Maronda communal area in Mwenezi District (Zimbabwe). Her husband was a long-term labour migrant in South Africa. Her in-laws chased her away from their home when she had a relationship with another man and got pregnant. She moved in with her sister in Chiredzi where she became an active member of the ZANU (PF) women's league and was amongst the first to settle on Fair Range. She admits to working as a prostitute in the resettlement area – raising money to purchase goods in South Africa for resale. As she puts it: 'I do not care (what other people think) as I now have my plot here and I am taking care of my children ... I no longer bother my sister and I am now independent'.

(Chaumba *et al.* 2003: 591)

Women's land rights and the agrarian question in Southern Africa

In the curious interface between donors, national governments and consultants that defines the policy agenda around agrarian issues in Southern Africa today, the security of women's land rights has become a central preoccupation.[1] At one level it appears as a consensus issue, driven by the antipoverty agenda and human rights advocacy. Heightened by gender- and generationally skewed patterns of AIDS mortality, who could oppose the proposition that rural women who cultivate land should have access to it, or that widows should be able to claim the property to which their labour has contributed?

Yet behind these apparently uncontroversial appeals to gender justice lie facets of the postcolonial agrarian question in Southern Africa. The contributors to this volume do not necessarily share precisely the same vision of what the agrarian question is, or on what currently constitutes an acceptable range of answers to it, but all focus on its three elements: class, politics and accumulation. They further agree that it is a strategic question that links the politics of class alliances to processes of accumulation, agricultural production to industry, and country to city. Moreover, most contributors to this book would also argue that the agrarian question of the twenty-first century does not concern the transition from precapitalist modes of production to capitalism, but rather the position of rural people and agricultural production within global capitalism. The contradictions of contemporary capitalism have given rise to a renewal of non-capitalist forms of production, downward pressures on wages, informality and unemployment. The implication of this position is a radical rejection of all analytical oppositions: capitalist versus precapitalist, market versus non-marketed, traditional versus modern, formal versus informal. Each of these oppositions captures part of the descriptive empirical reality, but analytically they are – and this must be stressed – interdependent.

The postcolonial agrarian question in Southern Africa raises three particularly thorny questions. What is to be done about the enormous economic inequality, not just of income but of conditions of living, that is the heritage of the regional system of migrant labour? What is to be done about the continuing racial divide in land ownership, particularly in South Africa and Zimbabwe, where the political weight of the question seems to go beyond its economic importance? Finally, what is to be done about the link between forms of landed property and governance expressed in the divide between customary and freehold statutory tenure, between 'citizen and subject' (Mamdani 1996)?

It may seem anachronistic to suggest that the literature on the agrarian question and the issues it raises in Southern Africa could provide any guidance in the debate on women's land rights. Historically, gender relations have received short shrift in Marxist discussions of rural property rights, so one might not expect much help. However, gender is clearly implicated in all three aspects of the agrarian question, whether class, politics or accumulation, although protagonists have not always been willing to recognize that this is so. Moreover, the rejection of radical oppositions and the stress on analytical interdependence has long been understood by those working on the political economy of gender. The boundary between reproductive labour and the productive labour that formally produces surplus value is extremely fluid. Although the preoccupation of capital is necessarily with the sphere of marketed production, the dynamics of capital accumulation also depend on how non-marketed work affects the real wage and the prices of commodities that enter the circuit of capital. Above all, from the perspective of labour, a livelihood does not depend on wage income alone, for it includes the unmarketed labour of women, children and men. There is, in short, a need to both engender the agrarian question and bring the issues raised by the agrarian question into the analysis of gender relations. If such is the case, then, the debate on women's land rights in Southern Africa needs to be reassessed in light of the concerns of the agrarian question.

This chapter argues that the issue of women's land rights has been deployed in the policy discourse on agrarian change in Southern Africa to reinforce the moral claims of a liberal capitalist project that misrepresents and simplifies the political and economic history of the region. It discusses the ways in which a class-based understanding yields more complex and varied questions about the relations between gender, land and livelihood. It also suggests, however, that the liberal misconstrual of gender relations has been facilitated by the avoidance of gender issues in the Marxist analysis of accumulation, class and agrarian politics. These have, I think, particular importance for what is arguably the central concern of a critical Marxist political economy in Southern Africa: constructing a politically viable counter-hegemonic response to the agrarian question, one that will challenge market fundamentalism in a way that liberalism cannot be expected to do.

Agrarian crisis

Regional boundaries are always approximations – political constructs. Southern Africa is a diverse region, but many of its commonalities today were delimited by the boundaries of colonial empire and defined by its distinctive political economy. These commonalities include the concentration of capital accumulation in certain key sectors in particular locations – manufacturing, mines and plantations in South Africa, Zimbabwe and the Zambian copperbelt and some urban centres; the appropriation of land with most commercial potential by settlers; the constitution of the remaining rural areas as labour reserves for the recruitment of migrant male wage labourers; a dualistic and racially based political and legal system; and a late and protracted struggle for decolonization.

For several generations, the urban and industrial labour force was unevenly gendered, with migrant men living in hostels, and women farming and raising children in rural areas. Migrants travelled long distances to do waged work, sometimes contracted for fixed periods and sometimes searching out better jobs on their own. Families were divided, or sometimes never firmly established. Women also migrated to urban centres, particularly in South Africa, but gendered pass laws, identity cards and border restrictions regulated their mobility, and that of children, more tightly than that of men.

These gendered patterns of migration are reflected in the high incidence of female-headed households in Southern Africa: households headed by widows, divorcees, grandmothers or single mothers, caring for children on their own. Female-headed households range from 24.8 per cent of all households in Zambia to 50.1 per cent of all households in Botswana, with Malawi, Mozambique, Lesotho, Zimbabwe, Namibia and South Africa falling in between these two proportions, according to Macro International (2007). The high incidence of female-headed households, particularly in rural areas, is not just a matter of missing migrant husbands or early male mortality. There are also many men who never succeed in forming a stable conjugal household.

AIDS is, like drought and famine, a revelatory crisis in southern Africa (Solway 1994). Writing in 1989, before the AIDS epidemic was so evident in South Africa, Hunt (1989) argued that the distribution of HIV/AIDS in Southern and Eastern Africa suggested that the best explanation for the epidemic lay in the history of the migrant labour system: protracted absences of men, family breakdown, and a high number of sexual partners. He noted that, historically, people of the region have suffered from epidemics of sexually transmitted diseases that make women particularly vulnerable to AIDS. Deep inequalities within the region, of class, race and gender, also undermine prevention and the capacity to treat the disease. As one would expect from such migration patterns, the incidence of HIV/AIDS was initially higher in urban areas and among men; however, women are now disproportionately victims of the disease, and it has become endemic in rural areas.

There is thus a terrible irony in the situation of rural Southern Africa today. Rural livelihoods came to depend heavily on regular remittances, making some form of wage labour a way to invest in agriculture and cattle, to weather the uncertainties of harvests, or simply to survive while working very small plots of land. However, capital no longer searches out unskilled labour to hire, in either rural or urban areas. Mining and capitalist agriculture have mechanized, and liberalization has undercut domestic industry, except in South Africa. Investors focus on tourist complexes, including the establishment of privately run nature reserves and game parks, the cutting of timber, and outgrower schemes. As a result, while rural areas have come to depend on wage labour, the reality is that of chronic unemployment or underemployment in both rural and urban areas, insecure livelihoods, and agrarian crisis.

There is, of course, great intraregional diversity and varied local history. Some former labour recruitment areas have found alternatives to migration: in north-eastern Zambia some redundant miners became growers of hybrid maize (Moore and Vaughan 1994); and in central Mozambique the sons of former plantation workers are now bicycle traders. There are parts of South Africa and Botswana where 'urban villages' sit in a countryside that appears rural but has little agricultural production outside large farms or ranches. In some places, men continue to migrate and women continue farming in rural areas, but in others young women move to urban areas to work in industry or as domestic servants. There are rural areas supported by remittances, old-age pensions and government food banks; there are others where the only forms of external social assistance come from local non-governmental organizations (NGOs) dependent on fickle donor funding. Yet beneath these real differences, there is a fundamental unity of labour markets across the Southern African region that makes change in one part reverberate in others.

Conflicting approaches to the agrarian question

There are two principal, contrasting ways of understanding the nature of agrarian crisis in Southern Africa today: liberal and Marxist. Each has roots in the classical literature on the agrarian question, which (as noted by Akram-Lodhi and Kay in Chapter 1) addressed the political dilemmas of urban classes in early modern Europe. Both the liberal bourgeoisie and working class movements had to determine what kinds of class alliance were appropriate for the advancement of their own economic and political agenda. For both, the question of alliances involved deciding what stand to take on agrarian land reform. The relationship between land and the agrarian question was predicated on the fact that land was the most important means of production in the countryside, and that its ownership and control was very unevenly distributed. Thus the liberal bourgeoisie balanced its concern with the freeing of labour and the development of the home market against the substantial political power of rural landlords. By way of contrast, working class movements were clear in their support for the emancipatory demands of enserfed or bound workers, and thus against feudal ties to land, but were not so convinced about the conversion of these bonds to individual property rights. To do so seemed to be promoting a class that would necessarily identify itself with capitalists, whose control over the means of production would be protected by bourgeois property rights.

Land in the liberal vision of the agrarian question

From a liberal perspective, agrarian crisis in Southern Africa today has universal causes: the absence or failure of liberal institutions such as private property, free markets, voluntary association, free information, free expression of individual opinion, the rule of law and parliamentary democracy. The liberal vision captures much of the reality of Southern Africa; its history has indeed been a negation of liberal values under *apartheid*, protracted colonialism, and some very illiberal postcolonial regimes. Pass laws and forced labour regimes impeded the development of labour markets, and state intervention disrupted or even suppressed the development of capital and commodity markets. Politically, the exclusion of the vast majority of the population from the rights of citizenship under colonialism and *apartheid* lingered on in rural areas under postcolonial regimes.

The neoliberal consensus forged in the 1980s focused on the regulation, fragmentation, closure or absence of markets as barriers to capital accumulation, and thus as causes of poverty. Rural poverty was attributed to urban bias in market interventions: the protection of domestic industry and urban consumption. Granted, the liberal ascendancy in the 1990s has given great attention to a broader range of human rights and to the political dimensions of poverty. Its charter text could be Amartya Sen's (1999) *Development as Freedom*, with its emphasis on freedom as individual autonomy and choice. However, despite this shift in emphasis, the liberal economic agenda maintains neoliberalism's prescriptive emphasis on the development of markets.

Private property is a basic human right in a liberal approach, because without it the individual has no basis for autonomy and thus freedom of choice. Almost everything in human life can be understood as individual property: knowledge is human capital; kin and friendship networks are social capital. Clear and discrete relations of property and transparent information about the terms of exchange are needed to reconcile myriad individual choices in an outcome that maximizes welfare for all. Institutional barriers, such as gender inequality, that prevent agents from maximizing their own utility or hamper the free flow of information, lead markets to work imperfectly. If allowed to function without institutional fetters, however, the freely functioning market creates the best possible moral universe.

This set of assumptions goes beyond economics. It also grounds the moral language of individual rights, permeating the discourse of the human rights movement and organizations such as Human Rights Watch. In a liberal moral order, the proper rule of law is to allow each individual the right of free choice, to protect individual autonomy and rights of property, and to assure the free flow of commodities and ideas.

The neoliberal political agenda has dominated the region since the 1990s, including formal political institutions – if not repressive political practice – in Zimbabwe. Constitutions were written or revised along liberal lines (Mozambique's postsocialist constitution includes, for example, a specific commitment to a market economy); multiparty elections have been held; independent media are present, if somewhat uneasily so; trade unions have been nursed away from ruling parties; local NGOs function as both advocacy groups and service providers; parastatals have been sold off and private sector investment, whether domestic or foreign, is encouraged. The rhetoric of rights-based development has displaced the aspirations of socialist revolution. South Africa was once a glaring anomaly in the liberal vision of the region, as it combined relatively healthy economic growth with the denial of democratic rights to the entire black population. Today it appears to be the most secure embodiment of liberal values, judging by the extent of commodification, the sway of private property, and the independence of liberal institutions.

In the 1990s there was substantial pressure from bilateral donors, the International Monetary Fund and the World Bank to draft land laws that would give investors greater security of tenure and codify liberal notions of governance and the rule of law (McAuslan 1998; 2003). In areas not covered by freehold tenure, the principal issue has been land tenure reform. Followers of de Soto (2001) in particular argue that the combination of state ownership of land and the maintenance of communal access under customary tenure regimes in the labour reserves has hindered both the free flow of labour and the allocation of land to more efficient forms of production.

The current liberal economic consensus does not assume that large-scale holdings are more efficient than small-scale holdings, and thus does not oppose redistributive land reform (Brink 2002). It also recognizes that individual tenure and the commodification of rights over land have developed within customary tenure regimes in Southern Africa. However, it does assume that the overlapping of property rights associated with such systems impedes security of tenure and thus ultimately reinforces poverty, inequality and economic stagnation.

The new land laws stopped short of instituting full private landed property or the extension of freehold rights to all who occupied land. Forms of communal or collective rights were maintained for those areas governed in the colonial period or under *apartheid* by customary authorities. Indeed, the political reforms of the 1990s strengthened the formal role of chiefs in both local government and the allocation of land in South Africa, Zimbabwe and Mozambique. Nonetheless, the state remains the ultimate owner or arbiter of access to land in many countries.

The apparent anomalous inclusion of customary hereditary authority within liberal land laws was, in part, due to pressure by NGOs that took part in the 'participatory' processes that accompanied the drafting of the laws. They were concerned to ensure that existing forms of land use and occupation by the broad mass of the rural population had a legal defence against land grabbing by big investors and political elites.[2] World Bank tolerance of customary land rights under what was essentially a neoliberal consensus reflected a new appreciation for the security of individual control of land, the capacity for innovation and investment under existing customary tenure arrangements in Africa, and the difficulties of titling (World Bank 2003). African smallholder farmers had thus invested in land without private title; individual title to land has not been an important determinant of access to credit in a context where most holdings are very small; and land titling schemes are also expensive to implement, demanding a capacity for cadastral registry.

The consensus around maintaining customary tenure has, however, proven to be unstable. In the name of a new 'Green Revolution for Africa', many within international financial institutions, donors, domestic capital and political elites have returned to their demands for full privatization, permanent title and the unrestricted negotiability of land. However, security of title under the extension of freehold tenure is not just a concern of potential investors. Some argue that subjecting transactions in informal land markets to legal regulation would limit land grabbing and protect both buyers and sellers of land, tenants as well as landlords. Others argue, though, that freehold registry will favour the rich and powerful, and that distress sales of titled land will fuel the dispossession of the rural poor. Titles demarcate and assign discrete rights to certain individuals; in doing so, they exclude others, many of whom may be landless or very poor.

The liberal argument for women's independent land rights

In this context of political uncertainty over the impact of titling on rural poverty, the present gender injustice of land rights – and the particular vulnerability of AIDS widows – has come to be a mantra for those who support the privatization of land.

Liberalism has no difficulty in accommodating demands for independent land rights for women. In its incarnation in neoclassical economics, liberalism for many years took the unitary household as a unit of analysis, although as Hart (1995) has pointed out, its methodological individualism would appear to mandate discriminating between women and men.

In line with its focus on equality under the law and rights of property, the liberal approach to women's land rights focuses on the content of law, particularly family and inheritance law, and the functioning of legal institutions. Liberal analysts point out that traditional systems of African customary law are inequitable because they give women only secondary land rights, particularly in Southern Africa where descent is often patrilineally traced (whereas in much of the Northern part of the region, matrilineal descent predominates). They note that even where women have land, their tenure is insecure or fuzzy because other people may have claims to the same plot.

Statutory law makes much clearer provision for gender equity in ownership and inheritance of property, particularly after the wave of liberal constitutional and legal reform of the 1990s. Women are often not able to claim their statutory rights, however, particularly in rural areas. Ikdahl *et al.* (2005) reviewed women's land rights in Southern Africa from a human rights point of view, focusing principally on the content of legislation and its implementation. They found that, although there were some differences in the quality of legislation, the main problem was women's lack of information on the property rights they legally enjoyed. To exercise their freedom, women must know their rights.

The crisis of AIDS has strengthened demands for women's independent land rights on human rights grounds. As part of their general review of gender inequality in ownership of assets, Deere and Doss (2006: 40) suggest that in the context of HIV/AIDS in Africa 'owning assets may even be a matter of life and death'. They emphasize that current inheritance laws deprive women of property that would both protect their livelihoods after the death of their husbands, and help them resist risky sex and domestic violence. Various regional NGOs support will-writing projects to assist men in writing wills that favour their own wives and children and exclude their patrilineal kin.

Bina Agarwal (1994, 2003a, 2003b) has provided the most worked out theoretical account of the liberal argument for women's land rights. She brings together a rights-based approach to gender equity and the efficiency concerns of neoclassical economics. Her argument that women need fields of their own is somewhat predictable, given the emphasis that liberalism placed on individual autonomy as the basis of freedom, but she argues with such clarity that her work has acquired great legitimacy both in World Bank circles and among land activists. Applying Agarwal's arguments, for example, the World Bank Gender Unit advocated the formalization of women's land rights as an important contribution to poverty reduction, particularly in Africa.[3] Although Agarwal's own research focuses on South Asia, it easily extends to Africa, where the high proportion of farm work done by women on small plots provides a strong ethical, economic and political basis for arguing that control over land is an essential right for women. However, the question remains whether this is best done by formalizing individual tenure.

Using a bargaining model approach derived from neoclassical economics, Agarwal provides the theoretical grounding for three main arguments in support of the formalization of women's independent land rights. First, if women's land rights are not derived from those of men, their greater autonomy will give them stronger bargaining positions within households and greater respect in public domains. Second, women manage what they own differently from men, using it in ways that provide better for overall household wellbeing; separate title allows women to manage their land particularly with regard to the nourishment of children. Third, formalizing land rights for women will lead to greater economic efficiency: women will be able to mortgage their land for credit, thus obtaining access to technologies and information currently open only to men. Women will also be more assiduous in their work on the land if they know their hold on it is secure.

Agarwal does not entirely dismiss the idea of joint registration of household land, but she argues that individual title of some kind – 'a field of one's own' – gives women greater protection. Thus, with formal individual title, women are able to maintain land rights after the break-up of marriage. Moreover, having an exit option may protect women from domestic violence. Finally, separate title facilitates deviating from their husbands' patterns of land use and gives women better control over the produce of the land.

More recently, Agarwal (2003b: 573), in response to charges of individualism in her work, has said that she is not necessarily wedded to individual ownership. She suggests that women might join their plots in group farming schemes with state-provided credit and support. This rejoinder is, however, not very convincing. Apart from a substantial literature showing how much investment and long-term effort must be put in to make group farming work, the proposal also compromises some of the advantages to women that are said to flow from individual land rights. Exit options are not so easy to follow when women's property is held collectively with that of other women, nor is inheritance a transparent issue.

Agarwal links the campaign for women's independent land rights to the broader liberal political project of achieving women's citizenship rights. She recognizes that land rights in themselves will not transform women's lives, but argues that 'it is not just an increase in women's command over economic resources, but also the process by which that increase occurs that has a crucial bearing on gender relations' (Agarwal 2003b: 573).

If we return to the description of Loveness, the Zimbwean single mother, with which this chapter begins, we can see in some ways that she is the embodiment of Agarwal's liberal vision. Spurned and dispossessed by her in-laws, she was nonetheless able to care for her children as an autonomous woman once she had her own field.

Marxist views on land and the agrarian question

Marxist approaches provide a critical alternative to the liberal understanding of agrarian crisis in Southern Africa, and thus to the question of land reform and gendered land rights. In a Marxist approach, Southern Africa's agrarian crisis is rooted not in what it does not have – liberal economic and political institutions – but in what it does have: a history of integration into global markets and the class relations of capitalism through violence and colonial domination, as examined by Amiya Kumar Bagchi (Chapter 4). The meaning of land reform and the importance of women's land rights must thus be read through the lens of class.

Marxism is like liberalism, in that it is both a mode of analysis and a political programme.[4] It provides an alternative discourse for claims to social justice and human rights. It is politically concerned with collective agency, and thus maintains a conception of human rights that does not begin with an autonomous individual able to dispose of property according to her or his own preferences. So pervasive is the language of liberalism in contemporary everyday life that it is sometimes difficult to remember that it is possible to conceive of human rights without making private property a fundamental right. Rather than a universal right to property – even to land or water – one might have a right to a livelihood and decent health. From this alternative viewpoint, then, it can be strongly argued that prescriptive commodification of everything, and the privileged legal status of the right to hold property, constitutes the defence of class privilege in a capitalist world.

Not all those who address the agrarian question from a Marxist perspective answer it in the same way. Some think that the call for redistribution of land to small farmers is a neopopulist fantasy attempting to recreate a non-existent peasantry, while others would say it is an appropriate political and economic response to the new inequalities of globalization.[5] There is, however, general agreement that the answer requires us to deal with the historical dynamic of three interdependent aspects: accumulation, class and politics (Byres 1982). Taking account of the dynamics of accumulation means attending to the structure of the economy, an unpopular term as far as contemporary development economics is concerned. That implies, in turn, that no agrarian question is purely about agriculture or rural life.

In formal terms, the agrarian question in Southern Africa today is not so different from that in nineteenth century Europe. The merits of redistributive land reform and individual land demarcation and titling are under discussion across the region. The context of global capital accumulation, in which the question is posed, is however very different, and so will be the answers. The clarity of older categories of property and class has been compromised, and it is no longer the case that one finds capitalists hungry for cheap labour tearing peasants away from the fabric of rural life.[6] Today, a fragmented proletariat confronts informal labour markets and sub-contracting. Individuals and households combine farming with off-farm labour, while others float between rural and urban areas, or between different rural areas. Old linear sequences are destabilized as workers may move from industry back to small-scale farming, and families retreat – or are driven – from urban areas to the countryside. There are powerful national and multinational capitalist firms, but there are also NGOs and government agencies undertaking service provision according to commercial principles, and donor governments carrying out the functions of finance capital.

Whereas liberalism sees markets yet to develop, Marxist political economy sees workers displaced from labour markets by mechanization in mining and the demise of manufacturing in many parts of the region as a consequence of the adoption of liberal trade policies over the past 30 years. It highlights the feedback effects of unemployment on agriculture through the interrupted flow of remittance income that has come to be necessary to invest in ploughs, inputs, irrigation pumps, boreholes and cattle, and to hire casual labour. The break between agricultural and industrial accumulation explains why, even in the context of land shortage in areas such as north-eastern Zimbabwe, where some people are landless, land can still lie vacant or poorly cultivated, and why rural producers speak of labour shortages. It follows that forms of land ownership *per se* cannot explain poverty in Southern Africa.

Shifting patterns of accumulation in rural areas are related both to contradiction and change in class relations over time, and to shifts in global patterns of accumulation. The relation between capital and labour has come to be the central determinant of rural life in Southern Africa, not because agrarian capital is strong, but because proletarianization rooted in non-farm labour is so deep. Rural proletarianization is reflected in out-migration and in the large numbers of women who do casual wage labour where there are commercial farms and plantations, even though some have access to land (Sender 2002; Sender *et al.* 2006). For them, the core poverty issue may not be land, but rather instability in employment, low wages or wretched conditions of work. These are the processes of change that Bernstein (Chapter 10) refers to when he suggests that, while the classical agrarian question was the question of capital, the new agrarian question is that of labour. In a time of structural unemployment, proletarianization is reflected in the concern rural people have with jobs, in the proliferation of small vendors, and in the desperation and anger of unemployed youth.

There is growing class differentiation within rural communities, evident not only in income and housing, but also in the size of herds and land-holdings, in the type of agricultural techniques employed, and in the yields achieved. This differentiation is reflected in the growth of informal land markets, even in areas held under customary tenure, particularly when these are areas of good commercial potential (Chimhowu and Woodhouse 2006; Peters and Kambewa 2007). Rentals are an important part of this market. There are also increasing numbers of direct land sales, particularly wetlands or land near cities, in areas administered by local chiefs throughout southern Africa. Part of this informal commodification is chiefs selling off land under their control, but there are also direct sales by those occupying the land.

Tellingly, there are reports of HIV/AIDS driving distress sales of land to pay medical expenses in South Africa, Swaziland and Zambia (Chimhowu and Woodhouse 2006: 360–361; Wiegers *et al.* 2006).

The condition of landlessness, the experience of agricultural production and the meaning of poverty vary widely across the region. James' (2007) in-depth study of one case of restitutive land reform in Mpumalanga, South Africa showed that very high levels of government support would be needed to provide the semiurban living conditions that even the poor expected from their life in the reserves. She also pointed out that not all those hungry for land are poor. She argued that focusing land reform on the land rights of the poor cuts out other landless, but more prosperous, groups with the resources and skills needed to make a financial success of farming. Moreover, the meaning of land reform would be quite different just across the border in Southern Mozambique, where rural people see themselves as farmers.

Class, gender and land

In a context so shaped by migrant labour, the relation between land, gender and class is complex and historically shifting. For much of the nineteenth century, women worked the land in rural areas while men migrated, a pattern that still holds in many parts of the region. Now, however, the gendered patterns of semiproletarianization are unstable. There are many women migrating to cities and living on their own. There are people, women and men, living in rural communities trying to scratch a living from very small plots, or without any land at all, particularly in South Africa, Zimbabwe and in periurban areas throughout the region.

Even in conditions of great land scarcity, there are women and men who have land, but leave it fallow or badly cultivated. They may be too ill to work it, or they are urban migrants who want to maintain their home base, or they do not have the cash to buy inputs. In this case, holding onto land may mean letting or lending the land to someone else. Paradza, in her unpublished research on women's land rights in north-eastern Zimbabwe, found that despite general agreement that land was scarce, there were many plots lying fallow. Widows were lent these plots; their tenure was insecure, but the deaths of their husbands did not mean that they were expelled from the community or left landless.

There are also people who have owned land, but have lost it because they could not keep it under cultivation. Vijfhuizen (2001) explains how single women in one arid area of Southern Mozambique came to lose their land. First, their rainfed plots were included in an irrigation scheme built by an Italian aid project. To keep their plots in the project, they had be able to pay water and maintenance fees. Those who succeeded belonged to households that had some form of off-farm income: mainly households headed by men. In addition, Mutangadura (2004) observes that many AIDS widows who have lost their land to their husbands' landless patrilineal kin have done so not always because they have been expelled, but rather because many HIV/ AIDS-affected families have not been able to make productive use of their landholdings. When a woman has nothing but a plot of land, that plot may well be full of weeds.

There are thus many ways in which women and men obtain – and lose – access to land in non-freehold areas in Southern Africa. They may receive land in gift or inheritance from their own parents or members of their parents' descent group. They may be granted land by a local chief or land board, often with some kind of payment. They may join a government resettlement scheme or a church community. They may be lent land by kin or friends, or they may buy it. The insecurity of these rights means they cannot be used to raise a mortgage, but most of the holdings are so small that, even with formal freehold, a bank would not be interested.

This multiplicity of ways that women and men obtain land is not new in Southern Africa; Cheater (1990) challenged the ideology of communal tenure and the idea that patrilineal descent barred women from access to land on the basis of her research in Zimbabwe in the 1980s. Research in Mozambique in the 1970s and 1980s similarly showed that land was obtained in many different ways. Robertson (1987) underlined the importance of different forms of share contract in Southern Africa in 1987.

The diversity of class processes affecting access to land thus undercuts the simplistic notion that gender bias in customary law is the main constraint on women's land rights. Descent groups, chiefs, district administrators, parliamentarians, judges and ministers all function within a crosscutting class structure. Communities in Mozambique found that, when dealing with a potential outside investor accompanied by someone from government, they felt they could not refuse requests for their land or its forest cover – they were just hoping to get something out of an undesirable situation (Tanner *et al.* 2006). Claiming one's constitutional rights, or using a will to contest an inheritance settlement, requires access to courts and lawyers, a right most often claimed by those who have substantial property.

Manji (2006: 99) observed that African NGOs and legal networks working on women's land issues in Africa tended to focus on the statutory reforms and legal institutions that consolidated the property rights of middle-class women. The liberal rhetoric of the donor-driven consensus – good governance and the rule of law (and, it might be said, human rights) – papered over the lines of class division and rural urban difference that matter for the relations of different groups of women and men to land. The problem was not their robust and contested defence of legal principles of gender equality, but what was not raised – the distributional choices implied by an agenda of land reform (Ntsebeza 2004).

Locating the question of land tenure reform in Southern Africa within the context of the agrarian question thus leads to a much more sceptical assessment of the likely impact of formalizing women's independent land rights than the liberal argument would suggest. Formal title simply will not resolve the problems of rural poverty in Southern Africa. These have to do with structural problems of accumulation, class relations, and politics that cross the rural–urban divide.

As to whether formal titling would improve the immediate situation of the poor, whether men or women, there is no single answer; whether holding legal title to a field of one's own benefits the poor will depend on the particular economic and political contexts within which it arises. Even in the same context, there are no easy answers. Ntsebeza (2004), for example, thinks that those living in the former Bantustans would be better off if their permits to occupy could be converted into freehold tenure. Cousins (2007: 293), while like Ntsebeza rejecting chiefs' control over land allocation, recently suggested that some kind of individual title that did not imply exclusive rights would be better. Yet some things are clear: for those who are landless, titling is meaningless outside some sort of redistributive land reform; and holding title to a piece of land means little for the poor without some kind of regular non-agricultural income.

A narrow emphasis on legalizing women's individual right to land embeds a standard neoliberal proposition – the centrality of privatization and the commodification of land – within the liberal language of human rights. It focuses our attention on gender inequality in inheritance of property, of which the rural poor, women and men, have very little. Concerned with securing the property of those who have, titling excludes those who have not. We are led away from the fundamental questions of restructuring a migrant labour system and redistributing wealth and power in postcolonial Southern Africa, and away from the global, regional and national inequalities embedded in the enormous gaps between rural and urban areas.

So, returning to the story of Loveness, from a class perspective one might ask how long it had been since her ex-husband returned or sent remittances, when she had her affair with another man. Many in Southern Africa now claim the profession of miner who do not really have the job. Moreover, fast-tracking gave Loveness a piece of land, but she is dependent on the off-farm earnings of commercial sex work to complement what she gets from her field.

Gender reconstrued: the political economy of land reform

Class analysis makes it clear that, in the context of Southern Africa, some gender inequalities are inextricable from class. Are appeals to formalize women's land rights no more than an ideological screen masking the fundamental inequalities underlying poverty in rural Southern Africa? Is the question of women's land rights reducible to class? This is where feminists begin to develop an uncomfortable sense of *déjà vu*. Marxist political practice was historically slow to oppose gender inequality, tending to regard feminist movements as bourgeois deviations from the main questions of class struggle.[7] Both worker and peasant in the early literature on the agrarian question were generic ungendered subjects. Feminists would strongly dispute the proposition that the relative positions of women and men can be simply read off their respective class positions.

On the other hand, as Molyneux and Razavi (2003) have pointed out, feminists working in developing countries remain deeply ambivalent about the liberal reforms of the 1990s, and liberalism more generally.[8] Greater emphasis on democracy and rights provided a political space that women's groups have actively used, but the use of this political space has not resulted in any decisive rupture with the neoliberal market fundamentalism of 1980s structural adjustment programmes. These did not address the poverty and inequality in which most women, and men, live in developing countries, and have often intensified women's burden of care. Many feminists do not wish to find their political allies at the cutting edge of neoliberal reforms. Individual registry of women's land rights is a good case in point, as many feminists share the concerns raised by class analysis: that it will legitimate titling exercises that promise nothing for the vast numbers of rural poor, men and women, who have little or no land on which to claim title; and that it exposes the land currently occupied under some form of customary tenure to enclosure by those who have the economic and political power to manipulate the registration process.

Feminist theory has, however, been particularly critical of both liberalism and Marxism for focusing attention so narrowly on commodified work and public space, and ignoring contradictory relations of gender that cut across the commodified/non-commodified and public/private divides. I emphasize contradictory, for feminists have also pointed out that, to the extent that both liberals and Marxists historically dealt with gender, they treated it as a part of a functionally harmonic and natural order of things – the sexual division of labour. On the contrary, gender, much like class, is a concept that recognizes both domination and resistance. This feminist critique has implications for the three main aspects of the agrarian question in Southern Africa – accumulation, class and politics – and hence for the question of land rights in general, and women's land rights in particular.

The contribution of non-commodified labour to accumulation

Feminist political economy emphasizes the continuing importance of non-commodified work within capitalist economies, and the fluidity of the boundary between commodified and non-commodified spheres. Both liberal economics and Marxist political economy locate the dynamic of accumulation in the sphere of commodities where value is realized. As with liberal modernization theory, there has also been a certain dose of residual teleological evolutionism in Marxist political economy; commodification was thought to be a unilinear and irreversible process, and non-commodified forms would disappear.

The current crisis of unemployment in Southern Africa makes it clear that the inevitable march of commodification, while possibly true in the long run, is not presently an analytically useful proposition in Southern Africa. Feminists would probably point out that Marx never really explored the question of how the reserve army of labour sustained itself. Whereas one once could see wage labour as the best form of social security, given the vagaries of agricultural production in semi-arid Southern Africa, one might now suggest that the opposite applies – a plot of land is, in many places, the best form of social security against the vagaries of wage employment.

How we look at the interdependence of commodified and non-commodified labour in the process of accumulation affects how we see different forms of land tenure. Women's access to land may have implications that go beyond the formal importance of agriculture in national output. In socialist practice in Southern Africa, non-commodification has usually been understood as backwardness. Mozambique's socialist agricultural policy, for example, focused on marketed production; the rest was subsistence production and, by definition, could take care of itself. In deciding what to do with the land left by departing settlers, both Mozambique's and Angola's socialist governments initially opted for establishing state farms and cooperatives rather than redistributing land to peasants, and provided extension support only for commercial crops. Similarly, in early resettlement projects, the Zimbabwean government refused to allocate land to households that included members with full-time urban employment, and wanted resettlement land to be used exclusively for growing cash crops (Potts and Mutambirwa 1997). Bernstein (1996: 32) pointed out that the joint African National Congress/ Congress of South African Trades Unions' sponsored Macroeconomic Research Group report, one of the most radical economic strategy documents to date, proposed a limited allocation of land to women who belonged to landless households on opportunistic welfarist grounds.

Any major political assault on the massive inequalities of Southern African societies would imply great economic dislocation. There are many people in Southern Africa, particularly in South Africa, for whom non-commodified agricultural production is non-existent. Thus allocating land for it would not even be a very useful welfare measure. For others, however, land redistribution and/or explicit protection of smallholders' land rights, including those of women and including land for non-commodified production, would be important for any broad social and economic programme.

Attending to the interdependence of non-commodified and commodified forms of work highlights another area that can be seen as unproductive labour – that of healthcare – which could matter as much as women's land rights for the agrarian question of labour in some areas of rural Southern Africa. *Apartheid*'s two-tier system based on race has given way to a two-tier system based on class, with 60 per cent of health expenditure focused on the 18 per cent of the population covered by private insurance (Benatar 2004: 81). That excludes most of the population in rural areas, putting great pressure on government facilities and on rural home care, carried out mainly by women, many of whom are ill themselves. This burden has of course been exacerbated by AIDS.

Gender as a relation of production: cooperation and contradiction

Feminists have emphasized that gender is a social relation and thus inter-twined with, but not reducible to, class. Like class, it is a relation of inequality, and thus a site of contradiction and resistance. However, gender is also a relation of cooperation based on a gendered division of labour. The realm of family and household is not a utopian private space, but none-theless it depends on practices of sharing and mutuality. Thus women can recognize, resist and change relations of gender inequality within institutions to which they remain committed and from which they gain support. Feminist theory is particularly concerned with the ways in which collective agency arising from the commonality of experience can transform a division of labour rooted in inequality. Both Marxist and liberal approaches have had some analytical difficulty in dealing with this concern.

Marxist political economy easily recognizes collective agency within rela-tions of inequality – that is, after all, the meaning of the concept of class struggle – but, in the context of Southern Africa, generally focused on how gender relations mirrored class. Socialist movements in Southern Africa were historically suspicious of any cross-class collective agency exercised by women that was not tightly linked to a socialist party. Indeed, as we have seen, class does explain a lot about the gendering of experience in a migrant labour system. Women's oppression was good for capital's need for cheap labour. However, Bozzoli (1983, 1991) has argued that this functionalist analysis of the migrant labour system ignored the ways that gender contra-dictions in rural households and communities historically affected the tra-jectories of change. Women confronted oppression by chiefs, husbands and brothers as well as by employers and pass laws. The high proportion of female-headed households in Southern Africa is thus not a reflection just of the fact that men left and women remained behind, but also of women's protest against the terms of their remaining. These contradictions of gender often implicated tensions of generation and pitted younger women against their mothers-in-law.

Liberals have no difficulty recognizing that gender relations are con-tentious, but the importance that is given to individual autonomy makes it difficult to appreciate the importance of cooperation within relations of domination. The brisk exchange between Jackson (2003, 2004) and Agarwal (2003b) illustrates the liberal dilemma. Jackson observed that one did not find rural women in Southern Africa pressing for separate land rights, as Agarwal's argument would suggest. She argued that that this reflects the advantages that women gain from cooperation with men, rather than misperception of interest.[9] Agarwal responded – accurately – that her bargaining framework takes account of the fact that household members do cooperate, if cooperative arrangements make each of them better off than non-cooperation does. However, here cooperation is epiphenomenal: the result of the calculation of individual interest, which can, according to liberal theory, be optimizing only if everyone has clear individual entitlement to resources.

A different way of seeing rural land rights in Southern African is to recognize that the fuzziness of land rights arises from overlapping socially embedded – and not strictly bounded – forms of cooperation that include descent groups and residential communities as well as households. The fact that women's and men's land entitlements are not discrete opens a space for contestation and renegotiation that individual titling systems restrict.

In insisting that only discrete, individually delimited rights constitute rights to land, diminishing the importance of collective, more openly defined rights, the liberal literature on women's land rights underestimates rural women's access to land in Southern Africa. On the basis of research done in Magude, southern Mozambique, Gengenbach (1998) challenged the stereotype that customary law invariably discriminates against women's land access. Women emphasized that their rights derived from their membership in the cultivating community: those married into various different descent groups who had everyday control over land management. Land demarcation and individual titling, particularly in the wetlands, were associated with the intrusion of settler farms, and later dislocation and resettlement during the war. These processes had not deprived the women of Magude of land, but had weakened the collective rights they held as the cultivating community to decide how land would be used. Contrary to what Agarwal might predict, they felt that individual control had lessened, and not increased, their power to be managers of land.[10]

Collective support from other women of the community is critical in getting by and keeping agricultural production going in times of adversity. In the context of AIDS mortality, pushing for legal enforcement of a strict conjugal model of inheritance of land, and excluding the claims of descent group, could easily heighten vulnerability rather than secure women's livelihoods. For poor rural widows to be on their own is potentially deadly; they need the help of members of their own and their husbands' descent groups. Church groups, external NGOs, mutual help organizations and local party chapters provide some support, but less formal links of reciprocity between kin and friend within the community remain important.

The gendering of formal and informal political institutions

Feminists working on land issues in Africa have been particularly critical of analytical dualism implicit in discussions of legal pluralism (Nyamu-Musembi 2007). They see customary and statutory law as intertwined and hybrid. They have also observed that discussions of land tenure reform have focused political attention almost entirely on formal political institutions, their constitutional charters and their codified laws. In her critique of de Soto, Nyamu-Musembi (2007) observes that he addresses only formal legal institutions, discounting the web of informal legality that governs property relations in developing countries. Even some feminist legal analysts minimize the importance of rural African women's land rights, because these rights are not recognized by statutory law.

Such an approach is criticized by Khadiagala (2003: 102) in her work on rural Uganda. She disputes the idea that customary courts necessarily marginalize the land rights of women. She argues that a common set of principles for adjudicating the property rights of both men and women has emerged from women's claims to property. These are based on universal norms of justice that recognize cooperation and relative labour contributions (Khadiagala 2003: 102). In other words, the rights of the custodian and user of the land implied by the notion of the cultivating community in Magude (Gengenbach 1998) also enter into the process of formal adjudication, which partially explains why women are not always willing to trade customary judgment for statutory procedures.

Informal power infuses formal legal processes. Indeed, this is what Scott (1985) was getting at with the 'weapons of the weak', although those who are not weak do not, of course, abstain from using both formal and informal power. In the land demarcations following from the 1997 land law in Mozambique, for example, women rarely spoke in the formal consultation sessions, but had a great deal of influence outside (Tanner *et al.* 2006). The formal process is often so rapid, however, that there is little time for persuasion or lobbying. Therefore, politically, any counter-hegemonic project for rural areas will have to recover the space of tradition, to go beyond chiefdom and descent to invoke less formal but nonetheless material practices and norms. After all, the claim 'land to the tiller' is not so different from the notion of the cultivating community.

Land, class and gender justice

Returning for the last time to the story of Loveness, feminists would, I think, share liberal respect for her independence, but would also recognize the limitations of her autonomy. They would, like Marxists, note that a plot of her own has certainly not made it possible for Loveness to abandon commercial sex work, but they would also point out that it has cushioned her vulnerability and that of her children. They might suggest that, despite her protests, Loveness clearly does care what people say, and they would suspect that the voices that matter are those of the other women with whom she lives and works. They would point out the help Loveness received from joining the women's league of the ruling political party, and suggest that repeated electoral victories in rural areas might reflect the ways it has addressed contradictions of gender, not just the political alliances it has made with local chiefs, and certainly not generic rural traditionalism.

Like Loveness, throughout Southern Africa, people in many rural households and communities are impoverished – in everyday consumption, in their conditions of work, in their access to healthcare, and in education. In many rural areas, over half of all households are headed by women, many of them poor, some landless, and some without the capacity to work the land they have. Many women living in conjugal unions do not share equally in the resources of the household and community. These are important issues of class and gender justice; land titling will not resolve them. In areas where most land is already held under freehold, women should have the same legal rights of title as heir or spouse that men enjoy. However, outside South Africa, Zimbabwe and perhaps Namibia and Malawi, the main land issues are the defence of existing rights of access by smallholding producers and their capacity to draw a livelihood from the land they now hold.

The implications of full conversion to freehold are unclear, and will certainly differ from place to place. Previous titling schemes in the region have not invariably resulted in the displacement of the poor from their land – some people never even bothered to pick up their titles. The current titling process is, however, driven principally by concern for investor guarantees, and applies both to agricultural land and to large expanses cut out for logging rights, tourist facilities or private game reserves. In the areas affected, it is certain that the titling process implies rigid boundaries to use. Formal individual titling of fixed plots can also erode the kinds of informal rights that women have to land through residence and their work.

Despite the ambiguous implications of formalizing land rights, class analysis makes one thing very clear: abolishing customary tenure and introducing universal freehold will not answer the agrarian question in Southern Africa. Addressing the inequalities linked to the migrant labour system will require major economic restructuring and very substantial redistribution of wealth, neither of which is presently a high priority in regional macroeconomic policies. Instead, we are offered de Soto's pale prescription for economic growth: full commodification and the privatization of land.

The liberal account finds the roots of rural poverty principally in the absence of liberal institutions and in the ways that rural people in Southern Africa treat each other in general, and women in particular. The remedy proposed, to give each one a right to her or his individual piece of property, disguises the ways that contemporary liberal legal institutions based on the protection of private property give priority to the rights of capital in their everyday functioning. To force them to do otherwise requires concentrated forms of political action based on collective agency and strong class alliances. In constructing such alliances, it would be useful to have a political analysis that recognizes both class and collective forms of gendered agency that are not reducible to class. This would mean recognizing non-commodified work as more than unproductive labour; integrating collective rights based in non-commodified work in class demands; and mobilizing the political power of forms of political agency – however fragmentary or transient –

that have been illegitimized by formal politics. In short, the answer to the agrarian question in Southern Africa necessitates challenging market fundamentalism by addressing the gender dynamics of class, accumulation and politics.

Notes

1 I would like to thank Haroon Akram-Lodhi, Wicky Meynen, Dubravka Zharkov and Ruth Castel-Branco for comments on earlier versions of this chapter.
2 This was not true in South Africa, where the political clout of the Congress of Traditional Leaders of South Africa, known as Contralesa, was criticized by many land activists.
3 See Blackden and Bhanu (1999) and World Bank (2001). For a critical discussion of these reports see O'Laughlin (2007).
4 The many failures in the realization of that political programme explain why some now prefer to use terms such as 'critical political economy', but because of its importance in the anticolonial struggle, Marxism still enjoys some legitimacy among academics and oppositional movements in the region.
5 See the special 2004 issue of the *Journal of Agrarian Change* 4 (1/2), particularly the introductory essay by Terry Byres (2004).
6 These changes are discussed by Bernstein, specifically in relation to South Africa (Bernstein 1996); Southern Africa (Bernstein 2003); and globally (Chapter 10 in this volume).
7 For an early but still pertinent review of the issues see Hartmann (1979).
8 See Nussbaum's (1999) defence of liberal feminism; Phillips (2001) offers a robust critique.
9 Jackson (2003) also draws on the work of Rao (2005, 2006) on India. For a similar point on cooperation within gender inequality see Yngstrom (2002) and O'Laughlin (1995).
10 Similar evidence on the importance of community recognition of the land rights that women enjoy as cultivators comes from Eastern Africa, particularly Uganda, Tanzania and Kenya (Khadiagala 2003; Daley 2005 and Aliber and Walker 2006). The Aliber and Walker study is particularly interesting because it is one of the few that used survey research to look specifically at widows' land rights in the context of AIDS.

References

Agarwal, B. (1994) *A Field of One's Own: Gender and Land Rights in South Asia*, Cambridge: Cambridge University Press.
—— (2003a) 'Gender and land rights revisited: exploring new prospects via the state, family and market', *Journal of Agrarian Change*, 3 (1/2): 184–224.
—— (2003b) 'Women's land rights and the trap of neo-conservatism: a response to Jackson', *Journal of Agrarian Change*, 3 (4): 571–585.
Aliber, M. and C. Walker (2006) 'The impact of HIV/AIDS on land rights: perspectives from Kenya', *World Development*, 24 (4): 704–727.
Benatar, S.R. (2004) 'Health care reform and the crisis of HIV and AIDS in South Africa', *New England Journal of Medicine*, 351 (1): 81–92.
Bernstein, H. (1996) 'South Africa's agrarian question: extreme and exceptional?', *Journal of Peasant Studies*, 23 (2/3): 1–52.

—— (2003) 'Land reform in southern Africa in world-historical perspective', *Review of African Political Economy*, 96: 203–227.

Blackden, C.M. and C. Bhanu (1999) *Gender, Growth, and Poverty Reduction*, Washington, DC: World Bank.

Bozzoli, B. (1983) 'Marxism, feminism and South African studies', *Journal of Southern African Studies*, 9 (2): 139–171.

—— (1991) *Women of Phokeng: Consciousness, Life Strategy, and Migrancy in South Africa, 1900–1983*, London: Heinemann.

van den Brink, R. (2002) 'Land policy and land reform in Sub-Saharan Africa: consensus, confusion and controversy', Presentation to the Symposium on Land Redistribution in Southern Africa, Pretoria, South Africa, 6–7 November 2002, online: http://www.sarpn.org.za/documents/d0000115/index.php

Byres, T.J. (1982) 'Agrarian transition and the agrarian question', in J. Harriss (ed.), *Rural Development: Theories of Peasant Economy and Agrarian Change*, London: Hutchinson.

—— (2004) 'Introduction: contextualizing and interrogating the GKI case for redistributive land reform', *Journal of Agrarian Change*, 4 (1/2): 1–16.

Chaumba, J., I. Scoones and W. Wolmer (2003) 'New politics, new livelihoods: agrarian change in Zimbabwe', *Review of African Political Economy*, 30 (98): 585–608.

Cheater, A. (1990) 'The ideology of "communal" land tenure in Zimbabwe: mythogenesis enacted?', *Africa*, 60 (2): 188–206.

Chimhowu, A. and P. Woodhouse (2006) 'Customary vs. private property rights? Dynamics and trajectories of vernacular land markets in Sub-Saharan Africa', *Journal of Agrarian Change*, 6 (3): 346–371.

Cousins, B. (2007) 'More than socially embedded: the distinctive character of "communal tenure" regimes in South Africa and its implications for land policy', *Journal of Agrarian Change*, 7 (3): 281–315.

Daley, E. (2005) 'Land and social change in a Tanzanian village 1: Kinyanambo, 1920s–1990', *Journal of Agrarian Change*, 5 (3): 363–404.

Deere, C.D. and C.R. Doss (2006) 'The gender asset gap: what do we know and why does it matter?', *Feminist Economics*, 12 (1/2): 1–50.

Gengenbach, H. (1998) '"I'll bury you in the border!": women's land struggles in post-war Facazisse (Magude District), Mozambique', *Journal of Southern African Studies*, 24 (1): 7–36.

Hart, G. (1995) 'Gender and household dynamics: recent theories and their implications', in M.G. Quiriba (ed.), *Critical Issues in Asian Development Theories Experiences and Policies*, Hong Kong: Oxford University Press.

Hartmann, H. (1979) 'The unhappy marriage of Marxism and feminism: towards a more progressive union', *Capital and Class*, 8: 1–33.

Hunt, C.W. (1989) 'Migrant labor and sexually transmitted disease: AIDS in Africa', *Journal of Health and Social Behavior*, 30 (4): 353–373.

Ikdahl, I., A. Hellum, R. Kaarhus, T.A. Benjaminsen and P. Kameri-Mbote (2005) *Human Rights, Formalization and Women's Land Rights in Southern and Eastern Africa*, Studies in Women's Law No. 57, Oslo: Institute of Women's Law, University of Oslo.

Jackson, C. (2003) 'Gender analysis of land: beyond land rights for women?', *Journal of Agrarian Change*, 3 (4): 453–480.

—— (2004) 'Projections and labels: a reply to Bina Agarwal', *Journal of Agrarian Change* 4 (3): 387–388.

James, D. (2007) *Gaining Ground? 'Rights' and 'Property' in South African Land Reform*, Abingdon/New York: RoutledgeCavendish.

Khadiagala, L.S. (2003) 'Justice and power in the adjudication of women's property rights in Uganda', *Africa Today*, 49 (2): 101–121.

Macro International (2007) 'Measure DHS STATcompiler', online: www.measuredhs.com

Mamdani, M. (1996) *Citizen and Subject: Contemporary Africa and the Legacy of Late Colonialism*, Oxford: James Currey.

Manji, A. (2006) *The Politics of Land Reform in Africa: From Communal Tenure to Free Markets*, London: Zed Books.

McAuslan, P. (1998) 'Making law work: restructuring land relations in Africa', *Development and Change*, 29 (3): 525–552.

—— (2003) 'Only the name of the country changes: the diaspora of "European" land law in Commonwealth Africa', in *Bringing the Law Back In: Essays on Land, Law and Development*, London: Ashgate.

Molyneux, M. and S. Razavi (2003) 'Introduction', in *Gender Justice, Development, and Rights*, Oxford: Oxford University Press.

Moore, H.L. and M. Vaughan (1994) *Cutting Down Trees: Gender, Nutrition, and Agricultural Change in the Northern Province of Zambia, 1890–1990*, Lusaka: University of Zambia Press.

Mutangadura, G. (2004) 'Women and land tenure rights in Southern Africa: a human rights-based approach', prepared for the workshop 'Land in Africa: Market Asset or Secure Livelihood', Westminster, London, November 8–9.

Ntsebeza, L. (2004) 'Democratic decentralisation and traditional authority: dilemmas of land administration in rural South Africa', *European Journal of Development Research*, 16 (1): 71–89.

Nussbaum, M.C. (1999) *Sex and Social Justice*, Oxford: Oxford University Press.

Nyamu-Musembi, C. (2007) 'Breathing life into dead theories about property rights: de Soto and land relations in rural Africa', *Third World Quarterly*, 28 (8): 1457–1478.

O'Laughlin, B. (1995) 'The myth of the African family in the world of development', in D.F. Bryceson (ed.), *Women Wielding the Hoe: Lessons from Rural Africa for Feminist Theory and Development Practice*, Oxford: Berg Publishers.

—— (2007) 'A bigger piece of a very small pie: intrahousehold resource allocation and poverty reduction in Africa', *Development and Change*, 38 (1): 21–44.

Peters, P.E. and D. Kambewa (2007) 'Whose security? Deepening social conflict over "customary" land in the shadow of land tenure reform in Malawi', *Journal of Modern African Studies*, 45 (3): 447–472.

Phillips, A. (2001) 'Review essay: feminism and liberalism revisited – has Martha Nussbaum got it right?', *Constellations*, 8 (2): 249–266.

Potts, D. and C. Mutambirwa (1997) '"The government must not dictate": rural–urban migrants' perceptions of Zimbabwe's land resettlement programme', *Review of African Political Economy*, 74: 549–566.

Rao, N. (2005) 'Questioning women's solidarity: the case of land rights, Santal Parganas, Jharkhand, India', *Journal of Development Studies*, 41 (3): 353–375.

—— (2006) 'Land rights, gender equality and household food security: exploring the conceptual links in the case of India', *Food Policy* 31 (2): 180–193.

Robertson, A.F. (1987) *The Dynamics of Productive Relations: African Share Contracts in Comparative Perspective*, Cambridge: Cambridge University Press.

Scott, J.C. (1985) *Weapons of the Weak: Everyday Forms of Peasant Resistance*, New Haven, CT: Yale University Press.

Sen, A.K. (1999) *Development as Freedom*, Oxford: Oxford University Press.

Sender, J. (2002) 'Women's struggle to escape rural poverty in South Africa', *Journal of Agrarian Change*, 2 (1): 1–49.

Sender, J., C. Oya and C. Cramer (2006) 'Women working for wages: putting flesh on the bones of a rural labour market survey in Mozambique', *Journal of Southern African Studies*, 32 (2): 313–333.

Solway, J. (1994) 'Drought as a "revelatory crisis": an exploration of shifting entitlements and hierarchies in the Kalahari', *Development and Change*, 25 (3): 471 – 95.

de Soto, H. (2001) *The Mystery of Capital: Why Capitalism Triumphs in the West and Fails Everywhere Else*, New York: Basic Books.

Tanner, C., S. Baleira, S. Norfolk, B. Cau and J. Assulai (2006) *Making Rights a Reality: Participation in Practice and Lessons Learned in Mozambique*, FAO Livelihood Support Programme Working Paper No. 27, Rome: Food and Agriculture Organization.

Vijfhuizen, C. (2001) 'Losing control, gender and land in Massaca irrigation scheme', in R. Waterhouse and C. Vijfhuizen (eds), *Strategic Women Gainful Men: Gender, Land and Natural Resources in Different Rural Contexts in Mozambique*, Maputo: Land Studies Unit, Faculty of Agronomy and Forestry Engineering.

Whitehead, A. and D. Tsikata (2003) 'Policy discourses on women's land rights in Sub-Saharan Africa: the implications of the re-turn to the customary', *Journal of Agrarian Change*, 3 (1/2): 67–112.

Wiegers, E., J. Curry, A. Garbero and J. Hourihan (2006) 'Patterns of vulnerability to AIDS impacts in Zambian households', *Development and Change*, 37 (5): 1073–1092.

World Bank (2001) *Engendering Development: Through Gender Equality in Rights, Resources and Voice*, New York: Oxford University Press.

—— (2003) *Land Policies for Growth and Development*, Washington, DC: World Bank.

Yngstrom, I. (2002) 'Women, wives and land rights in Africa: situating gender beyond the household in the debate over land policy and changing tenure systems', *Oxford Development Studies*, 30 (1): 21–40.

9 The political economy of land and the agrarian question in an era of neoliberal globalization

A. Haroon Akram-Lodhi, Cristóbal Kay and Saturnino M. Borras, Jr

Land, neoliberalism and the agrarian question

This purpose of this book is to explore alternative interpretations of the historical meaning and contemporary relevance of the agrarian question. A common aspect of the various interpretations of the agrarian question contained in this volume is the use, as noted in the Introduction, of the balance of forces, locally, nationally, and internationally, between capital and labour, as the critical analytical variable. The purpose of this chapter is to examine the validity of some of the claims advanced by those engaged within this debate, both in this book and elsewhere, but not to do so by focusing on the balance of forces, important as these are for all of the protagonists and positions in this debate. Rather, this chapter uses the political economy of land, the principal agrarian asset, as the fulcrum by which to examine these claims. We do this because, in our view, prior to the complete maturation of capitalism in agriculture, and hence the alienation of land as a commodity, it can be argued that land is inexorably relational in character. Social relations are reflected in the structure of property rights and the character of the security attached to such rights. Social relations are also exposed by the distribution of land between individuals within communities, a distribution that is established through the structure of property rights. Social relations surrounding the terms and conditions by which land is accessed affect how farmers decide to organize the on-farm production process as well as their off-farm activities. In so doing, social relations affect the terms and conditions by which labour and other non-land resources are used in production. As a consequence, social relations that are embedded within the terms and conditions governing access to land affect and reflect ongoing processes of accumulation and depeasantization, which in turn underpin structural transformation and the development of rural capitalism. Finally, a cumulative consequence of this array of relations is that the principal object of rural politics commonly revolves around altering the social relations that shape, and are shaped by, access to land. Land is thus, in its impact on production, accumulation and politics, central to the agrarian question as it was classically conceived. Indeed, in these senses, and in the specific context of a less than fully developed capitalist agriculture, land is like capital – as rural capitalism emerges out of the messy array of precapitalist agrarian relations, it embodies those relations. Thus the distribution of property, power and privilege is, in many rural economies, both a cause and a consequence of the social relations and struggles surrounding land.

In this chapter, the changing character of access to land in the rural economy of contemporary developing and transition economies is evaluated from perspectives that reflect both the classical concerns of the agrarian question and the current context within which it is now located. The current context is, in our view, critical. For more than a quarter of a century, a broad set of policies have been introduced across developing and transition countries that have sought to liberalize international trade in food and agricultural products, deregulate the operation of domestic agricultural markets, privatize parastatals that function in the rural economy, and formalize the ownership and control of property that had been held in public, in common or, in some cases, privately. This project was first introduced under the aegis of World Bank and International Monetary Fund interventions in rural political economies, in the form of structural adjustment programmes, and has continued under their successor, poverty reduction strategy papers. Its most complete statement is perhaps contained in the World Bank's (2007) *World Development Report 2008: Agriculture for Development*. In this chapter we call this project 'neoliberal agrarian restructuring'.

Broadly our argument is that, despite obvious complexity in the characterization of the contemporary agrarian question, some general similarities can be seen to underpin an understanding of the processes at work in rural economies in developing and transition countries undergoing neoliberal agrarian restructuring. Thus we will demonstrate that neoliberal agrarian restructuring has had the effect of reconfiguring rural production processes in relatively more capital- or more labour-intensive patterns, fostering, as a general if not exclusive rule, the emergence of new processes of segmentation, inequality and exclusion. This results in the realignment and deepening of a 'bifurcated' agrarian structure, in which an export-oriented agrarian subsector sits beside a peasant producer subsector, which may itself be subject to processes of differentiation. The realignment of the bifurcated agrarian structure is an outcome of the emergence of a new global politics of land in which, in particular, dominant global class forces and their representatives seek to promote, through free trade agreements and poverty reduction strategy papers, a market-led, and hence neoliberal, appropriation of land, in an effort to respond to a broadened and deepened market imperative, so as to promote the improvements in productive efficiency that boost capitalist competitiveness.

Central to the reconfiguration of this bifurcated agrarian structure have been processes facilitating the expanded commodification of products, labour, nature and space, which affect the relationship between the export and peasant-production subsectors, and which clearly differ in specific contexts, as a result of historically embedded trajectories of agrarian change generating differential incorporation into capitalism as it increasingly operates on a world scale. The key to understanding these processes, we argue, is not the relationship between production for export and production for the home market and self-provisioning, but rather reconfigurations between production for the market, the stubborn persistence of peasant production for use, and the deepening of semiproletarianization. However, it is nonetheless the case that production for export is the main driving force of the increasingly exclusionary and unequal nature of the rural development process under neoliberal globalization (Kay 1995). This is because production for export has the effect of raising, globally, the rate of relative surplus value for capital. Thus the main dynamism in global agricultural production in developing and transition countries is from non-traditional agricultural exports that are produced by either the capitalist farm sector, such as soyabeans, or by agro-industry, such as fresh fruits and vegetables. It must be stressed, however, that these processes are subject to a substantive diversity that is rooted in the contingent and conjunctural complexity that arises out of processes of uneven development. It must also be stressed that, in these processes, some clear outliers can be identified. Thus we argue that while it is possible to make general statements about the contemporary character of the agrarian question, it is not possible to produce universal 'truths'.

The treatment offered in this chapter is theoretical and analytical. Space precludes detailed presentation of the ample evidence that can be used to substantiate the many arguments that are advanced. However, country-based case study evidence that backs up many of the propositions that are made can be found in our earlier work (Akram-Lodhi *et al.* 2007); see also de Janvry *et al.* (2001); Rosset *et al.* (2006); some articles found in a recent special issue of *Third World Quarterly* (Borras *et al.* 2007); and some of the background papers for World Bank (2007). Cumulatively, we believe that through the focus on the relational quality of land, the contemporary character of the agrarian question will become manifest.

Neoliberal globalization, agrarian restructuring and land

Agrarian political economy is concerned with teasing out the underlying laws of motion of contemporary capitalism and its relationship to the countryside and, in particular, whether capital is transforming the forces and relations of production in agriculture in general, and among those who own and/or control property in particular (Kautsky 1988, first published 1899). Whether capital is, or is not, revolutionizing agriculture in general, or at different paces in different times and spaces, is both shaped by, and shapes, the socially embedded terms and conditions governing access to land, in that land is the principle agrarian means of production and form of property. In other words, the way in which land is held will affect the capacity of capital to transform agriculture. For agrarian political economy, then, forming a critical aspect of the emergence of rural capitalism are what one might call 'agrarian questions of land': who controls it, how it is controlled, and the purpose for which it is controlled will determine and reflect the distribution of power, property and privilege in the countryside and the capability of capital to overcome these limits. In seeking to understand the answers to these questions, then, the key terrain of analysis is not the terms and conditions under which property rights are transferred between individuals and social classes; rather, it is the terms and conditions under which property rights are vested in individuals and social classes.

Neoliberal globalization dates from the 1980s, and has witnessed a sustained reconfiguration of rural livelihoods in the South as the terms and conditions under which property rights are vested in individuals and social classes have been transformed. In this volume, Araghi (Chapter 5) reiterates his memorable observation that it is 'the great global enclosure of our times' (Araghi 2000). Dominant classes in the South, working in conjunction with neoconservative dominant classes in the North, have used the policy conditionalities imposed with their agreement upon the countries in the South, in the form of structural adjustment programmes and poverty reduction strategy papers, to compress the state and to enhance the role of markets in social and cultural life, and in so doing to broaden and deepen the role of capital and the capitalist mode of production in the countries of the South (Akram-Lodhi 2005, 2006). They have also used multilateral trade agreements, in the form of the Uruguay Round's Agreement on Agriculture, regional trade agreements such as the deepening of Mercosur, and bilateral trade agreements, such as that signed between the USA and Costa Rica, to substantially broaden and deepen the scope of supposedly free trade, and thus notably widen the reach of the market imperative. In this sense, neoliberal globalization has sought to promote the further and deeper capitalist transformation of societies and cultures in the South, in the form of a marked sharpening of capitalist social property relations. Neoliberal agrarian restructuring is therefore, in this perspective, an intrinsic part of the global logic of capital and hence the law of value, in which 'territorial restructuring' is demonstrated: a reconfiguration of the 'control over the places and spaces where surplus is produced by shaping and controlling the institutions and social relations that govern production, extraction and accumulation' (Holt-Giménez 2007: 2; Assies 2006).

Neoliberal globalization has, as a consequence, promulgated changes in the character of the rural economy in many countries, most vividly, perhaps, around access to land. These alterations commenced with a series of legislative changes in several countries that sought to terminate or roll back a wide variety of state-led land and agrarian reforms produced during the first three-quarters of the twentieth century. The most famous examples of this roll back were witnessed with Chinese and Vietnamese decollectivization, as well as with the collapse of collective agriculture in the former Soviet Union; the former created opportunities for capitalist farming on a relatively egalitarian scale, while the latter created opportunities for large-scale capitalist farming. However, neoliberalism was equally hostile to state-led land and agrarian reforms that distributed land non-collectively to individual peasant households, such as in Bolivia, Brazil, Chile, Egypt, India, and Pakistan, among others. Thus a less well known but equally dramatic roll back of state-led land and agrarian 'counter-enclosure' occurred; Egypt (Bush 2002) and Chile (Bellisario 2007a, 2007b) offer stark examples. Often predicated on the subdivision and privatization of the cooperatives that had emerged out of a state-led agrarian reform process, such as the *ejidos* in Mexico, and with the common objective of seeking to attract foreign direct investment in landscapes that were not yet fully privatized, these transformations were a result of direct action by the state designed to facilitate a process of market-led appropriation of land under conditions 'regulated' – that is, shaped – by dominant classes (Bernstein 1996). Thus neoliberal globalization has produced changes in the agricultural sector and in rural life that have, as a general if not universal rule, reshaped the rural production process, in that there have been, to differing degrees, in some cases a reinforcement and in other cases a resurrection of inequalities in access to land. This has resulted in the reassertion of a bias in the pattern of rural accumulation so that it works to the benefit of a minority.

Neoliberal agrarian restructuring can be differentiated from previous forms of agrarian restructuring in that its objective is not to impose capitalist social property relations where such did not previously exist. One of the hallmarks of the current period is that these can now be considered globally established. Rather, neoliberal agrarian restructuring seeks to widen the scope of already established and prevailing capitalist social property relations by broadening and deepening the sway of capitalist social property relations into areas of social, cultural, political and economic life that have yet to be fully commodified, exposing an even greater number of people to the market imperative. The broadening and deepening of capitalist social property relations requires, as a necessary condition, diminishing the relative power of peasants and workers in favour of local and/or global dominant classes. This is achieved principally through the use of market-based processes, supplemented by the direct action of the state, and in this sense neoliberal agrarian restructuring is commonly a byproduct of a market-led accumulation process, using capitalist economic rationality, and in particular the imperatives of cost reductions and technical change, as a mechanism to achieve its ends: reconfiguring the set of social relations that sustains the systematic transfer of agricultural surpluses to the land-controlling dominant class and its agents in order to deepen such transfers. However, neoliberal agrarian restructuring required, in the first instance, fundamental alterations by the state in the structure of extra-economic socially constructed and enforced rights to property in the juridical and legal sphere that it monopolized, and which thus reflected the power of dominant class forces to regulate the underlying social relations that govern the extraction of surplus labour and, in fully capitalized agriculture, surplus value.

Notwithstanding common aspects in processes of neoliberal agrarian restructuring, the impact of such transformations demonstrates significant taxonomies of variation, which must be evaluated contextually. Thus neoliberal agrarian restructuring can be geographically specific, as in the Bolivian region of Santa Cruz, Punjab and Haryana in India, the southern coastal region of Mozambique, or the Central Highlands region of Vietnam, among others. It can also be commodity-specific, as in the case of cut flower exports in Ecuador and Kenya, coffee production in Nicaragua and Vietnam, or game farming in Namibia. Neoliberal agrarian restructuring can be market-specific, as in the case of export-oriented agricultural production in Chile, Iran, Kenya, the Philippines and Uzbekistan, among others. Finally, it can be ownership-specific, as in the case of state-owned enterprises in Vietnam, newly privatized agro-enterprises in Uzbekistan, and the political elite's private takeover of what had been European settler farms in, for example, Mozambique and Zimbabwe, a process that led to fractions of the elite being effectively transformed into a class of protocapitalist farmers. Moreover, there are, in some instances, cases in which multiple and overlapping processes of neoliberal agrarian restructuring are found. These taxonomic complexities, within what we suggest are a common set of underlying processes largely derived from the immanent if not immutable drive of capital, helps explain why neoliberal agrarian restructuring has resulted in substantive trajectories of variation in changing access to land and landscapes. Thus, notwithstanding Araghi's argument in this volume and elsewhere (Araghi 2000: 147) that the great global enclosure of our times is witnessed in a near-universal process of dispossession through displacement, we would argue that neoliberal agrarian restructuring has generated a wide array of procedurally similar yet historically specific processes of differential incorporation into global capitalism. This is uneven rural development on a world scale.

The global politics of land

Processes of neoliberal agrarian restructuring have not only reshaped rural production. They have also, ironically, reopened debates around the global politics of land and, in particular, reinvigorated arguments for land and agrarian reform, albeit in ways that differ remarkably from earlier arguments in support of redistributive land reform. Previously, extensive peasant mobilization and collective struggles around access to land were, in many instances, a key factor in the struggle for national liberation and political independence from the start of the 1950s through to the mid-1960s. Moreover, peasant struggles provided an important reason for the formulation of rural development strategies by states in which redistributive land reform, in particular, was perceived to be capable of playing a significant strategic role in stimulating accumulation with equity, by transforming the rural production process so as to increase agrarian productivity and incomes. Thus, within the context of an emerging capitalist economy, rural redistribution with rural growth was believed to be possible. As a consequence, during the classic 'heyday' of land reform, the balance of forces played a critical role in setting the stage for the development and implementation of land and agrarian reform policies in a host of countries that were predicated on a Keynesian-inspired redistribution-with-growth paradigm, even when it was often couched in vaguely Marxist language. Nonetheless, as a result of reforms being the outcome of the balance of forces, they were often embedded within an ideological framework that reflected the oppositions of the Cold War, with both socialist and capitalist political elites launching land-reform projects as a means of consolidating claims to state power, building state capacity, managing rural unrest, and accruing international support from the competing global powers in the Cold War.

That era has irrevocably vanished. The Cold War has been superseded by the period of neoliberal globalization, which might be seen as the latest in a series of long waves of world development, in which international capital develops a new, deeper round of increased integration of the global circuits of trade, production and finance. In this latest wave, the scope for formulating and implementing development strategies predicated upon an emphasis on the construction of national capacity and redistribution, whether in agricultural or non-agricultural activities, has been successively eroded, to be replaced by an emphasis on comparative advantage, international interdependence and the need, in such circumstances, for a supposedly level playing field between actors and institutions in the global economy.

It might be thought that, with the arrival of this supposedly new economic paradigm, struggles over the global politics of land might vanish just as profoundly as it was central to the previous global economic regime, but such has not been the case. If anything, the period of neoliberal globalization and the resulting process of neoliberal agrarian restructuring have seen the most significant reassertion of the primacy of struggles over the global politics of land since the early 1950s. A significant factor behind the re-emergence of land within development struggles and strategies has been the negative social and economic consequences of neoliberal economic policies when applied to developing and transition countries in general, and the agrarian economy in particular, as has been done since the early 1980s. At the same time, however, there has been a major change in the proposed content of land and agrarian reform emerging out of the global politics of land between the 1950s and the late 1990s. Then, there was extensive debate on the comparative merits of state ownership versus private ownership or, as it was sometimes put, in the comparative merits of vesting property rights in individuals versus the comparative merits of vesting property rights in collectives. The need for redistribution was taken for granted, in part because in the post-war years land and agrarian reform was also seen as a way to finance a process of import-substituting industrialization and thus structural transformation.[1] Now, however, the terms of the debate admit little discussion of the comparative merits of alternative property rights structures. At this juncture, it is highly unlikely that a state-led collectivist land reform can be implemented (Kay 1998). Rather, private individual ownership is seen as the exclusive long-term target to which contemporary market-led land and agrarian reforms should be directed. Thus in many instances contemporary land and agrarian reforms seek to deepen and broaden a set of social property relations that are already supportive of global capitalism, in that they offer one means of partially accommodating the exclusionary character of neoliberal reforms and the struggles they have provoked.

Actors, agency and the building of markets

In seeking to promote private individual landownership, contemporary land and agrarian reforms are heavily oriented towards 'market-led agrarian reform' (MLAR) (World Bank 2003, 2007; Borras 2007). Early versions of MLAR commenced in the 1970s and 1980s, including an important episode in Guatemala in the mid-1980s that was designed under the auspices of the US Agency for International Development (Wittman and Saldivar-Tanaka 2006). Later, in the 1990s, it was implemented under the guidance of the World Bank in countries as diverse as Brazil, Colombia, South Africa and the Philippines (Borras 2006). Following the clear assignment of property rights, 'textbook' MLAR sees landlords being paid the full market value for land that they are voluntarily willing to sell privately to smaller farmers and the landless. Buyers usually bear the full costs of the land transfer that they demand, in the form of a debt that is acquired from a rural financial institution or the state, a debt that must be repaid over time. However, in some 'non-textbook' versions of MLAR, such as South Africa, the costs of land acquisition may take the form of a one-off, non-repayable grant. In both cases, MLAR seeks to replace previous state-led land and agrarian reform efforts with a 'willing buyer, willing seller' model of rural change in which market-facilitated and price-mediated transactions are undertaken in order to generate improvements in capitalist economic efficiency and social welfare (Deininger and Binswanger 1999; World Bank 2003, 2005, 2007).

The effective reassertion of the centrality of land and agrarian reform, albeit in the form of MLAR, in the era of neoliberal globalization was buttressed by two contingent events. The first was the collapse of the Soviet Union and its system of collective agriculture, which, because of its early 1990s emphasis on the privatization of previously socialized assets, required on its demise a massive, market-oriented, market-building land reform as a means of dealing with struggles for the control of land. The second was the potential role of land reform as a means of building political stability in fragile political environments that were subject to possible natural resource-based conflict, focusing particularly on struggles over land. Here the transition in post-*apartheid* South Africa was an absolutely pivotal event.

In addition to these contingent factors, an important empirical phenomenon explaining the reassertion of the global politics of land, albeit in a market-led guise, in the 1990s were the struggles of capital's key player in the process of neoliberal globalization, the transnational corporation. Access to secure land was a necessary condition for profit-seeking transnational corporations, as well as local rural capitalists, operating particularly but not exclusively in the non-traditional agro-food export sector. Transnational agro-food corporations and local capitalists wanted locally procured sub-contracting producers to be secure in their production arrangements, so that supply could be ensured; struggles by transnational corporations to support land titling facilitated that security. Alternatively, transnational agro-food corporations and local capitalists wanted to be able to secure land in their own right; structural adjustment in its various guises, including neoliberal globalization, deepened the operation of land markets in the 1990s, and in many instances widened the scope for international and national capitalists to own land, making this a much stronger possibility than was previously the case. Only in cases where control of land creates social tensions and conflict that have the potential to challenge the power of transnational agro-food corporations – cases that are, in any event, spatially localized around specific grievances, and not, by and large, generalized – do transnational agro-food corporations seek other ways to extract the agricultural surplus. Thus struggles over the meaning and content of the global politics of land have often reflected the accumulation imperatives of dominant classes in the world economy.

Not surprisingly, it is in this reconfigured global context that land and agrarian reform has reappeared as an objective among the major multilateral agencies, bilateral donors, and some international non-governmental organizations (NGOs). Without doubt, the World Bank played an instrumental role in this rediscovery. A key impetus behind the reassertion of the need for land and agrarian reform within the Bank was the clear failure of strict neoliberal policy prescriptions to boost accumulation and reduce poverty in developing economies since the early 1980s, particularly in Sub-Saharan Africa, but also in large parts of Latin America, rural China and rural India. Increases in the absolute number of those who are food-insecure, the marked deepening of inequality, environmental degradation and social exclusion, when combined with the inability of neoliberal economic policies to foster productive efficiency improvements in agriculture and the attendant supply response, led to a search for theoretical explanations for this failure and a willingness to consider redistributing access to land as a means of transcending the social and economic failures of the 1980s and 1990s (World Bank 2003).

However, rather than questioning the neoliberal paradigm in the light of its failure, an economic argument that had had wide currency in the 1960s and early 1970s was rediscovered: that there was an inverse relationship between productivity per unit of land and the size of the holding.[2] This argument provided intellectual support for the suggestion that improving access to land among smallholder farmers by promoting some type of land reform could, in fact, raise the level of productive efficiency in the economy as a whole, and in so doing facilitate a transformation in the growth pattern of an agrarian economy. However, in order to be effective, small farmers had to be capable of capturing the fruits of productivity improvements. Here, a critical intervention was made by Hernando de Soto (2000), who argued simply that poor people were poor because they did not formally own the resources they used. Therefore, it was argued by de Soto and others, it was necessary to vest clear and enforceable private individual property rights among farmers, at the expense of collective and communal arrangements of the type witnessed in the formerly centrally planned economies, or in much of Sub-Saharan Africa. The clear suggestion of these 'neoliberal populists' (Byres 2004) was that the negative consequences of neoliberal globalization could be offset in ways that, by improving equity and securing private property rights, could foster productive efficiency improvements and rural accumulation, while at the same time enhancing the stability of a prevailing set of capitalist social property relations that had been both deepened and broadened.

In the 1980s and 1990s, the emphasis in a great deal of development research undertaken by the principal research institutions in international development was on enhancing the capacity of rural people to better use their principal productive asset, their labour-power, in market relationships. But by the late 1990s it had become a 'stylized fact' of international development analysis that there was a primary need to secure access for poor people to a more diverse set of productive assets than labour-power, including land, so as to foster a wider set of specialization-predicated, market-oriented livelihood activities rooted in productive, efficiency-enhancing labour regimes. This, it was argued, was necessary in order to foster enhanced specialization, rural diversification, accumulation and agrarian transition – a phrase now sometimes used by researchers in the international financial institutions (Ravallion and van de Walle 2006).

Moreover, it came to be argued by multilateral and bilateral donors that the need for improved, secure private access to land, in particular, could be tied, critically, to the building of markets, which had been the focus of growth-dominated neoliberal economics in the 1980s and early 1990s, and which are a central feature of neoliberal globalization. Thus, by providing secure private individual titles to land, asset markets could be developed in comparatively underdeveloped settings, which in turn could facilitate an expansion of market-based resource allocation and induce the onset of the accumulation-promoting productive efficiency improvements that were sought in the 1980s and early 1990s, but which failed to be realized. The provision of private individual titles could, moreover, be expected to lead over time to a reallocation of land from the comparatively less efficient to the comparatively more efficient as the market imperatives described by Wood (Chapter 2) forced specialization on more efficient producers, and the exit from farming of less efficient producers.

Such a market-led appropriation of land on the basis of comparative advantage is viewed by neoliberals as a strong rationale to support private individual titles and the establishment of functioning land markets, even though a market-led appropriation of land could foster market-led land concentration. This is because concentration is not, in and of itself, seen to be negative if it promotes improvements in capitalist economic efficiency. Such improvements were to be expected of capitalist farms that, under the market imperative, generated the yield increases that brought forth the resources to modernize. However, as a consequence of neoliberal agrarian restructuring, peasant farms no longer had access to state support in the form of subsidies, financial credit, technical assistance, and marketing, and this had an impact on farm yields. There was thus a marked divergence of yields, and hence revenues, between capitalist and peasant farms. Market-led land concentration and yield divergence is not explicitly stated by neoliberals because of the potential political ramifications that such an argument would generate. In this context, it was not coincidental that the rediscovery of land and agrarian reform occurred alongside a new emphasis on the economic aspects of institutions, within the context of the discovery of social capital and, more specifically, the socioeconomic setting in which rural poor people sought to build a sustainable rural livelihood (Ellis 2000). This supposedly new approach to rural development was one in which the issue of rural deprivation and social exclusion was seen exclusively as an outcome of an inappropriate set of choices made by individual peasants, given the environment in which they operated. In its lack of attention to structures of deprivation, power relations, and its emphasis on methodologically individualistic asset portfolio management, it was an approach that was deeply neoclassical in nature and neoliberal in orientation (O'Laughlin 2004).

It should be noted, though, that struggles over access to land never disappeared from the set of objectives of activist-based and advocacy-oriented civil society organizations and national NGOs (Rosset *et al.* 2006; Desmarais 2007). As De Angelis stresses, 'the fact that capital encloses … [generates] real social struggles against the many forms of capitalist enclosure' (De Angelis 2004: 65, 67). Struggles seek to defend existing commons, to create new ones and, more generally, to spread the spatial coordinates within which peasants have the possibility of obtaining 'non-commodified means to fulfil social needs, e.g. to obtain social wealth and to organize production'; these are 'created and sustained by communities' and 'are not reduced to the market form' (De Angelis 2003: 1). Those engaged in the struggle now consciously engage in transnational action and advocacy,[3] an engagement that demonstrates the diverse character of the actors and institutions involved in struggles around the land and agrarian reform process in the early part of the 2000s (Borras, Edelman and Kay 2008). This makes the analysis of struggles over access to land even more complex now than previously.

Neoliberalism and agrarian structure

Analytical distinctions

The process of neoliberal agrarian restructuring witnessed over the course of the past two decades has reshaped the character of the agrarian political economy in developing and transition countries. In particular, changes in access to land altered the relationship of the rural population to the principal productive asset, and consequently further restructured the rural production process. This is squarely the terrain of the agrarian question as it was classically understood. The result, in a diverse set of countries, has been the reconfiguration of an agrarian structure that we will term 'bifurcated'.

A bifurcated agrarian structure can be distinguished from a bimodal rural system in the sense that the latter is epitomized by Latin American *latifundio* and *minifundio* existing side-by-side, in a figurative and sometimes empirical sense, in such a way as to ensure that both are, in purely neoclassical economic terms, inefficient. In a bifurcated structure, however, while two quite different productive subsectors remain located side-by-side, figuratively and sometimes empirically, and indeed can be quite closely connected with each other, such need not be the case. It is precisely this possibility – that linkages between the two productive subsectors can be varied – that opens up the prospect of substantive variation in the differential ways by which rural economies are incorporated into global capitalism.

It is important to stress that our key analytical distinctions are twofold, and both are important to an agrarian political economy perspective. The first distinction is that of commodification. In particular, the two productive subsectors can be distinguished by the relative extent to which they produce for use or produce for sale; this is a key marker of the development of rural capitalism. Production for use and production for sale between the two subsectors can be strongly linked, but need not be. Our second distinction is related to the extent of commodification, in that one productive subsector strives under the market imperative to improve its competitive profitability within an increasingly globalized circuit of capital. By way of contrast, the market imperative for the other productive subsector is often, but not exclusively, that of the market for labour-power rather than commodities. Granted, food imports can intensify the crisis of this productive subsector, and in this sense global market imperatives can have an impact on the sector. However, this is, in our view, not as binding a market imperative as that generated by the market for labour-power. Within historically specific processes of change, these two distinctions can produce continued if differential incorporation into global capitalism, an uneven development that results, not surprisingly, in substantive diversity.

Bifurcation clearly describes much of African, Asian and Latin American agriculture over the past century. Under neoliberal agrarian restructuring, however, bifurcated agrarian structures have been reconfigured, in the sense that the market imperative to improve competitive profitability within an increasingly globalized circuit of capital has become far, far sharper than was previously the case. This has resulted in the emergence of an export-oriented capitalist subsector that is both more closely integrated into the global agro-food system than ever before, and more important to the inter-nationalized circuit of capital. This is because it acts both as a provider of agro-food commodities that lower the value of labour-power in the advanced capitalist countries – and hence raise the rate of relative surplus value – and as a source of the agrifuels that have the potential to power capitalist pro-duction. By way of contrast, for the peasantry the market imperative that has become more binding than previously is that of the market for labour-power, which is, often for the first time, productive of surplus value. Food imports tighten the market imperative facing the peasantry, and in so doing intensify the agrarian crisis. However, the way this crisis plays out is increasingly by forcing peasants into the market for labour-power that is productive of surplus value, and it is for this reason that labour market imperatives are more strongly binding on the peasantry.

The emerging export-oriented capitalist subsector

The export-oriented subsector is emerging, or may be about to emerge, as capitalist. It is more capital-intensive and less labour-absorbing in its tech-nical coefficients of production, seeking to utilize those economies of scale and scope that can be unlocked in the production of crops principally, but not singularly, destined for export markets that are primarily, but not exclu-sively, located in the advanced capitalist economies.[4] As such, understanding the characteristics of this productive subsector relies not so much on under-standing access to land, as on the location of the productive subsector within the circuit of capital. As it produces almost exclusively for the market, this productive subsector is subject to the logic of the market imperative, in that it must strive continually to improve competitiveness by reducing per-unit costs and improving per-unit quality in order to generate the surplus value that sustains enhanced profitability. However, the markets in which the pro-ductive subsector participates are heavily regulated by dominant class forces. Thus the productive subsector is often closely linked to transnational agro-food corporations operating in the spheres of production, processing, dis-tribution, retailing and finance in what is now a buyer-driven global agro-food system.

The linkages between transnational agro-food corporations and emerging export-oriented capitalist farms may be direct, through the physical owner-ship of capitalist farms or the control of production through contract farm-ing. However, they may also be indirect, operating through public or private intermediaries that arbitrate between on-farm production, global processing, and global wholesale and retail distribution. In this sense, transnational agro-food corporations play a key role in shaping the configuration of this productive subsector, imposing, as it were, 'capitalism from above' (Byres 2003).

This productive subsector often has limited backward linkages, but that need not be always the case. Thus in contemporary Vietnam, intensified commodification was predicated on growth in which transnational agro-food corporations played a key intermediary role for an export-oriented emerging capitalist subsector that, nonetheless, has extensive backward linkages, particularly in employment. Forward linkages in this productive subsector into domestic markets may also be limited, in that crops are not necessarily produced for local consumption, although again this need not be the case, as the dynamic commodification of domestic food markets witnessed, for example, in China, Vietnam and parts of Sub-Saharan Africa demonstrate.

Linkages into export markets are, however, exceedingly important and much more diverse, albeit in a manner that is restricted by the regulatory activities of transnational capital. These include, very importantly, the global supermarket chains that have increasing influence on what should be produced, how, and by whom. They are seeking providers of agro-food commodities that lower the value of labour-power in the advanced capitalist countries, and in so doing enhance the rate of relative surplus value. They also include the seed and chemical companies that are in the midst of turning themselves into energy companies producing agrifuels to replace the hydrocarbons that fuel capitalist production within internationalized circuits of capital.

In general, then, the emerging export-oriented capitalist subsector witnesses the generation of surplus value and agricultural profitability under a market imperative regulated by dominant classes. This demonstrates sharpened global value relations, as Araghi (Chapter 5) argues, in a world food system governed by highly internationalized circuits of capital seeking to raise the rate of relative surplus value. The key point is that the array of interventions that come about as a result of neoliberal agrarian restructuring enhance the rate of relative surplus value and, in so doing, of capital accumulation on a global scale.

The peasant subsector

While the second productive subsector resembles a 'classic' peasant-producing farm sector, it is important to be nuanced in recognizing some of its characteristics. For a start, and importantly, in this subsector the social, political and ecological characteristics of landscapes may shape behaviour and identity, and in this sense economic relations are refracted through a broader set of social relations. Nonetheless, in terms of its economic characteristics, this productive subsector is far more labour-intensive in its technical coefficients of production, with correspondingly lower levels of capitalization and greater challenges involved in reaping economies of scale and scope. This productive subsector is not homogeneous; even marginal differences in the technical coefficients of production and the ability to capture incremental economies of scale and scope can lead to the emergence of stratification among farms, as the capacity to produce output surplus to consumption requirements generates processes of differentiation. The peasant subsector produces a greater diversity of crops, principally but far from exclusively for direct consumption by the producing household, or for sales in the home market, whether local or regional. Through its impact on product as well as on labour markets, the peasant subsector thus has significant forward and backward linkages into the domestic economy.

However, as farmers within this productive subsector produce for the market, for use or for both, farms within the peasant subsector may be differentially incorporated into the logic of the market imperative, which nonetheless remains regulated by dominant classes. There are thus peasants who are relatively more strongly incorporated into dynamic markets for farm commodities that are regulated by dominant classes, and who must seek to improve competitiveness as rural capitalism slowly emerges 'from below'. For these farmers, the ownership of land and other means of production must be set beside the fact that the capacity of dominant classes to regulate markets has resulted in the effective loss of control of much of the labour process, and hence an emerging loss of access to non-market-based subsistence as surpluses are transferred from the direct producer to dominant classes, and production is therefore carried out 'by the peasantry ... but not for the peasantry' under the logic of capital (Araghi 2000: 151).

For those peasants who are less incorporated into the market, the issue of control of land is critical for their very survival. The control of land can bring with it the possibility of production for direct use, a non-commodified subsistence guarantee that gives peasants a degree of autonomy from capital that may secure a livelihood – although it will not open up the possibility of accumulation. At the same time, however, if the control of land relies on landowners for that access despite a subsistence guarantee, surpluses will, as in the case of those peasants who are more strongly integrated into market processes, be transferred from the direct producer to the dominant classes. Production for those who rely on landowners is thus once again by peasants, but not for peasants.

The characteristics of the peasant subsector thus demonstrate how the issue of access to land, by shaping the rural labour process, extends far beyond the immediate terrain of social struggles over land and into the more general terrain of rural social relations. Such relations include social property relations and the processes by which surpluses generated within the political economy can be accumulated by the direct producer, as rural capitalism emerges from below, or be transferred from the direct producer to the owner of land in ways that may, or may not, facilitate the emergence of rural capitalism.

Semiproletarianization

Standing beside those in this bifurcated agrarian structure is a significant and increasing proportion of the global peasantry who are seeking, day by day, refuge in their small plot of land, producing agricultural products for food security reasons while increasingly engaging in selling their labour-power to capitalist farmers, to richer peasants or to non-farm capitalists (Kay 2000). These peasants try to retreat from the market imperative in terms of their food production, as they can no longer compete with food imports or with local capitalist farmers. Nonetheless, for these peasants the market imperative holds – in order to survive, they must be able to sell their increasingly commodified labour-power, which is productive of surplus value, and an inability to sell labour-power results in pauperization. This is why these peasants are not included within the productive subsectors: with insufficient means of production, they do not produce, but rather sell their ability to work and their potential to produce surplus value.

This stratum was described by Lenin as being semiproletarian, which he defined as

> peasants who till tiny plots of land, i.e. those who obtain their livelihood partly as wage-labourers ... and partly by working their own rented plots of land, which provide their families only with part of their means of subsistence ... the lot of these semiproletarians is a very hard one.

> (Lenin 1966: 153, first published 1920)

While neither peasant nor proletarian, this part of the rural population is nonetheless the result of the immanent, if not immutable, drive of capital to separate producers, to a greater or lesser extent, from the means of production.[5] It can therefore be suggested that context-specific factors contributing to or constraining semiproletarianization are very important, in that they can help explain a significant fraction of the variation in processes of agrarian change in contemporary developing and transition countries, or indeed the lack thereof. For example, in countries where an MLAR has been implemented, rural labour that is settled on inadequate amounts of land would work the land highly intensively, increasing the relative surplus value that they would generate when working off-farm, but with an inability to accumulate that could lead, over time, to a process of socio-economic differentiation that would eventually force them to sell part or all of their holding to richer peasants or rural capitalists. In this way, despite the confidence of neoliberal populists such as de Soto, MLAR can facilitate market-led land appropriation by capital by deepening the capitalist market imperative when labour is fragmenting into a semiproletarian class (Bernstein 2006).

Contrasts and outliers

It is important not to overgeneralize, and (in addition to the areas of comparability) to stress the areas of contrast that may be witnessed in the contemporary bifurcated agrarian structure that has emerged under neoliberal globalization. Thus the specific forms of the capital-intensive, export-oriented emerging capitalist subsector can differ significantly. In some instances, farms in this productive subsector are classic capitalist farms, such as in Bolivia. In other instances, they may be more traditional plantations, such as in Vietnam. Clearly, these two forms of production can exist alongside each other, as in Kenya. In addition, the export-oriented emerging capitalist subsector may utilize the surplus redistributive characteristics of landlord–peasant relationships, with the result that the peasant subsector, even when internally differentiated, may seek to produce for export, such as in the Philippines.

There are outliers to these general processes: for example, countries in the Caucasus such as Armenia, and Ethiopia. Each case is similar, in that the agricultural sector is not bifurcated; a petty peasant sector dominates the rural economy of each, with high degrees of labour absorption in labour-intensive technical coefficients of production, limited links to local and global capital, and pervasive linkages across the rural economy. Even here, however, the sectors are not homogeneous. Once again, marginal differences in the technical coefficients of production and the ability to capture even incremental economies of scale and scope can lead to the emergence of stratification among farms, as the capacity to produce output surplus to consumption requirements generates processes of differentiation. In this context, even outliers may, in particular instances and contexts, generate processes promoting the eventual capitalization of some agrarian producers as neoliberal agrarian restructuring deepens.

Neoliberal agrarian restructuring and expanded commodification

Within the context of neoliberal agrarian restructuring, the reconfiguration of a predominantly bifurcated agrarian structure, along with processes of economic and social stratification within the peasant economy and semi-proletarianization, appear to have shaped, and been shaped by, processes of expanded commodification. Expanded commodification is part of the immanent drive of capital to accumulate. Expanded commodification has occurred in terms of products, of labour, of nature and of space. Thus in terms of products, in a multiplicity of countries, state development policies as 'a particular historical form of capital's inherent drive' (De Angelis 2004: 76) have focused on promoting the expanded commodification of the outputs of the rural economy, and have thus been biased, in particular, towards the production of higher-value agricultural products destined for export markets. This promotion often occurred as a direct consequence of neoliberal structural adjustment programmes initiated in the 1980s, and thus can be directly linked to processes of globalization and neoliberal agrarian restructuring. Indeed, it can be argued that MLAR is integrally and intimately intertwined with expanded commodification, in that within the context of neoliberal agrarian restructuring MLAR seeks to deepen land markets and hence the status of land as an alienable commodity.

Capital has expanded commodification of products for two interrelated reasons. The first reason has been to facilitate a continued expansion of an increasingly diversified set of agricultural exports destined for wealthier markets, especially in the North, even when nominally left-of-centre governments have been in power, as in Brazil under the Worker's Party and in Vietnam under the Communist Party. Structural adjustment programmes and their successor poverty reduction strategy papers were thus constructed around what could be termed a 'neoliberal agricultural export bias', a bias designed to raise the rate of relative surplus value and thus offset the tendency for the organic composition of capital to rise in the advanced capitalist economies. In some instances there can be little doubt that the promotion of agricultural exports has made a significant contribution to the rate of accumulation in developing and transition countries, although the actual percentage change in poverty reduction with respect to the percentage change in growth commonly remains far less impressive, as evidenced by the contrast between Brazil and Vietnam.

The second reason the expanded commodification of products was undertaken was to boost agricultural productivity and profits within the international circuit of capital. Expanded commodification creates new markets and thus stimulates increased investment in specific branches of agriculture. This has led to the further and more deeply imposed market imperatives of continual specialization, per-unit cost reductions, technological innovations, improved competitiveness, and hence the enhanced production of surplus value upon which accumulation is predicated.

Another aspect of expanded commodification that has shaped, and been shaped by, processes of economic and social stratification within and between the emerging export-oriented capitalist and peasant rural economy has been the expanded privatization of state-held rural productive and distributive assets, particularly in activities necessary to sustain agricultural production such as marketing, storage and processing facilities, as well the provision of credit and technical assistance. This phenomenon is complementary to the previous two, in that a principal motivation behind rural privatization has been an expansion of commodification, an increase in agricultural exports, and improved agricultural productivity and profitability. Thus rural privatization has expanded dramatically in much of Sub-Saharan Africa, where the role of the state in marketing and distribution has been circumvented by the privatization of parastatals, leading to a socially regressive redistribution of surplus labour within the circuit of capital away from the direct producers and towards the dominant classes as surplus value.

However, it should be noted that the privatization of productive and distributive assets is not the only demonstration of privatization. Perhaps most wide-ranging in its impact has been the fact that, in many countries, the private sector has been allowed to commence activities in operations that were once the exclusive preserve of public sector enterprises, thus effectively commodifying economic 'space' and transferring it from the public sector to capital, a clear sign of an enclosure of space that had been held in common. The result has been the establishment of private input companies and private companies involved in marketing and distribution, both nationally and internationally, as a near-global phenomenon dominated by transnational corporations.

The transfer of assets and space from public hands to capital has not, in many instances, been reflected in a marked increase in the rate of accumulation, either in the rural economy or in the economy as a whole. Granted, there are some cases, such as Vietnam, where there can be little doubt that the effective privatization of land sparked dramatic increases in poverty-reducing economic growth during the 1990s. However, there are other cases, such as Armenia, where the privatization of land has not been reflected in economic growth, while in countries such as Bolivia, the privatization of state enterprises in marketing and distribution has had, if anything, a negative impact on economic growth.

The reconfiguration of a bifurcated agrarian structure and the process of neoliberal agrarian restructuring has also been accompanied by widespread de-agrarianization, in which rural people become increasingly less reliant on farming as a source of their livelihood, resulting in the expanded commodification of labour (Bryceson 2000). This process is the outcome of the shift towards more capital- and land-intensive technical coefficients of production, often for the purpose of export, and mediated by transnational corporations. Such a shift has commonly led to the expulsion of some small farmers from the land and the simultaneous concentration of land in fewer hands, often as a result of appropriation through the operation of land markets regulated by dominant classes or, in some circumstances, as a consequence of some other byproduct of neoliberal accumulation processes such as debt and taxation. This is Araghi's process, explained in Chapter 5, of 'dispossession through displacement'. It can be witnessed most starkly in Vietnam, China, Brazil, Argentina and Bolivia, among others, with the result that, as a consequence of the logic of capital, an increasing proportion of the rural population is becoming semi-proletarian (Kay 2000). These trends have been reinforced by population growth and the accompanying subdivision of land. As a result, people have become increasingly reliant on labour markets as a mechanism by which to construct a livelihood, although in many cases the amount of available employment is far less than the demand for employment. The outcome has thus been an expansion of the global reserve army of labour, with implications for the rate of exploitation, as well as both intra- and international migration and, in some cases, remittances exceeding the value of agricultural exports.[6]

Again, within these general processes it is possible to identify outliers: for example, countries in the Caucasus where, in part as a result of land privatization, extensive re-agrarianization has taken place in order to facilitate the production of staples for the immediate use of the producing household, rather than expand production of the principal export crop. Despite the commodification of land, however, the re-agrarianization of production for use has restricted wider processes of commodification in rural economies. This sets it apart, starkly, from what has been discussed above, which describes the general processes at work as neoliberal globalization reconfigures land, and the social property relations within which control of the land is embedded.

Expanded commodification is also reflected in a changing balance between the market, the state and civil society. In a clear demonstration of a transformed economic, social and cultural environment, in most instances, despite an absence of a complete set of 'properly developed' markets and supporting institutions, product, labour and land markets have become structurally dominant institutions with regard to the activities of the state and civil society in rural social settings. Thus, in parts of Argentina for example, by fostering a tremendously increased concentration of operational holdings in a country that had historically low rates of land concentration, the operation of land markets has come to play a major role in rural livelihoods and to dominate rural social relations (see Chapter 6). Similarly, in Uzbekistan the lack of formal land titles being bestowed on rural households has not prevented a rise in incremental market-led land concentration. In Zimbabwe, by way of contrast, the political elite used a combination of land markets, state redistributive policy and coercion to obtain large quantities of land. Even in Brazil, where in the past 10 years an expanded role for the state in sustaining a degree of social protection within the peasant farm sector has taken place, this expansion has occurred in the context of an increasing use of land markets and a lack of debate concerning the social efficiency of land markets. Thus, overall, markets relations have, as a general if not universal rule, come to structurally dominate the actions of the state and civil society.

In short, neoliberal globalization has thus, through a process of privatization, land grabbing and (principally) the land market, facilitated the process of neoliberal agrarian restructuring in the agrarian production systems that have already been described. This alteration in the character of the agrarian structure has reshaped the rural production process, in many cases facilitating the reconfiguration of a bifurcated agrarian production system and the expanded commodification of rural economic activity. However, while there is much that is similar in these transformations of the rural production process, there is nonetheless substantive diversity that can be witnessed, and this diversity, when placed within a historically specific path of contingent and conjunctural transformation, helps in explaining the significant trajectories of variation in the pattern of growth and accumulation in the agrarian sector, as a consequence of a continued if differential incorporation into global capitalism. This helps explain, we suggest, a significant fraction of the variance in the process of agrarian transition, or the lack thereof. If this argument is correct, as we suggest it is, then the agrarian question, as it was classically understood, continues to be relevant in that it is capable of capturing the substantive diversity witnessed during a protracted process of differential incorporation into capitalism operating on a world scale.

Conclusions

Land both shapes, and is shaped by, its place within social relations. Thus, in the context of a less than fully developed agrarian capitalism, land is like capital – as rural capitalism emerges out of precapitalist agrarian relations, it is both a thing and a relation, structuring the distribution of property, power and privilege. In this chapter we have focused on the changing character of access to land as a means by which to consider the veracity of some claims advanced within the contemporary debate on the character of the agrarian question.

The argument we have developed is that, despite obvious complexity in the characterization of the contemporary agrarian question, some broad similarities can be seen to underpin an understanding of the processes at work in rural economies in developing economies and transition countries. The latest wave of neoliberal globalization has expanded world trade in agricultural commodities and integrated world agricultural markets that are increasingly dominated by transnational agro-food corporations. This has resulted in transformations in access to land as a result of processes of neoliberal agrarian restructuring, which works through both extra-economic and economic mechanisms to seize spaces of peasant reproduction. The effect has been to restructure rural production processes in relatively more capital- or more labour-intensive patterns, fostering (as a general if not exclusive rule) the reconfiguration of a bifurcated agrarian structure in which an export-oriented agrarian subsector sits beside a peasant-producer subsector with the peasantry increasingly dislocated from livelihood security. This reconfiguration is an outcome of the emergence of a new global political economy of land in which, in particular, dominant global class forces and their representatives seek to promote a market-led appropriation of land, in an effort to promote improvements in productive efficiency under the market imperative.

Central to the reconfiguration of this bifurcated agrarian structure have been processes of expanded commodification of products, labour, nature and space, which affect the relationship between the export and peasant-production subsectors, and which clearly differ in specific contexts. In this regard, factors contributing to or constraining semiproletarianization have been of critical import. This helps explain, we suggest, a significant fraction of the variance in the process of agrarian transition or the lack thereof. It must be stressed, however, that these processes are subject to substantive diversity rooted in contingent and conjunctural complexity.

It must also be stressed that, in these processes, some clear outliers to these aggregate processes can be identified; we do not claim that the agrarian question allows one to capture conclusively all the facets of the conjunctural complexity fostered by differential incorporation, for we are not positivists. However, neither were the classic theorists of the agrarian question.

Thus, we argue that while it is possible to make general statements about the reconfiguration of production, accumulation and politics that underpins the contemporary character of the agrarian question, it is not possible, nor is it advisable, to produce universal 'truths'. Agrarian political economy is not concerned with offering an all-embracing account of the totality of social relations within and between social formations. Rather, agrarian political economy is concerned with teasing out the underlying laws of motion of contemporary capitalism and its relationship to the countryside. In this regard, the agrarian question continues to have significant contemporary resonance.

Notes

1 As argued by Kay (2002), in the post-war years land and agrarian reform was conceptualized within a process of overall structural transformation, in which rural change underpinned industrialization. The difference, then, between Latin America's and East Asia's attempts at import-substituting industrialization was one of sequencing. In Latin America, land and agrarian reform came at the conclusion of the first phase of import substitution, whereas in East Asia, land and agrarian reform came either before or at the start of import substitution. Thus there is a clear difference in the timing of land and agrarian reform within a project of structural transformation (Kay 2006).

2 This debate can be reviewed in Griffin, Khan and Ickowitz (2002) and a special issue of the *Journal of Agrarian Change* (Byres 2004). Also see Johnston and Le Roux (2007), who, in our view decisively, introduce the gender dimension into the debate.

3 For further discussion about the global–local dynamics of these transnational agrarian reform campaigns, and how issues are framed, demands made, and actions launched, see Borras (2004).

4 China is becoming an important actor in world food markets, in terms of both its dynamic domestic production and its international trade, but it is important not to underestimate the role of agro-food transnational corporations in the internationalization of Chinese agricultural production and markets.

5 Some might describe this segment of the rural population as one of 'disguised wage labour', but in our view Harriss-White (2005) and Banaji (2003), the two principal proponents of the disguised wage labour thesis, mean something different from Lenin's concept of semiproletarian. Contrary to Harriss-White and Banaji, Lenin's semiproletarians are not disguised: they rely on their insufficient plot and on wage labour.

6 While Davis (2006) is correct to assert that enforced labour migration has created a 'planet of slums', the key process at work in the creation of a planet of slums is

the capitalization of agriculture as a result of neoliberal globalization, and the consequent expulsion of small farmers from much of the rural economy through neoliberal agrarian restructuring, with the result that rural people, needing to survive, migrate in order to try to sell their labour-power (Akram-Lodhi and Kay forthcoming).

References

Akram-Lodhi, A.H. (2005) 'Neoconservative economic policy, governance and alternative budgets', in A.H. Akram-Lodhi, R. Chernomas and A. Sepehri (eds), *Globalization, Neoconservative Policies and Democratic Alternatives*, Winnipeg: Arbeiter Ring.

—— (2006) 'What's in a name? Neo-conservative ideology, neoliberalism and globalisation', in R. Robison (ed.), *The Neoliberal Revolution: Forging the Market State*, London: Palgrave.

Akram-Lodhi, A.H. and C. Kay (eds) (forthcoming) *Footloose Workers and Dissolving Peasantries*, London: Routledge.

Akram-Lodhi, A.H., S. Borras, Jr and C. Kay (eds) (2007) *Land, Poverty and Livelihoods in an Era of Globalization: Perspectives from Developing and Transition Countries*, London/New York: Routledge.

Araghi, F. (2000) 'The great global enclosure of our times: peasants and the agrarian question at the end of the twentieth century', in F. Magdoff, J.B. Foster and F. Buttel (eds), *Hungry for Profit: The Agribusiness Threat to Farmers, Food and the Environment*, New York: Monthly Review Press.

—— (2003) 'Food regimes and the production of value: some methodological issues', *Journal of Peasant Studies*, 30 (2): 41–70.

Assies, W. (2006) 'Land tenure legislation in a pluri-cultural and multi-ethnic society: the case of Bolivia', *Journal of Peasant Studies*, 33 (4): 569–611.

Banaji, J. (2003) 'The fictions of free labour: contract, coercion and so-called unfree labour', *Historical Materialism*, 11 (3): 69–95.

Bellisario, A. (2007a) 'The Chilean agrarian transformation: agrarian reform and capitalist "partial" counter-agrarian reform, 1964–1980 – Part 1: reformism, socialism and free-market neoliberalism', *Journal of Agrarian Change*, 7 (1): 1–34.

—— (2007b) 'The Chilean agrarian transformation: agrarian reform and capitalist "partial" counter-agrarian reform, 1964–1980 – Part 2: CORA, post-1980 outcomes and the emerging agrarian class structure', *Journal of Agrarian Change*, 7 (2): 145–182.

Bernstein, H. (1996) 'The political economy of the maize *filière*', in H. Bernstein (ed.), *The Agrarian Question in South Africa*, London: Frank Cass.

—— (2006) 'Is there an agrarian question in the 21st century?', *Canadian Journal of Development Studies*, 27 (4): 449–460.

Borras, S.M., Jr (2004) *La Via Campesina: An Evolving Transnational Social Movement*, Briefing Series No. 2004/6, Amsterdam: Transnational Institute.

—— (2006) 'The Philippine land reform experience in comparative perspective: some theoretical and methodological implications', *Journal of Agrarian Change*, 6 (1): 69–101.

—— (2007) *Pro-Poor Land Reform: A Critique*, Ottawa: University of Ottawa Press.

Borras, S.M, Jr, M. Edelman and C. Kay (eds) (2008) *Transnational Agrarian Movements Confronting Globalization*, Oxford: Blackwell Publishing.

Borras, S.M., Jr, C. Kay and E. Lahiff (eds) (2007) 'Market-led agrarian reform: trajectories and contestations', special issue of *Third World Quarterly* 28 (8).

Bryceson, D.F. (2000) 'Peasant theories and smallholder policies: past and present', in D.F. Bryceson, C. Kay and J. Mooij (eds), *Disappearing Peasantries? Rural Labour in Africa, Asia and Latin America*, London: ITDG Publishing.

Bush, R. (ed.) (2002) *Counter Revolution in the Egyptian Countryside*, London: Zed Books.

Byres, T.J. (2003) 'Paths of capitalist agrarian transition in the past and in the contemporary world', in V.K. Ramachandran and M. Swaminathan (eds), *Agrarian Studies: Essays on Agrarian Relations in Less-Developed Countries*, London: Zed Press.

—— (ed.) (2004) 'Redistributive land reform today', special issue of *Journal of Agrarian Change* 4 (1/2).

Davis, M. (2006) *Planet of Slums*, London: Verso.

De Angelis, M. (2003) 'Reflections on alternatives, commons and communities, or building a new world from the bottom up', *The Commoner* (6) winter.

—— (2004) 'Separating the doing and the deed: capital and the continuous character of enclosures', *Historical Materialism*, 12 (2): 57–87.

Deininger, K. and H. Binswanger (1999) 'The evolution of the World Bank's land policy: principles, experience and future challenges', *The World Bank Research Observer* 14 (2): 247–276.

Desmarais, A. (2007) *La Via Campesina: Globalization and the Power of Peasants*, London: Pluto Books.

Ellis, F. (2000) *Rural Livelihoods and Diversity in Developing Countries*, Oxford: Oxford University Press.

Griffin, K., A.R. Khan and A. Ickowitz (2002) 'Poverty and the distribution of land', *Journal of Agrarian Change*, 2 (3): 279–330.

Harriss-White, B. (2005) *Poverty and Capitalism*, Queen Elizabeth House Working Paper Series No. 134, Oxford: Department of International Development, University of Oxford.

Holt-Giménez, E. (2007) 'Territorial restructuring and the grounding of agrarian reform: indigenous communities, gold mining and the World Bank', paper presented to the Canadian Association for the Study of International Development Annual Congress, University of Saskatchewan, Saskatoon, Canada, 1 June.

de Janvry, A., G. Gordillo, J.-P. Platteau and E. Sadoulet (eds) (2001) *Access to Land, Rural Poverty and Public Action*, Oxford: Oxford University Press.

Johnston, D. and H. Le Roux (2007) 'Leaving the household out of family labour? The implications for the size–efficiency debate', *European Journal of Development Research*, 19 (3): 355–371.

Kautsky, K. (1988) *The Agrarian Question*, London: Zwan Publications (first published in 1899).

Kay, C. (1995) 'Rural Latin America: exclusionary and uneven agricultural development', in S. Halebsky and R.L. Harris (eds), *Capital, Power, and Inequality in Latin America*, Boulder, CO: Westview Press.

—— (1998) 'Rural development: from agrarian reform to neoliberalism and beyond', *Land Reform, Land Settlement and Cooperatives*, 2: 8–31.

—— (2000) 'Latin America's agrarian transformation: peasantization and proletarianization', in D.F. Bryceson, C. Kay and J. Mooij (eds), *Disappearing Peasantries? Rural Labour in Africa, Asia and Latin America*, London: ITDG Publishing.

—— (2002) 'Why East Asia overtook Latin America: agrarian reform, industrialization and development', *Third World Quarterly*, 23 (6): 1073–1102.

—— (2006) 'Rural poverty and development strategies in Latin America', *Journal of Agrarian Change* 6 (4): 455–508.

Lenin, V.I. (1966) 'Preliminary draft theses on the agrarian question', in *Collected Works, Volume XXXI* (4th edn), Moscow: Progress Publishers (first published in 1920).

O'Laughlin, B. (2004) 'Review of several rural livelihood books', *Development and Change,* 35 (2): 385–392.

Ravallion, M. and D. van de Walle (2006) 'Does rising landlessness signal the success or failure of Vietnam's agrarian transition?', Policy Research Working Paper No 3871, Washington, DC: World Bank.

Rosset, P., R. Patel and M. Courville (eds) (2006) *Promised Land: Competing Visions of Agrarian Reform*, Oakland, CA: Food First Books.

de Soto, H. (2000) *The Mystery of Capital: Why Capitalism Triumphs in the West and Fails Everywhere Else*, New York: Basic Books.

Wittman, H. and L. Saldivar-Tanaka (2006) 'The agrarian question in Guatemala', in P. Rosset, R. Patel and M. Courville (eds), *Promised Land: Competing Visions of Agrarian Reform*, Oakland, CA: Food First Books.

World Bank (2003) *Land Policies for Growth and Poverty Reduction*, Washington, DC and Oxford: World Bank/Oxford University Press.

—— (2005) *World Development Report 2006: Equity and Development*, Oxford: Oxford University Press.

—— (2007) *World Development Report 2008: Agriculture for Development*, Oxford: Oxford University Press.

10 Agrarian questions from transition to globalization

Henry Bernstein

Introduction[1]

I begin at the point where Terence J. Byres finishes Chapter 3 in this volume, with this quote from Rodney Hilton:

> ... historians and sociologists are engaged in comparative studies of peasant societies in different epochs. It would be very risky to transfer any generalizations about peasant societies of medieval Europe to any other time. For example, the capitalist farmers who were to be an important element in the history of early European capitalism emerged in a general environment of small-scale enterprise. What could the fate of peasant societies in the present world of almost world-wide commercial and industrial monopoly capitalism have in common with that of peasant societies of the late medieval world? Clearly, the tasks of leadership in contemporary peasant society have nothing in common with the tasks of the past, except in the recognition that conflict is part of existence and that nothing is gained without struggle.
>
> (Hilton 1973: 236)

The three moments highlighted in these observations by Hilton provide key signposts to the sources of the 'agrarian question', and implicitly to the mutations and trajectories of how it has been conceived in modern history. At the same time, of course, they are only the briefest of signposts. The direction they suggest takes us through the long, complex, and varied paths of:

(i)   the transition(s) to capitalism in particular social formations in different parts of the world;
(ii) the historical development of capitalism at a global level; and
(iii) the connections between the two.

Cursory as Hilton's observations are, they suggest two dimensions of increasing scale definitive of the development of capitalism. One is spatial and explicit: the world-historical distance between Hilton's second and third signposts, from early European capitalism to what he terms 'almost world-wide ... monopoly capitalism' – in effect, imperialism. The second, more implicit, is that of economic scale: from the emergence of early European capitalism 'in a general environment of small-scale enterprise' to the drive of capitalism, once established, towards economies of scale in production, and towards concentration and centralization in the organization and functioning of capital itself, to the point of the emergence and global domination of 'monopoly capitalism'. Once that point is reached, and in the processes of reaching it, a rupture between the 'peasant societies' that characterized late European feudalism and contemporary 'peasant societies' is completed. That rupture is not only historical, but has some fundamental implications for theorizing paths of transition to capitalist farming in other times and places, and indeed for their politics, as Hilton's last sentence recognizes.

This chapter aims to explore some of those implications for agrarian questions today. The first section considers the transition to agrarian capitalism, and its contributions to industrialization, in the agrarian question of classic Marxism, and how the concerns and approach of the classic agrarian question were mapped onto key processes and moments in the formation of a capitalist world economy. The second suggests why, and how, globalization challenges the assumptions of the classic agrarian question. The third and fourth sections note and comment on notions of new agrarian questions in the conditions of contemporary globalization. I hope that the violence to properly historical investigation incurred by the highly schematic exposition of the chapter is compensated, at least in part, by some benefit to fresh theoretical reflection on today's circumstances and challenges.

Transition(s) to capitalism: the classic agrarian question and its applications

The classic agrarian question: three aspects

What was the classic agrarian question, or agrarian question of classic Marxism, that haunts the agenda and concerns of this book? Following the seminal work of Byres (1991, 1996), it is useful to distinguish three aspects or connected questions.[2] I rearrange the order of these in a suggested sequence of their historical appearance as preoccupations within: first, Marxist theory; second, political movements that drew on and developed Marxist theory; and third, states claiming the support of Marxist theory and movements for projects of socialist construction, otherwise known as development.

> Q1: What constitutes a transition to capitalist agriculture and what drives it? In effect, what are the forms and trajectories of class struggle that, sooner or later, transform precapitalist social relations of production as a basis for the development of the productive forces in farming?

Q2: What is the role of agrarian classes of labour – peasant classes, small farmers and agricultural workers – in struggles for democracy and socialism?

Q3: How do transitions to capitalist agriculture contribute (or otherwise) to the accumulation necessary for industrialization – what Byres terms 'agrarian transition'?

These three questions may be conveniently summarized as centred on the problematics of agricultural production, contemporary politics and industrial accumulation, respectively. Clearly, they are connected with each other, and even more so as the era of modern capitalism proceeded, but the historical sequence proposed is somewhat different from what might be considered a logical ordering, which would proceed from Q1 to Q3 to Q2. The reasons for this may begin to shed light on some of the tensions intrinsic to the intellectual and political lineages of the agrarian question established in, and inherited from, classic Marxism.

The basis of Q1 was established by Marx himself. Writing in the midst of the massive transformations wrought by nineteenth century industrial capitalism, which he investigated and sought to explain, Marx provided a compelling historical, as well as theoretical, account of the primitive accumulation that produced the first agrarian capitalism, and subsequently the first industrial capitalism, in England, and a theoretical account of the class basis and dynamics of capitalist farming, including capitalist landed property and the theory of rent. This, then, was the original source of what later became known as the agrarian question: Q1 as an object of Marxist theory first established by Marx himself, and subsequently developed considerably by Kautsky (1988, orig. 1899) and Lenin (1964, orig. 1899) in works that drew on a great deal of recent empirical material.

Q2 was placed centrally on the agenda first by Engels (1970, orig. 1894) in his *The Peasant Question in France and Germany*. The striking point of this timing is that Engels sought to address the political challenges confronting mass political movements based in a growing industrial working class in countries where 'the peasant is a very essential factor of the population, production and political power'; that is, he noted, all European countries at that time except Britain and Prussia east of the Elbe (Engels 1970: 381). Issues of the role of rural classes in relation to the programme of a mass working-class party in Germany, and to the strategic considerations of an underground vanguard party in Russia, informed the classic works on agrarian political economy by Kautsky and Lenin, respectively, both published in 1899, which did much to define the agrarian question as it was understood subsequently.[3]

While Marx and Engels, Kautsky and Lenin were, of course, all aware of the connections between transitions to capitalist agriculture and subsequent industrialization, Q3 did not emerge as a distinct focus of theory and action until economic transformation became a central preoccupation of the first communist state, the USSR, in the 1920s. Byres (1991) provided this key insight, together with the observation that the founding text of Q3 in these conditions was Preobrazhensky's *The New Economics*, published in 1926, which formulated 'the law of primitive socialist accumulation' as, in effect, a substitution for capitalist primitive accumulation (Preobrazhensky 1965).

Iterations of the classic agrarian question: the place(s) of the peasantry

Q1 focuses above all on the transformation – or elimination – of the definitive agrarian classes of feudalism: feudal landed property and the peasantry. Transformations of the peasantry can follow a path of dispossession by emergent landed property or a path of internal differentiation towards classes of agrarian capital and labour. The former may be summarized as the enclosure model emphasized by Marx; the latter was established by Lenin's (1964) *The Development of Capitalism in Russia*.

The legacy of Engels, Kautsky and Lenin in the original constitution of Q2 establishes a formulation of the contemporary politics of the agrarian question as, indeed, the 'peasant question' in those circumstances where, as noted above, 'the peasant is a very essential factor of the population, production and political power'. This is likely to apply *a fortiori* to formations at much earlier stages of transition to capitalism; for example, Tsarist Russia in the 1890s relative to France and Germany at that time.

The significance of Q3 was established in the highly distinctive conditions of the first attempt at socialist construction, centred on rapid industrialization in a primarily agrarian or peasant society. That significance can be highlighted by the nature of Lenin's *The Development of Capitalism in Russia* and the Soviet collectivization of agriculture, separated by only three decades, albeit spanning exceptional social and political upheaval. It has been little remarked that Lenin's study – the fullest in classic Marxism of contemporary processes of development in a 'backward' country – proceeds with virtually no reference to the international capitalist economy in which late-nineteenth century Russia was located, and by which its 'backwardness' was defined, nor to its effects on capitalist development in Russia. In effect, it was a study of capitalism in one country, as it were, following the internalist framework of studies of the emergence of 'early European capitalism'. By this I mean internal to:

- agrarian modes/forms of production such as feudalism;
- class struggle between exclusively agrarian classes of landed property and labour, that is to say, the peasantry; and
- individual social formations outside any international framework.[4]

A greater, and most painful, irony – among many which mark the problematic histories of the agrarian question – is registered in the passage from capitalism in one country to Stalin's claims for socialism in one country, and the strategic place within it of the collectivization of agriculture. Preobrazhensky (1965) had already proposed, in uniquely explicit fashion, a strategy for the taxation of agriculture, which was now in the hands of peasant farmers freed from the exactions of landed property, as the basis of early socialist industrialization. However, he had not advocated collectivization, which under Stalin's leadership marked a definitive resolution, of a certain kind, of the classic agrarian question in Soviet conditions. Q1 was to be resolved through the dispossession of the Russian peasantry, to establish forms of production that could reap the economies of scale and development of the productive forces hitherto exemplified by capitalist farming. Development of the productive forces through mechanization on large farms would not only boost the agricultural surplus available to an industrial accumulation fund, but also provide the greatly enlarged labour force needed for rapid industrialization – that is, Q3. Moreover, and by no means least, ostensibly collectivization would resolve the tensions of the worker–peasant alliance, of the union of hammer and sickle, in the moment of October 1917 and its aftermath; that is, the politics of Q2. It can be suggested that this experience, including Soviet views of the peasantry that fed into the extraordinary force applied to its dispossession, cast the longest, and deepest, shadow over those extensive zones of the world where the issues of the classic agrarian question, with all their underlying contradictions, asserted themselves subsequently in the course of the twentieth century.

In short, these iterations of the classic agrarian question highlight world-historical issues of the fate of the peasantry in transitions to capitalism and, once, socialism; its dispossession or its decomposition via class differentiation; its political roles and options, strengths and weaknesses, in processes of profound social change wrought by the development of capitalism and in relation to projects of capitalist and, once, socialist accumulation and industrialization ('development'). I next sketch, albeit in all too schematic a fashion, some of the contexts defined by such issues.

Extensions and applications of the classic agrarian question: imperialism during and after the colonial era

As suggested above, from its original focus on the first transition to capitalist agriculture in England, with its source in Marx, the concerns of the classic agrarian question were extended to the contemporary industrializing countries of Western Europe by Engels and Kautsky, and then further afield to its eastern and southern peripheries by Lenin, as well as to Ireland. Thereafter it came to encompass most of the major zones of the old agrarian civilizations of North Africa and across Asia during the period of colonial imperialism, and likewise to the social formations of Latin America – including, retrospectively, to their periods of colonial rule, from which they had inherited their agrarian class structures of landed property and peasantry.

Social upheaval and political struggle across the South revealed further the tensions of the classic agrarian question – and their Soviet resolution of the 1930s – in the different and changing historical circumstances of colonial empire and, even more broadly, the global development of capitalism during and after the colonial era. Q1 was marked above all by the tensions accompanying its two constitutive moments, and especially the passage from the first to the second: the transformation/elimination of feudal, or other precapitalist, landed property, and the subsequent fate of the peasantry. These tensions were witnessed in:

- its transformation by the dynamic of agrarian capital, whether deriving from within the peasantry via its class differentiation (Byres' English case) or from other social sources;
- some form or other of collectivization; or
- successful resistance by peasantries to dispossession by emergent agrarian capital (Byres' French case) and/or – to extend the range of possibilities to the twentieth century and now – dispossession by established agrarian, and indeed agribusiness, capital, or by state development schemes, or by some combination of the two.

These tensions, intrinsic to the drama of transition, and the different historical paths and outcomes that registered them, had a crucial impact on Q2, centred on class alliances, and on Q3, centred on the contributions of agriculture to industrialization – just as class struggle beyond the countryside, as well as within it, and industrialization, as both immanent dynamic and state project, had effects for the rhythms, trajectories and forms of Q1.

Central to all this, as the Soviet experience suggests, is the politics of how precapitalist landed property was dispossessed (or transformed into capitalist landed property, as happened in very different ways in England and Prussia, and subsequently in parts of Latin America and South Asia), and how this affected what happened to the peasantry subsequently. Of particular interest here is the dispossession of precapitalist landed property by land reforms following longer or shorter episodes of typically intense class struggle in the countryside. The defeat of predatory landed property was a major goal and/ or outcome of peasant movements – and later of state policies – in a series of momentous social upheavals that traverse modern history from the French revolution onwards, and which culminated with particular intensity across much of the world in a period from the 1910s to the 1970s: the period *par excellence* of Eric Wolf's 'peasant wars of the twentieth century' (Wolf 1969). Examples include Mexico and Russia in the 1910s, Eastern and Southern Europe and China in the interwar period (continuing in China into the 1940s and 1950s), and in the postwar period, Bolivia in the 1950s, Vietnam and Algeria in the 1950s and 1960s, Peru in the 1960s, Mozambique in the 1970s and Nicaragua in the 1980s. In all these instances, peasants contributed to land reform, in some cases undertaking it more or less autonomously, more or less spontaneously, by their own political action, and in some crucial instances combining struggles against large landed property and its social power with anticolonial or anti-imperialist struggles, in which socialist and communist parties often had an important, and sometimes leading, role.

The resonances of land reform effected by peasant wars thus remained potent in the period of state-led development initiated, and generalized, in the postwar conjuncture of decolonization in Asia and Africa and super-power rivalry between the USA and USSR for influence in the South. In effect, the period from the 1940s to the 1970s was simultaneously the last phase of Wolf's peasant wars and, as discussed by Araghi (Chapter 5), of the golden age of land reform in recent history, which also coincided with, and helped shape, the period of state-led developmentalism following decoloni-zation. This was manifested in land reforms of very different types during this period, driven by continuing – or renewed – impulses of social revolu-tion (as in China and Vietnam); strategies to pre-empt the possibility – or threat – of social revolution (as in Italy, Japan and Korea in the 1940s and 1950s under US military occupation, and in the US-led Alliance for Progress in Latin America in the 1960s following the Cuban revolution); and other state-led development strategies pursued by modernizing regimes of varying nationalist complexions, from Nehru's India and Nasser's Egypt to the Iran of the last Shah, between the 1950s and 1970s.

This wide range of examples from the different zones and times of Wolf's period of peasant wars suggests that more and less comprehensive land reforms were pursued for different purposes, by different social and political forces, through more and less radical means, and with various outcomes. Some modernizing nationalist land reforms accelerated the pace of capitalist development in agriculture, which was often part of their rationale, while, on the other side of the same coin, landless workers and poorer farmers mostly obtained less land, if any, than richer peasants and embryonic capitalist farmers – in India, Egypt, Iran and much of Latin America, for example – and especially women farmers and agricultural workers, who generally con-tinue to have the weakest land rights (Razavi 2003). In short, land reforms in the name of land to the tiller, a slogan shared across a wide ideological spectrum, seldom led to comprehensive redistribution in terms of who received land, except perhaps in the most dramatic instances of social revo-lution. Rather, who got land, what land, how much land, and what they were able to do with it, was contested along – and often followed – the contours of existing, typically intricate structures of differentiation in agrarian popu-lations beyond that represented by landed property: most ubiquitously, inequalities of class and gender among the peasantry, as well as, in some cases, those of ethnicity and caste.

In other instances of major historical significance, the initial dispossession and division of large feudal or colonial–commercial landholdings in favour of land to the (peasant) tiller was quickly followed by collectivization under communist regimes, notably the adaptations of the Soviet model in China and Vietnam. As suggested earlier, this may be considered the equivalent in socialist construction to the formation of large-scale farming and its contributions to industrialization, in the agrarian transition to capitalism conceived in the classic schema, albeit now highly focused by political intent and highly compressed in time. In another kind of scenario, exemplified by generally later cases, when large commercial estates and plantations (often foreign-owned) were expropriated by socialist and radical nationalist regimes brought to power by national liberation struggles, they were immediately converted into state farms rather than divided for distribution to peasants/ small farmers – for example in Cuba, Algeria, Mozambique and Nicaragua.

The most virtuous realization of the logic of the classic agrarian question, in transitions to both capitalism and, once, socialism, is when rapid agricultural productivity growth can help finance an initial accumulation fund for industrialization without severely undermining investment in farming and the living standards of its classes of labour. Sadly, such virtue is historically rare by contrast with far more vicious ways of trying to effect agriculture's contribution to industrialization. This typically proceeds through one form or another of taxing agriculture, regardless of its levels of productivity and investment and the conditions of labour in the countryside, and/or otherwise intensifying state control over peasant production, and/or promoting/intensifying production and accumulation by agrarian capital, including progressive, that is to say, richer, strata of the peasantry. All these measures were deployed, to varying degrees and in various forms and combinations, in projects of national development pursued in the moment of independence from colonial rule in Asia and Africa (and also in Latin America, long politically independent), albeit without the consistency and force, and extreme circumstances, of the Soviet experience, and without generating the levels of industrialization achieved in the USSR.

In sum, land reforms, often driven by peasant political action, played a key historical role in a number of agrarian transitions, both capitalist and socialist, by overturning precapitalist landed property and its predatory grip on agricultural production and producers. Such land reforms were followed more or less quickly, more or less brutally, by subsequent change in the forms of farming and whether and how agriculture – or more precisely different agrarian classes – could be pressed into the service of a project of industrial accumulation pursued with more or less clarity, coherence and effect by a range of modernizing regimes. It remains doubtful, however, whether (with the rather distinctive exception of England, in Byres' interpretation, as discussed in this volume) Q1 and its subsequent contributions to Q3 were ever resolved in a path of agrarian transition through class differentiation of the peasantry that generated either full-blown capitalist agriculture or comprehensive industrialization, let alone both (Byres 1991, 1996; Bernstein 1996).

The processes and paths so schematically sketched here stretched across the world-historical distance – as I called it earlier – from Hilton's early

European capitalism to global monopoly capitalism, or imperialism. Once a capitalist world economy, and its constituent international divisions of labour and markets, started to be shaped by industrialization in the course of the nineteenth century, and by modern imperialism by the end of that century, this was bound to have effects for the realization, or otherwise, of the logic of capitalist development outlined in the schema of the classic agrarian question.[5] To put it somewhat differently, the trajectories and forms of the transition to capitalism in social formations where it is deemed yet incomplete are affected by both earlier transitions to capitalism elsewhere, and subsequent transformations within capitalism in its dominant formations and global circuits – the latter is exemplified by contemporary globalization.

My proposition here is that from the 1970s – the advent of the moment of current globalization, the end of the golden period of land reform, and the beginning of the end of developmentalism in the South – the historic notion of redistributive land reform as a gravedigger of feudal, or feudal-like, landed property was no longer applicable to the countrysides of the South. Above all, this was because of changes in the development of capitalism on a world scale and of its effects for the range of agrarian structures and dynamics it contains.

Globalization: the agrarian question of capital resolved

While controversy rages, and will continue to do so, concerning the causes, mechanisms and implications, including new contradictions, of changes in world economy, politics and culture since the 1970s – as registered in debates about globalization – there is little doubt that important shifts with far-reaching ramifications have occurred, of which that decade, in retrospect, was a crucible. A familiar list would include: the deregulation of financial markets; shifts in the production, sourcing and sales strategies and technologies of transnational manufacturing and agribusiness corporations; the massive new possibilities attendant on information technologies, not least for mass communications, and how they are exploited by the corporate capital that controls them; the demise of the Soviet Union and finally of any plausible socialist model of development; and the ideological and political ascendancy of neoliberalism in a highly selective rolling back of the state, including the structural adjustment programmes, economic liberalization, and state reform/good governance agendas imposed on the countries of the South and, more recently, the former Soviet bloc. This is the context, and some of its key markers, that spelled the end of state-led development, or what Araghi (Chapter 5) calls national developmentalism.

Here I sketch some broad theses relevant to changing conditions, which reconsideration of the classic agrarian question in the present period needs to take into account. Some of the theses imply qualification of elements of the classic agrarian question as applied historically – for example, its internalist problematic – and hence even more so as applied to conditions

today. Some concern processes that pre-date the current period of globalization but are necessary to understanding its impact and which, in many
respects, have intensified as direct or indirect effects of its dynamics.

Thesis 1 By the time of independence from colonial rule in Asia and
   Africa, the economies of their former colonial territories were permeated, like those of Latin America, by generalized commodity production – capitalist social relations of production and reproduction.

Thesis 2 Generalized commodity production includes both the inter-
   nalization of capitalist social relations in the organization of economic
   activity, including peasant production; and how economies are located
   in international divisions of labour, markets and circuits of capital and
   commodities.

Thesis 3 Agrarian capital can have a range of sources beyond the countryside and its original, localized, indigenous rural classes of landed
   property and peasantry. The range of non-agrarian, non-indigenous
   sources of agrarian capital is likely to expand and diversify, and their
   significance to increase, over the history of capitalism.

Thesis 4 Different types of agrarian capital, in capitalist and petty commodity
   production, and among different peasant classes, are increasingly likely
   to be combined or articulated with forms of activity and income in non-
   agricultural sectors, or spaces in social divisions of labour, with variant
   effects for the specific forms of organization, scale, economic performance and simple or expanded reproduction of farming enterprises.

Thesis 5 There are similar tendencies to the decomposition of notionally
   once pure classes of agrarian labour, including that combined with
   capital in petty commodity production, that have to diversify their
   forms, and spaces, of employment and self-employment to meet their
   simple reproduction needs as labour ('survival'), and in the case of
   petty commodity producers, as capital too.

Thesis 6 The agricultural sector in capitalism today is not simply a set of
   relations between agrarian classes – landed property, agrarian capital,
   labour – nor an aggregation of farm enterprises of different types, but is
   increasingly, if unevenly, integrated, organized and regulated by the
   relations between agrarian classes and types of farms, on one hand, and
   often highly concentrated capital upstream and downstream of farming, on the other hand. Moreover, such integration and regulation
   operates through global as well as national and, indeed, more local
   social divisions of labour, circuits of capital, commodity chains and
   sources and types of technical change, including in transport and
   industrial processing, as well as farming.

Thesis 7 Important globalizing tendencies that affect agriculture in capitalism
   today include: new strategies of sourcing by transnational agribusiness;
   new forms of organization and regulation of global commodity chains
   for agricultural products; the high profile of agricultural trade and

its regulation in the agenda of, first, the General Agreement on Tariffs and Trade (GATT) from the mid-1980s and now of the World Trade Organization; and the drive of transnational agribusiness chemical and seed companies to patent, monopolize, produce and sell genetic plant and animal material, and to lock in farmers in both North and South to its use.

Of these theses, 1–5 suggest some reasons why nothing is gained, and much is obscured, by characterizing social formations in the South today as peasant societies, or contemporary classes of petty commodity-producing small farmers as peasants. The use of such terms typically resonates a notion of deep continuity with past worlds: the persistence or survival of some essential precapitalist social category or form that is emblematic of most of recorded history into the era of current globalization or imperialism (Bernstein 2000).

Theses 6 and 7 recommend bringing the capitalist development of the USA into the narrative of this chapter for the first time, if only to illustrate a proposition about modern capitalist agriculture central to the consideration of globalization. So far, the terms 'agriculture' and 'farming' may have appeared to be interchangeable, and they are all too commonly used thus. I now want to emphasize that the classic agrarian question was concerned, above all, with the emergence of capitalist farming as conceived for the original transition of sixteenth century England and thereafter. It can be suggested, however, that it was the nineteenth century USA that pioneered the organizational forms of modern capitalist agriculture, not least Chicago and its hinterland, with its closely associated industrial manufacture of farm equipment, emergence of corporate agribusiness, infrastructure for handling and transporting agricultural commodities in unprecedented quantities over long distances, and futures markets in farm commodities and other institutional innovations, all traced in William Cronon's seminal *Nature's Metropolis* (1991). In effect, in the formation of a home market across its continental distances, including the dynamic linkages of agriculture with industry, and in its rapid emergence as a leading grain exporter, not least to Europe, the USA developed many aspects of modern corporate agribusiness and how it incorporates and regulates farming.[6] This is a world of capitalist organization and operation far beyond the struggles between landed property and peasantry over enclosure or rents that marked the passage to 'early European capitalism'. These constantly evolving modes of organization and operation of agribusiness, exemplifying the concentration and centralization of capital, were later to be internationalized, and indeed are central to current processes of globalization (Friedmann 1993).

The salience of the processes and tendencies sketched in the theses above for particular branches and types of agricultural production, and forms of agrarian capital and labour, in different times and places, is a matter of investigation that is bound to reveal massive unevenness and variation. Nonetheless, recognition of such processes and tendencies, as of others relevant to the world of contemporary capitalism, can inform the agenda of identifying, and seeking to explain, what may be 'changing before our very eyes' (Bernstein 2004; Byres 2004a).

Here is a further, and final, thesis. In effect, the classic agrarian question was the agrarian question of capital: first of an emergent agrarian capital, and then of emergent industrial capital. With contemporary globalization and the massive development of the productive forces in advanced capitalist agriculture, the centrality of any agrarian question to industrialization is no longer significant for international capital. In this sense, then, there is no longer an agrarian question of capital on a world scale, even when the agrarian question – as a basis of national accumulation and industrialization – has not been resolved in many countries of the South.

To reiterate, and to avoid misunderstanding: for capital on a global scale, the definitive questions of continuously raising the productivity of labour in farming, the production of cheap food staples, and the agrarian sources of industrial accumulation have been resolved, albeit with all the customary – and intensifying – contradictions of combined and uneven development that characterizes contemporary imperialism. This is not inconsistent with, and indeed helps explain, novel forms of the expanded reproduction of capital in agriculture, as defined earlier, in the current moment of globalization and its 'massive assault on the remaining peasant formations of the world' (Friedmann 2006: 462).[7]

The final sections of this chapter consider whether, in this context, there might be other, new agrarian questions.

Agrarian questions of labour?

The reverse side of the thesis that globalization today represents a new phase of the international centralization and concentration, as well as mobility and financialization, of capital, is that it also generates an intensification of the fragmentation of classes of labour. I prefer the term 'classes of labour' to the inherited vocabulary of proletarianization and proletariat, semiproletarianization and semiproletariat, as it is less encumbered with problematic assumptions and associations in both political economy, such as functionalist readings of Marx's concept of the reserve army of labour, and political theory and ideology, such as constructions of an idealized, Hegelian collective class subject.

Classes of labour comprise 'the growing numbers ... who now depend – directly and indirectly – on the sale of their labour power for their own daily reproduction' (Panitch and Leys 2000: ix). The term fragmentation signals the effects of how classes of labour in global capitalism, and especially in the South, pursue their reproduction, through insecure and oppressive – and in many places increasingly scarce – wage employment, often combined with a range of likewise precarious small-scale farming and insecure informal-sector ('survival') activity, subject to its own forms of differentiation and oppression along intersecting lines of class, gender, generation, caste and ethnicity (Harriss-White and Gooptu 2000; Harriss-White 2003). Additionally, many pursue their means of reproduction across different sites of the social division of labour: urban and rural, agricultural and non-agricultural, wage employment and self-employment – 'footloose labour' indeed (Breman 1996). This is one aspect of the fifth thesis sketched above, and its links with the third and fourth theses.

The most vivid concrete exploration I have come across of the dynamics and effects of the fragmentation of classes of labour is in an urban, rather than rural, context: Mike Davis's *Planet of Slums* (2006, especially Ch 8). There is a strong affinity between what I designate classes of labour and their intensified fragmentation, and Davis's notion of an 'informal working class'; moreover, Davis's emphasis on the dramatic increase of 'economic informality' – with its intimate association with the fragmentation of labour – in Latin American cities since 1980 also applies to the countrysides of the South with all their diversity.[8]

It is thus the crisis of labour as a crisis of reproduction – hardly unique to capitalism today, but undoubtedly intensified by its globalizing tendencies – that compels attention; a point that is also stressed, albeit differently, by Araghi (Chapter 5). In the schema of the classic agrarian question, the development of the productive forces in agriculture and its manifestation in the rising productivity of farm labour has the function, among others, of releasing/expelling labour required by the growth of industry and associated urban branches of activity. However, what if capitalism, including industrialization – 'to the extent that it is proceeding' (Byres 2003: 200) – in the South today is incapable of generating sufficient, and sufficiently secure, employment to provide a living wage to the great majority? This is not to deny *a priori* that significant industrialization in some zones of the South in today's world of globalizing capitalism may be possible, but rather to approach its possibilities with appropriate caution. First, the times and places – the when and where, and also how – of past histories of comprehensive capitalist industrialization themselves have to be problematized and explored, in terms of both their internal and international conditions, class dynamics and mechanisms of accumulation. Second, it cannot be doubted that poorer countries today confront more formidable barriers to comprehensive industrialization – and *a fortiori* to the generation of comparable levels of industrial employment – than did the advanced industrial countries in the past.[9] Third: 'the underlying contradiction of a world capitalist system that promotes the formation of a world proletariat but cannot accommodate a generalized living wage (that is, the most basic of reproduction costs), far from being solved, has become more acute than ever' (Arrighi and Moore 2001: 75).

One basis, then, from which to consider an agrarian question of labour is provided by popular struggles over land today that are driven by experiences of the fragmentation of labour. These include losses of relatively stable wage

employment in manufacturing and mining, as well as agriculture, by contestations of class inequality, and by collective demands and actions for
better conditions of living – 'survival', stability of livelihoods and economic
security – of which the most dramatic instances are land invasions and
occupations. Is it an index of the end of the agrarian question of capital and
the generation of an agrarian question – or questions – of labour in the
current moment of globalization that redistributive land reform is now (as
discussed by Akram-Lodhi *et al.* in Chapter 9) back on the agenda after a
hiatus since the 1970s; that is, on the neoliberal agenda as well as that of
radical politics?[10]

While of wider relevance, this revival of interest on the left in struggles
over land incorporates a strong Latin American lineage, all the more strikingly so given the massive rates of continuing rural–urban migration over the
past three decades in Latin America, as well as the continent's generally
much more developed capitalist agriculture and industry relative to South
Asia and Sub-Saharan Africa. In these conditions, writers such as Petras
(1997), Edelman (2002) and Veltmeyer (2005) emphasize that the social
bases of contemporary land struggles in Latin America are significantly different from those of the classic peasant movements of the past, while
others – notably Moyo and Yeros (2005) – argue that land struggles more
generally today are generated by the semiproletarian condition, defined by
Yeros (2002: 9) as that of 'a workforce in motion, within rural areas, across
the rural–urban divide, and beyond international boundaries'.

If a case can be made for agrarian questions of labour today, understanding and assessing them should be disciplined by some important qualifications, in contrast to enthusiastic, and at times triumphalist, celebrations
of popular struggles over land. First, such struggles do not have the same
structural or world-historical significance as the agrarian question of capital,
once central to conceptions of the transition to capitalism, and are marked
by the contradictions that permeate the fragmentation of classes of labour
and their crises of reproduction, to which I will come back. Second, I am
unconvinced by the sweeping nature of the semiproletarianization thesis,
which tends to rest on a view of global capitalism based in dependency
theory (as in Moyo and Yeros 2005), and the political struggles of classes of
labour evidently range across far wider terrains than issues of land, important as those are in particular places to particular groups of the labouring
poor. In this sense, I am not sympathetic to the argument of Akram-Lodhi
et al. in Chapter 9. Indeed, contemporary struggles over land applauded by
advocates of the semiproletarianization approach are typically far more
complex and contradictory, and by extension more diverse, than they allow.
In part, this reflects the always difficult – and unpredictable – process of
'translating social facts into political ones', especially when 'the many ways
in which power fragment(s) the circumstances and experiences of the
oppressed' (Mamdani 1996: 219, 272) are so pervasive an aspect of the
'social facts'. This is compounded by the structural fragmentation of labour

in the conditions of its pursuit of means of reproduction, proposed here as a central feature of globalization. On one hand, there is a pervasive dynamic of class relations at work; on the other hand, those class relations are not manifested in, or as, self-evident or unambiguous class categories and subjects/agents in the manner of purist class analysis. Popular struggles over land are more likely to embody uneasy and erratic, contradictory and shifting alliances of different class elements and tendencies than to express the interests of some notionally unambiguous and unitary class subject, be it proletarian or peasant, semiproletarian or worker-peasant.[11]

Third, the vast range of combinations of wage labour with petty commodity production in the pursuit of means of reproduction by the labouring poor discloses another, distinctive, source of fragmentation among classes of labour. This is that petty commodity production in farming and other informal-sector activities always contain the possibility of social class differentiation. As proposed earlier, petty commodity production within capitalism is constituted as a contradictory combination of the 'class places' of capital and labour, both of which have their own circuits and disciplines of reproduction. Moreover, petty commodity production, especially when founded on access to means of production – notably farm land in this context – typically contains an aspiration to accumulation, even when this is likely to be realized by only a small minority of petty producers.[12] Petty production embroils the labouring poor in a world of 'relentless micro-capitalism', in Davis's formulation. He further remarks that 'petty exploitation (endlessly franchised) is its essence, and there is growing inequality *within* the informal sector', including how it permeates 'the sphere of the household' (Davis 2006: 181). While his observations concern the urban informal economy, they describe dynamics that typically apply to petty commodity production in farming and other activities in the countryside. Champions of the semiproletarianization thesis seem to aspire to liberate worker-peasants from the subsumption by capital – that is, workers employed by others – and to restore them to full peasantness. In Marx's terms, this means enabling them to work for themselves by dint of their possession of capital. It also subjects them to the vagaries of 'relentless micro-capitalism' which generate tendencies to individualization: the pursuit of individual solutions to the contradictions of social existence, through securing and setting in motion private property in means of production. This also includes the more or less overt forms of exploitation that permeate patriarchal farming households and relations between households, as well as aspirations to accumulation, noted earlier.

Back to the future? The 'new agrarian question' and the 'peasant way'

If agrarian questions of labour lack the systemic or world-historical scope and significance that the agrarian question of capital once occupied in the problematic of transitions to capitalism, this is not the case for 'the new agrarian question', as Philip McMichael (Chapter 12) formulates it. The new agrarian question, in an earlier version of this account, opposes 'the cor-poratization of agriculture ... (which) has been globally synchronized to the detriment of farming populations everywhere' by 'revalorizing rural cultural-ecology as a global good' (McMichael 2006a: 473, 472). The agents of the latter comprise a global agrarian resistance, an agrarian counter-movement, that strives to preserve or reclaim 'the peasant way' – and indeed La Via Campesina appears as its emblematic manifestation, and a principal source, of McMichael's vision of an alternative agrarian future (McMichael 2006a: 474, 480, *passim*). The new agrarian question is world-historical in that, first, it transcends the capital–labour relation; and, second, the social forces of global agrarian resistance that it mobilizes have the capacity, at least poten-tially, to generate that transformation, according to McMichael and others.

Marx, of course, would recognize transcending the capital–labour relation as the sense of a world-historical movement beyond capitalism, even if he would not have accepted that this could be driven by the contradiction between capital and peasants, family farmers or 'people of the land' mobi-lized in global agrarian resistance. Notions of 'the peasant way' resonate lineages of agrarian populism that have always appeared and reappeared in the long histories of modern capitalism. When counterposed to what is undoubtedly, in key respects, a new phase in the globalization of agriculture, advocates of the peasant way argue that it does not represent nostalgia – worlds we have lost – but that contemporary peasant movements incorporate and express specific, novel and strategic conceptions of, and aspirations to, modernity, and visions of modernity alternative to that inscribed in the neoliberal common sense of the current epoch. This is a plausible thesis, always worth investigating in particular circumstances, but the principal weakness of the new agrarian question *qua* the peasant way, as articulated to date, is its lack of an adequate political economy.

First, it tends to present farming populations everywhere as a single social category that serves, or is necessary to, both the analytical and political purposes of resistance to globalization and neoliberalism.[13] Indeed, farmers thus constitute not only a single category but a singular one: they are deemed to experience, to challenge, and to seek to transcend the social and ecological contradictions of a globalizing capitalism in a uniquely combined fashion. While differences within and between farming populations – differ-ences of North and South, of market conditions, of gender relations, and sometimes even class relations – are acknowledged, this tends to be gestural in the absence of any deeper theorization and more systematic empirical investigation of the conditions in which farming and agriculture are con-stituted by specific forms and dynamics of the capital–labour relation, not least how they express, generate, reproduce and shape class differentiation. For the new agrarian question, whether by explicit intent or by implicit default, class and other social differentiation is subordinate to what all family farmers and their struggles have in common: exploitation by capital (which they share with labour?), and a special relation with and respect for nature (which distinguishes them from non-agrarian classes of labour, or simply from urbanites?). This is evident in many statements by advocates of this vision that represent contemporary variations on long-established themes of agrarianism. For example, Annette Desmarais refers to 'people of the land' as a unitary global social bloc, also known as 'peasants', apparently, as when she applauds 'over 5,000 farmers including European, Canadian, American, Japanese, Indian and Latin American peasants' marching on a GATT meeting in Geneva in 1993 (Desmarais 2002: 93).

Second, there is little specification of the alternative systems of production that the peasant way may generate as the basis of a future postcapitalist, ecologically friendly social order. Rural community, and an associated localism, are championed: antithesis to the thesis of the global corporatization of agribusiness and the drive to individualization of neoliberal ideology; but where is any plausible formulation of the social and material coordinates of a synthesis, or what used to be called the negation of the negation?[14] Further, in this respect, advocacy of the peasant way largely ignores issues of feeding the world's population, which has grown so greatly almost everywhere in the modern epoch, in significant part because of the revolutions in agricultural productivity achieved by the development of capitalism. In response to provocations by the present author on this matter of the demographic – or, better, population/productivity – challenge, McMichael (2006b: 415) observes that 'longer-term questions of raising agricultural productivity to provision cities are yet to be resolved'. Why is this longer-term, and how might it be resolved?[15] Similarly, Friedmann's 'brief formulation of the population question of today' concludes that 'we may be heading for … demographic collapse. What this means for the "global" phase of capitalism, capitalism *tout court*, and even human survival is what we need to think about now' (Friedmann 2006: 464). This, once more, is to restate a problem, however fundamental, rather than point to its resolution.[16]

Third, and similarly to my criticisms of triumphalist versions of an agrarian question of labour discussed above, celebrations of global agrarian resistance and the transformational aspirations attached to it lack any plausible formulation and analysis of how it could work as a political project (Scott 2005; Bernstein 2005 on Martinez-Alier's 'environmentalism of the poor'). Interestingly, the *Movimento dos Trabalhadores Rurais Sem Terra* (Landless Rural Worker's Movement, or MST) in Brazil is especially emblematic for both those who advocate land struggles as the cutting edge of semiproletarian politics and agrarian questions of labour, and those who aspire to transcend the capital–labour relation through revalorizing rural cultural ecology as a global good. Both are frequently given to long quotes from MST documents in ways that elide that necessary distinction or distance between sympathy with the programmatic statements of the organization and its leadership, and the demands of analysis. As Wendy Wolford

(2003) points out in one of her fine articles on the MST, many discussions of the MST refer to the imagined community articulated in such statements as accurate representations of the experiences, beliefs and practices of its socially heterogeneous membership, in effect attributing to the movement a unity of vision and purpose that is unwarranted and unhelpful. Too many accept the official ideology of the MST, as of La Via Campesina, at face value from political sympathy, rather than combining sympathy with the demands of critical inquiry necessary to adequate investigation, analysis and assessment.[17] In effect, the contemporary movements held to exemplify global agrarian resistance are no less permeated by the class and other social complexities and contradictions signalled earlier in relation to struggles that exemplify agrarian questions of labour.

Conclusions

For all their shortcomings and difficulties, as briefly outlined, formulations of both agrarian questions of labour and a 'new agrarian question', which combats and seeks to transcend globalizing tendencies of the organization of agriculture, raise fundamental issues about what is changing in the world of contemporary capitalism: the former with respect to the fragmentation of classes of labour, the latter with respect to the modes of operation and powers of corporate agribusiness and their social and ecological effects. By the same token, both challenge the agrarian question inherited from classic Marxism, and especially its capacity to address a world so different from that which generated its original concerns with paths of transition from pre-capitalist agrarian social formations to capitalist agriculture and industry, as well as to state socialism in the unique adaptation and impact of the classic agrarian question registered by the Soviet experience.

The classic agrarian question of Marxism at its most doctrinaire, and in its often-attenuated current applications, can reduce to a strongly deductive model of the virtues of economies of scale in farming. Reconsideration by historical materialism of its historic, and uncritical, attachment to the benefits of large-scale farming is long overdue for various reasons, including the following. First, it is salutary to recover a properly materialist, rather than technicist, conception of scale in agriculture as an effect of specific and variant forms of social relations. Second, the scale and distribution – and uses – of capitalist landed property in particular circumstances are often shaped by speculative rather than productive investment. Third, the productive superiority of larger-scale farming is often contingent on conditions of profitability underwritten by direct and hidden subsidy and forms of economic rent, and indeed ecological rents. Fourth, materialist political economy needs to take much more seriously the environmental consequences and full social costs of the technologies that give modern capitalist farming the astonishing levels of productivity it often achieves. Finally, in considering these issues, it should be evident that the internalist problematic, within which the transition to capitalism was framed in classic Marxism, is no longer adequate, if indeed it ever was, beyond the much-debated instances of 'early European capitalism' – above all England, and later France and Prussia/Germany (Brenner 1976; Aston and Philpin 1985; Bernstein 1996; Byres, Chapter 3).

These types of issue illustrate the challenges of, and demands on, an agrarian political economy less confined by its historic sources and pre-occupations, and more committed to problematizing and investigating what is changing in today's globalizing capitalism. They are not presented as elements of a general argument against large-scale farming, as I am sceptical about any models of virtuous farm scale constructed on deductive or *a priori* grounds. Nor is the political economy in this chapter deployed in any anti-peasant spirit nor, more to the point, in any prescriptive stance on petty commodity production. Nor do any of my observations in the previous two sections suggest withdrawing political sympathy and support for progressive struggles because they fail to satisfy the demands of an idealized, class purist or other model of political action. Rather, I have suggested that part of the problem with the new agrarian questions sketched is how they posit a unitary and idealized, and ostensibly world-historical, subject: 'semiproletarian' in one case, 'farmers'/'peasants'/'people of the land' in the other. The point is, first to recognize, and second to be able to analyse, the contradictory sources and impulses – and typically multiclass character – of contemporary struggles over land and ways of farming that can inform a realistic and politically responsible assessment of them.

To paraphrase Hilton for the last time: the tasks of today 'have nothing in common with the tasks of the past, except in the recognition that conflict is part of existence and that nothing is gained without struggle'. In relation to agrarian change in contemporary capitalism, some of the original theory of the agrarian question retains a unique value if it can be adapted and applied to the tasks of today: to identify and analyse the changing realities of a globalizing capitalist agriculture, including how its dense and complex determinations bear on the conditions and prospects of peasant/petty commodity production in farming. It is better equipped to do so if it is able to recognize new forms of popular struggle in agrarian social movements without the distorting lens of Leninist vanguardism, and to unburden itself of the legacy of states that once claimed to promote some version of socialist transformation of agriculture and the countryside.

Notes

1 This chapter draws on a paper presented to the conference on 'Land, Poverty, Social Justice and Development' at the Institute of Social Studies, The Hague, the Netherlands, 12–14 January 2006, and also on Bernstein (2006).

2 The extent of my debt to the work of T.J. Byres, if not always in agreement with it, should be evident in this section.

3 The title of Kautsky's book, *Die Agrarfrage*, is the source of the term 'agrarian question'. The problem of detaching any particular question from the totalities of

social reality and historical change in which it is constituted is remarked on by Araghi (Chapter 5), as well as by Murmis (2006), who offers other critical comments on Bernstein (2006). My response to both is that I try to locate the agrarian question in its broadest world-historical dimensions. Inevitably, this makes for a highly schematic exposition with certain intellectual costs. Whether the utility of this for certain purposes outweighs such costs is for others to judge.

4 Although Lenin's study was as much about industrialization as about agrarian change, it is the third aspect of an internalist problematic that is most apposite here.

5 As explored in the seminal paper by Friedmann and McMichael (1989) and their other individually authored work on international divisions of labour in agriculture and 'food regimes' from the nineteenth century.

6 From somewhat different perspectives in political economy, Post (1995) and Friedmann and McMichael (1989) provide accounts of the extraordinary dynamism of US agriculture in the earlier and later nineteenth century, respectively, that are exemplary in their theoretical depth and precision.

7 This is not reiterated in any futile attempt to command agreement, but to clarify the nature of disagreement so as to pursue and debate it fruitfully. For example, Goodman and Watts (1997), in their flamboyant essay, miss the point of this line of argument about the end of the agrarian question of capital: a thesis about the periodization of capitalism on a world scale that does not propose the end of history in capital's activities in agriculture and the many contradictions they generate and confront, as Goodman and Watts seem to think.

8 Indeed, Davis acknowledges his debt to the ethnography of Jan Breman, which explores the circuits of 'footloose labour' within and between countryside and town in India to such illuminating effect. Davis cites Breman's (2003) *The Labouring Poor in India* among his prolific publications.

9 Summarized by Kitching (2001: 152) in terms of the constraints of industrial technology and its employment effects, of population growth, and of the international terms of trade for agricultural exports, in the early twenty-first century compared with the late nineteenth century.

10 For current neoliberal/neopopulist land redistribution policies and their critique, see Borras (2003) and Byres (2004b), among others.

11 As I have tried to argue in the case of Zimbabwe (Bernstein 2004: 210–220).

12 The Bolshevik notion that all peasants *qua* petty commodity producers, while differentiated by class relations, are 'ideological *kulaks*' has a rational kernel, if hardly one that justified the extraordinary force applied to the dispossession of the Russian peasantry in the name of building socialism.

13 I distinguish globalization in the sense of both new forms of the restructuring of capital and neoliberalism as an ideological and political project. Conflating the two, which is unfortunately all too common, precludes the possibility that the former can proceed in the future without the latter, despite their close connection in the current conjuncture.

14 Some lines of thought in considering this question are sketched by McMichael (2006b: 186–187), as usual with reference to the manifestos of La Via Campesina and its central notion of 'food sovereignty'.

15 Elsewhere – as an instance of 'global agrarian resistance' – McMichael (2006c: 186) asserts that urban gardens 'provision 35 million people in the US alone' without specifying what 'provision' means here.

16 From their earlier work (Friedmann and McMichael 1989), Friedmann and McMichael have sought to incorporate an ecological dimension as central to the history of international food regimes. The use of titles such as 'Feeding the empire … ' (Friedmann 2004) and 'Feeding the world … ' (McMichael 2006b) makes the absence of any demographic consideration the more surprising, and I have pointed out (Bernstein 2006: 458) that 'issues of population … are (so far) completely

absent from the historical political economy of international food regimes' they have developed. Interestingly, the population question is central to the ecological economics of Martinez-Alier (2002), who seeks to wrest it from its Malthusian heritage, while insisting that global environmental sustainability requires fewer people (and, possibly, zero economic growth). At the same time, he is among the most evidently romantic, and unhistorical, advocates of 'the peasant way' (see Bernstein 2005).

17 As does Marc Edelman (2002) in his outstanding monograph on Costa Rica, including the valuable methodological reflections of his final chapter on 'Peasant movements of the late twentieth century'.

References

Arrighi, G. and J.W. Moore (2001) 'Capitalist development in world historical perspective', in R. Albritton, M. Itoh, R. Westra and A. Zuege (eds), *Phases of Capitalist Development: Booms, Crises and Globalizations*, London: Palgrave.

Aston, T.H. and C.H.E. Philpin (eds) (1985) *The Brenner Debate: Agrarian Class Structure and Economic Development in Pre-industrial Europe*, Cambridge: Cambridge University Press.

Bernstein, H. (1996) 'Agrarian questions then and now', in H. Bernstein and T. Brass (eds), *Agrarian Questions: Essays in Appreciation of T.J. Byres*, London: Frank Cass.

—— (2000) '"The peasantry" in global capitalism: who, where and why?', in L. Panitch and C. Leys (eds), *The Socialist Register 2001*, London: Merlin Press.

—— (2004) '"Changing before our very eyes": agrarian questions and the politics of land in capitalism today', in T.J. Byres (ed.), *Redistributive Land Reform Today*, special issue of *Journal of Agrarian Change*, 4 (1/2): 190–225.

—— (2005) Review of J. Martinez-Alier, *The Environmentalism of the Poor*, *Journal of Agrarian Change*, 5 (3): 429–436.

—— (2006) 'Is there an agrarian question in the 21st century?', *Canadian Journal of Development Studies*, 27 (4): 449–460.

Borras, S.M., Jr (2003) 'Questioning market-led agrarian reform: experiences from Brazil, Colombia and South Africa', *Journal of Agrarian Change*, 3 (3): 367–394.

Breman, J. (1996) *Footloose Labour: Working in India's Informal Economy*, Cambridge: Cambridge University Press.

Breman, J. (2003) *The Labouring Poor in India: Patterns of Exploitation, Subordination, and Exclusion*, New Delhi: Oxford University Press.

Brenner, R. (1976) 'Agrarian class structure and economic development in pre-industrial Europe', *Past and Present*, 70: 30–74.

Byres, T.J. (1991) 'The agrarian question and differing forms of capitalist transition: an essay with reference to Asia', in J. Breman and S. Mundle (eds), *Rural Transformation in Asia*, Delhi: Oxford University Press.

—— (1996) *Capitalism From Above and Capitalism From Below: An Essay in Comparative Political Economy*, London: Macmillan.

—— (2003) 'Structural change, the agrarian question, and the possible impact of globalisation', in C.P. Chandrasekhar and J. Ghosh (eds), *And Yet the Centre Holds: Essays on Globalisation, Structural Change and Income Distribution*, Delhi: Tulika Books.

—— (2004a) 'Neo-classical neo-populism 25 years on: *déjà vu* and *déjà passé*. Towards a critique', in T.J. Byres (ed.), *Redistributive Land Reform Today*, special issue of *Journal of Agrarian Change*, 4 (1/2): 17–44.

—— (ed.) (2004b) *Redistributive Land Reform Today*, special issue of *Journal of Agrarian Change*, 4 (1/2).

Cronon, W. (1991) *Nature's Metropolis: Chicago and the Great West*, New York: W. W. Norton.

Davis, M. (2006) *Planet of Slums*, London: Verso.

Desmarais, A.-A. (2002) 'The Vía Campesina: consolidating an international peasant and farm movement', *Journal of Peasant Studies*, 29 (2): 91–124.

Edelman, M. (2002) *Peasants Against Globalization: Rural Social Movements in Costa Rica*, Stanford, CT, USA: Stanford University Press.

Engels, F. (1970) *The Peasant Question in France and Germany*, in K. Marx and F. Engels, *Selected Works, Vol. 2*, Moscow: Progress Publishers (first published in 1894).

Friedmann, H. (1993) 'The political economy of food: a global crisis', *New Left Review*, 197: 29–57.

—— (2004) 'Feeding the empire: the pathologies of globalized agriculture', in L. Panitch and C. Leys (eds), *The Socialist Register 2005*, London: Merlin Press.

—— (2006) 'Focusing on agriculture: a comment of Henry Bernstein's "Is there an agrarian question in the 21st century?"', *Canadian Journal of Development Studies*, 27 (4): 461–465.

Friedmann, H. and P. McMichael (1989) 'Agriculture and the state system: the rise and decline of national agricultures, 1870 to the present', *Sociologica Ruralis*, 29 (2): 93–117.

Goodman, D. and M.J. Watts (1997) 'Agrarian questions: global appetite, local metabolism: nature, culture, and industry in *fin-de-siècle* agro-food systems', in D. Goodman and M.J. Watts (eds), *Globalising Food: Agrarian Questions and Global Restructuring*, London: Routledge.

Harriss-White, B. (2003) *India Working: Essays on Society and Economy*, Cambridge: Cambridge University Press.

Harriss-White, B. and N. Gooptu (2000) 'Mapping India's world of unorganized labour', in L. Panitch and C. Leys (eds) *The Socialist Register 2001*, London: Merlin Press.

Hilton, R. (1973) *Bond Men Made Free: Medieval Peasant Movements and the English Rising of 1381*, London: Temple Smith.

Kautsky, K. (1988) *The Agrarian Question*, translated by P. Burgess, London: Zwan (first published in 1899).

Kitching, G. (2001) *Seeking Social Justice through Globalization*, University Park, PA, USA: Pennsylvania State University Press.

Lenin, V.I. (1964) *The Development of Capitalism in Russia, Collected Works, Vol. 3*, Moscow: Progress Publishers (first published in 1899).

Mamdani, M. (1996) *Citizen and Subject: Contemporary Africa and the Legacy of Late Colonialism*, Cape Town: David Philip.

Martinez-Alier, J. (2002) *The Environmentalism of the Poor*, Cheltenham: Edward Elgar.

McMichael, P. (2006a) 'Reframing development: global peasant movements and the new agrarian question', *Canadian Journal of Development Studies*, 27 (4): 471–483.

—— (2006b) 'Feeding the world: agriculture, development and ecology', in L. Panitch and C. Leys (eds), *The Socialist Register 2007*, London: Merlin Press.

—— (2006c) 'Peasant prospects in the neoliberal age', *New Political Economy*, 11 (3): 407–418.

Moyo, S. and P. Yeros, (2005) 'The resurgence of rural movements under neoliberalism', in S. Moyo and P. Yeros (eds), *Reclaiming the Land: The Resurgence of Rural Movements in Africa, Asia and Latin America*, London: Zed Books.

Murmis, M. (2006) '"Is there an agrarian question in the 21st century?": a commentary', *Canadian Journal of Development Studies*, 27 (4): 467–70.

Panitch, L. and C. Leys (eds) (2000) 'Preface', in *The Socialist Register 2001*, London: Merlin Press.

Petras, J. (1997) 'Latin America: the resurgence of the left', *New Left Review*, 223: 27–47.

Post, C. (1995) 'The agrarian origins of US capitalism: the transformation of the northern countryside before the Civil War', *Journal of Peasant Studies*, 22 (3): 380–445.

Preobrazhensky, E. (1965) *The New Economics*, translated by B. Pearce, Oxford: Clarendon Press (first published in 1926).

Razavi, S. (ed.) (2003) *Agrarian Change, Gender and Land Rights*, special issue of *Journal of Agrarian Change*, 3 (1/2).

Scott, J. (2005) 'Afterword to "Moral economies, state spaces and categorical violence"', *American Anthropologist*, 107 (3): 395–402.

Veltmeyer, H. (2005) 'The dynamics of land occupation in Latin America', in S. Moyo and P. Yeros (eds), *Reclaiming the Land: The Resurgence of Rural Movements in Africa, Asia and Latin America*, London: Zed Books.

Wolf, E. (1969) *Peasant Wars of the Twentieth Century*, New York: Harper and Row.

Wolford, W. (2003) 'Producing community: the MST and land reform settlements in Brazil', *Journal of Agrarian Change*, 3 (4): 500–520.

Yeros, P. (2002) 'Zimbabwe and the dilemmas of the left', *Historical Materialism*, 10 (2): 3–15.

11 The Southern question

Agrarian questions of labour and capital

Michael J. Watts

We have said that Southern Italy (the Southern question) is an area of extreme social disintegration. This formula can apply to the intellectuals as well as the peasants.

(Gramsci 1957: 47, first published 1926)

Bernstein and the Bank

Perhaps a place to begin is Henry Bernstein's provocative suggestion in Chapter 10 that the classical Marxist account of the agrarian question is, in fact, the 'agrarian question of capital'; that is, the agrarian question concerns the transformation of precapitalist agrarian social formations and, more specifically, how capital is taking hold of production, as Karl Kautsky (1988, first published 1899) put it.[1] By the 1970s, suggests Bernstein, partially as a product of the land reforms undertaken in response to what Eric Wolf (1969) termed 'peasant wars', the key index of the agrarian question of capital – namely, predatory landed property – had largely vanished. As a consequence, on a global scale, the agrarian question of capital had, Bernstein argues, ended; a process whose completion, on a world scale, had been reached in conjunction with 'the implosion of state-led development', the productivity revolution in capitalist agriculture, and the globalization of agribusiness (Bernstein 2006: 452). Once this is recognized, says Bernstein, the key question turns to the fate of the peasant, or what he properly calls the 'rural labouring classes'.

However, this question, which he calls 'the agrarian question of labour', is, it turns out, not about peasants at all; nor is it about the classic agrarian question of capital. For Bernstein, the very invocation of peasants suggests a deep, and in many ways apparently illogical, continuity with the past; a past that is, for many, characterized by persistence, survival and resistance.[2] Rather, according to Bernstein, it is necessary to recognize that peasants are simply one expression of generalized commodity production, an expression that is, in this instance, internalized within peasant household production. Further, agrarian capitalism is no longer about farming, narrowly construed. Agrarian capitalism is instead about global corporate agribusiness and its upstream and downstream domination of the circuits of appropriation and substitution (Goodman *et al.* 1987) which are, in complex and uneven ways, linked to agrarian classes and enterprises; global commodity chains might be the avatar of agrarian capitalism. The fate of the peasant, in Bernstein's view, is thus really about the fragmentation of labour under generalized commodity production.

Bernstein says that this question has been compellingly posed, in a different setting, by Mike Davis (2006), in his analysis of the slum world.[3] The fragmentation of rural labour turns in part on land, although Bernstein is deeply skeptical about the land politics that derive from what he calls 'the semi-proletarianization thesis' and, more generally, from the panoply of new land reform movements that originate from below. Much more importantly, it profoundly turns on the ways in which 'relentless micro-capitalism' is pulverizing all forms of household production through individuation, interhousehold competition and individual property rights. It is primitive accumulation all over again, but this time the global enclosure movement – accumulation by dispossession, as Farshad Araghi terms it in Chapter 5, or as David Harvey (2003) might say – is armed with massive corporate power, a rural sector beaten into submission by neoliberalism and structural adjustment, and supplicant developing world states no longer concerned with national markets. This is a sort of synoptic aerial view of the heavy armour of capital at work.

The first thing that needs to be said is that this sort of analysis would come as no surprise to the World Bank. The new World Bank (2007) *World Development Report 2008: Agriculture for Development* – the first on agrarian issues in 25 years – starts from an almost identical set of presuppositions, although it offers quite different theoretical and prescriptive analyses. First, like Bernstein, there is an acknowledgement of the rural 'slum world', using this term metaphorically: 75 per cent of the poor in the developing world live in rural areas, and agriculture is a source of livelihood for 86 per cent of rural people. Thus 2.1 billion live on less than $2 a day. Unlike Africa, in which self-employment dominates, in Asia and Latin America at least 50 per cent of the rural labour force is engaged in the agricultural and rural non-farm labour market. Agriculture is thus, in the perspective of the Bank, vastly underused for development and poverty alleviation. The result is a deep reservoir of rural poor; temporary and casualized rural workforces and land-poor peasants trapped by what de Janvry *et al.* (1989) called 'the double development squeeze'.

Second, the Bank stresses, like Bernstein, the historic ascendancy and dominance of what it dubs the 'corporate global agri-food business chain', whose massive capitalist concentration is dryly noted as 'a cause for concern'. Third, and not least, the depth of poverty within the rural sector is marked by a massive diversification of rural household livelihood strategies, in which wage labour is paramount; what the Bank calls 'pervasive heterogeneity', Bernstein, following Davis, would call micro-capitalism and the fragmentation of labour. Fourth, the Bank also seems to share Bernstein's Malthusian concerns with population growth. There is a shared concern regarding the need to feed the projected growth in the slum world of the South, along with the productivity and accumulation consequences of the biogenetic revolution.[4]

In addressing these issues, the Bank has, as expected, a predictable menu of concerns: raising smallholder productivity; improving access to markets, in part because staple foods are apparently still remarkably undertraded; making use of high-value agricultural commodity chains; making the most of biofuels, carbon trading and environmental services; and moving beyond agriculture in the provision of employment for rural workers. Bernstein, conversely, turns his eye to wider, and not simply land-based, 'social and political struggles of labour'. Nonetheless, the affinities between the two at the level of agrarian dynamics are striking.

I am broadly in sympathy with Bernstein's two moments of the agrarian question, that of capital and of labour, although I do not share his hostility to the use of the term 'peasant', as it does not, in my view, have to carry the freight of precapitalism or residual traits. Likewise, it is not clear to me that something called the 'semi-proletarianization thesis' uncritically applauds all aspirations to land or is simply 'functionalist'. The work of Bryceson *et al.* (2000), for example, looks carefully at the complexity of both the fragmentation of labour and of the politics of land, but suggests that these complex forms of livelihood can be stable or at least self-reproducing in ways that, as the World Bank acknowledges, can persist over long periods of time. In this light, it is not surprising that Bramall and Jones (2000) talk of Chinese peasants being alive and well into the next century.

All of that said, posing the question of the rural world that Mike Davis posed of the megacity in the South – highlighting the contradictions between urban economic recession, neoliberalism, ecological calamity and rapid demographic growth amidst limited infrastructural investment – is very generative for agriculture. Not least, it highlights the vast array of opinion on the contemporary agrarian question, for which this volume is evidence; hence my invocation of Gramsci's reference to the social disintegration of the intellectuals as much as the peasants. At one pole is the identification of alternatives and the rise of multiperspective, globally networked movements (McMichael 2006); at the other pole are those like Bernstein, who suggests that current land-based movements are not systemic, are not world-historical, and are not worthy of triumphalist thinking. It is also entirely unclear what a critical normative stance might be with regard to the sort of agriculture to which aspiration could be made – Bernstein simply says he has no belief in any models – at a moment of extraordinary productive and technical change within the global agro-food system.

It seems to me that the danger of talking about the end of the agrarian question of capital on a world scale is the same as that identified by Arendt (1951) in her discussion of primitive accumulation; namely, that it is repeated historically. This is not to say that predatory landed property might reappear, although this is clearly possible, as the experience in some parts of postsocialist Eastern Europe revealed in the 'refeudalization' of some agrarian settings. Rather, it is to say that capitalist landed property is itself not a static entity: there are always new frontiers and conditions it must confront. If there is an argument to be made about peasants and their historical baggage, this is surely also the case with the category of 'landed elites', as Bobrow-Strain's (2007) new book shows. It is one thing to say there is no precapitalist landed property of any weight, but quite another to understand the forms that capitalist landed property actually assumes.

How have the crashing waves of neoliberalism – accumulation by dispossession – transformed the ways in which capital is further taking hold of production and fragmenting or reconstituting labour? Let's recall that Davis's key points of departure were not only urban involution through ever-deeper forms of fragmentation, individuation and immiserization. He also has two other great insights, both with agrarian parallels. The first was the crisis of urban ecology. The second was ideological: that the politics of the slum world were not of Marx and the revolutionary lumpenproletariat, but of 'the Holy Ghost', as embodied in the spirit world of Islamism and the evangelical churches. Davis's points of departure flag for me much of the complexity that is passed over so quickly in the language of the end of the agrarian question of capital and, for that matter, the fragmentation of labour – what Bernstein recognizes as the more or less organized and articulated social and political struggle of labour. Thus, from the vantage point of what Paul Collier (2007) calls 'the bottom billion', the end of predatory landed property has not necessarily translated into strong commercial impulses in eastern Congo, large swathes of the Indonesian archipelago, or even parts of inland China. It seems to me that the end of the agrarian question of capital says very little about the dynamics of generalized commodity production or integration with upstream capital, when set within the context of civil war, extractive enclaves or geographical isolation. By the same token, given the complex forms of class and social differentiation across the pervasive heterogeneity of the rural sector, how can we understand the 'more or less organized politics' associated with the new frontiers of agrarian labour: the biofuels revolution; environmental services; new sorts of supply chains, with their attendant institutional (contract) and accumulation (quality) strategies (Daviron and Ponte 2005); the massive constraints imposed around access to water, compounded by global climate change; the next wave of genetically modified organisms and corporate integration (Walker 2004); the politics of consumption, so-called 'ethical sourcing' and the so-called 'fair trade' movement (Fridell 2006; Jaffee 2007). Mapping what Bernstein (2006: 459) calls 'class impulses' along these multiple fronts might shed some light on how the agrarian question of labour is currently constituted. This is obviously what Gramsci had in mind in his 'Southern question'. None of this is inconsistent with Bernstein's call for an

understanding of the complex, contradictory and multiclass struggles surrounding the agrarian question of labour – Gramsci was certainly struggling
with this too; it is simply that we have hardly begun.

The death of the peasantry?

Modernity's victims?

One place to begin examining the current constitution of the agrarian question of labour is with the great Brazilian photographer Sebastião Salgado
and his latest visual monument to the world's poor and excluded. *Migrations*
(Salgado 2000) can be read as a photographic communist manifesto for our
times, a searing indictment of globalization and the making of a world proletariat. Its central figure is the deracinated subject: the Vietnamese migrant;
the Rwandan refugee; the displaced Kurd. Salgado's images capture something of the phenomenology of the homeless; the impoverished millions
buffeted in the high seas of contemporary capitalism, propelled from one
place to another by the great, crashing waves of war, the free market and
civil strife. Mobility, which is so often seen as a source of freedom and
emancipation, is, in Salgado's eyes, a form of coercion and victimization,
both of which are marked by a worldwide exodus from the countryside.

In its attention to the lethal intersection of globalization and dispossession, Salgado's documentation of the contemporary global enclosure movement echoes the sentiments of another powerful book, Mike Davis's *Late
Victorian Holocausts* (2000). Davis is concerned with a prior moment of
global proletarianization and dispossession in the last quarter of the nineteenth century, which was marked by the confluence of worldwide drought
and a string of massive famines and subsistence crises. The El Niño droughts,
and more precisely the warm phase of the active ocean component of a vast
oscillation in air mass and ocean temperature across the Pacific Basin (El
Niño Southern Oscillation, ENSO), devastated China, Brazil, India and
parts of Africa. It proved to be one in a series of synchronous climatic per-
turbations between 1876 and 1902, which in turn set the environmental stage
for a serial trio of global subsistence crises between 1876 and 1879; 1889 and
1891; and 1896 and 1902. It is the burden of *Late Victorian Holocausts* to
show that the fate of tropical humanity – principally peasants – between
1870 and 1914 was harnessed not to natural disasters or to the spectre of
Malthusian grain shortage, but rather to the unnecessary deaths of millions
of peasants and landless workers. In Davis's hands, this fate must be located
at the ground zero of the late imperial order, namely a world economy
centred on London. Subsistence crises have social origins, he argues, best
grasped through a sort of causal triangulation encompassing: the depletion
or loss of ecological entitlements; a radical deepening of household poverty;
and state decapacitation. Each of these is the precipitate of a lethal suturing
of market utopianism to the neo-Darwinism of a new imperial order. The

famine holocausts were thus no accident of climatic history. Rather, they were overdetermined artefacts of the workshop of nineteenth century liberal capitalism, forged by profit, primitive accumulation and state extraction. In stitching together economic long waves, the ENSO and the new imperialism, Davis argues that famines and subsistence crises were forcing dispossession and impoverishment: one part colonial enclosure, one part incubator of a colonial proletariat.

Both Salgado and Davis provide compelling accounts of primitive accumulation in its colonial and postcolonial forms. Both the commodification of labour and the severing of proprietary rights to land, which constitutes the freeing of labour in the Marxian sense, serves to highlight the centrality of the peasantry in both moments of globalization. One way to read *Migrations* and *Late Victorian Holocausts*, then, is to see each as a memorial to the pain and suffering – the fire and blood, as Marx put it – associated with the agrarian question of labour. Moreover, both works recapitulate a much deeper history of posing the peasantry as 'modernity's victims' (Moore 1966) within an act of historical erasure: the disappearance of the peasant.

For Eric Hobsbawm, who also sees the peasantry as the victims of modernity, this twentieth century death sentence is signalled by rural exodus and the proliferation of vast developing world cities and, correlatively, the loss of access to land:

> The most dramatic and far-reaching social change of the second half of the twentieth century, and the one which cuts us off for ever from the world of the past, is the death of the peasantry ... The strange thing about this massive and silent exodus from the land ... is that it was only partly due to agricultural progress, at least in the former peasant areas.
>
> (Hobsbawm 1994: 292)

Postpeasants?

For Michael Kearney, this death is deeper, in that it is discursive and material:

> The category peasant has outlived the conditions that brought it into being. And what are those conditions? First ... are the changing realities of rural life, that are refracted through the lenses of social theory. And second social theory itself ... is also undergoing transformations characteristic to this particular historic moment.
>
> (Kearney 1996: 245)

On the one hand, rural life has been transformed by globalization, principally through transnational movement and the genesis of what Kearney refers to as networks and reticula. On the other hand, the end of developmentalism in the 1960s and 1970s, by which he means the failure of postcolonial modernization, and the termination of left- and right-wing Cold War modernization, decisively removed the historical conditions from which the peasant category was invented. As a response to the crisis of development and modernity, the 1980s and 1990s witnessed, in Kearney's account, a romantic, populist peasant revivalism, marked by calls for peasant persistence and smallholder development; that is to say, a reappearance of what Tom Brass (1997, 2000) memorably calls 'the agrarian myth'. For Kearney, however, the conditions of transnational globalization and the death of modernism are no longer congruent with the category of peasant, typified by essentialist notions of subsistence, autonomy and land ownership. In its place he substitutes a 'postpeasant', a condition of 'postdevelopmentalism', and an intellectual and academic shift from the 'external differentiations of types of peasants (which are but reified objects) to the internal differentiations of subjects ... [That is,] from unitary subjects to complex subjects' (Kearney 1996: 7).

Contemporary narratives on the death of the peasantry, or what John Berger calls an act of historical elimination, appear a century and more after the publication of the foundational text in peasant studies, Karl Kautsky's *Die Agrarfrage* (1988, first published 1899), which posed the same question, and which rather dramatically disconfirmed it. Drafted amidst European social democratic debates on the democratic question and the consequences of the extension of the parliamentary franchise – and at a moment of quite fundamental technological and financial innovation – Kautsky's orthodox Marxism precisely anticipated the displacement of European peasantries at the hands of large-scale capitalists, as capital took hold of production. In a striking description, with obvious echoes in the present, he put it this way:

> What (agriculture) is spared from overseas competition [it] is threatened by industrial development at home. The transformation of agricultural production into industrial production is still in its infancy. [But] bold prophets, namely those chemists gifted with an imagination, already are dreaming of the day when bread will be made from stones and when all the requirements of the human diet will be assembled in chemical factories ... But one thing is certain. Agricultural production has already been transformed into industrial production in a large number of fields ... This does not mean that the time has arrived when one can reasonably speak of the imminent demise of agriculture ... [But] economic life even in the open countryside, once trapped in such eternally rigid routines, is now caught up in the constant revolution which is the hallmark of the capitalist mode of production ... The revolutionizing of agriculture is setting in train a remorseless chase. Its participants are whipped on and until they collapse exhausted – aside from a small number of aggressive and thrusting types who manage to clamber over the bodies of the fallen and join the ranks of the chief whippers, the big capitalists.
>
> (Kautsky 1988: 297)

The originality of Kautsky resided in the fact that he discovered an alternative to the disappearance of the peasantry, which had been anticipated by classical Marxism as proletarianization and the growth of capitalist enterprises proceeded; contrarily, he uncovered the possibility of the consolidation of at least a segment of the middle peasantry, and indeed the stability of what Lenin called 'propertied proletarians'. At any rate, European peasants were not, in any simple sense, disappearing.

Kautsky's book is as salient for the contemporary moment of globalization as it was for the classic phase of imperialism at the end of the nineteenth century (Watts 2002). However, what is more relevant for my purposes is that his text offers a note of necessary caution for the sorts of apocalyptic and grandiose claims made by Hobsbawm and Kearney, and indeed for any account of the agrarian question of labour that simply identifies world-historical trends of enclosure and primitive accumulation. It is curious that Hobsbawm, for example, after pronouncing the death of the peasantry, ignores the extraordinary events of the early 1980s in China, when decollectivization produced over 100 million new peasant households (Oi 1999). He also ignores the 'revolutions' of 1989 and the epochal events thereafter, when the collapse of actually existing socialisms in Eastern Europe and the former Soviet Union also created, admittedly in an uneven and often chaotic fashion, millions of small-scale agrarian property owners, even as it created capitalist estates *pur et dur* (Verdery 1996; Kitching 2001). One can legitimately argue about the complexities of agrarian postsocialist transitions; but to claim that the death of socialism equals the death of the peasantry is unsustainable, and in statistical terms has perhaps added half a billion persons to the ranks of the global peasantry.

The same might be said of South Asia. The empirical evidence suggests that the Green Revolution may have done little to improve the lot of the landless and the 'footloose labour' (Breman 1996) of the Indian agrarian economy, but it has not heralded a mass dispossession. Quite the contrary; if Harriss-White's (1995) work is any indication, under conditions of mercantile dominance, productivity increases have been associated with a reinforcement and consolidation of poor and middle peasants and the continuance of forms of 'unfree labour' (Byres 1995). None of this is to suggest that the dispossession of the world's peasantry is somehow permanently on hold, or that the global forces of accumulation and market deepening are not reshaping peasant relations of production, community structure and cultural identifications. What, though, is being thrown up in the name of the new in these turbulent neoliberal settings?

Trajectories of class formation?

While Kearney believes that globalization has transformed rural conditions, very little evidence is provided regarding the new relations of production, forms of surplus appropriation and disposition, which have attended the supposedly postpeasant condition. Tellingly, this includes Mexico, his principal case. We are provided with no apparatus for understanding the forms of transformation in the local political economy and the patterns of class differentiation that are in train in Oaxaca or Chiapas. Conversely, a study by Geraldo Otero (1999) entitled, appropriately, *Farewell to the Peasantry?*, suggests the continuing centrality of the old peasant economic questions; what Bernstein (2006: 454) refers to as 'massive unevenness and variation'. Otero seeks both to transcend the Lenin–Chayanov debates, which have stimulated much controversy in Latin America agrarian circles since the 1970s, and to distinguish himself from the multiple variants of both proponents of the *campesinismo* approach, which is focused on struggles over and access to land, and proponents of the *proletarismo* approach, which accentuates the role of wages, in understanding Mexican agricultural transformation. His treatment turns equally on a different account of the forms and character of social differentiation in the countryside, and on an alternative model of political class formation. The general purpose, says Otero, is to question class reductionist assumptions in variants of both Marxism and populism through a comparative analysis of three regional case studies.

Common to Puebla, Sonora and Coahuila/Durango is the fact that capitalist agriculture was installed during the 1930s, and that such installation provided the original focus of agrarian struggles. Through careful historical analysis, contemporary survey data and field work conducted in the 1980s and 1990s, Otero shows three different trajectories of class formation from ostensibly similar points of origin. His comparative political economy approach emphasizes process rather than structure. This is done in order to accentuate how the economic location of rural producers does not determine political class formation which is, rather, mediated by the state, regional culture and the type and form of leadership. As he puts it, class formation cannot be deduced from class position alone, but is overdetermined by the content of demands and struggles, the character of class organizations, and the degree of autonomy of the movements.

Underlying this approach is an implicit political project: that there is a space for what he calls 'market-oriented but non-capitalist culture' (Otero 1999: 25). Market-oriented non-capitalist culture can, according to Otero, be given expression through two alternatives to proletarianization and the wage form: peasant entrepreneurship, which is essentially the deepening of petty commodity production; and postcapitalist production, which includes self-managed cooperatives and collective forms of organization. Nonetheless, in rural Mexico the heterogeneity of economic class positions are capable of generating a panoply of differing political outcomes depending on the state, culture and leadership. All of this, in other words, reinforces the claim by Bernstein (2006: 459) that we should be attentive to the multiple and prismatic forms of class impulses in the contemporary agrarian question.

Farewell to the Peasantry? represents a challenge to Kearney in particular, in two ways. First, Otero sees postrevolutionary Mexico as the product of a land redistribution harnessed to bourgeois development and state hegemony. However, the reforms to the Constitution in 1992, in tandem with neoliberal policies, represented a major overhaul of the original agrarian reform programme. He therefore provides an analysis of social differentiation between 1930 and 1990 and confirms the analysis of Alain de Janvry referred to previously: that the middle peasantry is indeed disappearing in the double crisis of capitalist agriculture and the peasant economy; that the majority of direct producers are relatively stable semiproletarians; and that uneven development has fostered marked regional and class heterogeneity.

Second, through the three case studies he explores the idea of depeasantization without full proletarianization in relation to the direction and content of their class conflicts and struggles. In the case of Laguna, agricultural workers struggled for typically proletarian demands but received land from the state, and the *ejidatarios* unleashed a programme of self-management and democratic production in the newly collectivized *ejidos*. However, the state and the agrarian bourgeoisie crushed these initiatives, which, in turn, produced political fragmentation and an impoverished semiproletariat. By way of contrast, in Atencingo the collective *ejidos* were dismantled and individual household production stimulated a process of internal social differentiation, from which emerged peasant entrepreneurs on the one side and a deeply impoverished semiproletariat dependent on migratory income on the other. Finally, in the Yaqui Valley, Otero sees the emergence of post-capitalist struggle in response to aggressive capitalist penetration in the region and *mestizo* in-migration. New demands involved not only land, but other means of production and the democratic self-management of the productive process. All three trajectories were notable because they contained differing forms of political discourse and contrasting alliances and solidarities with progressive and democratic forces in Mexico. The analysis of *Farewell to the Peasantry?* is thus, in some regards, an unfashionable sort of political economy in the light of Kearney's claims, but it is nonetheless a model of rigorous comparative analysis that adds precisely the complexity that Kearney invokes, using the classical tools of the agrarian question to explain why class agents that started out in similar positions followed differing paths and destinies.

Postdevelopmentalism?

Kearney claims that the category of peasant has evaporated. This claim reflects a larger concern within social theory toward discursive analysis and the conditions of possibility for particular sorts of representations and practices. Poststructural analysis of a Foucauldian sort has shed much light on, and can deepen, the study of the peasantry, as revealed by, for example, Mitchell's (2002) studies of the uses and abuses of the Egyptian peasantry and Moore's (2006) analysis of peasant identity politics in Zimbabwe (Li 2007). Kearney, however, wishes to place the peasantry on the landscape of

modernization, of development as a post-1945 invention, in which the category of peasant fulfilled a function of containment; that is to say, the ambiguity of the peasant as half-developed and half-underdeveloped was
apparently witnessed in ties to the land driven by the logic of subsistence, a
form of essentialism, argues Kearney, that is peculiar to both Leninism and
bourgeois forms of modernism.

Containment both made sense of peasant ambiguity – and hence stabi-
lized the category – and 'served to organize the political and military projects aimed at developing – read controlling and containing – rural
populations' (Kearney 1996: 62). With the advent of the crises of development and modernity, both are which are left unexplained, the category of
peasant is exploded even though 'peasant-like' attributes still inhere among
rural populations. Thus, rather than the unitary peasant, we now have new
forms of postpeasant politics, representations and identifications constituting
a complex subject. Where Kearney ends up is ironically on the same ground
as the agrarian question of labour posed by Bernstein: what, now, in the
postpeasant world, are the wider social and political struggles?

Is this demolition of the peasant, as form of representation and as political
agent, plausible? The figure of the peasant has a long and complex history in
the English language – as Raymond Williams (1983) has noted, dating back
to the fifteenth century – but the figure began to decline around the 1830s against
the backdrop of the consolidation of three centuries of enclosure. The term
has had a number of specialist deployments, as the work of Kautsky, Lenin
and the multiplicity of European populisms of the nineteenth and early
twentieth centuries reveal. Peasants figured centrally in the nation-building
of postcolonial states (Gupta 1998) and were interpolated in quite different
ways along the multiple axes of the Cold War; one thinks of the revolutionary peasant of Fanon and Mao, the penny-capitalist of Sol Tax, the risk-
averse peasant of the neo-Chayanovians, and so on. Nonetheless, all this is
rendered reductive by Kearney to containment at the hands of the West.

Equally questionable is Kearney's claim that the crisis of developmentalism in the 1960s and 1970s produced a populist, romantic reaction
asserting the virtues of the peasant. Populism is indeed a powerful narrative
running across the histories of peasantries, and is central to Brass's (1997,
2000) work and to the romantic politics of the land that Bernstein (2006)
identifies, but is it helpful to see, as Kearney does, Alexander Chayanov and
James C. Scott as romantic conservatives? Is it possible that the *Journal of
Peasant Studies* in the 1970s and 1980s can be grasped as being part of the
peasant studies boom of the 1960s, funded by the 'vast resources' of 'government and corporations', and 'fostered by Western political interests'?
(Kearney 1996: 137). There is, of course, an important originary moment in
the 1960s, when the confluence of Maoist and guerilla forms of political
practice, peasant revolutionary insurrection (most obviously in Vietnam),
and the academic appearance of foundational works in English by Franz
Fanon (1962), Alexander Chayanov (1966) and Eric Wolf (1969) unleashed

something of a peasant boom – which stood as a counterpoint to the backward peasant of 1950s modernization theory. Nonetheless, Kearney's mapping, and his narrow focus on anthropology and English language studies, seems questionable.

Kearney wades into even deeper water in his vision of the postpeasant emerging from postdevelopment; that is to say, from the ashes of development and modernity. Here he joins hands with a body of work operating under the sign of 'alternatives to development'. Postdevelopmentalism is a form of postmodernism/poststructuralism, although it traces its lineage to the work in the 1960s of Ivan Illich (1971), and earlier still to some of the populist and civic theory associated with Proudhon, the Owenite socialists and others. Associated with a number of public intellectuals and activists largely but not wholly from the South, it is a variegated community. The intellectual field that constitutes these radical critiques of development – one thinks of the work of Arturo Escobar, Gustavo Esteva and Wolfgang Sachs, with *The Post-Development Reader* (Rahnema and Bawtree 1997) as its compendium – is replete with the language of crisis, failure, apocalypse and renewal, and most especially of subaltern insurgencies that are purportedly the markers of new histories, social structures and political subjectivities (Nederveen Pieterse 1997). To invoke one important and visible cluster of these erstwhile antidevelopment Jacobins, latterly referred to by Fred Dallmayr (1996) as a 'Third World Frankfurt School', the Delhi Center for Developing Societies includes among its pantheon the likes of Ashis Nandy, Rajni Kothari and Shiv Visvanathan, all of whom, in their own way, represent a veritable heteroglossia of alternative voices from the South, encompassing a massive swath of intellectual and political territory, on which there is often precious little agreement.

There is a sort of unity to these postdevelopmental critiques – drawn variously from post-Marxism, ecofeminism, narrative analysis, poststructuralism, postcolonial theory and postmodernism – by emphasizing their confluences around development as a flawed, and in some quarters a catastrophically failed, modernist project. Much but by no means all of this critique draws sustenance from the idea of the third leg of modernity – the dark side of modernity and the Enlightenment, which produced the new human sciences and the disciplines – as well as from the Marxian leg of capitalist exploitation and the Weberian and Habermasian leg of the colonization of the lifeworld by monetization, rationalization, calculation and bureaucratization. This tale of disenchantment carries much of the tenor, and timbre, of earlier critiques of development; most vividly of the 1960s, but indeed also of the 1890s and earlier, as Michael Cowen and Robert Shenton (1996) have admirably demonstrated in *Doctrines of Development*, readily assigning blame to the multinational behemoths, both corporate and multilateral, of global capitalism.

Running across this body of work is the notion of development as an essentially Western doctrine whose normalizing assumptions must be rejected: 'it (development) is the problem not the solution', as notably suggested by Rist (2002). The sacred cows of development, which Esteva and Prakash (1998) denote as 'the myth of global thinking', 'the myth of the universality of human rights', and 'the myth of the individual self', must be substituted by what could be called grassroots postmodernism.

Arturo Escobar's (1995) book *Encountering Development* famously offered an account of postdevelopment thinking. He provided, like Kearney, a vision of subaltern and indigenous social movements as vehicles for other ways of doing politics, ways that were non-party, non-mass, and self-organizing. He also provided another way of doing postdevelopment that was decentralized, community-based, participatory, indigenous and autonomous. Interestingly, this postdevelopment movement met up with, and was cross-fertilized with, a largely Western academic development community energized by what was dubbed the 'impasse in development' debate of the 1980s and 1990s. In effect, this was a debate within the walls of Marxist development theory between its 'neo' and 'structural' schools; a debate over the extent to which developing world socialism suffered from many of the trappings of industrial capitalism, as well as the extent to which such theory had been captured by economic essentialism, class reductionism and teleological thinking.

One can argue whether this characterization of Marxist development theory is plausible or indeed an adequate account of Marxism itself in its panoply of guises. Nonetheless, the impasse debate spawned important new intersections between postcolonial and post-Marxist thinking, providing a fertile ground on which development could be refigured by a careful reading of Ranajit Guha or Gyatri Spivak or Edward Said. There is, though, little theoretical coherence in the 'impasse work', as is demonstrated by its discussions on actor–network approaches, its focus on identity politics and the cultural construction of class, and its shift to 'responsible politics'. Corbridge (1998: 95) is, however, right to emphasize that it, like the postdevelopment work, reinforced the need to see 'the ways in which the West represents its non-western others' and forces us to ask 'what is development? Who says that is what it is? Who aims to direct it and for whom?'

For the postdevelopmentalists as a varied group, diversity and identity became the new watchword. However, at the same time the postcolonialist's proper emphasis on writing history differently, which signaled, as Stuart Hall (1995: 248) says, the 'proliferation of histories and temporalities, the intrusion of difference and specificity into generalizing Eurocentric post-Enlightenment grand narratives', in turn often mistook the word for the world, populist incantation for new politics, and opted for a heavy dose of wishful thinking. Thus, claimed David Slater (1993: 106), 'in the heartlands of the West modernity is in question and the fixed horizons for development and progress [are melting away]'!

There is no doubt that this postdevelopment corpus has opened up, initially through Esobar's provocation, important new avenues for understanding development, and peasant, practices. Clearly, though, it has left its own problematic legacy, as is obvious in a close reading of Kearney's ideas on postpeasant politics and practice. First, there is the curious, and perhaps appropriately ironic, way in which a postmodern or poststructural sensibility is attached to claims of extraordinary totalizing power, certainty and rectitude. Development, as Escobar has it, is 'a historically singular experience'; 'the death of modernism spelled the death of developmentalism' says Kearney (1996: 118). Second, the unalloyed celebration of the popular energies of grassroots movements – new social movements and multiple identities in Kearney's lexicon – is not subject to the sort of hypercritical discourse analysis that might permit an understanding of their achievements, their political strategies, and the limits of their horizons and vision. Third, there is a curious confluence between elements of the neoliberal counter-revolution and the uncritical celebration (and often naive acceptance) of postdevelopment's new social movements. For example, the similarities are striking between this and the World Bank's account of Africa's postcolonial modernization failure, its antistatism and the need to harness the energies of the people. Finally, the important critique of economic reduction and class determinism (the Marxian master narrative), along with the deconstruction of the free-market myopia (the Smithian master narrative), has produced, to quote Stuart Hall (1995: 258), not alternative ways of thinking about basic economic questions, but instead 'a massive, gigantic and eloquent disavowal'.

As I have tried to emphasize, Kearney's arguments on the disappearance of the peasant and the emergence of a new postpeasant condition do speak to important issues. Globalization and transnationalism have, by and large, provided new coordinates for the study of the agrarian question. There has been a growing concern with identity questions – whether of gender or ethnicity or religion – emerging out of the deepening and thickening of civil society in the period since 1980. In this sense there has been, one might say, a shift from the agrarian question to the 'indigeneity question' in peasant studies (Warren 1998). It is the figure of the indigenous movement – the Ogoni struggle, the *Ejército Zapatista de la Liberación Nacional* (EZLN), Quechua confederations, the Mayan struggle – rather than the class and accumulation question that now dominates the academic landscape. To put the matter crudely, one might say there has been an abandonment of one aspect of Kautsky's agrarian question – how is capital taking hold of agriculture? – and a corresponding rise of Gramsci's 'Southern question': what might new forms of global accumulation and imperialism mean for the politics of the rural sector? Unlike Gramsci's references to agrarian blocs, syndicalism and worker–peasant alliances, however, we now have indigenous subalterns, the World Social Forum and fair trade cooperatives.

In what follows, I want to very briefly identify four ways in which the political complexity of the agrarian question of labour is being explored, which are sensitive to what Bernstein calls 'the contradictory sources and impulses of agrarian struggles' (Bernstein 2006: 459).

The coordinates of the Southern question

New agricultures and new peasants?

One of the presumptions of new research focused on transnational processes and agrarian food orders is that the old or classical international division of labour within the agro-food system has been irretrievably altered in the past 25 years. Classical export commodities such as coffee, tea, sugar, tobacco, cocoa and so on have been increasingly displaced by so-called 'high-value foods', including fruits and vegetables, poultry, dairy products and shellfish. During the 1980s, the aggregate value of world trade in cereals, sugar and tropical beverages declined quite dramatically in some cases; conversely, high-value foods grew by 8 per cent per annum. Thus even as early as 1989, high-value food represented 5 per cent of world commodity trade, roughly equivalent to crude petroleum (World Bank 2007). Developing economies currently account for over one-third of high-value food production by value, roughly twice the value of developing world exports of coffee, tea, sugar, cotton, cocoa and tobacco. In 1990, there were 24 low- and middle-income countries, mostly located in Latin America and Asia, which annually exported high-value foods worth more than US$500 million. However, four of these countries actually accounted for 40 per cent of total high-value food exports from developing states. These countries correspond to what Friedmann (1993) refers to as 'new agricultural countries' – the agro-industrial counterparts of the newly industrializing countries – that occupy a central location in what she calls the durable foods, fresh fruits and vegetable and livestock/feed complexes. Archetypical examples of these new agro-food systems are Brazilian citrus, Mexican 'non-traditionals' and 'exotics', Argentinean soy, Kenyan off-season vegetables, and Chinese shrimp (Friedland 1994: 210–231; Watts 1994: 21–77).

Dietary changes, trade reform and technical changes in the food industry all contributed to the growth of the high-value food sector. At the same time, there are issues intrinsic to the sector, including perishability, heterogeneity, seasonality, long gestation periods, the externalities associated with marketing, and more, which lead many commentators, most notably the World Bank (2007), to focus on the problems of production and market risk, asymmetrical information, logistical bottlenecks and high transaction costs. What is striking about the new agricultural countries is the extent to which the high-value food strategy rests on highly favourable international market conditions during the initial boom periods, in some cases precipitated by market vacuums as a result of trade embargoes or problems with traditional suppliers (Raynolds *et al.* 1993). The competitiveness of the high-value food sectors clearly rests on the low costs of production, particularly labour costs (Collins 1993), but also on the extent to which quality can be established within heterogeneous commodities as a way of establishing dominance within niche markets. Given the concerns with quality and market niches, contract production is a fundamental way in which the division of labour in these global commodity systems, or value chains, is organized. These 'post-fordist' qualities raise important questions about the very notion of quality, standards and value in international markets when the organic heterogeneity of commodities are their distinctive feature, and places considerable weight on the point of consumption insofar as high-value foods have to be culturally constituted for particular sorts of taste, diet and vanities.

The debate over the rise of the new agricultural countries turns on the purported successes of commodities such as Mexican tomatoes, Central American exotics, Brazilian soy, and so on. What is striking in all these cases is the prominence of peasant contract production and/or vertical integration in linking farm-level production and downstream processing and trade. The rise of contracted high-value food through agribusiness has had the effect of integrating peasants juridically as much as economically into both the global market and the transnational firm. It is rarely the poorest of peasants, but Lenin's middle and rich peasants, who become part of increasingly mechanized and highly regimented work regimes, growing quality fresh produce to order. A number of studies focusing on this supposedly 'new peasant' suggest that the household economy resembles a piecework system in which one of the tenets of 'peasantness' – the autonomy of the labour process – is radically compromised by the demands of the contract, which specifies with reasonable precision the details of the labour process. In the same way, labour demands for new sorts of contract production are then internalized within domestic relations of production, which often produce tensions over access to labour and property, tensions that are explored by Bridget O'Laughlin (Chapter 8). At the very least, the subsumption of peasants directly into the firm as growers represents a distinctive, although not necessarily totally original, way in which peasants may persist, producing low-cost commodities in the midst of advanced global capitalism. The fact that a number of commodities in the US agricultural sector, including poultry, hogs and fresh fruit, among others, are currently produced by 'family farms' (here defined as petty commodity producers), and of which peasants are clearly a variant, suggests that this trajectory of agrarian change may deepen and expand as more markets open to agribusiness investment.

The emergence of high-value agriculture is highly uneven – like developing world manufacturing, as Kiely demonstrates in Chapter 7 – and the underbelly of the new agricultural countries is the agricultural marginality stressed by Araghi in Chapter 5. Much of Sub-Saharan Africa has returned to an agro-export model dependent largely on classical commodities, the market future of which looks extremely grim; much of the region has, as of now, been relatively marginal to high-value foods. In other cases, structural adjustment and deregulation has drawn investment out of agriculture all together (Marsden 1992). Another variant of this global marginalization is the process in Bangladesh, described by Wood (1995), where agricultural involution under conditions of capital investment has generated an 'agricultural reformation' in which private service networks and associations of various sorts gain from productivity increases on the land, and compromise the very idea of the family farm as the decision-making unit over a range of decisions on land formally held by the family.

The agrarian question comes to town

Some of the most exciting recent Marxist-inspired work in peasant studies draws sustenance from the confluence of two related bodies of research: one focuses on the question of flexibility and networks in peasant agriculture in a way that sheds light on debates within industrial geography; another draws on the growing body of work on rural industrialization in the developing world and related peasant non-farm work. Both these trends point to the continued importance of Kautsky, among others, and the agrarian origins of industrialization. Chari's (2004) work on industrial districts around Tirupur in south India is especially important as a case study of developing world flexible specialization and of what can be called 'amoebic capitalism'. The genesis of this form of industrialization is inseparable from rural–urban linkages in a regional economy dominated by specialized towns, and specifically how the capture of textiles by an agrarian capitalist caste, the *Gounders*, brought with it migration and a consequent refashioning of a variety of agrarian institutions of labour control and discipline, which are central to the contemporary organization of a dynamic small-firm textile sector. Harriss-White (1995) has explored these rural–urban linkages as part of what she calls the 'rural urbanization of agrarian economies'. Here, the economic linkages are regarded as the outcome of social relations shaped by local institutions, but embedded in relations of power, trust and reputation.

These aspects of the agrarian question are central in understanding the newly emerging rural industrial districts in a variety of social and institutional contexts. Certainly, a part of the explanation of the dispersed and decentralized character of Taiwanese flexible family capitalism is rooted in the politics of agriculture and post-war agrarian reform. The Chinese case is also relevant here, because it shows how remarkable rates of rural industrialization can combine collective property rights at the township level with market discipline and local institutions emerging from the creation of a post-reform peasantry (Oi 1999). Hart (2002) has documented cases of what she calls 'interstitial spaces' – foreign capital investing in the quite specific milieus of rural South Africa – in which local networks and institutions are central to understanding the hybrid and multiple trajectories of capitalist development. These studies go beyond the old rural–urban consumption linkages debate, in which small-farm growth produced local demand for services, equipment or local consumer goods, to an examination of both the role of agrarian investment in industry and the ways in which agriculture, either through the provision of industrial wage labour from peasant households or through local institutions of labour recruitment and discipline, is a key local ingredient in the emergence of globalized rural industrial districts in various parts of the developing world. These developments can be argued to explain, in part, why land reform has re-emerged as a central plank of current development policy debates, although it is also a function of recognition of the need to deal with the deepening problems of rural inequality in the wake of structural adjustment. What Hart calls interstitial spaces, and what Marsden (1992), in describing locations such as the São Fernando valley in Brazil, calls 'agricultural districts', are both illustrations of how land-based activities in globalized sites are constituted by complex social networks, and how the agrarian question is a constituent part of the flexible forms of industrialization that are emerging in newly deregulated and internationalized economies.

Postsocialist peasants

If the history of actually existing socialisms is indeed the long road to capitalism, the experience of postsocialist transitions should provide a compelling experiment for understanding agrarian transitions. They represent a curious inversion of the second half of Kautsky's *Agrarian Question,* in which he lays out the social democratic route to socialist agriculture, the so-called *Erfurt Programm.* Much work has already been undertaken on the macroeconomic aspects of postsocialist transitions, which is a subject of as much interest to the World Bank *apparatchiks* as to academic political economists; on the merits of shock therapy versus gradualism; and on the political legacies of the past as impediments to some form of meaningful liberalization. Michael Burawoy (1994) has provided a useful typology of this work in terms of two axes: the tempo of change (revolutionary versus gradual), and the time horizon (origins and destinations). This yields a fourfold matrix of transitions: the totalitarian theory, or monolithic party state, which collapses entirely at the moment of transition; the neoliberal theory, which demands radical surgery to institute markets *de novo*; the evolutionary theorists, who emphasize the role of institutions, some of which can be used even though they are from the socialist past; and the legacy theory, which, *contra* totalitarianism, sees a vibrant civil society amidst the wreckage of the socialist state fundamentally shaping the development trajectory of capitalism. These contrasting trajectories are relevant to the study of decollectivized agriculture as much as to privatized industry or the democratization of the party-state, but agrarian transitions have typically received much less attention (Pryor 1992).

It is to be expected that, insofar as the practice of something called socialist agriculture was quite variegated – 'many shades of red', as Meurs (1998) memorably puts it – the forms and trajectories of decollectivization are equally diverse. One can easily contrast, for example, China, Russia and Cuba. China privatized collectives gradually, but early, and is typically seen as a success in output terms. Russia privatized its already decrepit state farms rapidly, but with chaotic and uneven consequences. Cuba's reforms have had important consequences in the realm of marketing and monetary relations, but have left much of the socialist productive structures largely intact.

One of the key questions in understanding postsocialist agriculture is whether decollectivization is returning agriculture to its prerevolutionary condition, and thus whether, as Szelenyi (1998) says, socialism simply interrupted a trajectory to which market reform has returned postsocialist states. This is Szelenyi's thesis of 're-embourgeoisement'. This turns, in part, on the question of the restitution of property and land reform. In many of these cases, however, property rights tend, in Verdery's (1996) phrase, to be 'elastic', either because they are hybrid or because the juridical and legal frameworks are incapable of imposing particular forms of land legislation.

There does seem to be a striking polarity between cases in which, to employ Kornai's (1992) language, 'transformational recession' produces agrarian crisis, often amidst a flurry of legislation intended to remove subsidies, abolish parastatals and institute legal reform. Here, one typically sees an increase in rural unemployment, cooperative and state farms that stagger along largely because workers have no obvious alternative employment, and the tardy production of an underequipped class of peasants or family farms. Albania, Bulgaria and, most notably, Russia are clearly exemplary cases; it is, one might argue, the fragile, brittle and chaotic character of the socialist state in Russia that has created the transformational recession in former Soviet agriculture. Even despite the so-called success of earlier reforms in Hungary and of its purportedly efficient collectives, its agrarian sector is also lurching from one crisis to another. Not surprisingly, in these varied circumstances, decollectivization has often produced populist peasant parties that, in view of the numbers in the rural sector, emerge as key actors in the democratic transition; as, for example, in Poland and Hungary. In some cases the chaotic political environment of weak postsocialist states, typified by Romania and Albania, witnesses peasant politics taking on a 'feudal' character as new forms of the parcelized sovereignty, discussed by Wood in Chapter 2, emerge at the local level.

Conversely, China and Vietnam seem to be the success stories. The increase in output between 1978 and 1984 in China is often claimed to be the product of the rapid collapse of the collectives. In fact, China has maintained a two-tiered property system, with private and collective forms, a relatively equitable redistribution of land values if not land, and highly generative forms of non-farm employment in the rural sector (Ho 1994; Oi 1999). The heart of this rural revolution has been industries set up by collectives and local governments, and only subsequently by private enterprises employing reinvested capital from agriculture. These reforms produced not a collapse of local government, but its strengthening, through its ability to tax non-farm income. Vietnam, and especially the old north, has implemented a more rapid and thoroughgoing land reform, partly as a function of the strength of the Communist Party at the local level, producing a sort of highly egalitarian Chayanovian peasant economy, but without the same unleashing of market forces (Watts 1996). Despite differences, though, in both cases the agro-food system has been quite dynamic; in China's case it has been a central component of its capitalist growth. Neither of these cases illustrates what Lenin called 'the American Path', in which agrarian capitalism emerges 'from below', in part because property rights are hybrid and complex and because the strength of the state has been central to their productive success (Bowles and Xiao 1994).

Indigenous communitarians

The indigeneity movements are striking because peasant identity is substituted by the invocation of indigenous or ethnic custom and tradition in which land, territory and state recognition figures centrally as a basis for resource control. Chiapas and the struggle of the Zapotec peoples is a paradigmatic case, but represents only the most visible expression of a much longer history of indigenous struggles by indigenous communities in South America and elsewhere. These movements are global in the sense that many are now linked virtually, through the internet, and through multilateral organizations, regulations and law: for example, the International Labour Organization's Convention 169 on Indigenous and Tribal Peoples; and the Unrepresented Nations and Peoples Organization (Nelson 1999).

The case of Chiapas is instructive if one is examining Kearney's post-development and the postpeasantry. First, Chiapas was unthinkable outside the democratic processes unfurled by the slaughter of Mexican students in Tlateloco Square. Second, the genesis of the Chiapas rebellion must be traced to the maelstrom of the 1960s, throwing together the church, indigenous movements and left activism. The long fuse of the EZLN was ignited by Bishop Ruiz and the Catechist Apostles movement, which was liberated by the Medellin Episcopal Assembly of 1968, by Maoist insurgents in Monterrey and Chichuaha in the late 1960s, who helped form the *Unión de Uniones/Asociación Rural de Interés Colectivo* and other radical organizations, and of course by the burgeoning of indigenous movements brought together in the 1974 Indian Conference. The trail from the Armed Forces of National Liberation to the EZLN can, and must, be traced to the late 1960s, even if it was in the period between 1983 and 1989 when these elements started to work together, a combination that proved to be the revolutionary crucible in which the events of 1994 matured and, ultimately, combusted. At the same time, Chiapas is surely unthinkable outside the world market that the North American Free Trade Area anointed on 1 January 1994. That is to say, indigeneity has all manner of connections to an earlier history of political practice, including the organized left and the church, and is both a reaction to and a product of the world market. In many cases, indigeneity is strikingly modernist and displays many of the essentialist peasant deployments around land, territory and autonomy that Kearney derides as products of a now-defunct modernizing Cold War epoch. However, none of this is to suggest that indigenous movements simply reproduce a prior history of peasant politics; rather, it is to radically question the grandiose claims of a new postpeasant landscape. There is within the indigenous movements a local and global discursive creativity; what Tania Li (2007) calls the occupation of the 'tribal slot'. Whether this stands in opposition to the material and discursive sense of being a peasant is, however, another question entirely.

The community looms large in this new concern with peasant identities and indigeneity. However, the community turns out to be, along with its lexical affines, namely tradition, custom, and indigenous, a sort of keyword whose meanings, always unstable and contested, are wrapped up in complex ways with the problems it is used to discuss. The community is important because it is typically seen as: a locus of knowledge; a site of regulation and management; a source of identity and a repository of 'tradition'; the embodiment of various institutions such as, for example, property rights, which necessarily turn on questions of representation, power, authority, governance and accountability; an object of state control; and a theatre of resistance and struggle, of social movement, and potentially of alternate visions of development. It is often invoked as a unity, as an undifferentiated entity with intrinsic powers, which speaks with a single voice to the state, to transnational non-governmental organizations, or to the World Court. However, communities turn out to be nothing of the sort.

A claim to be a peasant community typically involves: a territorialization of history, in which land and resources can be traced in relation to a set of founding events; and a naturalized history of a people and not their relations to other peoples. Communities fabricate, and refabricate through their unique histories, the claims they take to be naturally and self-evidently their own. This is why communities have to be understood in terms of hegemonies: not everyone participates or benefits equally in the construction and reproduction of communities, or from the claims made in the name of community interest. This is exactly what is at stake in current work on the infamous peasant tree-hugging *Chipko* movement in north India (Rangan 1995). The mythic community of tree-hugging, unified, undifferentiated women articulating alternative subaltern knowledges for an alternative development supposedly witnesses forest protection and conservation by women in defence of customary rights against timber extraction. Actuality is far from this myth. There are several *Chipko* movements, each standing in a quite different relationship to development, modernity, sustainability, the state and local management. It was, and is, a movement with a long history of market involvement, of links to other political organizing in Garawhal, and with aspirations for regional autonomy.

Similarly, Brosius's (1997) work in Indonesia, in two seemingly comparable local communities, shows how the type and fact of indigenous resistance varied dramatically between the two communities, which were in many respects identical cultural communities, and how these differences turn on a combination of contingent but nonetheless important historical events. Brosius found that radical differences in resistance to logging companies between two indigenous peasant communities turned on their histories with respect to colonial forces, their internal social structure, their autonomy and closed, corporate structure, and the role of transnational forces, environmentalists in particular. The point is that some communities do not resist and may not have, or have any interest in, local knowledge; a point that disappoints the foreign or local academic. Some peasants within communities are happy to take on board essentialism and wrong-headed local 'traditions' pedalled by foreign activists or investors, in order to further local struggles. Tradition or custom hardly captures what is at stake in the definition of the community.

Chronicle of a death foretold

> The process of dissolution which turns a mass of individuals in a nation etc., into potential free wage labourers ... does not presuppose the disappearance of the previous sources of income or (in part) of the previous conditions of property of these individuals.
>
> (Marx 1964: 105, first published 1952)

To draw, one last time, an analogy from Mike Davis's (2006) account of the slum world, does the agrarian question of labour resemble a rural slum characterized by: a relentless micro-capitalism of subsistence; an absence of rights and contracts; the failure of bootstrap development; forced entrepreneurialism; the fragmentation of work; the abuse of women; declining social capital; corruption; anomie; individuation; gothic involution; ecological catastrophism; gambling; witchcraft; and ethnic violence? In sum, does the agrarian question of labour resemble a disposable humanity with only the protection of religion? Whether or not this Hobbesian vision has some applicability throughout the slum world, or indeed is an adequate account of the dynamics of being poor in the developing world city, it hardly represents, to return to Bernstein, a nuanced and place-specific mapping of the wider social and political struggles of labour.

The World Bank (2007) suggests that urban poverty is insignificant in comparison with armies of the rural poor; its picture of the rural world is bleak, but it lacks any account of the sorts of politics thrown up in and around land and labour, in contract farming schemes in Kenya, on the tea estates of Kerala, or in the land seizures in Brazil. I have not attempted to map such complexity in this chapter, but only to point to the multiple trajectories along which the contemporary Southern question is currently advancing. To say that the agrarian question of capital is dead, or that the agrarian question of labour generates struggles not of world-historical significance, may be plausible abstractions derived from a rigorous materialism, but they offer little in the way of thinking beyond, and indeed the routes out of, the catastrophism – whether ecological, demographic, social or material – that confronts the rural and agrarian poor.

Notes

1 A quite different version of this essay was published as part of a debate with Michael Kearney concerning a number of issues raised in his book *Reconceptualizing the Peasantry*, and appeared as Watts (2002). I am grateful for suggestions provided by Cristóbal Kay and Haroon Akram-Lodhi.
2 This is, of course, an old argument – Polly Hill railed against the use of the term 'peasant' 30 years ago – but to suggest that anyone who deploys this term is necessarily guilty of a series of populist sins seems rather odd; it is like saying that the deployment of the term 'simple commodity production' signifies nothing more than the *pur et dur* of the 'logic of capital'.
3 It should be said, though, that Davis provides a structural account of urban catastrophism in which Lagos serves as the model for all cities in the developing world, and in which the world of the slum is totally Hobbesian; the only counterweight is Pentecostalism and political Islam, which sanctifies those who 'live in exile'.
4 Perhaps these affinities should come as no surprise; the World Bank's (2007) *World Development Report 2008: Agriculture for Development* was directed by Alain de Janvry, a person who knows a thing or two about Marx, Lenin, Kautsky and the agrarian question.

References

Arendt, H. (1951) *Imperialism*, New York: Harcourt.
Bernstein, H. (2006) 'Is there an agrarian question in the 21st century?', *Canadian Journal of Development Studies*, 27 (4): 449–465.
Bobrow-Strain, A. (2007) *Intimate Enemies: Landowners, Power and Violence in Chiapas*, Durham, NC, USA: Duke University Press.
Bowles, P. and Dong Xiao (1994) 'Current successes and future challenges in China's economic reform', *New Left Review*, 208: 77–97.
Bramall, C. and M.E. Jones (2000) 'The fate of the Chinese peasantry since 1978', in D. Bryceson, C. Kay and J. Mooij (eds), *Disappearing Peasantries? Rural Labour in Africa, Asia and Latin America*, London: Intermediate Technology Publications.
Brass, T. (1997) 'The agrarian myth, the new populism and the new right', *Journal of Peasant Studies*, 24 (4): 201–224.
—— (2000) *Peasants, Populism and Postmodernism*, London: Frank Cass.
Breman, J. (1996) *Footloose Labour: Working in India's Informal Economy*, Cambridge: Cambridge University Press.
Brosius, P. (1997) 'Prior transcripts, divergent paths', *Comparative Studies in Society and History*, 39 (1): 468–510.
Bryceson, D., C. Kay and J. Mooij, (2000) *Disappearing Peasantries? Rural Labour in Africa, Asia and Latin America*, London: Intermediate Technology Publications.
Burawoy, M. (1996) 'The state and economic involution: Russia through a China lens', *World Development*, 24 (6): 1105–1117.

Byres, T. (1995) 'Political economy, the agrarian question and comparative method', *Economic and Political Weekly*, 30 (10): 507–513.

Chari, S. (2004) *Fraternal Capital: Peasant-Workers, Self-Made Men, and Globalization in Provincial India*, Stanford, CA, USA: Stanford University Press.

Chayanov, A. (1966) *The Theory of Peasant Economy*, Madison, WI: University of Wisconsin Press.

Collier, P. (2007) *The Bottom Billion*, New York: Oxford University Press.

Collins, J. (1993) 'Gender, contracts and wage work: agricultural restructuring in Brazil's Sao Francisco valley', *Development and Change*, 24 (1): 53–82.

Corbridge, S. (1998) *Development Studies: A Reader*, London: Hodder Arnold.

Cowen, M. and R. Shenton (1996) *Doctrines of Development*, London: Routledge.

Dallmayr, F. (1996) 'Global development?', *Alternatives*, 21 (2): 259–282.

Daviron B. and S. Ponte (2005) *The Coffee Paradox: Global Markets, Commodity Trade and the Elusive Promise of Development*, London: Zed Books.

Davis, M. (2000) *Late Victorian Holocausts: El Niño Famines and the Making of the Third World*, London: Verso.

—— (2006) *Planet of Slums*, London: Verso.

Escobar, A. (1995) *Encountering Development: The Making and Unmaking of the Third World*, Princeton, NJ, USA: Princeton University Press.

Esteva G. and M. Prakhash, (1998) *Grassroots Postmodernism: Remaking the Soil of Cultures*, London: Zed Books.

Fanon, F. (1962) *The Wretched of the Earth*, London: Penguin.

Fridell, G. (2006) *Fair Trade Coffee: The Prospects and Pitfall of Market-Driven Social Justice*, Toronto: University of Toronto Press.

Friedland, W. (1994) 'The new globalization: the case of fresh produce', in A. Bonnano, L. Busch, W. Friedland L. Gouveia and E. Mingione (eds), *From Columbus to Conagra: The Globalization of Agriculture and Food*, Lawrence, KS: University Press of Kansas.

Friedmann, H. (1993) 'The political economy of food', *New Left Review*, 197: 29–57.

Goodman, D., B. Sorj and D. Wilkinson (1987) *From Farming to Biotechnology*, Oxford: Blackwell.

Gramsci, A. (1957) 'The Southern question', in *The Modern Prince*, New York: International Publishers (first published in 1926).

Gupta, A. (1998) *Postcolonial Developments: Agriculture in the Making of Modern India*, Durham, NC, USA: Duke University Press.

Hall, S. (1995) 'When was the postcolonial?', in I. Chambers and L. Curti (eds), *The Post Colonial Question*, London: Routledge.

Harriss-White, B. (1995) *A Political Economy of Agricultural Markets in South India*, New Delhi: Sage.

Hart, G. (2002) *Disabling Globalization: Places of Power in Post-Apartheid South Africa*, Berkeley, CA, USA: University of California Press.

Harvey, D. (2003) *The New Imperialism*, Oxford: Oxford University Press.

Ho, S. (1994) *Rural China in Transition: Non-agricultural Development in Rural Jiangsu, 1978–90*, London: Routledge.

Hobsbawm, E. (1994) *Age of Extremes: The Short Twentieth Century 1914–1991*, London: Michael Joseph.

Illich, I. (1971) *Celebration of Awareness*, London: Methuen.

Jaffee, D. (2007) *Brewing Justice: Fair Trade Coffee, Sustainability, and Survival*, Berkeley, CA: University of California Press.

de Janvry, A., E. Sadoulet and L. Young (1989) 'Land and labour in Latin American agriculture', *Journal of Peasant Studies*, 16 (3): 396–424.

Kautsky, K. (1988) *The Agrarian Question*, London: Zwan (first published in 1899).

Kearney, M. (1996) *Reconceptualizing the Peasantry*, Boulder, CO: Westview Press.

Kitching, G. (2001) 'The concept of *Sebestoimost* in Russian farm accounting', *Journal of Agrarian Change*, 1 (1): 57–80.

Kornai, J. (1992) *The Socialist System*, Princeton, NJ, USA: Princeton University Press.

Li, T. (2007) *The Will to Improve: Governmentality, Development, and the Practice of Politics*, Durham, NC: Duke University Press.

Marsden, T. (1992) 'Creating space for food', in D. Goodman and M. Watts (eds), *Globalising Food: Agrarian Questions and Global Restructuring*, London: Routledge.

Marx, K. (1964) *Pre-capitalist Economic Formations*, London: Lawrence and Wishart (first published in 1952).

McMichael, P. (2006) 'Reframing development: global peasant movements and the new agrarian question', *Canadian Journal of Development Studies*, 27 (4): 470–483.

Meurs, M. (ed.) (1998) *Many Shades of Red*, Toronto: Allanheld.

Mitchell, T. (2002) *Rule of Experts: Egypt, Techno-Politics, Modernity*, Berkeley, CA: University of California Press.

Moore, B. (1966) *Social Origins of Dictatorship and Democracy*, Boston, MA: Beacon.

Moore, D. (2006) *Suffering for Territory: Race, Place and Power in Zimbabwe*, Durham, NC: Duke University Press.

Nederveen Pieterse, P. (1996) *My Paradigm or Yours? Alternative Development, Post Development, Reflexive Development*, Working Paper Series No. 229, The Hague: Institute of Social Studies.

Nelson, D. (1999) *A Finger in the Wound: Body Politics in Quincentennial Guatemala*, Berkeley, CA: University of California Press.

Oi, J. (1999) *Rural China Takes Off: Institutional Foundations of Economic Reform*, Berkeley, CA: University of California Press.

Otero, G. (1999) *Farewell to the Peasantry?*, Boulder, CO: Westview Press.

Pryor, F. (1992) *The Red and Green: The Rise and Fall of Collectivized Agriculture in Marxist Regimes*, Princeton, NJ: Princeton University Press.

Rahnema, M. and V. Bawtree (eds) (1997) *The Post-Development Reader*, London: Zed Books.

Rangan, P. (1995) 'Contesting boundaries', *Antipode*, 27 (4): 343–362.

Raynolds L., D. Myhre, P. McMichael, V. Carro-Figueroa and F.H. Buttel (1993) 'The new internationalization of agriculture: a reformulation', *World Development*, 21 (6): 1101–1121.

Rist, G. (2002) *The History of Development: From Western Origins to Global Faith*, London: Zed Books.

Salgado, S. (2000) *Migrations*, New York: Aperture.

Slater, D. (1993) 'The political meanings of development', in F. Schuurman (ed.), *Beyond the Impasse: New Directions in Development Theory*, London: Zed Books.

Szelenyi, I. (ed.) (1998) *Reforming Collectivized Agriculture: Failures and Successes*, London: Routledge.

Verdery, K. (1996) *What Was Socialism and What Comes Next?*, Princeton, NJ: Princeton University Press.

Warren, K. (1998) *Indigenous Movements and their Critics*, Princeton, NJ: Princeton University Press.

Walker, R. (2004) *The Conquest of Bread: 150 Years of Agribusiness in California*, Boston, MA, USA: New Press.

Watts, M.J. (1994) 'Life under contract', in P. Little and M. Watts (eds), *Living Under Contract: Contract Farming and Agrarian Transformation in Sub-Saharan Africa*, Madison, WI, USA: University of Wisconsin Press.

—— (1996) 'Agrarian thermidor: the agrarian transition in Vietnam in comparative context', in J. Pickles and A. Wood (eds), *Theorizing Transition*, London: Routledge.

—— (2002) 'Chronicle of a death foretold: some thought on peasants and the agrarian question', *Österreichische Zeitschrift für Geschichtswissenschaften*, 13 (4): 22–50.

Williams, R. (1983) *Keywords: A Vocabulary of Culture and Society* (new edn), London: Flamingo.

Wolf, E. (1969) *Peasant Wars of the 20th Century*, New York: HarperTrade.

Wood, G. (1995) *From Farms to Services*, Occasional Paper, Bath: Centre for Development Studies, University of Bath.

World Bank (2007) *World Development Report 2008: Agriculture for Development*, Oxford: Oxford University Press.

12 Food sovereignty, social reproduction and the agrarian question

Philip McMichael

Introduction

There should be no doubt that the agrarian question needs re-asking today.[1] Not only is the political history of capitalism continuing to unfold, but also the subject of the question is important to revisit. The agrarian question, in history, cannot be generic, and needs to address changing political–economic conditions and changing problematics related to subquestions concerning land, urban-rural ecology, peasants, production and circulation, and reproduction.[2] Broadly, as the era of state-building has yielded to the era of globalization, the question concerning the changing role of agriculture in accumulation and attendant political forces has been displaced from the national to the international arena, while capital's deepening global reach has accentuated the associated 'peasant question'. Henry Bernstein (Chapter 10) has addressed this transition very creatively through his reformulation of the classic agrarian question as the 'agrarian question of labour'. To the extent that the fate of today's peasantries is intimately connected with a process of proletarianization on a world scale, marked by the cycles of dispossession and displacement discussed in Chapter 5 by Farshad Araghi, Bernstein underlines the absence or demise of an effective transfer of surplus labour from a commercializing rural sector to urban manufacturing employment calibrated to developing a home market for capital (Lenin 1972, first published 1899). The original problematic of peasant differentiation and/or disintegration has been replaced by a new problematic of dispossession and/or displacement, as Araghi stresses. Of course, the landscape has changed since the era of state-building between 1870 and 1970, as the globalization project has dismantled national economic sectors and installed a truly 'world agriculture' (McMichael 2005a). Seemingly superfluous peasantries or rural household members have been compelled to leave the land permanently or cyclically as wage labour, to intensify self-exploitation in order to remain on the land, and/or to mobilize for land rights via appeals to sociocultural justice and ecological sustainability.

This chapter argues a simple proposition: that the agrarian question is ultimately more about the political history of capitalism than its trajectories of transition. That is to say, while the agrarian question is embedded within processes of capital accumulation, these processes are politicized in time and space. Accordingly, the agrarian question cannot be reduced to a question formed within the terms of capital theory itself. The historical conditions of accumulation are not equivalent to the theoretical conditions of accumulation, just as the subjects of accumulation impart a historical sensibility that cannot be deduced from a categorical representation of the processes of accumulation. In the latter regard, the agrarian question has, in general, viewed peasants as external to the accumulation process, insofar as they are understood to inhabit precapitalist relations. As such, their role in the capitalist transition of the 'classic' agrarian question of emergent capital and emergent wage labour is similar to that of landed property: a social form to be overcome, subordinated or eliminated by capital.

To the extent that peasantries – and landowning classes more generally – have resisted capital and defied their fate (Wolf 1969), the political history of capitalism has shown considerable variation in its processes and outcomes *vis-à-vis* landed property (Moore 1967). Indeed, Byres highlights variation in his contribution to this book (Chapter 3). There is, then, no reason to assume that variation is anomalous; rather, variation expresses the politicized history of capital. While the concept of uneven development interprets this variation, it tends to work with a deductive base/superstructure episteme by externalizing non-capitalist relations as precapitalist. My point is that once we accept Marx's methodological injunction not to mystify the economy as devoid of political relations, we enter a methodological space that allows a politicized and historical understanding of capitalist relations. Here, rather than posing the agrarian question as a question of how capital forms a labour force through transforming agriculture, and whether and to what extent capital reproduces that labour force in gainful employment, it can be posed alternatively from the perspective of agrarians subject to these transforming processes. This is not an essentialist perspective of a besieged peasantry; rather, it is a perspective shaped by the historical conditions in which they find themselves, conditions that are not limited to the failures of neoliberal capitalism to develop the global South, to regulate the transfer of labour from rural to urban sectors, or to preserve the peasant way of life. The agrarian question today is conditioned by the political history of capitalism, which includes struggles to exercise, obtain and defend a complex of rights. Put simply, rights struggles include workplace conditions, civil and social rights in the state, and human rights in and for representation in global society. Contemporary peasant movements – in all their heterogeneity as subsistence producers, *kulaks*, landless peasants and contract farmers, among others – as and like labour movements today, combine all three domains of rights in their struggles, and more, as we shall see.

Peasant resistance to capital occurs within its relations, but not its terms, of subjection (Beverley 2004). That is, beyond offering alternatives, what is described below as 'food sovereignty' politics engages critically with the political infrastructure of contemporary global capitalism, within and through which rights discourse and struggles operate. As a consequence, food sovereignty combines a formal politics of citizenship and the social contract with a substantive politics of rights expressed through a reformulation of multilateralism, combined with a revaluing of agrarian relationships. This chapter examines the conditions of peasant mobilization today from the perspective of how these conditions express historical relations embedded in global capitalism, even as peasant movements seek to transcend the projection of capitalist ontology into the agrarian context.

Historical capitalism

As several contributors to this volume have stressed, at the turn of the twentieth century the agrarian question concerned the politics of capitalist transition in agriculture, and specifically how peasantries would interpret their political allegiances in revolutionary times. In turn, this 'peasant question', as Engels put it, concerned political identity under conditions of differentiation, or disintegration, of the peasantry (Lenin 1972). Karl Kautsky in particular observed:

> What decides whether a farmer is ready to join the ranks of the proletariat in struggle is not whether he is starving or indebted, but whether he comes to market as a seller of labour-power or as a seller of food. Hunger and indebtedness by themselves do not create a community of interests with the proletariat as a whole; in fact they can sharpen the contradiction between peasant and proletarian once this hunger has been stilled and debts repaid, should food prices rise and make it impossible for workers to enjoy cheap food.
>
> (Kautsky 1988: 317, first published 1899)

Kautsky linked this question of allegiance to the reversal of food prices from the 1870s to the interests of agrarian producers. German agriculture experienced the ripple effects of the creation of a world wheat market as a consequence of the British state's mid-century abolition of the Corn Laws. As Harriet Friedmann (1978) has documented, the particular historical conditions of New World agricultural frontiers posed a profound competitive threat, through a falling price of wheat, to European farmers following the American Civil War. Kautsky wrote:

> It was not the volume of imported food which threatened European agriculture, but rather the conditions under which it was produced. Such produce did not have to bear the burdens imposed on agriculture by the capitalist mode of production. Its appearance on the market made it impossible for European agriculture to continue shifting the rising burdens imposed by private property in land and capitalist commodity

production on to the mass of the consumers. European agriculture had to bear them itself. And this is what is at the heart of the current agrarian crisis.

(Kautsky 1988: 243)

While the agrarian question was posed in state-centric terms, in Western Europe it was clearly conditioned by the late-nineteenth century food regime, which Friedmann (2005) has aptly labelled 'colonial–diasporic'. In fact, this food regime, based on agricultural outsourcing to the settler colonies, in reducing food prices both on tropical products such as sugar, tea and fruit, and on temperate products such as wheat and meat, lowered wage costs for capital during a critical period of European industrialization, as Araghi discusses in Chapter 5 (Friedmann and McMichael 1989). Rural producers and the industrial proletariat shared a common experience in low food prices, but they also shared a deepening exposure to market relations, which treated land and labour, artificially, as commodities. The separate but combined countermovements of agrarians and workers to protect these social substances contributed to the formation of the twentieth century social-democratic state (Polanyi 1957).

Related historically to this state form was agricultural protectionism, in a successor, mercantilist, food regime lasting from the 1940s through the 1970s. In effect, Kautsky identified the conditions in the late nineteenth century that gave rise to mid-twentieth century agricultural protectionism. These were the incorporation of the New World and the colonial world into circuits of capital dedicated to food provisioning to depress industrial wage costs. In addition, twentieth century agricultural protectionism derived largely from the US dust bowl experience of the 1930s, which brought to an ecological halt the soil-exhaustive agriculture associated with the settler frontier. In reconstructing the post-war world economy, the USA elaborated an international development project, premised on an idealized form of accumulation in the national articulation of industry and agriculture (McMichael 2004). National farm sectors, particularly that of the USA, were protected from cheap agricultural imports by a post-war General Agreement on Tariffs and Trade (GATT) regime focused only on liberalization of trade in manufactures.

The agrarian crisis identified by Kautsky was thereby contained behind mercantilist structures. These, however, nurtured an overproduction of agricultural commodities in the first world, whose management of food surpluses instituted a dynamic of dumping that continues today. First deployed by the US state, via the Public Law 480 programme of concessional food aid to strategic third world states on the Cold War perimeter (Friedmann 1982), food surplus dumping was generalized as a commercial weapon by states in the European Union as the American agribusiness model took hold in Europe, and the global South was opened up by structural adjustment as a dumping ground. In effect, the mercantilist resolution of Kautsky's agrarian crisis for the first world was the condition for a new agrarian crisis in the global South, as artificially cheapened foodstuff imports from the global North have steadily decimated Southern peasant agricultures (McMichael 2005a). The World Trade Organization's (WTO) Agreement on Agriculture institutionalized this residual dynamic from the postwar food regime, with the minimum import rule and liberalization of farm protection in the global South, while Northern producers continue to depend on huge subsidies invisibilized through a shell game of coloured boxes (Rosset 2006: 84).

Beyond trade relations, mercantilist structures fostered the rise of agribusiness corporations – food producers, traders, processors and retailers – that have progressively concentrated commodity sectors of the agro-food system, coordinated global trading, and built integrated global supply chains (Heffernan and Constance 1994). The postwar food regime was characterized by an intensive accumulation process geared not to cheapening wage-food consumption, but rather to incorporating consumption relations into the accumulation process itself (Friedmann and McMichael 1989). Accordingly, a food culture centred on animal protein consumption, and identified with a 'developed' lifestyle, emerged in the USA and as a target for emulation across Europe, Japan and eventually the growing middle-class strata in the third world. This development spurred a second wave of agricultural outsourcing, as consumer markets for processed food, fast food and fresh counter-seasonal food emerged, and food corporations responded by developing joint ventures and transnational supply chains (Friedland 1994). Thus, an increasingly integrated world agriculture emerged, maturing through the devices of the debt regime, which normalized agro-exporting as the new ingredient of financial orthodoxy and global development.

In this vortex of relentless dumping of agricultural surpluses from the North, abetted by proliferating free trade agreements and the displacement of Southern staple foods by agro-exports, a new agrarian crisis materialized. Although time and space relations differ, the similarity with Kautsky's late-nineteenth century agrarian crisis is the exposure of agrarian communities to competitive market forces that undermine their agriculture – the market imperatives that Wood discusses in Chapter 2. The difference is that agrarian communities everywhere are under threat from agribusiness. Kautsky, in focusing on the European agrarian crisis and not its manifestations in the colonial world (Davis 2001), implicitly privileged the path-dependent model of agrarian transition stemming from capital theory. For example, extrapolating forward from the late-nineteenth century agrarian crisis, Kautsky surmised:

> But should the time ever come when all the wheat or rye lands are full, and grain prices inexorably begin to rise, the spirit of invention would immediately throw itself upon the problem of replacing customary cereals with surrogates made from tropical products. Those tropical countries which are not suited to wheat cultivation – Central America,

northern Brazil, large parts of Africa, India, Southeastern Asia – would then also join the ranks of the European grain farmers' competitors.

Eventually, this competition will have to lose its ruinous character. The surface of the earth is finite and the capitalist mode of production is expanding at a dizzy pace. As the product of the competition between the backward agricultural countries and the advanced industrial countries, the agrarian crisis must therefore eventually come to an end. But the end of this competition will also spell the end of the capitalist mode of production's possibilities of further expansion. Constant expansion is the life principle of capitalism: technical revolution and the accumulation of capital are unceasing; production becomes increasingly mass production, whilst the share of the masses in their own product steadily diminishes. The agrarian crisis can therefore only end with a general crisis of capitalist society as a whole. This point may arrive earlier or later; but as long as capitalist society continues, agrarian crisis will be its permanent accompaniment. And if the capitalist burdens which once depressed agriculture in Western Europe now begin to do the same to its competitors in the USA, Russia, and so on, this is not proof that the crisis in Western European agriculture is coming to an end. It simply proves that the crisis is extending its grip.

(Kautsky 1988: 252)

While this is not an unreasonable scenario – perhaps in both senses of the term – its path-dependent assumption is unable to anticipate the mercantilist interlude of the postwar food regime, and its consequences: for stemming agrarian crisis in the first world; for undermining third world agricultures; and for installing first world agribusiness models. In other words, it is a projection devoid of political contingency in the manipulation of a chronic agrarian crisis. As such, a deductively theorized perspective such as this cannot accommodate transformation of the political conditions of capital accumulation, and especially the changing world-historical context and content of the politics of landed property.

Time and space relations do matter, and of particular importance is that while the model of colonial provisioning of metropolitan food needs continues and deepens, the appearance of agrarian crisis in the global South is overdetermined by the effects of its resolution in the North in the form of agricultural mercantilism. This mercantilism originated in the USA as the dominant state – ironically, the source of Kautsky's agrarian crisis – which used its agricultural surpluses and, later, global food sourcing as a vehicle of hegemony as it built food dependency, dietary emulation and a global food consumer culture across the world. The transnational grain traders, processors and retailers that have intensified food circuits have simultaneously dislodged millions of peasants and small farmers. As La Via Campesina (2000a) puts it: 'the massive movement of food around the world is forcing the increased movement of people'. Both circuits mark the construction of a world agriculture, governed by corporate technologies, supplying differentiated consumer markets, and outsourcing to the global South, as labour costs, land rents and Northern environmental regulations rise and encourage the spread of agribusiness estates and food-processing plants across the South – a foundation on which the recent retailing revolution is being built (McMichael and Friedmann 2007).

What is striking about La Via Campesina's observation is that it is the foundation for an understanding of capitalist agrarian transition that goes beyond that of the classic agrarian question. Whereas the latter focused on changing class relations in agriculture and their implications for national political alliances, La Via Campesina complements this with analysis of the politics of circulation. Not only does this complete the analysis of capitalist relations, but it also allows a world-historical specification of agrarian transition and the nexus between capital and the nation-state system in transforming agriculture.

Food sovereignty

The food sovereignty movement can be viewed, in the first instance, as a protectionist countermovement in the context of the contemporary agrarian crisis. It is a politicized movement of agrarians, including landless movements, seed savers, Slow Food practitioners, and farmer/peasants threatened universally by declining public support, food imports and land seizures for agro-industrial estates. La Via Campesina (2001) defines food sovereignty in the following way:

> In order to guarantee the independence and food sovereignty of all of the world's peoples, it is essential that food be produced through diversified, farmer-based production systems. Food sovereignty is the right of peoples to define their own agriculture and food policies, to protect and regulate domestic agricultural production and trade in order to achieve sustainable development objectives, to determine the extent to which they want to be self reliant, and to restrict the dumping of products in their markets. Food sovereignty does not negate trade, but rather it promotes the formulation of trade policies and practices that serve the rights of peoples to safe, healthy and ecologically sustainable production.

Trade is thus not ruled out in this vision; rather, it is a question of the regime under which trade occurs. Neither does the anticapitalist resistance represented by La Via Campesina reject the global for the local; rather, it redefines the global in terms appropriate to democratic conditions of food production and distribution. Interpreting the conflict between the French Farmers' Confederation and McDonalds in 1999, Judit Bodnar notes that Jose Bové and his followers destroyed transgenic corn produced by global firms 'not because the seeds are produced by "others" but because of the way they are produced' (Bodnar 2003: 141). Bové and La Via Campesina work from two central premises: first, that the international tensions surrounding food politics ultimately derive not from intergovernmental conflict but from conflict between models of production and rural development – 'a conflict that exists in both the North and the South' (La Via Campesina 2003: 5); and second, that while the struggle is global it is decentralized in content and leadership. Bové thus observes:

> The strength of this global movement is precisely that it differs from place to place ... The world is a complex place, and it would be a mistake to look for a single answer to complex and different phenomena. We have to provide answers at different levels – not just the international level, but local and national levels too.
>
> (Bové and Dufour 2001: 168)

The movement's polycentrism means it simultaneously addresses both state and interstate political relations. In addition, La Via Campesina has created an institutional effect insofar as it 'has emerged as an important arena of actions, debate and exchanges between different national and sub-national peasant and farmers' groups' (Borras 2004: 4–5). When Bové (2001: 96) claims that 'for the people of the South, food sovereignty means the right to protect themselves against imports. For us, it means fighting against export aid and against intensive farming', he identifies the uneven and combined political conditions precipitating the current agrarian crisis. In other words, the food sovereignty movement is not about recovering a mythical peasant past; rather, it is about politicizing the current global food system and its agnostic model of 'food security' (Patel 2007: 90). The food sovereignty movement recognizes that multilateral arrangements have given content to this agnostic form by institutionalizing food security as a private relation through corporate-structured markets (McMichael 2003), and it represents a self-conscious peasant politics in the present for the future. As such, it also transgresses classic agrarian question assumptions about peasant proletarianization (McMichael 2006a).

Returning, then, to Bernstein, for purposes of exposition, he suggests that the classic agrarian question, framed by the various determinations of a developing home market for capital, was

> the agrarian question of capital, and specifically industrial capital. In the context of transition(s) to capitalism, this was also assumed to be the agrarian question of labour as well as capital, inasmuch as these two definitive classes of an emergent capitalism shared a common interest in the overthrow/transformation of feudalism, and of precapitalist social relations and practices more generally.
>
> (Bernstein 2003: 209)

By contrast, today, on a global scale, Bernstein argues that the classic agrarian question is no longer capital's concern, resolved by the over-production of Northern farming, even if unresolved in most of the South, where home markets are undeveloped and labour is chronically fragmented (Bernstein 2003: 210). The common interest of capital and labour in the agrarian question is thereby fractured, leaving only the 'agrarian question of labour' (Bernstein 2004). This representation is apt as far as it goes, but it is constrained by its capital accumulation lens on agrarian relations. Certainly, Bernstein's creative resolution of this agrarian transition as the labour question is informed by the observation that peasantries today 'become petty commodity producers ... when they are unable to reproduce themselves outside the relations and processes of capitalist commodity production, when the latter become the conditions of existence of peasant farming and are internalized in its organization and activity' (Bernstein 2000: 29). While this characterization may not be universally applicable, even the majority to whom it does apply may not subjectively have so much internalized as uti-lized commodity markets to supplement their material needs and/or sustain a frugal and fragile peasant agriculture (Jaffee 2007: 39)[3] – that is, being a petty commodity producer may be necessary, but not sufficient, in defining peasant possibility (McMichael 2006b: 411). More to the point, peasant possibility is actively being redefined and reconstituted through various agrarian mobilizations. Such mobilizations typically involve negotiating a politics of solidarity that goes beyond the particular class positions of indi-viduals, or individual chapters, in the movement (Desmarais 2007: 56).

When the *O Movimento dos Trabalhadores Rurais Sem-Terra* (Landless Rural Workers' Movement, MST) engages in producing staple foods for the Brazilian working poor, rather than foods for affluent consumers, under an arrangement with the da Silva government for the direct purchase of settlement produce for Lula's Zero Hunger campaign (Jardim 2003), the supposedly 'classic' common interest between capital and labour in eliminating pre-capitalist relations has dissipated. It has been replaced by a common interest between peasants and wage labour in reconstituting social reproduction. This is food sovereignty in action. The terms of reference have changed. Certainly wage labour and social reproduction are prominent, but the MST represents one face of the new *campesino* politics that connects not only with other agrarian and indigenous movements advocating cultural sustainability, but also with those with whom peasants share the exclusionary consequences of the neoliberal model. Here, 'the *sem-terra*, the "without-land" movement, has given rise to an urban version, called the *sem-toto* ("without-roof") movement of homeless people' (Wright and Wolford 2003: 429).

Situating food sovereignty

In what follows, I examine two seemingly contradictory relationships defin-ing the food sovereignty movement. The first concerns the strategic location of peasant politics today, and in particular the form of the agrarian question, which I shall provisionally term the 'agrarian question of food', and which centres on a straightforward question: how can a peasant politics make sense in a world-historical conjuncture overwhelmingly dominated by capital? The second concerns the association of peasant politics with the land, which is viewed not as an economic asset but as a cultural relation.

In his method of political economy, Marx critiques the bourgeois tendency to construct economic categories via a developmentalist narrative, where the 'latest form regards the previous ones as steps leading up to itself, and ... it always conceives of them one-sidedly' (Marx 1973: 106, first published 1939–41). This is an epistemological point, which Marx then complicates with his well known methodological directive:

> Capital is the all-dominating economic power of bourgeois society. It must form the starting-point as well as the finishing-point, and must be dealt with before landed property ... It would therefore be unfeasible and wrong to let the economic categories follow one another in the same sequence as that in which they were historically decisive. Their sequence is determined, rather, by their relation to one another in modern bourgeois society, which is precisely the opposite of that which seems to be their natural order or which corresponds to historical development.
>
> (Marx 1973: 107)

In other words, to avoid conceiving of landed property one-sidedly requires an analysis that takes capital as its point of departure. It is not now so much a prior form as it is subsumed by, or incorporated into, the relations of capital. The food sovereignty movement appears to invert this method by privileging landed property – through agrarian reform – and/or preserving precapitalist landed relations: 'Land provides the base for all human life. Land, appropriately called Mother Earth by the natives of the Americas, feeds us: men, women, boys and girls; and we are deeply bound to her' (La Via Campesina 2000b). However, at the same time, as modelled by the MST, beyond the task of settling hundreds of thousands of families on recovered land, the significance of this movement lies in 'linking up what it calls the struggle for the land with the struggle on the land' (Flavio de Almeida and Ruiz Sanchez 2000) – that is, combining a political/ideological struggle with the basic economic struggle of gaining access to land. This involves, as suggested above, both a politics of cooperative labour and rural education in the settlements, and a politics of critique of the agribusiness and neoliberal models through national and transnational alliance-building informed by the concept of food sovereignty. Put another way, MST leader João Pedro Stédile observes:

> From the time of Zapata in Mexico, or of Julião in Brazil, the inspiration for agrarian reform was the idea that the land belonged to those

who worked it. Today we need to go beyond this. It's not enough to argue that if you work the land, you have proprietary rights over it ... We want an agrarian practice that transforms farmers into guardians of the land, and a different way of farming, that ensures an ecological equilibrium and also guarantees that land is not seen as private property.

(Stédile 2002: 100)[4]

In this sense, capital is the point of departure of the food sovereignty movement, in its strategic analysis and political intervention – but this does not mean it accepts a capitalist teleology for agrarian relations. Rather than consign agrarian relations to a narrative of industrial subordination and elimination, or marginalization, of peasant-farmers, the food sovereignty movement constructs an alternative narrative, which works within the context, but against the dictates, of corporate globalization. Just as labour struggles to limit the working day revealed that 'for Marx the history of capital is not a teleology independent of class struggle' (Beverley 2004: 265–266), so peasant resistance – which includes elements of class struggle – seeks to transform, as well as transcend, capital's relations of subjection and its developmentalist teleology. In particular, La Via Campesina seeks to reverse, or denaturalize, dispossession and thereby limit peasant subjection to capital – both materially and discursively. I have argued elsewhere that this is 'the' new agrarian question (McMichael 2006a). Here I posit an 'agrarian question of food' as a way of understanding why a peasant movement has salience in a capital-dominated world.

In the classic agrarian question, food is invisible except insofar as its price affects political relationships and accumulation patterns. In other words, it features only as a commodity, where social relations are expressed in and shaped by objectified exchange relations. Such economic reductionism is consistent with an accumulation fetish. Certainly, Marx's politicization of capital animates analysis of the agrarian transition, insofar as the classic agrarian question was about the political consequences of proletarianization. However, the terms of reference were limited to the narrative of expanded reproduction, notably industrialization. The food sovereignty movement, by contrast, contests these terms of reference, restoring the critique of fetishism. Its historical point of entry is the critique of the concept of food security (McMichael 2003).

The 1996 World Food Summit declared the existence of food security 'at the individual, household, national, regional and global levels ... when all people, at all times, have physical and economic access to sufficient, safe and nutritious food to meet their dietary needs and food preferences for an active and healthy life' (quoted by Patel 2007: 90). As Raj Patel observes, food security 'is agnostic about the production regime, about the social and economic conditions under which food ends up on the table' (Patel 2007: 90). In fact, food security has been appropriated as a private relation ever since US Agriculture Secretary John Block argued in 1986, at the start of the GATT Uruguay Round: 'The idea that developing countries should feed themselves is an anachronism from a bygone era. They could better ensure their food security by relying on US agricultural products, which are available in most cases at lower cost' (quoted by Schaeffer 1995: 269). In the same year, US corn dumped in Zimbabwe forced its grain marketing board to cut domestic farmers' prices almost in half and to reduce its purchase quota from them (Watkins 1996: 43). In this way, food security initiatives passed from Zimbabwean farmers to the international grain traders. The WTO's Agreement on Agriculture institutionalized this relationship in 1995, establishing an artificially cheapened world market price for agricultural commodities. The US Agricultural Secretary's reference to lower-cost product availability was shorthand for a corporate food regime whose discourse naturalizes the market as a site of agricultural efficiency for heavily subsidized and institutionally protected (through free trade agreements) corporate producers. This privileging of the price form through the discourse of food security acts as midwife to capital in general by subordinating agriculture and food to corporate commodity relations (McMichael 2003).

It is this capitalist political conjuncture that food sovereignty politics takes as its point of departure. Its critique of the corporate food regime is levelled squarely at the fetishization of agriculture as a source of cheap market inputs for a mythical global consumer society. Such commodity fetishism subordinates a public good for private profit. The subordination of landed property to capital reproduces everywhere a fundamental contradiction, whereby 'free' markets exclude and/or starve populations dispossessed as a consequence of their implementation, in the name of food security. An associated contradiction is the threat to food cultures and ecologies. Whether the food regime is eliminating peasant culture, generating a 'planet of slums' (Davis 2006), or undermining sustainable biodiversities, its narrative of development essentially invisibilizes a broad swathe of humanity destined for the silent and marginal space of informality, reproduced through a global process of labour casualization (McMichael 1999). In other words, the conceptual universe of the home market, or capital accumulation, is unable to account for such 'structurally redundant' people (Bauman 1999: 22). While this reality is addressed by Bernstein's agrarian question of labour, the conditions giving rise to this question, and the question itself, can only be resolved, justly, by fully awakening Marx's dialectic, by transcending the fetishism of agricultural commodities. In this regard, the food sovereignty movement's genius is to insert a political economy of representation that promises just that (Patel 2006). As Nettie Wiebe stresses,

> that is what the Via Campesina is. It's a movement of people of the land who share a progressive agenda. Which means we share the view that people – small farmers, peasants, people of the land – have a right to be there … That it's our job to look after the earth and our people. We must defend it and we have to defend it in the global context.
>
> (quoted by Desmarais 2002: 98)

It might appear from this that we have a new 'agrarian question of land', a point that is explored by Akram-Lodhi *et al.* in Chapter 9. However, my point is that the 'practical ethic of peasant movement solidarity' (Patel 2006), which advocates the 'peasant way', is not just about land. As La Via Campesina claim, in Polanyian terms:

> We therefore reject the ideology that only considers land as merchandise ... when governments fail to keep their commitment to agrarian reform and just allow the market to govern the distribution of land, they violate the human rights of peasant families who need access to land to fulfill their right to feed themselves as well as other economic, social and cultural human rights.
>
> (La Via Campesina 2000b)

That is, the movement focuses on land reform as a vehicle of food security for those experiencing physical and psychic displacement in the name of a globalized model of agribusiness that, in commodifying nature and food, systematically disrupts peasant and societal social reproduction as a condition of capital's reproduction through processes of 'accumulation by dispossession' (Harvey 2003). The commodification of food, via agro-industrialization, is thus not just about the substitution of industrial, or wage-foods, for peasant foods; it is also fundamentally about how this food regime generates redundant populations and destabilizes social and ecological relationships. For this reason, it is possible to conceive of a contemporary agrarian question of food: first, as a politicization of the corporate discourse of food security; and second, as a politicization of, and fundamental challenge to, the development narrative of agrarian transition at a time when that narrative is increasingly moribund and planet-threatening.

The food sovereignty movement's elaboration of an agrarian narrative includes the revaluing of land as a cultural relation. By this I mean a combination of a politics of place that includes the bioregional and the ancestral with a politics of space that can be expressed in the concept of 'agrarian citizenship' (Wittman 2005). In this, food sovereignty expresses a subjectivity formed historically by the processes of subordination of landed property to capital, including the quickening contradictions of the present world order. Not only is the capitalization of land via market-led agrarian reform, agro-industrial estate zoning, and land accumulation by dispossession displacing peasants; the food regime it fosters displaces food cultures, directly by supply-chain deepening, and indirectly by removal of public subsidies for peasant, and wage, foods. In short, access to land is ultimately a question of social reproduction of agrarian cultures whose self-definition centres on food production. Thus the International Planning Committee on Food Sovereignty noted:

> No agrarian reform is acceptable that is based only on land distribution. We believe that the new agrarian reform must include a cosmic vision of

the territories of communities of peasants, the landless, indigenous peoples, rural workers, fisherfolk, nomadic pastoralists, tribes, afrodescendents, ethnic minorities, and displaced peoples, who base their work on the production of food and who maintain a relationship of respect and harmony with Mother Earth and the oceans.

(La Via Campesina 2006)

The social reproduction of agrarian culture was absent in the classic agrarian question, as it focused on the conditions of social reproduction of capital and their political implications for state formation. Just as craft work was destined to disappear, so were peasantries. Food would be mass-produced through capitalist forms of social labour. Never mind that the conditions of social reproduction of capital depended also on the imperial division of labour, through which, as Mike Davis (2001: 26) remarks, 'Londoners were in effect eating India's bread' at the turn of the twentieth century. Here, the food security and sovereignty of rural India was deeply compromised by the penetration of commercial telegraphic communications that allowed merchants to purchase village grain reserves for sale on the London market. Little has changed, except that now the crisis of social reproduction in the global South is mediated by a politics of rights that was non-existent during colonial times.

In a pre-rights era, food was conceived as an input to lower accumulation costs and provision growing urban populations, as Araghi argues. Peasant mobilization today, in the name of food sovereignty, has brought food to the political centre. In this conjuncture, food is increasingly understood as a source of political identity and substantive rights. It is concretized in the politics of states, in terms of formal and substantive understandings of citizenship, and in the politics of the state system, in terms of formal and substantive understandings of rights. Thus the International Planning Committee on Food Sovereignty challenges states, as members of the inter-state system, to respect food sovereignty, observing that the 'state must play a strong role in policies of agrarian reform and food production', and to accomplish this 'states have the right and the obligation to sovereignty, to define, without external conditions, their own agrarian, agricultural, fishing and food policies in such a way as to guarantee the right to food and the other economic, social and cultural rights of the entire population' (La Via Campesina 2006). However, the obligation to sovereignty entails recognizing the 'laws, traditions, customs, tenure systems, and institutions, as well as the recognition of territorial borders and the cultures of peoples' (La Via Campesina 2006).

Strategically, the food sovereignty movement reasserts the formal Westphalian concept of sovereignty against corporate globalization, yet at the same time advocates a substantive reformulation of sovereignty. Politically, this represents a 'transgressive use of the discourse of rights' (Patel 2007: 91), where La Via Campesina has consistently called for context-specific rights to decide the content of food policy, through the principle of subsidiarity, operationalizing rights democratically. This 'approach to rights is transgressive, insofar as it orients itself not toward the institutions that enshrine, enforce, and police rights, but toward the people who are meant to hold them' (Patel 2007: 92). In this sense, sovereignty is a strategic weapon in a struggle committed to realizing a new politics of subjectivity geared to transforming the state. Historically, this represents an anticapitalist development narrative to reverse the social catastrophe of neoliberal capitalism, and reinsert a substantive agrarian political ecology in order to reconstruct an equitable and sustainable form of social reproduction. Thus the International Planning Committee on Food Sovereignty declares:

> In the context of food sovereignty, agrarian reform benefits all of society, providing healthy, accessible and culturally appropriate food, and social justice. Agrarian reform can put an end to the massive and forced rural exodus from the countryside to the city, which has made cities grow at unsustainable rates and under inhuman conditions.
>
> (La Via Campesina 2006)

More than redistributing land to the tiller, this politics directly addresses the crisis of modernity. In the first instance, the food sovereignty movement can be read as a classic Polanyian countermovement to protect society from the market, but its resolution requires more than this. Beyond a modernist outcome of states regulating markets, the food sovereignty vision potentially transcends the extant state, and its competitive interstate relations, substituting cooperative relations of communities of producers where political authority is multilayered, cosmopolitan and sustaining of social and ecological relationships (McMichael 2005b).

From this perspective, the food sovereignty movement embodies short-term tactical and long-term strategic goals. Short-term episodes of land redistribution and food provisioning for the excluded majority of humanity will continue to be necessary. Strategic reformulations are yet to be realized, but as the old order dies – and, as perhaps evidenced by WTO paralysis, neoliberalism is in its last throes – new possibilities present themselves. Corporate agriculture and its deepening food circuits, associated with the supermarket revolution, is inevitably interweaving social and environmental justice concerns as populations lose more habitat and access to food, water and other resources. Cascading forms of political mobilization – especially emergent in Latin America – and increasing visibility of environmental and economic refugees may, in the short run, promote protectionism, but in the longer run open up new political spaces as the crisis of social reproduction deepens, precipitating new multilateral political arrangements to protect populations, human rights and the ecology of the planet. Food sovereignty is fundamental to these concerns.

An agrarian question of food?

Re-posing the agrarian question is as much an exercise in critique as a preliminary statement of an epistemic shift. The classic agrarian question recognized that capitalist development was founded in the transformation of political relationships, interpreted within a state-centric perspective – despite, and perhaps because of, imperialism. As a question regarding the trajectory of capitalism, it was certainly time-bound, in the sense that revolutionary politics were focused in the first instance on the state. Not only was this period distinguished by state formation, but also the food regime was instrumental in constructing national economic sectors. The settler states, lacking a feudal past, emerged through a dynamic articulation of national farm and manufacturing sectors, assisted by access to foreign trade and investment (Friedmann and McMichael 1989). However, at the same time, this was a period in which the foundations for agricultural outsourcing emerged, and the historical structure of capital accumulation depended on a world market. For this reason, the characterization of Terry Byres' three-dimensional agrarian question, discussed by Bernstein (Chapter 10) – the historic confrontation of landed property by capital, the balance of political forces in relation to agrarian transition, and the role of agricultural capital in accumulation – requires qualification. All three dimensions are apposite, but insofar as they are interpreted through the national lens, they tend to dehistoricize capitalism, paradoxically promoting a historicist understanding of capitalist transition. In particular, they discount the world-historical relations underpinning agrarian transition in the European capitalist state.

These relations have since intensified, so that agrarian transformations are now profoundly global. Whether this is a logical maturation of capitalism as a world force, or a deepening of late-nineteenth century capitalist relations across a twentieth century protectionist interlude associated with the universalization of the state system (see, for example, Halperin 2004), the terms of reference of the classic agrarian question have altered profoundly. These terms now situate the peasant question within the multiple impacts of transnational circuits of money, food and labour on states and their citizen-subjects. The agrarian question continues to be about capital and labour relations. However, these relations, being historical, must be defined within and through the new world-historical conjuncture of financialization (Arrighi 1994), neoliberalism (Harvey 2005) and the corporate food regime (McMichael 2005a). Their historical specificity includes the transformation of the nation-state system, as a relation of production (Sayer 1987), under the combined institutions of privatization and liberalization to accommodate transnational capital mobility. As suggested above, the attention paid to the embedding of the relations of production in relations of circulation by La Via Campesina underscores the politics the food system.

Transforming the state in this way, as a relation of production, involves a dual process of accumulation by dispossession (Harvey 2003), which in turn precipitates the crisis of social reproduction. In the first instance, within the mandates of neoliberalism, as states author liberalization through free trade agreements, they privatize public assets and reformulate the terms of citizenship and development, defining them as the consumption of market services. In rural areas, peasant-farmers experience withdrawal of farm sector protections and rural subsidies, allowing land and agriculture itself to be accumulated in corporate hands as dispossession proceeds. Where episodes of land reform in the development era, inspired by peasant insurgency and Cold War politics, proclaimed a modernization and democratization of landed property relations, abandonment of this politics expresses a new, post-Cold War phase in the reconstitution of rural subjects as market entrepreneurs. The urban counterpart involves dismantling social programmes, under austerity conditions ostensibly to qualify for debt repayment loans, thus reneging on the social contract with citizen-subjects established in the era of the 'development project'.

In the second instance of accumulation by dispossession, the original process of primitive accumulation, which 'entails appropriation and co-optation of pre-existing cultural and social achievements' (Harvey 2003: 146), is enabled by states. Here non-capitalist social forms, including indigenous knowledges, genetic resources, and other natural resources such as biodiversity and water, are released into the corporate marketplace by new protocols and policies of the neoliberal moment. In the name of global food security, and with multilateral agency support and/or dictate, governments progressively privatize the commons in order to participate in the development of a world agriculture based on the promise of market efficiencies, contributing simultaneously to their foreign exchange reserves – typically for debt repayment – and the deepening of consumer-led development.

The precondition for private accumulation in, and through, commercialized agriculture is the elimination of alternative and pre-existing peasant agricultures. Such abstraction of food production accentuates hunger among, and dispossesses, rural majorities across the global South, deepening the role of states as population containment zones, and compromising their civic role. It is for this reason that the food sovereignty movement advocates an agrarian citizenship (Wittman 2005) dedicated to a tactic of reterritorializing states through revitalizing local food ecologies under the stewardship of the peasant way: 'The government should introduce policies to restore the economic condition of small farmers by providing fair allocation of these production resources to farmers, recognizing their rights as producers of society, and recognizing community rights in managing local resources' (La Via Campesina 2005: 31).

Agrarian citizenship is a tactic insofar as it appeals to the authority of the nation-state system to protect the farmers, as guardian of the commons. It is a strategic intervention in the politics of development insofar as it advocates for peasant-farmer rights to initiate social reproduction. In other words, the demand is for rights to be exercised as a means to a social end, rather than an end in itself. Whereas the United Nations Declaration on Human Rights defined citizenship as an individual right, as the 'realization, through national effort and international co-operation and in accordance with the organization and resources of each State, of the economic, social, and cultural rights indispensable for his dignity and the free development of his personality' (quoted by Clarke and Barlow 1997: 9), the agrarians view rights as a 'means to mobilizing' social relations (Patel 2007: 88). In this mobilization, food is at the centre of the social equation, and, as Raj Patel insists, this is

> a call for a mass re-politicization of food politics, through a call for people to figure out for themselves what they want the right to food to mean in their communities, bearing in mind the community's needs, climate, geography, food preferences, social mix, and history ... More important, though, is the building of a sustainable and widespread process of democracy that can provide political direction to the appropriate level of government required to see implementation through to completion.
>
> (Patel 2007: 91)

Arguably, while I may refer to this as an agrarian question of food, my point is that food is a touchstone for a potentially far more profound political intervention to transcend the depeasantization scenario embedded in the development narrative. An agrarian question of food, in reformulating the development episteme, symbolizes a politics that reaches beyond the conventional and extant coordinates of political and social life. Just as La Via Campesina opposes the G-20 demand for a uniform agricultural liberalization to equalize free trade for agro-exports from the global South, because it would only privilege agribusiness corporations under a WTO regime, so too the food sovereignty movement at large embodies a strategic transformation of political institutions based on a global moral economy. Thus, a revamped United Nations Commission on Trade and Development, and various multilateral agencies dedicated to fair trade and so forth, constitute part of the proposed infrastructure of an alternative food regime, in relation to which Jose Bové asks: 'Why should the global market escape the rule of international law or human rights conventions passed by the United Nations?' (Bové and Defour 2001: 165). Materially, the regulation of food production and circulation via principles of justice and equity implicates other social and political relationships. Symbolically, centering food in the development equation reframes it. Instead of viewing it as a complement, or an input, to the processes of accumulation and development, it moves to the centre of the plate, so to speak, in two senses.

An agrarian question of food represents a critique of extant relations of production and social reproduction. Echoing Peter Kropotkin's (1892) claim that the 'question of bread' was the pre-eminent social question of the time,

Amory Starr proposes that the global anticapitalist movement for diversity is best summarized as agricultural,

> encompassing first world farmers seeking market protection, farmers resisting genetic engineering, indigenous sovereignty movements seeking to control land and practices, sustainable development, localist economic visions, and third world peasant movements reacting to the failures of urbanization and neoliberalism by insisting on rights to land and subsistence. These movements have a variety of relationships to political economy, formal democracy and existing nations. But none imagines that growth, modernization or technology provide answers to their problems; indeed they see corporate technology as economically and ecologically dangerous.
>
> (Starr 2001: 224)

In this sense, the food sovereignty movement's challenge to the corporate food regime is embedded in a broader political challenge that anticipates Colin Duncan's (1996) social and ecological claims for the centrality of agriculture. Duncan suggests that

> the proper scaffolding for a well-founded, hence potentially permanent, socialism would be a complex pattern of federated interacting elements of the world's dispersed population, each of which would be aware that they severally and collectively live within a living environment into whose local cycles they must insert their agricultural and industrial activities. There would be a complex division of labour but it would involve several scales of social entity – neighbourhood, municipality, region, and so on up to global levels – many tied to places ... This conception, which accords centrality to agriculture, must explicitly deal with the obvious, albeit misconceived, charge that it tends to counsel an antimodern, even 'peasantist', approach to social questions ... The key point is denial of the claim that all cases of modernity depend(ed) necessarily on marginalizing agriculture.
>
> (Duncan 1996: 48–49)

The point of such blueprints is to envision ways in which social life can be reconstituted around alternative principles that respect the ecological relations through which social reproduction occurs. Whether, and to what extent, humanity will move in this direction is, in fact, what the agrarian question of food implies; it is recentering agriculture. The significance of the food sovereignty movement is that it comes, as it were, from the margins. In social science terms, as well as those of the market episteme, a 'peasantist' approach to social questions is almost incomprehensible, as marginalizing 'agro-culture' is so deeply embedded in the narratives of developmentalism and capitalism. Analysis of social movements routinely proceeds via the methodological tools at hand; that is, bourgeois categories of thought, which misread movements from the margins that, while framing their struggle in conventional discursive terms – such as sovereignty and agrarian reform – nevertheless may offer resolutions expressing an alternative ontology. The key to understanding the food sovereignty movement is precisely to recognize its peasantist ontology, so long as it is not confused with peasant essentialism (Brass 2000), and is understood as a method of posing an alternative modernity.

Conclusions

David Harvey (2005: 23) distinguishes contemporary antiglobalization resistances as 'movements against accumulation by dispossession'. In this conception, peasant mobilization, insofar as it resists displacement, declining public supports for small farming, and assaults on environments, knowledges and cultures, can be contrasted with movements around expanded reproduction, where the 'exploitation of wage labour and conditions defining the social wage are the central issues' (Harvey 2005: 23). His admonition that finding 'the organic link between these different movements is an urgent theoretical and practical task' (Harvey 2005: 23) is salutary, and points towards analysis of uneven development. My point is that these resistances are not separate, and that the organic link is implicit in La Via Campesina's linking of the accelerated circulation of food to the accelerated displacement and circulation of people, whether they are peasants or ex-peasants. That is, the corporate food regime conditions the trajectory of wage labour and the social wage precisely by reproducing an expendable global wage labour force (McMichael 1999, 2005a). In addition, if one views these dynamics solely through the capital/wage labour prism, the agrarian scenario is rendered inconsequential or invisible. Arguably, it takes the voice of the peasant movement to articulate a more complex perspective on the contemporary crisis of capitalism.

In generating a planet of slums, neoliberal capitalism has, in effect, inverted the problematic of the original agrarian question. Where capital may precede landed property as the proper methodological point of departure, capital's wholesale domination of landed property relations through agro-industrialization renders the politics of food – and the land – central to understanding the crisis of capitalism. La Via Campesina, as a contemporary political mobilization, forces acknowledgement of this nexus. This is because it is not just about class structure on the land – the classical agrarian question – nor simply about land reform, and it is certainly not about a 'romantic view of the ("peasant") alternative to contemporary capitalist agriculture/agribusiness' (Bernstein 2006: 458 fn). Beyond a simplistic either/or scenario, the agrarian countermovement engages with political economy writ large. It involves developing a praxis premised on a critique of the conditions of the global movement of capital at this historical moment.

It is a class politics with an ethical, historical and ecological sensibility aimed at the machinations of the state system in converting agriculture to a world industry for profit. As such, it concerns questions of rights, social reproduction and sustainability, rather than the questions of teleology, class and accumulation deriving from a productivist understanding of capital and its historical movement. For this reason, I suggest that the food sovereignty movement is an agrarian question of food, with all that this implies.

The food sovereignty movement not only introduces a substantive rights-driven food politics to 'move away from productivist language to a discourse of "growers and eaters"' (Patel 2007: 91), rendering food relations context-specific and subject to democratic practices at local, national and multi-lateral scales (Friedmann 2003). It also revalues agriculture and food, and, most of all, agrarian peoples, in an attempt to stem – and reverse – the dynamic and discourse of depeasantization that is associated with capitalist development (McMichael 2006a). To politicize and denaturalize food relations is to open up the question of the food regime itself, in a perspective combining its enabling conditions with its social and ecological consequences. Politicizing food relations takes capital as the point of analytical departure, but capital as a relation of production and of circulation. That is, the contradictions of the food regime are not simply about class relations, but are also about the associated political relations that enable the 'massive movement of food around the world' (La Via Campesina 2000a), dispossessing populations of their land and livelihood, and undermining social reproduction. A romantic would argue that the agrarian countermovement is a defensive manoeuvre, destined to fail. The argument here is that the transformation of rural subjectivity is not confined to defending property or territory, but includes re-envisioning the conditions necessary to develop sustainable and democratic forms of social reproduction.

The food sovereignty movement spotlights the relationship between corporate agriculture and the crisis of social reproduction, especially in the South, where the planet of slums catastrophe unfolds. This human ecological disaster will intensify as desertification in some regions, floods in others, salinization of depleted acquifers, rising sea levels in coastal regions, and so on, drive more environmental refugees into camps, slums and migrant labour streams. How these developments will affect the state system and generate new institutional relations to manage the global commons is an open question. However, the food sovereignty movement answers a key dimension of this question by demanding and practising a reversal of the cycles of dispossession in the name of, first, stabilizing social reproduction for the world's majority and, second, building an ethical complex of sovereignty, sufficiency and sustainability into a reformulated development paradigm. In this sense, an agrarian question of food is a key to unlocking the fetishism of accumulation and addressing its damaging socioecological consequences.

Notes

1 I am grateful to Raj Patel for thoughtful feedback on a previous version of this essay.

2 This can be compared with William Roseberry's (1982: 208) admonition that 'the "peasant" concept should not be discarded because the historical movement of which peasants have been a part is still unresolved'. In this sense, the agrarian question is really a question, with the 'peasant question' as a constituent part, posed and answered historically, rather than theoretically – meaning that there is every reason why the agrarian question can be asked by the peasantry, insofar as it is present in the making of history, rather than being the passive recipient, or theoretical residue, of history.

3 For example, Timothy Mitchell's account of a rural community in southern Egypt in the 1990s documents examples of peasant households which

> were involved in production for the market, but its purpose was to support the much larger system of self-provisioning. This was true for the village as a whole, and probably for the entire country ... Rather than a subsistence sector surviving in support of capitalism, market crops, protected and promoted by the state, survived in support of self-provisioning.
>
> (Mitchell 2002: 255)

Note that Cristóbal Kay (2006: 473) observes that for 'poor peasant households RNFE (rural non-farm employment) is a key mechanism to retain access to their small plot of land and to maintain a subsistence income. Meanwhile for rich peasant households it is a way to accumulate more capital'.

4 This can be compared with the argument made by Wendy Wolford (2007) that land reform is 'fundamentally about *labor*'. While I would not disagree with Wolford's argument regarding the right to labour, and appreciate her documentation of the confusion among MST settlers in north-eastern Brazil over according 'priority to property ownership or to labor on the land', her research, and this argument, demonstrate the inevitable tensions in a transnational movement such as La Via Campesina, which negotiates between immediate jurisdictional realities faced by its national chapters and a longer-term politics, articulated by Stédile, of attempting to 'transform the very political order in which they operate' (Alvarez *et al.* 1998: 8). There is a difference between leadership goals and rank and file subjectivities, where the latter often constitute a counterdiscourse in the process of land occupation – as cogently documented by Wolford (2006). Ultimately, Wolford (2007) and Bernstein (2004) appear to converge on the point that land reform is a condition for the exercise of labour on the land. Whether this is also a question of a new form and sensibility of a labour-based class politics is generally left unexplored – although see James Petras's suggestive characterization of Latin American new peasant movements as being 'strongly influenced by a blend of classical Marxism and, in differing contexts, by ethnic, gender, and ecological considerations' (Petras 1997: 21).

References

Alvarez, S.E., E. Dagnino and A. Escobar (eds) (1998) *Culture of Politics: Politics of Culture – Re-envisioning Latin American Social Movements*, Boulder, CO: Westview Press.

Arrighi, G. (1994) *The Long Twentieth Century: Money, Power and the Origins of Our Times*, London: Verso.

Bauman, Z. (1999) 'The burning of popular fear', *New Internationalist*, 310, 20–22.

Bernstein, H. (2000) '"The peasantry" in global capitalism: who, where, and why?', in L. Panitch, C. Leys, G. Albo and D. Coates (eds), *Socialist Register 2001: Working Classes, Global Realities*, London: Merlin.

—— (2003) 'Land reform in Southern Africa in world-historical perspective', *Review of African Political Economy*, 96: 203–226.

—— (2004) '"Changing before our very eyes": agrarian questions and the politics of land in capitalism today', *Journal of Agrarian Change*, 4 (1/2): 190–225.

—— (2006) 'Is there an agrarian question in the 21st century?', *Canadian Journal of Development Studies*, 27 (4): 449–460.

Beverley, J. (2004) 'Subaltern resistance in Latin America: a reply to Tom Brass', *Journal of Peasant Studies*, 31 (2): 261–275.

Bodnar, J. (2003) 'Roquefort vs Big Mac: globalization and its others', *Archives Européennes de Sociologie*, XLIV (1): 133–144.

Bové, J. (2001) 'A movement of movements? A farmers' international?', *New Left Review*, 12: 89–101.

Bové, J. and F. Dufour (2001) *The World Is Not For Sale*, London: Verso.

Borras, S.M., Jr (2004) *La Via Campesina: An Evolving Transnational Social Movement*, Briefing Series No. 2004/6, Amsterdam: Transnational Institute.

Brass, T. (2000) *Peasants, Populism and Postmodernism: The Return of the Agrarian Myth*, London: Frank Cass.

Clarke, T. and M. Barlow (1997) *MAI: The Multilateral Agreement on Investment and the Threat to Canadian Sovereignty*, Toronto: Stoddart.

Davis, M. (2001) *Late Victorian Holocausts: El Niño Famines and the Making of the Third World*, London: Verso.

—— (2006) *Planet of Slums*, London: Verso.

Desmarais, A.A. (2002) 'The Via Campesina: consolidating an international peasant and farm movement', *Journal of Peasant Studies*, 29 (2): 91–124.

—— (2007) *La Via Campesina: Globalization and the Power of Peasants*, Point Black/ Nova Scotia/London: Fernwood Books/Pluto Press.

Duncan, C. (1996) *The Centrality of Agriculture: Between Humankind and the Rest of Nature*, Montreal: McGill Queen's University Press.

Flavio de Almeida, L. and F. Ruiz Sanchez (2000) 'The landless workers' movement and social struggles against neoliberalism', *Latin American Perspectives*, 22 (5): 11–32.

Friedland, W. (1994) 'The new globalization: the case of fresh produce', in A. Bonanno, L. Busch, W. Friedland, L. Gouveia and E. Mingione (eds), *From Columbus to ConAgra: The Globalization of Agriculture and Food*, Lawrence, KS: University of Kansas Press.

Friedmann, H. (1978) 'World market, state and family farm: social bases of household production in an era of wage labour', *Comparative Studies in Society and History*, 20 (4): 545–586.

—— (1982) 'The political economy of food: the rise and fall of the postwar international food order', *American Journal of Sociology*, 88S: 248–286.

—— (2003) 'Eating in the gardens of Gaia: envisioning polycultural communities', in J. Adams (ed.), *Fighting for the Farm: Rural America Transformed*, Philadelphia, PA: University of Pennsylvania Press.

—— (2005) 'From colonialism to green capitalism: social movements and emergence of food regimes', in F.H. Buttel and P. McMichael (eds), *New Directions in the Sociology of Global Development*, Oxford: Elsevier.

Friedmann, H. and P. McMichael (1989) 'Agriculture and the state system: the rise and fall of national agricultures, 1870 to the present', *Sociologia Ruralis*, 29 (2): 93–117.

Halperin, S. (2004) *War and Social Change in Modern Europe: The Great Transformation Revisited*, Cambridge: Cambridge University Press.

Harvey, D. (2003) *The New Imperialism*, Oxford: Oxford University Press.

—— (2005) *A Brief History of Neoliberalism*, Oxford: Oxford University Press.

Heffernan, W. and D. Constance (1994) 'Transnational corporations and the globalization of the food system', in A. Bonanno, L. Busch, W. Friedland, L. Gouveia and E. Mingione (eds), *From Columbus to ConAgra: The Globalization of Agriculture and Food*, Lawrence, KS: University of Kansas Press.

Jaffee, D. (2007) *Brewing Justice: Fair Trade Coffee, Sustainability and Survival*, Berkeley, CA, USA: University of California Press.

Jardim, C. (2003) 'Interview with João Pedro Stédile (MST)', *Brasil de Fato*, 10–16 July.

Kautsky, K. (1988) *The Agrarian Question, Vol. 2*, London: Zwan Publications (first published in 1899).

Kay, C. (2006) 'Rural poverty and development strategies in Latin America', *Journal of Agrarian Change*, 6 (4): 455–508.

Kropotkin, P. (1892) *La Conquète du Pain*, Paris: Stock.

La Via Campesina (2000a) 'Declaration of the International Meeting of the Landless in San Pedro Sula', online: www.viacampesina.org/main_en/index.php?option = com_content&task = view&id = 87&Itemid = 27

—— (2000b) 'Bangalore Declaration of The Via Campesina', online: www.via-campesina.org/main_en/index.php?option = com_content&task = view&id = 53&Itemid = 28

—— (2001) 'Our world is not for sale: priority to peoples' food sovereignty', online: www.citizen.org/documents/wtooutoffood.pdf

—— (2003) 'Statement on agriculture after Cancun', online: www.viacampesina.org/main_en/index2.php?option = com_content&do_pdf = 1&id = 388

—— (2005) 'Impact of the WTO on peasants in South East Asia and East Asia', online: www.viacampesina.org/main_en/images/stories/lvcbooksonwto.pdf

—— (2006) 'For a new agrarian reform based on food sovereignty'. online: www.foodsovereignty.org/new/statement.pdf

Lenin, V.I. (1972) *The Development of Capitalism in Russia*, in *Collected Works, Vol. 3*, Moscow: Progress Publishers (first published in 1899).

Marx, K. (1973) *Grundrisse*, New York: Vintage (first published in 1939–41).

McMichael, P. (1999) 'The global crisis of wage labour', *Studies in Political Economy*, 58: 11–40.

—— (2003) 'Food security and social reproduction', in S. Gill and I. Bakker (eds), *Power, Production and Social Reproduction*, New York: Palgrave Macmillan.

—— (2004) *Development and Social Change: A Global Perspective* (3rd edn), Thousand Oaks, CA, USA: Pine Forge Press.

—— (2005a) 'Global development and the corporate food regime', in F.H. Buttel and P. McMichael (eds), *New Directions in the Sociology of Global Development*, Oxford: Elsevier.

—— (2005b) 'Globalization', in T. Janoski, R. Alford, A. Hicks and M. Schwartz (eds), *The Handbook of Political Sociology*, New York: Cambridge University Press.

—— (2006a) 'Reframing development: global peasant movements and the new agrarian question', *Canadian Journal of Development Studies*, 27 (4): 471–483.

—— (2006b) 'Peasant prospects in a neo-liberal age', *New Political Economy*, 11 (3): 407–418.

McMichael, P. and H. Friedmann (2007) 'Situating the retailing revolution', in G. Lawrence and D. Burch (eds), *Supermarkets and Agri-food Supply Chains: Transformations in the Production and Consumption of Foods*, Cheltenham: Elgar.

Mitchell, T. (2002) *Rule of Experts: Egypt, Techno-Politics, Modernity*, Berkeley, CA: University of California Press.

Moore Jr, B. (1967) *Social Origins of Dictatorship and Democracy: Lord and Peasant in the Making of the Modern World*, Boston, MA, USA: Beacon Press.

Patel, R. (2006) 'International agrarian restructuring and the practical ethics of peasant movement solidarity', *Journal of Asian and African Studies*, 41 (1/2): 71–93.

—— (2007) 'Transgressing rights: La Via Campesina's call for food sovereignty', *Feminist Economics*, 13 (1): 87–116.

Petras, J. (1997) 'Latin America: the resurgence of the left', *New Left Review*, 223: 17–47.

Polanyi, K. (1957) *The Great Transformation: The Political and Economic Origins of Our Times*, Boston, MA, USA: Beacon.

Roseberry, W. (1982) *Coffee and Capitalism in the Venezuelan Andes*, Austin, TX: University of Texas Press.

Rosset, P. (2006) *Food is Different: Why We Must Get the WTO out of Agriculture*, London: Zed Books.

Sayer, D. (1987) *The Violence of Abstraction*, London: Blackwell.

Schaeffer, R. (1995) 'Free trade agreements: their impact on agriculture and the environment', in P. McMichael (ed.), *Food and Agrarian Orders in the World-Economy*, Westport, CT, USA: Praeger.

Starr, A. (2001) *Naming the Enemy: Anti-Corporate Movements Confront Globalization,* London: Zed Books.

Stédile, J.P. (2002) 'Landless battalions', *New Left Review*, 15: 77–104.

Wolf, E. (1969) *Peasant Wars of the Twentieth Century*, New York/London: Harper and Row.

Watkins, K. (1996) 'Free trade and farm fallacies: from the Uruguay Round to the World Food Summit', *The Ecologist*, 26 (6): 244–255.

Wittman, H. (2005) 'The social ecology of agrarian reform: the Landless Rural Workers' Movement and agrarian citizenship in Mato Grosso, Brazil', PhD thesis, Development Sociology, Cornell University.

Wolford, W. (2006) 'The difference ethnography can make: understanding social mobilization and development in the Brazilian northeast', *Qualitative Sociology*, 29 (3): 335–352.

Wolford, W. (2007) 'Land reform in the time of neo-liberalism: a many splendored thing', *Antipode*, 39 (3): 550–570.

Wright, A. and W. Wolford (2003) *To Inherit the Earth: The Landless Movement and the Struggle for a New Brazil*, San Francisco, CA: Food First Books.

Part 4

The Agrarian Question, Past and Present

13 Neoliberal globalization, the traits of rural accumulation and rural politics

The agrarian question in the twenty-first century

A. Haroon Akram-Lodhi and Cristóbal Kay

Introduction

This book explores the fate of the peasantry in a contemporary world that is subject to apparently ceaseless agrarian change. Following the introductory chapter, in the second part of the book, the historical trajectories of agrarian change and their implications for peasant livelihoods in the contemporary world food system are examined, in contributions by Ellen Meiksins Wood, Terence J. Byres, Farshad Araghi, Amiya Kumar Bagchi and Miguel Teubal. The third part surveys a series of competing perspectives as to whether – and if so, how – changes in world agriculture have transformed the location of food and agricultural production within contemporary global capitalism, and in so doing are contributing to processes that will ultimately undermine the livelihoods of the global peasantry. This part includes contributions from Ray Kiely, Bridget O'Laughlin, Henry Bernstein, Michael J. Watts, Philip McMichael, and Haroon Akram-Lodhi, Cristóbal Kay and Saturnino M. Borras, Jr.

The analytical framework shared by the contributors to this volume, to a lesser or greater extent, is that of the 'agrarian question': the extent to which capitalism is or is not transforming agriculture, the impact of such transformation for accumulation, and the consequences for rural politics. In this book, six alternative interpretations of the contemporary relevance of the agrarian question, as it was classically conceived, have been explored. At the risk of oversimplification, the contributors to this volume can largely be located within one of these alternative interpretations – although admittedly they themselves might not subscribe to our categorization. Ray Kiely critically explores the terms and conditions of access to wage labour, in that it is, in the approach most famously laid out by Bill Warren, seen as the central dynamic process in the development of agrarian capitalism, a source of socioeconomic and spatial differentiation, and a propellant of capitalist industrialization. We label this approach the 'path-dependent agrarian question', or AQ1. Farshad Araghi focuses on the way in which the food regime of capital in the era of postcolonial neoliberal globalism is a direct continuation of that initially established during the period of colonial–liberal globalism, and argues that the peasant question of our times must emphasize the ways in which global value relations have simultaneously established the under-reproduction of surplus migratory labour and the subsidized consumption and overconsumption of dominant classes in the global North. We label this approach the 'global reserve army of labour agrarian question', or AQ2. Ellen Meiskins Wood, Amiya Bagchi, Terence Byres, Michael Watts, and Haroon Akram-Lodhi, Cristóbal Kay and Saturnino Borras, Jr broadly develop a set of arguments that are probably closest to the original terrain of the agrarian question as proposed by both Karl Kautsky and Vladimir Lenin, suggesting, in essence, that struggles within and between differentiating peasantries and emergent or dominant class forces are highly contingent, subject to substantive diversity, and are embedded within historical trajectories of variation that reflect processes of differential incorporation into capitalism operating both within capitalist states and on a global scale. We label this the 'class forces agrarian question', or AQ3. Henry Bernstein argues in essence that the contemporary struggle over rural livelihoods is spatially fragmented and is increasingly divorced from transnational capital, for which the agrarian question has been resolved as it allocates resources and technology globally in the quest for enhanced rates of surplus value. This reflects, in the case of Bernstein's reassertion of the centrality of the agrarian question of increasingly fragmented classes of rural labour struggling to construct a livelihood, an emphasis that shares Friedrich Engels' concern with the politics of the agrarian question. We label this the 'decoupled agrarian question', or AQ4. Bridget O'Laughlin argues strongly that, while there are elements of AQ1, AQ3 and AQ4 that can be witnessed in the Southern African region today, a failure to address the gender dimensions of production, accumulation and politics renders any understanding of the Southern African agrarian question, at best, highly partial. We label this the 'gendered agrarian question', or AQ5. Finally, Philip McMichael proposes that it is necessary to reframe the problematic of the agrarian question, defining it both within and through the new world-historical conjuncture of financialization, neoliberalism, and the establishment of a global corporate food regime, as well as situating capital as a relation of production and of circulation. Together, this allows, for McMichael, the politicization of the economic and the definition of the contemporary agrarian question as one of food. Doing this, he argues, addresses the fetishization of agriculture and politicizes a corporate food regime that subordinates public good for private profit. It also, critically, accommodates global peasant resistance, which has developed a praxis premised on a critique of the conditions of the global movement of capital at this historical conjuncture, focusing on the global politics of food in an effort to transform, as well as transcend, capital's relations of subjection and its developmentalist teleology. Thus, argues McMichael, the contemporary global agrarian crisis requires reframing the agrarian question as one of food, which embeds relations of production in relations of circulation, and in so doing opens up the possibility of rural transformation predicated on the social and ecological justice that is central to the food sovereignty movement. We label this the 'corporate food regime agrarian question', or AQ6, and it is a perspective also shared by Miguel Teubal.

This book thus focuses on: rural livelihoods in a contemporary world undergoing ongoing and incessant capitalist restructuring in farming; factors in restructuring that may contribute to or inhibit rural capital accumulation; and the political role of the balance of forces in both contributing to and being effected by these processes of restructuring. However, what have been, perhaps, less stressed are the traits of contemporary rural accumulation itself in an era of neoliberal globalization: its specific features, attributes and characteristics, and the implication of these traits for our understanding of the agrarian question. Granted, Henry Bernstein in this volume explores some of the traits of contemporary accumulation, arguing that rural accumulation is now not important for global capital, while Michael Watts has sought to clarify some of the specific characteristics of global agriculture, arguing in particular about the emergence of 'new agricultures and new peasants', the role of urban agriculture, postsocialist peasants and indigeneity. Both chapters serve to reinforce the point that understanding the traits of rural accumulation in an era of neoliberal globalization is extremely important when evaluating the salience or otherwise of the agrarian question in the contemporary period. This, then, is the purpose of this chapter: to explore the contemporary traits of accumulation in rural economies in developing and transition countries, in order to establish whether any generalities can be established and, as a consequence, to confirm or deny the continued salience of the agrarian question.

Neoliberal traits of accumulation

Neoliberal globalization and what in Chapter 9 we, along with Saturnino Borras, Jr, term 'neoliberal agrarian restructuring' has, as we have seen in this book, altered the land-, labour- and capital-intensity of production, reconfiguring the rural production process in ways that may, or may not, affect processes that expand the commodification of labour and alter the purpose of production from production for use to production for exchange. These changes effect and reflect deeper transformations in the relationship between people and rural production, and have thus profoundly altered the terrain on which the agrarian question is played out. This is witnessed particularly in the impact of neoliberal agrarian restructuring on rural accumulation strategies.

During the heyday of agrarian reform, particularly during the 1950s and early 1960s, an explicit objective of state policy was, as discussed by Farshad Araghi in his contribution to this book, in line with the prevailing Keynesianism of the period and in response to pressure from peasant movements, to use state intervention as a means of boosting domestic demand through an expansion of the home market. Increased domestic demand was expected, through its facilitation of growth, to be a principal transmission mechanism by which rural accumulation would proceed, and hence, in the explicitly articulated rhetoric of governments, poverty reduction would be achieved and income distribution improved.

The traits of accumulation have significantly changed in the past two decades as a consequence of neoliberal globalization. In particular, the emphasis on the expansion of the home market that previously prevailed during the mid-twentieth century has been largely, but not completely, replaced by an emphasis on the promotion of an agricultural export-led strategy as the principal means of enhancing rural accumulation. Thus, in a range of diverse countries in Africa, Asia and Latin America, efforts have been made to deepen agricultural integration into global economic flows and agro-food commodity chains as a means of boosting access to foreign resources, facilitating debt repayments, increasing funds for investment, promoting technological change, boosting rural productivity and profits, and, it was therefore proposed by governments and international development institutions, facilitating an expansion of the sway of the market in both agricultural and non-agricultural sectors. In other words, integration into the global economy – globalization – has been argued by neoliberals to be the most effective means of enhancing rates of accumulation, in the rural economy and more generally. This is starkly witnessed in the rural development policies flowing from the analysis contained in the World Bank's (2007) important *World Development Report 2008: Agriculture for Development*.

Conversely, our understanding of the contemporary traits of accumulation are derived from Marx's analysis of 'reproduction schemas' elaborated in *Capital Vol. II* (Marx 1956, first published 1885), as developed by E.V.K. Fitzgerald (1985), following Kalecki (1969). What is common in this lineage is that the traits of capital accumulation are understood to be a consequence of the character of the interrelationships between economic sectors. Here, rather than focusing on the relationship between the capital goods and wage goods sectors, as did Marx, or the relationship between three sectors in the 'peripheral socialist economy', as did Fitzgerald, we propose simply to focus on the relationship between agricultural export production and peasant production for the domestic market. Under neoliberal globalization, many countries in the South have sought to increase agricultural exports. What we suggest here is slightly different: that the character of the relationship between these two agricultural subsectors has important consequences for the dynamics of rural accumulation. In particular, we propose that those countries that have sought to foster increases in agricultural exports as a principal mechanism to increase rates of rural accumulation can be, admittedly crudely, subdivided into two groups, which have different traits of accumulation, and within which there is nonetheless substantive diversity. In the first group are countries with significant, if asymmetrical, linkages between the export and peasant production subsectors. In the second group are countries where linkages between the two subsectors are much weaker, if they exist at all. As we demonstrate in the following sections, differences in inter-subsectoral linkages appear to have an important impact on the traits of accumulation.

Accumulation with significant inter-subsectoral linkages

We identify a first group of countries, such as Brazil and Vietnam, where, notwithstanding the processes of market-led land concentration stressed by Akram-Lodhi *et al.* (Chapter 9), and termed by Araghi in this volume as 'accumulation by displacement and/or dispossession', significant linkages between the export-oriented and peasant production subsectors has facilitated an asymmetrical but nonetheless mutually reinforcing expansion of both subsectors, and consequently domestic demand (Carter and Barham 1996; Gwynne and Kay 2004).[1] In both, in terms of rates of rural accumulation, the agricultural export sector now drives growth that, through its impact on product prices and wages, fosters increases in domestic demand in the rural economy in the first instance, but also more generally in the economy as a whole.

In this process in Brazil, agro-food transnational corporations play an important role, whether through their direct involvement in rural production in the form of capitalist farming, plantations, contract farming or the engagement of wage labour; or whether through the somewhat more indirect marketing and distribution activities that link domestic capitalist farms, plantations and peasant production with the global agro-food complex and its buyer-driven commodity chains. These exchange relationships are hierarchical, with agro-food transnational corporations engaged in both production and distribution able to 'regulate', in Bernstein's (1996) sense of the word, the activities of domestic agents at earlier stages of the commodity chain. To reiterate the point of O'Laughlin, this regulation is subject to both class and gender dynamics. Brazil is notable for the degree of asymmetry between the export-oriented and peasant subsectors, in that alongside rapid rates of accumulation there are high degrees of poverty and inequality and, for many, marked food insecurity.

In Vietnam, by way of contrast, state-owned enterprises engaged principally in marketing and distribution play an important role in linking smallholder and state-owned plantation production to export markets, and thus domestic production with the global economy, even though the returns to smallholder and plantation production may be less than might be the case as a result of rent-seeking in state-owned enterprises. Despite these specificities, though, the benefits of enhanced rates of rural accumulation can be witnessed in Vietnam, particularly as a result of asymmetrical inter-subsectoral linkages that result in a wider, if gendered, distribution of the gains from rural accumulation, albeit one in which poverty reduction has been accompanied by rapid rises in rural inequality.

In this context, one final point must be stressed: that within both Brazil and Vietnam, rural accumulation continues to be of importance for both capital and labour and, in this sense, the classical concerns of the agrarian question remain salient, albeit within processes that have been asymmetrical. In this light, Bernstein's argument that only an agrarian question of labour remains, or McMichael's argument that the agrarian question is principally a peasant-led one of food, appear to be at best partial readings of the character of the agrarian question in the early years of the twenty-first century – readings with important insights about the contemporary character of rural livelihoods and struggles, but nonetheless partial. Additional insights are provided by Araghi's emphasis on the creation of a global reserve army of labour; by Watts' arguments concerning the establishment of new agri-cultures and new peasants, urban agriculture, postsocialist peasantries and indigeneity; and by Akram-Lodhi *et al.*'s arguments concerning trends in agrarian structure resulting from the expanded commodification witnessed under neoliberal globalization.

Accumulation with weaker inter-subsectoral linkages

The experience of the second group of countries stands in marked contrast to that of Brazil and Vietnam. For example, in countries as varied as Bolivia, Egypt, Ghana, Guatemala, Honduras, India, Indonesia, Kenya, Morocco, Namibia, Pakistan, Peru, the Philippines, South Africa, Tanzania, Tunisia, Uganda, Uzbekistan and Zimbabwe – in other words, large parts of Africa, Asia and Latin America – the processes of market-led land appropriation discussed by Akram-Lodhi *et al.* can be witnessed, but established yet con-tingent trajectories of variation have produced manifestly different outcomes in specific settings.[2] In particular, higher-value agricultural exports are an important determinant of aggregate rates of rural accumulation, but sub-stantially weaker linkages between the export and peasant subsectors have fostered a significantly weaker distribution of the gains from rural accumu-lation and thus equality-deteriorating patterns of rural growth in which, for many, food insecurity has deepened (Carter and Barham 1996; Gwynn and Kay 2004). Indeed, in some instances, as in much of Latin America and Africa, the greater emphasis on higher-value agricultural exports, coupled with devaluations and the removal of import restrictions resulting from ongoing structural adjustment in agriculture, has as a consequence effec-tively, and in some cases deliberately, neglected agricultural production for the home market. A neoliberal agricultural export bias has, in turn, led to rising food imports, with food imports rising faster than agricultural exports in some instances, and a resulting crisis of the domestic food sector.

An agrarian crisis has thus been fashioned as a consequence of the traits of accumulation: agro-food transnational corporations from the North, sub-sidized by capitalist states, as Araghi stresses, want increasingly uniform crops that are, in addition to entering the corporate-dominated Northern food system, exported to the South under terms and conditions by which local production is unable to compete. The corporate food regime discussed by McMichael has thus had a significant impact on commercial family farms in the North that are 'regulated' by dominant agro-food transnational corporations; on peasant farmers in the South producing for localized markets that are increasingly 'regulated' by agro-food transnational corporations; and in some instances on capitalist farms in the South that are unable to sustain their competitiveness with subsidized Northern imports from agro-food transnational corporations. This helps explain the perverse presence of food insecurity and hunger in the South simultaneously alongside obesity and overconsumption in the North, as discussed by Araghi in this volume, and highlighted by Weis (2007) and Patel (2007) in their recent books on the world food system.

However, as might be expected, there is 'differential uniformity', witnessed (as Akram-Lodhi *et al.* stress) in trends in agrarian structure under neoliberal globalization. Thus a range of countries in Africa, Asia and Latin America[3] are increasingly engaged in the production of specialist farm output for niche consumer markets in developed capitalist economies, usually under the aegis of agro-food transnational corporations operating upstream in the commodity chain, output that nonetheless often has little, if any, domestic demand. This is Watts' high-value food 'new agriculture', a process that may, in specific contexts and instances, in Teubal's words generate 'agriculture without farmers'.

Deeper sources of diversity in the traits of accumulation in this second group of countries can be noted. Thus, for example, in Bolivia there is a strong spatial dimension to this process, with rural accumulation being centred on the Santa Cruz region, where the agricultural export subsector is located. Similar spatial processes can be witnessed elsewhere – space is now a key factor in understanding agrarian structure and agrarian restructuring.[4]

By way of contrast, in Egypt and Pakistan the importance of domestic demand among workers and peasants in fostering sustainable rates of rural accumulation has, if anything, been largely ignored by those dominant classes that control the export subsector and who are in positions of social power, to the detriment of food security as the poverty of the poor sits alongside the overconsumption of the rich. Similar processes are also at work in Latin America and Africa.[5]

India and the Philippines offer, within a uniform set of overarching processes, a different experience in this second group: internal demand has expanded to a relatively greater degree than that witnessed in, for example, Bolivia, Egypt and Pakistan, but the emphasis by peasant producers on producing lower-value crops for export markets has, in both countries, fostered inter- and intra-subsectoral differentiation even as food imports have increased.

Alternatively, in some countries there are exports to regional markets that have higher levels of economic development. Thus in Namibia, specialist outputs for relatively wealthier consumers are exported, principally to South Africa, although the comparatively small size of the economy coupled with the large physical area of the country makes the establishment of linkages between the export and peasant production subsectors difficult. By way of contrast, in Zimbabwe the promotion of agricultural staple exports by international financial institutions resulted in restrictions on domestic supply, which, in turn, facilitated the onset of a food crisis that over time resulted in plummeting domestic food production and availability, even though exports could clearly have been consumed in the home market. Finally, in Uzbekistan cash crops are exported, largely because there is very limited domestic capacity to add value at later stages of the value chain, demonstrating the extent to which linkages between agricultural and non-agricultural production have failed to be established.

Therefore, it can be said that in many cases a lack of labour absorption within relatively more capital- and land-intensive export-oriented agricultural production, along with weak – or indeed absent – linkages between the export and peasant production subsectors, and a lesser ability of lower-value agricultural products produced within the peasant subsector to be exported, means that growth of the home market has been restricted and, in some cases, stagnant. Clear examples of these can be identified.[6] As a result, inter-subsectoral differentiation is occurring, between a relatively more rapidly accumulating export sector, and a relatively lesser accumulating peasant sector, on top of any intra-subsectoral differentiation that may be taking place in peasant production.

The result, in many countries, has been to generate a reproduction squeeze within the increasingly fragmented peasant sector as the conditions facing agrarian labour have deteriorated in terms of farming possibilities, employment opportunities, wages and other working terms and conditions; a point made by many contributors to this book. The manifest crisis of the peasant economy has fostered semiproletarianization and, in many cases, made labour redundant (Bryceson *et al.* 2000), both of which increase the reserve army of labour, with its attendant impact on wages. This commonly results in an enforced de-agrarianization that is witnessed in an outflow of labour from the peasant sector to urban centres (Davis 2006), as stressed by Araghi, O'Laughlin, Bernstein, Watts, McMichael and Akram-Lodhi *et al.*, or (if possible) international migration (Kay 2008).

In some instances, remittances that arise as a result of the enforced outflow of labour have a central role in sustaining peasant livelihoods. Thus, in the Southern African region, as noted by O'Laughlin, migrant remittances sustain farming, while in some countries, particularly in Latin America, international migrants' remittances provide more foreign exchange than agricultural exports. It is in these circumstances that Bernstein's AQ4 thesis of agrarian labour becoming 'decoupled' from capital accumulation is certainly strongest, and must be considered for its explanatory power. It is also in these circumstances, however, that McMichael's AQ6 'agrarian question of food' appears to be applicable, as the traits of accumulation have fostered an agrarian crisis of social reproduction that has resulted, in many places, in a political response in support of food sovereignty. Finally, though, Araghi's AQ2 'global reserve army of labour agrarian question' and the AQ3 'class forces agrarian question' also have clear relevance in understanding semi-proletarianization and the attendant global rural livelihoods crisis.

Outliers

It is important to note in these general processes what we, along with Saturnino Borras, Jr, earlier in this book term 'outliers'. For example, in the Caucasus in general, and Armenia in particular, the rural economy neither provides significant agricultural exports nor is an important component of domestic demand, which is driven by migrants' remittances and mineral rents. This is in part a function of the structure of the Armenian economy, with its reliance on labour migration and extractive activities, and in part a function of its relative isolation from global production and trading systems. As a consequence, the process of accumulation in rural Armenia is generally weak, and the countryside works, instead, through the process of re-agrarianization that we noted in an earlier chapter, to absorb surplus labour and thus act as a social safety net for the reserve army of labour in a period when employment has witnessed extensive labour shedding.

Similarly, in Ethiopia, as in Armenia, relative isolation from world markets has led the government to adopt an agriculture-led growth policy that is predicated on an expansion of domestic demand as a precursor to enhanced rural accumulation, increased agricultural exports, and eventual structural transformation. However, the expansion of the home market has been far less than that required to foster any kind of process of agrarian transformation. Poverty remains pervasive, and income distribution inequitable.

One final outlier should be stressed, not because of its relative isolation from world markets, but instead for its importance to global economic flows, including agriculture – and that is China. Watts, in particular, stresses the importance of accommodating the reality of postsocialist peasants in contemporary thinking on the agrarian question. In this light, it should be noted that China has not promoted an agricultural export-led strategy as a principal means of enhancing rural accumulation; rather, despite 'postsocialist repeasantization', the lack of a significant supply response in the rural economy for over 20 years has led to an emphasis by the state on rural diversification into specialist farming activities, with some limited success, and, more importantly, non-farm activities as the principal mechanism by which rural accumulation might proceed; an emphasis that the World Bank (2007) is now seeking to generalize. Some of this diversification in the countryside has been into agro-processing, although it is important to note the spatial dimensions to this process, and in particular the fact that the centre of gravity of diversification lies in the vastly wealthier east of the country.

China remains extremely important when considering the continued salience of the agrarian question because, as a consequence of neoliberal globalization, many agrarian economies have promoted an agricultural export-led strategy, and China is a very important source of demand for agricultural exports. Thus in many countries in Africa, Asia and Latin America,[7] China is a very important market for their agro-food commodity exports.

This has two implications. The first is that rural accumulation in many countries is reliant on China's ongoing capitalist transition. This is, in our view, not consistent with Bernstein's argument that agriculture does not 'matter' for global accumulation, because China's capitalist transition is now a global driver of accumulation in the North and in the South, especially as, at the time of writing, parts of the North slip into a cyclical recession. A collapse of China's access to imported agro-food commodities, whether for people or for animal consumption, would have a significant negative impact on global accumulation. Indeed, it might be argued that in many places in the South, China as a source of demand is facilitating the deepening of capitalist relations of production in export-oriented and peasant-based agriculture, and thus reconfiguring the agrarian question.

The second implication is that China's capitalist transition relies on continued and sustained access to agro-food commodities imported within what is still a global corporate food regime, as stressed by McMichael, because China's rural economy has witnessed disappointing production and productivity performance. Ironically, this is consistent with Bernstein's thesis: agriculture in China does not matter for China's capitalist transition, because accumulation in China is not linked to improved production and productivity in the rural economy as a source of capital, as a result of which the agrarian question that remains in a spatially and socially differentiating China is an agrarian question of labour.

Analytical implications of the traits of accumulation

A number of implications arise as a consequence of this review of the traits of rural accumulation under neoliberal globalization. The first implication is that, in the specific circumstances of strong complementary links between the agricultural export subsector and peasant production, there can be substantive if asymmetrical trickle-down of the gains from growth as rural accumulation proceeds, as in Vietnam. In Brazil, strong rural accumulation is accompanied by pervasive poverty and inequality, despite complementary links between the agricultural export subsector and peasant production, as a consequence of the 'conservative modernization' that has taken place.

However, complementary if asymmetrical inter-subsectoral linkages on a global scale are uncommon. The second implication is thus that the capital and land intensity of the agro-export subsector, and weak linkages between it and the peasant subsector, results in inter- and intra-subsectoral differentiation between export and peasant production. A wide variety of countries exhibit such characteristics. In such circumstances, the capacity of the rural economy, even if it is growing in the aggregate, to enhance peasant livelihoods is open to doubt. These are the places where the corporate food regime increasingly results in farmers in the South and in the North facing a livelihoods crisis that forces them to seek work, as footloose labour (Breman 2003), outside of agriculture and often even outside the country, as argued by many contributors to this book.

The third implication is the contradictory role played by China in both facilitating agrarian accumulation outside China, while at the same time being unable to facilitate agrarian accumulation within China. Finally, the fourth, analytical, implication is that although, in some instances, capital accumulation in developing and transition economies does not require agrarian capital accumulation to proceed, and thus the agrarian question of capital has been, in a sense, resolved, while an agrarian question of labour – and, for many, food – remains, this is not capable of being stated as an unambiguous 'stylized fact'. There are clearly historically-embedded processes that variably incorporate rural economies into capitalism operating on a world scale, or what used to be called uneven development. These processes generate a differential uniformity that the terrain of the agrarian question still allows us, in a simplified if not simplistic way, to capture.

Accumulation and rural poverty

The consequences of changes in the traits of rural accumulation for poverty and inequality can be inferred from the previous subsection, which has illustrated the complexity of the general processes at work and the impact of such complexity on the differential uniformity that can be witnessed. Despite such substantive diversity, however, it can be suggested that, overall, the impact of rural accumulation on poverty should be examined separately from the impact of rural accumulation on inequality. The reason for this is straightforward: rural inequality has, at best, experienced no change or has, in all likelihood, deepened during the current wave of neoliberal globalization (Held and Kaya 2006). This insight, when considered in light of contingent trajectories of variation that reflect processes of variable incorporation into capitalism, suggest a generalization: that neoliberal globalization does not improve equality. On the contrary, it fosters inequality.[8]

In contrast to inequality, in terms of rural poverty reduction it is, in general, possible to identify three very broad experiences in the period of neoliberal globalization. The first experience is that of Vietnam, which has witnessed, in official statistics, rapid poverty reduction that may be historically unprecedented.[9] The case of Vietnam suggests that initially equitable income and asset distributions, and in particular land, at the beginning of the period of neoliberal globalization may, in the context of complementary forward and backward linkages between the export and peasant production subsectors, generate traits of accumulation that foster rapid rates of poverty reduction. Indeed, it could be suggested that Vietnam may be undergoing a classic agrarian transition 'from below' (Akram-Lodhi 2007a).

This relative success can be set beside a second, more general set of experiences,[10] where poverty reduction has been at best limited, and at worst stagnant. Each of these experiences is notable for the counterpoint it provides to the Vietnamese example, in that, contrary to Vietnam's experience, each commenced the latest wave of neoliberal globalization subject to extremely skewed income and asset distribution. It should be noted that in some countries[11] this skewed distribution had a strong ethnic dimension. The impact of initially inequitable income and asset distributions was similar, and unsurprising: the benefits that accrued to the rural economy from traits of accumulation predicated on integration into the global economy were skewed in favour of those that initially controlled assets. In this way, the impact of neoliberal globalization on rural society has been to reinforce the social power of dominant classes acting, in true *comprador* fashion, in alliance with the agro-food transnational corporations that dominate the global corporate food regime.

The third broad set of experiences can be witnessed in countries such as Armenia, Uzbekistan and Zimbabwe, which have witnessed increased poverty during the current wave of neoliberal globalization. Clearly, increased poverty in Armenia and Uzbekistan can be traced back to the collapse of the Soviet Union, the economic shock that accompanied the independence of both, and the effective seizure of large parts of the state-owned economy by private interests with ties to the political elites that ran the countries both before and after independence. As a consequence of economic decline and deepening poverty, in Armenia many who had previously worked in cities, for the government or for state-owned enterprises found that their ability to construct a livelihood was coming under sustained pressure. They commenced smallholder farming as a means of coping, with the result that a widespread re-agrarianization was witnessed in Armenia during the 1990s.

By way of contrast, in Uzbekistan the large collectives and state farms that dominated cash-crop production prior to the collapse of the Soviet Union were effectively privatized during the 1990s, and increasingly sought to operate along the lines of capitalist agriculture. One outcome of this process was massive labour-shedding in a rural economy with limited labour absorption. As a consequence, poverty deepened.

Finally, in the case of Zimbabwe, the increase in agricultural staple exports decreed by the international financial institutions accompanied the partial re-enclosure of former settler farms by rent-seeking members of the political elite with strong ties to the ruling party. The result, in terms of farm productivity and eventually production, was a massive decline, even as agricultural staple exports meant that per capita food availability in the country declined. The resulting food crisis pushed much of rural Zimbabwe into chronic poverty for the first time in the country's history, from which it has yet to recover, and formed the backdrop to the land seizure movement of the early 2000s.

Once again, it is important to note outliers to these general processes. In terms of poverty reduction, for example, an outlier is Ethiopia. There, a record of stagnant poverty reduction cannot be laid at the door of an initial maldistribution of income and assets, as can be the case in other countries in Asia, Africa and Latin America.[12] There was inequality, to be sure; but the key factor inhibiting poverty reduction in Ethiopia since the collapse of the Derg has been the inability to transform agriculture technologically through the provision of water, appropriate biotechnologies and stable prices, which has had the consequence of sustaining the seasonality of Ethiopian agriculture and thus its poor productivity performance. Although Ethiopia pursues an agriculture-led development strategy, it is precisely the underdevelopment of agriculture's productive forces that constrains the rural economy and its ability to foster traits of accumulation that generate sustainable poverty reduction.

A second, very important outlier is China, which, despite postsocialist repeasantization, in terms of domestic agro-food production and productivity has witnessed stagnation since the mid-1980s. The lack of rural capital accumulation has not, however, inhibited capital accumulation more generally, as agro-food imports have provided the surpluses necessary for capital accumulation to take place at levels of world-historical significance.

Notwithstanding these outliers, the evidence emerging demonstrates some broad similarities that can be used to underpin a general understanding of the processes at work in rural economies. Neoliberal globalization has had the effect of restructuring rural production processes in relatively more capital- or more labour-intensive patterns, generating changes in agrarian structure, and altering traits and rates of accumulation in both export and peasant production subsectors, which in turn has affected both inequality and poverty. An important variable in this process has been the extent of forward and backward linkages between the export and peasant production subsectors, as demonstrated by Brazil and Vietnam, in contrast to a range of other countries.

However, the critical variable in this process, in our view, in terms of its impact on poverty, appears to be the degree of equality in the distribution of assets, incomes and resources at the start of the restructuring process. Vietnam was, without doubt, the most relatively egalitarian economy at the start of the process of rural transformation. It is (in our view), as a direct consequence, also the economy that has witnessed far and away the best performance in poverty reduction during what may be a fairly classical process of rural transformation.

These processes are not universal. They are, rather, subject to substantive diversity rooted in the contingent and conjunctural complexity arising out of historically embedded processes of variable incorporation of rural economies and societies into capitalism operating on a world scale.

Accumulation and rural politics

In the classical formulation of the agrarian question, it was argued that alterations in rural production processes and shifts in traits and rates of rural accumulation could be expected to have an effect on rural politics, because the fulcrum of rural politics is precisely the rural production process and rural accumulation. This aspect of the agrarian question is drawn directly from the analysis of Engels, who, as many contributors to this volume have noted, emphasized the political implications and possibilities of the peasant question. In considering rural political struggles in an era of neoliberal globalization, four central and interrelated issues need to be examined.

The first is the character of rural politics. Here, the focal issue is whether rural politics are dominated by highly individualistic, often indirect engagement with the formal rules and informal norms governing the production and allocation of resources, or what Kerkvliet (2005) calls 'everyday politics'; or by collective, usually direct, 'class-for-itself' struggles with dominant social actors that affect the production and distribution of resources, including the state, whether it be the bureaucracy or programmatic interventions. The distinction between everyday and collective action is often less than clear. Nonetheless, such a distinction is useful in understanding substantive diversity.

The second, strongly interrelated issue is whether ethnicity is used as a means of mobilizing everyday politics into collective action. In this regard, ethnicity may be used for potentially conservative or for potentially transformative mobilization. Thus there is extensive historical evidence that the use of ethnicity as a means of mobilizing collective action allows dominant elites to sustain their social control over communities (Akram-Lodhi 1987). Conversely, in Ecuador, Chiapas in Mexico and in Bolivia, the deployment of ethnicity has facilitated the mobilization of the indigenous peasantry for potentially transformative change, as Watts notes in Chapter 11. Indeed, the indigenous peasantry have, at times, changed their reference to themselves from *campesinos* to *indigenas*. An apparently key factor determining whether potentially transformative mobilizations are capable of successfully confronting dominant class forces is the extent to which indigenous movements are able to retain or develop the class character of their movement, and the extent to which they are able to develop alliances with non-indigenous groups. In Ecuador, the failure to achieve this has led to the failure of the indigenous movement; in Bolivia, the ability to achieve this has led to the success of the indigenous movement.

The third interrelated issue that has to be examined in order to understand the character of rural politics and struggle is the role of migration. Migration can serve to constrict the capacity of civil society to transform everyday politics into collective action, both by reducing the binding character of economic constraints on households, and by intensifying workloads among those who do not migrate, as implied by Araghi in Chapter 5.

The fourth, and final, issue that needs to be examined is the character of the state and its relationship to civil society. The processes and mechanisms by which the state formally and informally constructs, implements, transforms and avoids its interventions that affect the production and distribution of resources will have a profound impact on the character of rural politics and, in turn, on the terms and conditions by which the state governs and is governed by civil society (Akram-Lodhi 1992). There is thus a need to understand the specific articulation of consent and coercion by which the state and civil society collaborate or conflict with each other, in order to comprehend any trajectories of variation.

Everyday rural politics

All countries witness everyday politics. The issue here is rather different – whether everyday politics is the predominant form of rural political expression and, if so, why. Here it is possible to identify a number of countries in Asia and Africa[13] where 'the weapons of the weak' (Scott 1987) are the principal, but not exclusive, means by which dissent is expressed. The reason why rural political discourse is dominated by everyday politics has to do with the nature of dominant social forces. Each of these countries witnesses dominant social forces, including class forces, controlling political parties, popular mass organizations, and the state, and these social forces use their control of politics to tightly restrict political struggles, if necessary coercively, and thus control the activities of civil society in a manner that could be labelled 'neoauthoritarian'. Dominant social forces thus use the state to govern civil society strongly through the exercise of a degree of hegemony, although in most instances the state is capacity-constrained and this does allow limited amounts of political space for autonomous organization and struggle. Nonetheless, rural politics remains by-and-large everyday.

However, in these circumstances it is necessary to unravel the character of politics within dominant social forces. Here, some diversity emerges. Some countries[14] have strongly cohesive elites that dominate social relations in politics, economics and society. In Vietnam, this domination operates through diverse mechanisms designed to build and maintain reasonably consensual relations between the governing and the governed. By way of contrast, Ethiopia, Namibia and Zimbabwe have, on the surface, reasonably cohesive political and economic elites, but beneath this lies fractional divergence rooted in both political and ethnically mobilized differences. These differences, however, remain submerged under the political authority associated with liberation movements.

Rural collective action

A wide variety of countries in Asia, Africa and Latin America[15] offer a stark contrast. In these cases, the use of everyday politics remains widespread. However, everyday politics has been forged, through a long and diverse set of struggles, into collective action that seeks to alter the terms and conditions governing the production and distribution of rural resources by engaging with both dominant social forces and the state. Brazil offers the starkest example, with *O Movimento dos Trabalhadores Rurais Sem-Terra* (Landless

Rural Workers' Movement, MST) being but the best known of a host of rural advocacy and action groups that collectively struggle with rural elites and the state.

However, in Bolivia as well, everyday politics has been welded, collectively, into the *Movimiento al Socialismo* (Movement to Socialism) which is, again, one of a number of rural peasant movements that has moved beyond its peasant base, having established a political party that contests national elections, and that saw its leader elected to the presidency by an unexpectedly large margin in 2005. Similarly, the Philippines has a long history of rurally based collective struggle and armed insurgency involving a diverse plethora of political formations, non-governmental organizations and peasant movements, of which the most important is currently the National Coordination of Autonomous Local Rural People's Organizations. Collective action has witnessed rural elites being confronted and the state being challenged using both peaceful and non-peaceful tactics.

The substantive diversity demonstrated in these examples lies in the character of the rural elite. In Brazil, the elite are reasonably cohesive, with a clear vision of how the economy and society should be structured. In Bolivia and the Philippines, in contrast, the elite are subject to fractional fault lines. In the Philippines, these fault lines revolve around differential rent-seeking interests within the elite and its relationship to the state, as well as the differences witnessed between a modernizing, economically motivated, export-oriented rural elite interested in promoting higher-value agro-exports and a more conservative export-oriented rural elite that produces less valuable agro-exports and which is, through its use of patron–client relations in rural society, more (for lack of a better word) 'traditional' in its social, political and economic outlook. In Bolivia, fractional fault lines are spatially oriented, with an export-oriented modernizing fraction based in Santa Cruz engaged in conflictual struggles with the non-resource-rich highlands, where peasants are less interested in the economic possibilities offered by neoliberal globalization, or indeed reject it outright as a consequence of the negative impact of food imports.

Rural peasant movements, by entering into collective action, have had an impact on the state, but this impact differs in Bolivia, Brazil and the Philippines, partly because of the nature of the response of dominant social forces. In Brazil, the cohesive character of the dominant elite means that, while rural social movements are able to contest the state, it remains, despite the election of the *Partido dos Trabalhadores* (Workers' Party), dominated by the elite, who continue to use the state to pursue a project of conservative modernization. Nonetheless, the role of the *Partido dos Trabalhadores*, along with rural social movements, means that the dominant social elite struggles to exercise a degree of hegemony over society.

In the Philippines, a long-standing history of rural social organization and struggle, along with fractional fault lines within the dominant elite, has allowed civil society to seek to contest the state from within. This is witnessed, for example, in the internal struggles played out in the Department for Agrarian Reform between social activists and conservative modernizers. Once again, the ability to contest the state has meant that the rural elite have been unable to exercise an adequate degree of hegemony over society so as to shape the process of social and political change.

Finally, in Bolivia, fractional fault lines within the dominant elite have been exploited by strong rural social movements undertaking consistent and coherent collective action, with the result that the capacity of the state to govern civil society has been challenged. The state itself is thus the subject of contestation between rural civil society and the dominant social elite.

Peasant movements

The foregoing analysis of rural politics and the state suggests that Engels' original concern with the politics of the agrarian question remains of central analytical importance. Engels stressed the interrelationship between dominant classes, the state, and subaltern peasant and working classes undergoing processes of fragmentation and differentiation in understanding the political dynamics and possibilities of the 'peasant question'. These concerns remain of central relevance today even as the agrarian question transnationalizes. In Asia, Africa and, most explicitly, Latin America, with the MST, Chiapas, and *cocaleros* in Bolivia as the most prominent examples, the peasantry has, as powerfully argued by Teubal, McMichael and Watts in this book, led the struggle against neoliberal globalization, acting as a force for radical, progressive and ecologically sustainable transformative change.

Indeed, Latin America also indicates some of the conditions necessary for peasant struggles for progressive transformative change to be potentially successful: the ability to retain or develop an explicit class character to their movement; as well as the extent to which they are able to develop alliances with non-peasant groups such as the urban working class, ecologists, women's groups, advocacy groups and, critically, sympathetic elements within the state apparatus and fractions within dominant elites. In sustaining such alliances, maintaining an appropriate balance between immediate tactical demands and preoccupations and longer-run strategic commitments to deeper structural changes can be extremely difficult. Nonetheless, such a balance is possible, as exemplified by, on a global scale, La Via Campesina, the transnational peasant movement which is the largest social movement in the world. La Via Campesina, which seeks to alter the terms and conditions governing rural production, distribution and accumulation, and hence rural lives, is discussed by McMichael, Watts, and Bernstein in this volume (see also Borras 2004; Akram-Lodhi 2007b; Patel 2007; Borras, Edelman and Kay 2008).

None of the contributors to this volume would diminish the efforts of working people to improve the terms and conditions governing their access to a livelihood and employment, especially given an increasingly global fragmentation of classes of labour and the resultant survival squeeze as semiproletarianization without full proletarianization deepens, a point that Araghi, Bernstein, Watts, McMichael and Akram-Lodhi, Kay and Borras all emphasize, albeit in different ways.

In this sense, then, all contributors to this volume share Engels' original concern with the politics of the agrarian question; where they differ is in the relationship between political possibilities and structural constraints on action. Thus Philip McMichael, in AQ6, stakes out a position clearly different from that offered by Henry Bernstein in AQ4, who in turn offers a position different from that presented by, among others, Byres, Wood, Bagchi and Watts in AQ3, who also differ in their assessment from the perspective examined – and refuted – by Ray Kiely in AQ1. The contributors to this book clearly differ in their assessment of the relative possibilities offered by the struggles of peasants over land, livelihoods and labour.

The renewed relevance of the agrarian question

For much of the period described by Araghi as that of 'long national developmentalism', as well as the period of neoliberal globalization, the weight of food and agriculture in national and international circuits of capital accumulation was diminishing; agriculture was losing its relevance, a point that is central to Bernstein's argument. That may now be changing. In the last few years the importance of food and agricultural production within global circuits of accumulation has been of increasing concern to the actors and agents of international capitalism. Climate and other environmental change, particularly in Australia but also elsewhere, such as the Gangetic Plain, have led to plummeting world availability of wheat and, as a consequence, rising wheat prices. At the same time, rising demand for subsidized corn for the emerging, and also very heavily subsidized, American agrofuels sector has reduced world availability of corn and driven up the price. Finally, bad harvests in Latin America and crop diversification among other producers have left huge shortages in world soy markets. As these three crops are essential inputs in the corporate agro-food complex that rose to dominance during neoliberal globalization, changing agricultural supply and price dynamics have been witnessed throughout the world food system: in staple crops, in cash crops, in livestock, and in agro-industrial inputs (Patel 1997; Weis 2007). Reinforced by changing dietary patterns among elite consumers in China and India, with an attendant rise in meat consumption and processed foods, as well as by the increased transport costs incubated by oil that is over US$100 a barrel, agriculturally driven inflationary processes, or 'agflation', have increasingly become global: in China and India, to be sure, where food prices constitute 35 and 45 per cent of the consumer price index, respectively, but also throughout the South, in Europe, in the USA, and in other parts of the North (*The Economist*, 8 December 2007). Moreover, within global finance capital, there is increasing concern as to whether 'food inflation has moved from being cyclical to being driven by structural factors'

(*Financial Times*, 10 January 2008). Finally, and critically, these recent trends in the global agro-food complex are having political ramifications, with consumer and peasant protests being witnessed in Afghanistan, Bangladesh, Haiti, India, China, Indonesia, Italy, Mexico, Vietnam and Yemen, among others, and the UN Food and Agriculture Organization warning of serious threats to social and economic stability as a consequence of agflation (*Financial Times*, 20 November 2007).

In these circumstances, we argue that doubting the continued salience of the agrarian question is incorrect. We suggest that the agrarian question, in whatever form, far from diminishing, has assumed a new relevance in an era of neoliberal globalization. The renewed relevance of the agrarian question is witnessed in: postsocialist repeasantization through decollectivization; semiproletarianization and fragmentation without full proletarianization; the deepening of the market imperative around the globe under neoliberal globalization; the expanded commodification of natural resources, including land, labour-power and what Farshad Araghi has termed 'bio-enclosures', that is to say genetic resources; the strong spatial specificities to these processes, as cross-border megaregions transcend the state in driving substantial shares of global capital accumulation; and in response the global resurgence of peasant movements in Chiapas, Brazil, India, China and Indonesia, among others, as well as the critical, pivotal transnational response of La Via Campesina.

Clearly, rural transformation and its intersection with the development of capitalism – the agrarian question – impacts differentially on global labour, both rural and urban. With regard to classes of agrarian labour, uneven development has forced the rural poor to engage in a multiplicity of waged labour activities of a precarious and highly seasonal kind, even as they continue to cling to their land for reasons of security, and even though land no longer provides a subsistence guarantee, in part because increasingly casualized wage labour similarly fails to provide a subsistence guarantee. This process of semiproletarianization without full proletarianization is discussed by Araghi, Watts, and Akram-Lodhi, Kay and Borras, and is also addressed in the chapter by O'Laughlin. It bears strong affinities, in our view, to Bernstein's argument that 'peasants' are fragmenting into classes of agrarian labour, although Bernstein himself strongly disavows a somewhat different variant of semiproletarianization. In any event, the fragility of livelihoods of semiproletarians that have not fully proletarianized has forced classes of agrarian labour to migrate, both within countries and internationally, in order to use remittances to support precarious livelihoods. The crisis of the agrarian economy, accelerated as it is by food imports under a buyer-driven corporate food regime (explored by McMichael), has tightened the operation of the law of value on a global scale, and through migration has thus shifted poverty from the countryside to the city and the megacity, generating a 'planet of slums' (Davis 2006). These processes have been described, in a multiplicity of different ways, by the contributors to this volume.

Nonetheless, the attention paid to accumulation, inequality, poverty and politics in this chapter demonstrates that, when considering the renewed relevance of agrarian question in an era of neoliberal globalization, a number of common processes can be demonstrated, in which deviation from common processes – differential uniformity – in fact assists in explaining the historically embedded, contingent trajectories of variation that are witnessed. Therefore we suggest three reasonably coherent comparative conclusions that can be derived for this book as a whole.

The first is that neoliberal globalization has facilitated a process of change in agrarian production systems, and this alteration in the character of the agrarian structure has reshaped the rural production process and facilitated the expanded commodification of rural economic activity under the market imperative discussed by Wood. For example, neoliberal market-led concentration – effective accumulation by dispossession, in Araghi's arresting phrase – has been witnessed in access to land. However, it has also been witnessed in access to other natural resources, such as minerals, water and forests. Gender dimensions to these processes have been dissected succinctly by O'Laughlin. In particular, though, there has been, as part of this process, an emphasis on exports facilitated by the activities of transnational corporations operating in the agro-food sector under the corporate food regime discussed by McMichael and Teubal and, in different ways, by Araghi and Watts. However, there are substantial differences in how this process has taken place around the world.

The second comparative conclusion is that transformations in the rural production process have affected, and been affected by, processes of accumulation, poverty reduction and structural change. In particular, the traits of accumulation have been affected by the overarching process of globalization, by the entry of agro-food-based profit seeking transnational corporations into the South in an effort to reconfigure rural lives, and by the emphasis on agricultural exports as the motor of accumulation by the agro-food transnational corporations that dominate the global corporate food regime as well as international institutions and national governments. In a few instances, linkages exist between the export and peasant production subsectors. However, more commonly, these inter-subsectoral linkages are weak, and semiproletarianization without full proletarianization is witnessed widely, as discussed, in different ways, by Araghi, O'Laughlin, Bernstein, Watts, McMichael, and Akram-Lodhi, Kay and Borras. Nonetheless, these differences mean that there is not a set of standard, uniform lessons that can be learnt. Rather, historically specific paths of transition mean that it is necessary to undertake a historically informed, country-specific analysis of the process of accumulation or its lack thereof, set within the conditions governing international capital accumulation. The agrarian constraint to accumulation has become, internationally, more binding than at any time in the past 30 years, a phenomenon that must be fully integrated into an analysis of differential uniformity.

The third comparative conclusion is that country-specific alterations in rural production and accumulation invariably have an impact on rural politics, but the way in which this plays out will be, in part, a function of the relationship within and between the peasantry, the rural elite and the state – relationships that have clear gender dimensions. In particular, the relationship within and between the peasantry, the rural elite and the state can shape the extent to which rural politics remain everyday; take on a populist hue; or become collective expressions of transformational aspirations, whether nationally or, in the shape of La Via Campesina, transnationally. Clearly, when countries that have large peasant populations are able to transcend everyday politics and create and sustain collective alliances, the peasantry is capable of contesting the position of dominant social forces and the state to the point where the capacity of the state to govern in the interests of the elite is itself challenged and, in a very real sense, the peasantry seek to strike back (Petras 1997).

These three comparative conclusions suggest that the convergence of three key, interlinked, necessary but not sufficient conditions can facilitate struggles to undertake a transformation in social relationships. These interlinked conditions are, unsurprisingly, grounded in agrarian production systems, the traits of accumulation and the character of rural politics. Thus, in terms of the debate surrounding the contemporary character of the agrarian question in an era of neoliberal globalization, it appears that a clear perspective can, in the end, be offered for consideration.

The analysis of Bill Warren and his followers, as critically presented by Ray Kiely in his presentation of AQ1 in this book, stresses a contingent yet inexorable development of wage labour in the process of rural capitalist development. This appears to be too path-dependent to be able to grasp the complexity of rural social relations emerging out of the messy struggles between ascendant and emerging social forces. It also, as Kiely stresses, fails to explain the uneven character of capitalist industrialization on a world scale. The analysis offered by Farshad Araghi in AQ2, which stresses prolonged continuities confronting an increasingly global reserve army of labour as global value relations become entrenched, offers important insights into the world-historical development of capitalism, although in the breadth of its argument it is less capable of explaining historical specificity in the development of agrarian relations. The important arguments of Henry Bernstein contained in AQ4, which suggests that the agrarian question of capital has been resolved since the 1970s and all that remains is an agrarian question of labour, can explain some of the conditions witnessed in an era of neoliberal globalization, but at this time cannot, it appears to us, be offered as a globally stylized fact. This is partly because there can be no doubt that in some places, and in some spaces, the agrarian question of capital is still in the process of resolution in a fairly classical manner. Vietnam is evidence enough, while the impact of China on agrarian transitions outside China remains to be seen. The analysis of Philip McMichael in AQ6, which argues that the agrarian question is being reconstructed as one of food as transnational peasant movements confront the corporate food regime and global capital, does not, in our view, accord sufficient weight to the structural transformations in the forces of production that go hand in hand with ongoing struggles over land, labour and livelihoods and the national and international constraints that such transformations generate. These structural transformations in the forces of production may, just, be beginning to make their presence felt in global agriculture, as historically unparalleled changes in world food prices may indicate the beginnings of deeper shifts in the role of agriculture in global capital accumulation (*The Economist*, 8 December 2007).

In our view, only an analysis that stresses the contingent and conjunctural character of the manner in which forces and relations of production articulate to facilitate (or not) an agrarian transition offers a sufficiently nuanced account. This account must capture both the common processes at work in the countryside of developing and transition economies, and the substantive diversity, rooted in globally embedded, historically specific trajectories of variation, which cumulatively assist in understanding the challenge facing global peasant movements confronting global capital. This is the analysis put forward in AQ3, the class forces agrarian question. We would add, however, that the class forces agrarian question must be accompanied by a serious interrogation of the intersection of gender and class in rural transformation: AQ5, the gendered agrarian question. Admittedly, the lack of certainties that can be ascribed to this analysis might be, for some, a disappointment. For us, it is an indication of its theoretical and empirical coherence. Eclectic it may appear, but this analysis provides the analytical tools and analytical sensitivity necessary to understand the continuing relevance of the agrarian question in an era of neoliberal globalization. Moreover, it is clear to us that the political economy of rural social relations in an era of neoliberal globalization still has a profound impact on shaping the parameters of agrarian – and non-agrarian – change.

In short – in an era of neoliberal globalization, the importance of understanding agrarian change has become, paradoxically, even more context-specific than before. Granted, context must be located within the international conjuncture. Nonetheless, it is important to resume, continue and deepen the debate on the 'agrarian question', as this book attempts to do.

Notes

1 Evidence to substantiate the claims of this paragraph empirically can be found in Akram-Lodhi *et al.* (2007).
2 Country-based case study empirical evidence can be found in our earlier work (Akram-Lodhi *et al.* 2007); Rosset *et al.* (2006); de Janvry *et al.* (2001); Bryceson *et al.* (2000); some articles found in a recent special issue of *Third World Quarterly* (Borras *et al.* 2007), as well as some of the background papers for World Bank (2007), among others.

3 For example Bolivia, Egypt, Ghana, Guatemala, Honduras, Kenya, Morocco, Peru, the Philippines, South Africa, Tanzania, Tunisia and Uganda.
4 For example Ghana, Guatemala, Honduras, Kenya, Morocco, Peru, South Africa, Tanzania, Tunisia and Uganda.
5 For example Argentina, Guatemala, Honduras, Kenya, Morocco and Tunisia.
6 These include Bolivia, Egypt, Guatemala, Ghana, Honduras, Kenya, Pakistan, Peru and Uzbekistan.
7 These countries are as varied as Brazil, Egypt, Pakistan, the Philippines, South Africa and Vietnam, and this list is far from being exhaustive.
8 Akram-Lodhi (2005, 2006) argues that this was an objective of neoliberal globalization.
9 However, as emphasized by Akram-Lodhi (2007c), this conclusion must be evaluated very carefully.
10 This refers to countries such as Bolivia, Brazil, Egypt, Guatemala, Honduras, Kenya, Morocco, Namibia, Pakistan, Peru, the Philippines, South Africa and Tunisia, among others.
11 For example Bolivia, Brazil, Namibia and South Africa, among others.
12 Countries such as Bolivia, Brazil, Egypt, Namibia, Pakistan and the Philippines, among others.
13 Countries as diverse as Armenia, China, Egypt, Ethiopia, Morocco, Namibia, Tunisia, Vietnam, Uzbekistan and Zimbabwe, among others.
14 For example Armenia, China, Egypt, Morocco, Tunisia, Vietnam and Uzbekistan.
15 Including, among others, Bolivia, Brazil, Ghana, Guatemala, Honduras, Peru, the Philippines and Uganda.

References

Akram-Lodhi, A.H. (1987) 'Class and chauvinism in Sri Lanka', *Journal of Contemporary Asia*, 17 (2): 160–186.
—— (1992) 'Peasants and hegemony in the work of James C. Scott', *Peasant Studies*, 19 (3/4): 179–201.
—— (2005) 'Neoconservative economic policy, governance and alternative budgets', in A.H. Akram-Lodhi, R. Chernomas and A. Sepehri (eds), *Globalization, Neoconservative Policies and Democratic Alternatives*, Winnipeg: Arbeiter Ring Publishing.
—— (2006) 'What's in a name? Neo-conservative ideology, neoliberalism and globalisation', in R. Robison (ed.), *The Neoliberal Revolution: Forging the Market State*, London: Palgrave.
—— (2007a) 'Vietnam: an agrarian transition from below?', paper presented to the University of Toronto Munk Center for International Studies Development Studies Seminar, Toronto, 30 March 2007.
—— (2007b) 'Land reform, rural social relations and the peasantry', *Journal of Agrarian Change*, 7 (4): 554–562.
—— (2007c) 'Land markets and rural livelihoods in Vietnam', in A.H. Akram-Lodhi, S.M. Borras, Jr and C. Kay (eds), *Land, Poverty and Livelihoods in an Era of Globalization: Perspectives from Developing and Transition Economies*, London: Routledge.
Akram-Lodhi, A.H., S.M. Borras Jr and C. Kay (eds) (2007) *Land, Poverty and Livelihoods in an Era of Globalization: Perspectives from Developing and Transition Economies*, London: Routledge.
Bernstein, H. (1996) 'The political economy of the maize *filière*', in H. Bernstein (ed.), *The Agrarian Question in South Africa*, London: Frank Cass.

Borras, S. Jr (2004) *La Via Campesina: An Evolving Transnational Social Movement*, Briefing Series No. 6, Amsterdam: Transnational Institute.

Borras, S.M., Jr, M. Edelman and C. Kay (eds) (2008) *Transnational Agrarian Movements Confronting Globalization*, Oxford: Blackwell Publishing.

Borras, S.M., Jr, C. Kay and E. Lahiff (eds) (2007) 'Market-led agrarian reform: trajectories and contestations', special issue of *Third World Quarterly* 28 (8).

Breman, J. (2003) *The Labouring Poor in India*, Delhi: Oxford University Press.

Bryceson, D.F., C. Kay and J. Mooij (eds) (2000) *Disappearing Peasantries? Rural Labour in Africa, Asia and Latin America*, London: ITDG Publishing.

Carter, M.R. and B.L. Barham (1996) 'Level playing fields and laissez faire: postliberal development strategy in inegalitarian agrarian economies', *World Development* 24 (7): 1133–1149.

Davis, M. (2006) *Planet of Slums*, New York: Verso.

Fitzgerald, E.V.K. (1985) 'The problem of balance in the peripheral socialist economy: a conceptual note', *World Development*, 13 (1): 5–14.

Gwynne, R.N. and C. Kay (eds) (2004) *Latin America Transformed: Globalization and Modernity* (2nd edition), London: Arnold.

Held, D. and A. Kaya (eds) (2006) *Global Inequality*, London: Polity Press.

de Janvry, A., G. Gordillo, J.-P. Platteau and E. Sadoulet (eds) (2001) *Access to Land, Rural Poverty and Public Action*, Oxford: Oxford University Press.

Kalecki, M. (1969) *Introduction to the Theory of Growth in the Socialist Economy*, Oxford: Basil Blackwell.

Kay, C. (2008) 'Latin America's rural transformation: unequal development and persistent poverty', in R.L. Harris and J. Nef (eds) *Captial, Power and Inequality in Latin America and the Caribbean*, Lanham, MD: Rowman and Littlefield Publishers.

Kerkvliet, B. (2005) *The Power of Everyday Politics: How Vietnamese Peasants Transformed National Politics,* Ithaca, NY: Cornell University Press.

Marx, K. (1956) *Capital Vol. II*, Moscow: Progress Publishers (first published in 1885).

Patel, R. (2007) *Stuffed and Starved: Markets, Power and the Hidden Battle for the World's Food System*, London: Portobello.

Petras, J. (1997) 'Latin America: the resurgence of the left', *New Left Review*, (223): 17–47.

Rosset, P., R. Patel and M. Courville (eds) (2006) *Promised Land: Competing Visions of Agrarian Reform*, Oakland, CA: Food First Books.

Scott, J. (1987) *Weapons of the Weak: Everyday Forms of Peasant Resistance*, New Haven, CT: Yale University Press.

Weis, T. (2007) *The Global Food Economy: The Battle for the Future of Farming*, London: Zed Press.

World Bank (2007) *World Development Report 2008: Agriculture for Development*, Oxford: Oxford University Press.

Index